Nature in Common?

Edited by Ben A. Minteer

Nature in Common?

Environmental Ethics and the Contested
Foundations of Environmental Policy

TEMPLE UNIVERSITY PRESS
Philadelphia

Temple University Press
1601 North Broad Street
Philadelphia, PA 19122
www.temple.edu/tempress

⊛ The paper used in this publication meets the requirements of the American
National Standard for Information Sciences—Permanence of Paper for Printed Library
Materials, ANSI Z39.48-1992

Library of Congress Cataloging-in-Publication Data

Nature in common? : environmental ethics and the contested foundations of environmental
policy / edited by Ben A. Minteer.
        p. cm.
    Includes bibliographical references.
    ISBN 978-1-59213-703-9 (hardcover : alk. paper)—ISBN 978-1-59213-704-6 (pbk. : alk.
paper) 1. Human ecology—Philosophy.   2. Environmentalism—Philosophy.
3. Environmentalism—Moral and ethical aspects.   4. Environmental ethics.   I. Minteer,
Ben A., 1969–
    GF21.N36 2009
    179'.1—dc22
                                                                      2008034270

2 4 6 8 9 7 5 3 1

Contents

PART III   Expanding the Discussion: The Convergence Hypothesis Debate Today

PART IV   Reply by Bryan G. Norton

Acknowledgments

I would like to thank two publications for granting permission to reprint the essays that appear in Part II. Chapters 2, 3, 4, and 6 originally appeared in the journal *Environmental Ethics* (in, respectively, volume 17 (1995): 135–150; volume 19 (1997): 87–100; volume 19 (1997): 279–297; and volume 24 (2002): 135–148). Chapter 5 originally appeared in *Ethics, Place, and Environment* 3 (2000): 47–60. I would also like to convey my appreciation to those who contributed to this volume for all their good work, and in particular to Bryan Norton for giving us such interesting—and provocative—ideas to argue about. Finally, I thank Mick Gusinde-Duffy of Temple University Press for his enthusiastic support of this project.

Nature in Common?

I

Introduction

BEN A. MINTEER

Unity among Environmentalists?

Debating the Values-Policy Link
in Environmental Ethics

Introduction: A New Ethics for Environmental Protection

Environmental ethics emerged from the thickets of applied philosophy in the early 1970s as a rebuke to anthropocentrism, the human-centered outlook embedded within the Western ethical system. The anthropocentric worldview was singled out by the first generation of environmental philosophers for its failure to extend the boundaries of moral considerability—and the attribution of intrinsic value—to nonhumans (including animals and plants) and to larger ecological communities. These new *non*anthropocentric philosophers argued that the mainstream ethical traditions of the West—for example, Kantian ethics, utilitarianism, virtue ethics, and so forth—were not only insufficient as foundations for a new environmental ethic but also philosophically hostile to developing a more respectful relationship to nature. The conventional ethical theories, they argued, only considered human interests and harms worth recognizing. Nature itself was accorded only *instrumental* value; it was not deemed worthy of *direct* moral concern.

One of the earliest expressions of the desire to launch a new nonanthropocentric ethics of the environment appeared in a 1973 essay published by New Zealand philosopher Richard Routley, "Is There a Need for a New, an Environmental Ethic?"[1] There, Routley (who later changed his name to Sylvan) introduced what has since been referred to as the "last man" scenario, which he proposed as a kind of moral litmus test to separate the anthropocentrists from the nonanthropocentrists. According to the traditional ethical frameworks of the West, Routley argued, the last man surviving the collapse of the world system would be committing no wrong if he set about destroying every species of animal and plant on Earth. Since only humans have ultimate value in mainstream ethical theory, and since nature is therefore viewed as essentially valueless (in itself), Routley asserted that we have no established ethical principles that will allow us to condemn the destruction of nature on the grounds that it destroys intrinsic natural value. His essay was thus a strong rebuke of traditional ethical theorizing, particularly the "human chauvinism" Routley found in its exclusive concern for the interests of humans. We *do* need a new environmental ethic, Routley argued, and it should be nonanthropocentric in character.

Routley's indictment of anthropocentrism was shared by a growing number of environmental philosophers in the 1980s and 1990s. While some, such as Paul Taylor, advocated *biocentric* projects promoting the inherent worth of individual living organisms, most nonanthropocentric philosophers preferred to ground moral considerability and significance in more holistic understandings of natural populations, communities, and systems (an *ecocentric* position).[2] Also, during this same period, deep ecologists such as Arne Naess advanced a parallel critique of the dominant anthropocentric and industrial worldview, proposing as an alternative a nonanthropocentric cosmology and ethical curative to the "shallow" anthropocentric approach to environmental concern and protection.[3] In very short order, nonanthropocentrism (and the rejection of anthropocentrism) became the dominant, if not foundational, ethical commitment and philosophical move of academic environmental ethics and philosophy—its chief intellectual and political justification. Today, more than three decades removed from the academic founding of the field, the primary philosophical task for most mainstream environmental philosophers remains largely unchanged: the articulation of a new nature-centered or nonanthropocentric worldview and an alternative set of moral principles able to account directly for the good of nonhumans and the natural world as a whole.

This mandate to combat unbridled anthropocentrism via the philosophical platform of environmental ethics has, of course, always harbored a serious policy ambition, even if the practical implications of their theories and arguments did not receive as much attention from environmental philosophers as one might have expected. Indeed, by raising the flag of nonanthropocentrism, philosophers were also hoping to advance a persuasive moral justification for a robust environmental policy regime and a general rationalization of proenvironmental practices independent of the instrumental (i.e., human-serving) values of nature. If such a knockdown ethical defense could be successfully mounted, then public policies directing the protection of endangered species, wetlands, wilderness areas, and so on would appear to rest upon reassuringly solid, perhaps even unassailable foundations. Many environmental philosophers, in fact, became so convinced of the truth and necessity of the nonanthropocentric worldview that they insisted environmental policies and practices, to be truly principled and justified, *must* be underwritten by strong biocentric or ecocentric arguments.[4]

In making such arguments, however, nonanthropocentric philosophers were in many respects swimming upstream. A strong case can be made, for example, that most environmental activism, policy, and law in the United States (as well as in many other parts of the world) has been and continues to be motivated and explained by its advance of various *human* interests, especially health, welfare, and safety (but also property rights, aesthetics, and cultural/historical values). As Steve Cohen, a prominent environmental policy and management scholar at Columbia University puts it, "The environmental ethic that has had the greatest impact in the last three decades, at least in the United States and other Western countries, has been a form of enlightened self-interest."[5]

As a case in point, consider the cornerstone of U.S. environmental statutes: the National Environmental Policy Act (NEPA) of 1969.[6] Often described as purely procedural in nature due to its requirement that federal agencies prepare Environmental Impact Statements for proposals expected to have significant environmental consequences, NEPA is also notable for its more substantive emphasis on environmental values and its ambitious statement of vision. "What ought to be generally understood (and is not)," writes Lynton K. Caldwell, the dean of environmental policy scholars, "is that NEPA is basically legislation *about* values."[7] This is most obvious in the declaration of legislative intent in the Act's Section 2:

The purposes of this Act are: To declare a national policy which will encourage productive and enjoyable harmony between man and his environment; to promote efforts which will prevent or eliminate damage to the environment and biosphere and stimulate the health and welfare of man; to enrich the understanding of the ecological systems and natural resources important to the Nation.[8]

The Act goes on to pronounce that it is the "continuing policy of the Federal Government" to use all available means "in a manner calculated to foster and promote the general welfare, to create and maintain conditions under which man and nature can exist in productive harmony, and fulfill the social, economic, and other requirements of present and future generations of Americans."[9]

The values expressed in the text of NEPA are clearly anthropocentric, pertaining to the health and welfare (economic and physical) of humans, including future generations. As written, NEPA does not state or even seriously imply that the environment itself has any "interest" independent of human welfare, or that it might have a moral claim against human agents who wish to alter or destroy natural features, wild species, and the like. Moreover, the "harmony" with the environment described in the Act is modified by the term "productive," which—although it could possibly be stretched to refer to biological productivity—is surrounded here by references to human ownership ("man's environment") and anthropocentric designations of nonhuman nature ("natural resources"). In other words, the natural environment in NEPA is viewed instrumentally (though broadly, i.e., ecologically); it is not characterized as an intrinsically valuable entity apart from its contribution to human well-being.[10]

This broadly anthropocentric rationale is, moreover, not peculiar to NEPA. Indeed, if we examine the language of some of the other major U.S. environmental laws, we find that their value statements are overwhelmingly human-centered in character, emphasizing the myriad contributions of the environment to human health, safety, and economic welfare. Even the ostensibly "preservationist" natural resource laws advance primarily anthropocentric interests— including those trumpeted by environmentalists for providing strict and (seemingly) quasi-nonanthropocentric expressions of environmental concern. Take, for example, the federal wetlands policy outlined in Section 404 of the Clean Water Act, which regulates the physical alteration or destruction of wetlands.[11] As legal scholar Alyson Flourney observes, Section 404 itself is viewed as "one of the brightest stars of the environmental law constellation."[12] And yet the values expressed in Section 404, as with NEPA, may be generally described as anthropocentric in character, emphasizing economic productivity, property ownership, flood hazards, recreation, navigation, water supply, and the overall needs and welfare of the people.[13] Although these values do reflect a larger ecological context and thus go beyond narrow calculations of efficiency abstracted from natural systems, at the end of the day they still terminate in human interests and therefore are anthropocentric rather than biocentric or ecocentric in nature.[14]

The upshot is that many of the environmental protective policies set down in major U.S. environmental laws and regulations—concerning air and water quality, waste disposal, the release of toxic chemicals, and so on—reflect broadly anthropocentric concerns about human health, safety, welfare, and related social benefits. This normative trend, moreover, goes beyond the statutory language of policy. Anthropocentric (and, frequently, utilitarian) values also appear to be the dominant motivational elements of the major international environmental advocacy groups, at least to the degree that these are reflected in their vision and mission statements.[15]

Of course, just because the value expressions of environmental policy and regulation appear to be primarily anthropocentric in nature does not mean

that these values are easily harmonized, or that they are even roughly compatible or mutually consistent. Philosopher of public policy Mark Sagoff has
long argued, for example, that there are considerable tensions between, on
the one hand, prudential or efficiency-driven norms supporting the reliance
on economic analysis in environmental policy making and, on the other,
"moral" (in the Kantian sense, i.e., deontological) principles pertaining to
human health and safety that resist aggregation and comparison in any sort of
utility calculation.[16] However, Sagoff's utility versus rights axis in U.S. environmental policy still rests upon a solidly anthropocentric foundation: The
welfare, health, property, and safety of *humans*—not the interests of wetlands, wildlife, and wilderness—are recognized and promoted.

"Every idea about policy draws boundaries," writes Deborah Stone in her
influential book, *Policy Paradox.* "It tells what or who is included or excluded in a category. These boundaries are more than intellectual—they define people in and out of a conflict or place them on different sides."[17] And
nonanthropocentrists might argue that they define not just people but also
environmental entities and processes. While species, habitats, and the like
may "count" in environmental policy in the sense that their recovery and conservation are the codified targets of policy, they do not appear to count morally in the sense that policy and law codifies their moral standing or status.[18]
In other words, environmental policy at best seems to only reflect an *indirect*
regard for the environment; of *direct* ethical concern are the many *human* interests served by the provision of clean air and water, species conservation,
and so forth.

Nonanthropocentrists, though, want more than this. Philosopher Eric Katz
summarizes the general nonanthropocentrist position on the relationship between moral principle and environmental policy goals in the case of biodiversity protection: "The real solution to problems in environmental policy lies in
a specific transformation of values—the transcendence of human-based value
systems of ethics . . . Policies that ensure the preservation of planetary biodiversity must express values derived from a nonanthropocentric moral system."[19] For theorists like Katz and J. Baird Callicott, even the broad anthropocentrism expressed in NEPA and similar environmental statutes and
policies is not sufficient. As Callicott puts it, "Conservation policy based on
anthropocentrism alone—however broadened to include potential as well as
actual resources, ecosystem services, and the aesthetic, epistemic and spiritual uses of nature by present *and future* people—is less robust and inclusive
than conservation policy based on the intrinsic value of nature."[20]

Clearly, a major fear of the nonanthropocentrists regarding the anthropocentric defense of environmental policy—regardless of how enlightened it
may be—is that in the long run such rationales for policy choice will end up

supporting actions that do not adequately protect endangered species from harm or safeguard protected areas from encroaching development. Nonanthropocentric environmentalists presumably do not wish to see NEPA and the other pillars of environmental policy toppled because they reflect an anthropocentric pedigree. But they do want to argue that nonanthropocentrism is a *superior* moral foundation for environmental protection, and that it also supports, in many cases, a more ambitious policy agenda than a traditional, human-regarding moral outlook.

An illustration of this last point is the current "Rewilding" campaign to restore the wilderness values of North America by actively recolonizing the landscape with biological analogues—for example, elephants, cheetahs, and lions—of its long-lost charismatic megafauna of the Pleistocene Era.[21] Going well beyond the stated policy goals of the Wilderness Act and the Endangered Species Act (ESA), the proposed rewilding effort is, its authors assert, justified on "ethical" as well as ecological, aesthetic, and economic grounds. By "ethical," the rewilding advocates clearly mean to evoke the nonanthropocentric duty to restore biodiversity and wildness to the continent. Indeed, the Rewilding Institute, the umbrella organization for the Pleistocene Rewilding proposal, describes itself as driven by unabashedly biocentric values. As their Web site states, "We strive to protect and restore wild Nature and wild species for their own sake, not just because they are of use to humans."[22]

The upshot is that for many nonanthropocentrists (both within and outside academic environmental ethics), an alternative ethical system requiring deep value transformation—the shift from instrumental valuation of nature to seeing it as an end in itself—is necessary to motivate and justify sufficiently suitable environmental policy. Only assertions of the intrinsic value of nature, they argue, possess the kind of "trumping power" in environmental decision making that can defeat traditional, and traditionally powerful, economic arguments for the exploitation and liquidation of environmental assets. Without such moral authority, nonanthropocentrists worry that environmentalists will have to compete directly with economic interests in environmental decision making, a battle they fear is hopelessly lopsided but ultimately avoidable—that is, if there is recourse to nonanthropocentric arguments.[23]

Norton's *Toward Unity* among *Environmentalists* and the "Convergence Hypothesis"

Although it is still the dominant stance in the field, not all environmental ethicists have embraced the nonanthropocentric position and the view that it is essential to good environmental policy argument. For decades, the philosopher Bryan Norton has advanced an intellectual counteroffensive, arguing that the nonanthropocentric worldview is both conceptually flawed and pragmatically unnecessary within environmental ethics.[24] Specifically, Norton has challenged the popular notion that anthropocentrism is anathema to environmental protection by proposing an alternative and less-aggressive version of human-centeredness, what he termed "weak anthropocentrism." In its original formulation, Norton had in mind a kinder and gentler vision of humanist environmentalism that departed from the exploitative and economistic readings of the anthropocentric worldview within environmental ethics.[25]

For weak anthropocentrists, Norton wrote, nonhuman nature held an important, noneconomic instrumental quality, a good he later described as "transformative" value.[26] The direct experience of nature, he suggested, had the potential to transform selfish human preferences into more enlightened ones: Nature could in effect be "used" as a means to criticize ecologically irrational desires (such as destructively consumptive views of nature). This transformative experience could in turn encourage the formation of higher ideals that affirmed human harmony with the environment, now and in the future.[27] Among other things, Norton's argument demonstrated how the normative "widening" of anthropocentrism to countenance the full array of human goods in nature beyond narrow market values, and the temporal extension of these values so that they are properly understood as constraints imposed by the obligation to ensure resource sustainability for future generations, could put environmental humanism on much more solid ethical footing. It also showed that nonanthropocentric arguments were not necessary to criticize economistic views of nature; the latter could be shown to be deficient by appeal to other instrumental (but noneconomic) values in a reformed anthropocentric framework.

Norton's liberal humanism in environmental ethics was articulated in his influential 1991 book *Toward Unity among Environmentalists*, in which he broke new ground with his broadly pragmatic approach to environmental philosophy, a methodological orientation wherein the practical policy goals of environmentalists took center stage and ethical theorizing moved to the justificatory background.[28] Noting that environmentalists had not been able to rally around a consensus position about the ultimate value of endangered species, wetlands, wilderness, and so on, Norton's approach emphasized an important but frequently ignored distinction between the *values* of environmentalists and their policy *goals*:

> I will pursue a different strategy and look first for the common ground, the shared policy goals and objectives that might characterize the unity of environmentalists. To support this strategy, I will employ a useful, if

somewhat arbitrarily drawn, distinction between *values* and *objectives*. An objective will be understood as some concrete goal such as a change in policy or the designation of a particular area as a wilderness preserve. Values will be understood more abstractly as the basis for an estimation of worth, which can serve as a justification and explanation for more concrete objectives. Thus two environmentalists might work together to achieve the objective of prohibiting strip mining in a wilderness area, while justifying their activities by appeal to quite different values. One of them might, for example, value the wilderness as sacred, while the other wishes to perpetuate its recreational value for the use of the community. Differences in value may, therefore, lead to shifting coalitions regarding objectives; once strip mining is effectively prohibited, supporters of recreational values may find themselves allied with the local Chamber of Commerce in supporting a larger parking lot for the access to the wilderness, while their former ally opposes both, insisting that ease of access will cheapen and degrade the sacred place.[29]

Norton's focus on the "unity of environmentalists" at the level of policy preference—a view shaped by his analysis of key environmental decisions as well as interviews with leaders in the advocacy and policy-making communities—is the organizing principle of his 1991 book, a motif that resonates through a wide-ranging discussion of the values and objectives of population, energy, pollution control, land use, and biodiversity policy. It is also what led him to make the provocative claim that what had long been presented as *the* foundational rupture in the moral bedrock of environmental concern—that is, the deep chasm separating anthropocentrism and nonanthropocentrism—was greatly exaggerated. Norton wrote instead that nonanthropocentric claims and his own pluralistic, liberal reading of anthropocentrism should, in practice, actually "converge" on the same set of environmental policy goals. While he had advanced earlier versions of this idea in several publications, in *Toward Unity* Norton provided a robust expression of the argument, which by now had taken on a rather grand designation: the "convergence hypothesis."

Although he described the convergence hypothesis (CH) as an "article of environmentalists' faith," Norton suggested that it was also an empirical hypothesis that could be falsified by subjecting it to experimental text.[30] Logically, the CH is a hypothetical conditional: It predicts, for example, that if individual A is a consistently weak anthropocentrist (i.e., he or she embraces the full range of human values in the environment—aesthetic, spiritual, recreational, educational, etc.—over time) and if individual B is a nonanthropocentrist who endorses a consistent notion of the intrinsic value of the environment, then both A and B will end up supporting the same environmental policy positions. Norton predicted this convergence because he believed that, despite their different philosophical starting points, the weak anthropocentrist and the nonanthropocentrist embraced values that were ultimately dependent upon the long-term health or ecological sustainability of natural systems. The maintenance of multigenerational ecological processes, he argued, was the only way to protect ecological health, integrity, and biological diversity over the long run, whether these ends were justified by the comprehensive good of present and future generations of humans (the weak anthropocentrist position) or for the value that ecological health, integrity, biological diversity, and the like possesses in or for itself (the nonanthropocentrist position).

Norton briefly illustrated the CH in *Toward Unity* by referencing environmentalists' efforts to protect wetlands (as discussed above), a policy objective that he described as uniting advocates of a variety of ethical hues, including sportsmen and traditional conservation organizations (e.g., Ducks Unlimited, the National Wildlife Federation), as well as nature/wildlife appreciation societies like Audubon and Defenders of Wildlife.[31] As he wrote:

Information about the crucial role of wetlands in absorbing nutrients and limiting algae growth, information showing the crucial role of submerged aquatic vegetation in supporting migrating waterfowl, and facts about the importance of wetlands for migratory patterns generally—all focus attention on the policy goal of wetlands protection. Ecology therefore directs environmental concern to the *systematic* level, focusing attention on protecting whole complexes of wetlands. National and local groups espousing a wide variety of values and worldviews are therefore focused on the importance of habitat protection, even while some are polishing their field glasses and others are cleaning their shotguns.[32]

While Norton's prediction of the policy convergence of nonanthropocentric and anthropocentric positions was clearly a bold move in an environmental ethics field gripped by the view that these moral positions were polar opposites and thus irreconcilable, Norton soon drew a further conclusion in his argument that ensured the CH would become a lightning rod for criticism in the field. Since he believed in the empirical validity of the convergence thesis and he also believed that there were a number of thorny and insurmountable philosophical and practical problems afflicting nonanthropocentric theory, Norton concluded that it was more effective to argue for environmental policy goals from the weak anthropocentric point of view, that is, from the standpoint of the maintenance of options for future generations.[33] Norton's convergence thesis thus took a pragmatic and consequentialist line on value debates in environmental ethics. He favored those normative arguments—such as the claim that we should protect the environment for its ability to provide a harvest of cultural values for present and future generations—that he believed would most effectively lead to the resolution of actual environmental controversies. The CH's turn to naturalistic methods and empirical testing to resolve value disputes in environmental ethics, and Norton's work in the field more generally, have become fixtures in the pragmatist movement in environmental ethics and philosophy, an alternative set of approaches emphasizing value pluralism, experimentalism, and the search for policy consensus despite value differences.[34]

Norton's hypothesis with its implications for environmental ethical theorizing has generated a good deal of heat in the field since the early 1990s. In the years following the publication of *Toward Unity*, prominent nonanthropocentric philosophers such as J. Baird Callicott and Laura Westra came out strongly against Norton's convergence argument, declaring his prediction of the policy junction of weak anthropocentric and nonanthropocentric positions to be deeply suspect, or, in Callicott's words, "dead wrong." Along with Callicott and Westra, others of this persuasion insist that it makes a great practical difference whether one argues from anthropocentric or nonanthropocentric principles in real policy and conservation discussions. These "divergence" proponents in environmental ethics argue that humanist and nature-centered moral stances will ultimately lead to very different environmental policy agendas and practices.

Yet if Norton is right, the sharp value dualism—the anthropocentric-non anthropocentric cleavage—that has shaped the field of environmental ethics and much of the discourse of environmental advocacy has been for the most part unnecessary, and ethicists and environmental activists might do well to cease our internal squabbling over issues of moral purity and the misguided search for a final or universally "correct" expression of environmental values. We could then look toward building an integrative and pluralistic model of environmental ethics that places human and natural values within a more inclusive and commensurable value system, and devote more energy to the serious and more practical tasks of environmental policy analysis and political coalition building.

If, however, the "divergence" proponents are correct and it does indeed make a huge practical difference whether environmental policies are ultimately justified by nature-centered or human-centered principles and motivations, then maybe they are right to draw lines in the sand and hold fast to nonanthropocentric positions. Indeed, if the nonanthropocentrists are on target in the convergence debate, and the interests of humans and nature do not overlap in any appreciable sense, then environmental theorists and practitioners would seem (at the very least) irresponsible not to acknowledge the moral distinctiveness and practical significance of intrinsic-value-of-nature claims in environmental policy and conservation contexts. More significant, and as many of Norton's critics have argued, the failure to make strong nonanthropocentric defenses of environmental policy goals may even result in a serious weakening of environmental protection as the moral authority of "nature first" environmentalism is surrendered for less-absolutist anthropocentric justifications grounded in the shifting sands of enlightened human interests. The philosophical and practical stakes, in other words, are high.

A Brief Tour of the Book

Nature in Common? deepens and expands this important debate over the policy implications of environmental ethical theory. It does so by bringing together an ideologically diverse group of environmental ethicists and policy scholars to engage Norton's convergence argument and the issues it raises about the foundations and practical mission of environmental ethics as a branch of applied philosophy. Its contributors are among the most distinguished and influential writers in environmental ethics and policy studies today; collectively, their work has shaped and continues to shape the larger environmental philosophy agenda.

Given such philosophical breadth, it is probably not surprising that the authors of this volume are not of one mind regarding Norton's thesis and the policy import of environmental ethical arguments more generally. Chapters 2, 4, 6, 7, 9, and 11 provide a spirited defense of the nonanthropocentric tradition in environmental ethics and its necessary place in environmental policy argument. Others, however, including Chapters 3, 5, 8, 10, 12, 13, and 14, argue that a broad, pluralistic anthropocentrism is a legitimate approach to environmental ethical theorizing and an effective (if not the most effective) rationale for sound environmental policy goals. And while all of the contributors to this volume engage the convergence idea in one manner or another, many authors also use the debate over Norton's thesis as a mechanism to explore a number of additional themes and issues in environmental ethics and policy studies, ensuring that the following discussion is both philosophically interesting and politically vital.

The chapters in Part II, "The Convergence Hypothesis Debate in Environmental Ethics: The First Wave," lay out the original debate over Norton's thesis that emerged in the mid-1990s. Chapters 2 and 3 contain an interchange between Brian Steverson and Norton on the convergence idea, particularly its application to species conservation policy and Norton's attempt to operationalize his arguments via a contextualist decision procedure. Steverson claims that Norton's contextualism dooms his convergence argument because it violates the commitment of deep ecologists to preserve all species. For his part, Norton defends his convergence model and the contextualist method against Steverson's criticisms, elaborating in the process the logic and normative force of the "safe minimum standard" principle of conservation policy. The Steverson-Norton exchange was originally published in the journal *Environmental Ethics*.[35]

In Chapter 4 (also first published in *Environmental Ethics*), Laura Westra argues that both Norton's weak anthropocentrism and the convergence model are shaky foundations for environmental ethics and the shaping of environmental policy. Challenging in particular Norton's claim that there is little at stake in the debate between the anthropocentrists and the nonanthropocentrists for environmental policy choice, Westra argues that a strong nonanthropocentric holism (as expressed in her own "ethics of integrity") is required in order to fully protect natural systems and populations, and that intrinsic value claims are necessary to and effective in legislative and policy debates. In Chapter 5, Ben Minteer and Robert Manning respond to some of the assertions of Westra, Steverson, and others regarding Norton's theory by presenting the results of a social scientific study of the CH. Noting that many of his critics have not attempted to falsify what Norton originally intended to be a testable hypothesis about the actual policy implications of environmental ethics, Minteer and Manning argue that their inquiry into Vermont residents' environmental values and attitudes toward forest management policy provides empirical evidence for Norton's convergence claim. The chapter was originally published in *Ethics, Place and Environment*.

In Chapter 6, the final chapter in Part II, Mikael Stenmark keeps the debate over ethical convergence going by critically examining Norton's argument across a range of policy areas, including population policy, wilderness protection, and wildlife management. Stenmark suggests that, contrary to Norton's proposal, nonanthropocentrists (including both biocentrists and ecocentrists) and weak anthropocentrists do *not* share the same policy goals (both generally and in these specific domains) and that the value differences between nonanthropocentric and anthropocentric approaches are in fact highly relevant to the shaping and advocacy of general and specific policy agendas of environmental ethicists. Stenmark's chapter was originally published in *Environmental Ethics*.

Whereas Part II assembles important arguments in the first wave of the convergence-divergence debate in environmental ethics, Part III, "Expanding the Discussion: The Convergence Hypothesis Debate Today," brings together a new set of chapters written expressly for this volume. Authors in this section were tasked with exploring the contemporary relevance of Norton's thesis—including the questions it continues to raise for the discourse of environmental ethics as well as its status as normative policy argument.

In Chapter 7, Holmes Rolston, one of the founding figures of academic environmental ethics, argues that Norton's reformed anthropocentrism and the
CH actually reflect the extent to which weak anthropocentrists—and Norton
in particular—are moving closer to the nonanthropocentric position. The
biocentrists and ecocentrists, according to Rolston, are the ones enlightening
the moral sensibilities of the anthropocentrists, and Norton's argument for
convergence expresses (unconsciously, Rolston believes) the pull of the nonanthropocentric worldview. Rolston suggests that there is a convergence of values, and not just policy, taking place under the surface in Norton's work.

Douglas MacLean takes a different approach to the debate over environmental value theory and environmental policy, focusing in Chapter 8 on the
linkages between environmental and intergenerational ethics. Specifically,
MacLean identifies several issues of normative concern within economists'
approach to intertemporal environmental valuation. In doing so, he provides
one possible elaboration of the long-sighted anthropocentrism that stands as
a counterpoint to nonanthropocentric ethics. He also calls for more caution
among philosophers in making arguments about policy based on general metaphysical views. Even though MacLean is deeply critical of the reliance on
narrow economic reasoning in environmental decision making, he concludes
his chapter by suggesting that intrinsic-value-of-nature arguments do not add
much to the process of coming up with good reasons to protect the environment either today or in the future.

This conclusion is not shared by J. Baird Callicott, an ardent defender of
intrinsic-value-in-nature arguments and their role in justifying environmental
policy. In Chapter 9, Callicott argues that a careful interpretation of the ethical dimensions of legal decisions involving the ESA since its passage in 1973
effectively "falsifies" Norton's convergence hypothesis. According to Callicott,
while the ESA does not explicitly reference nonanthropocentric values, its citizen suit provision confers "implicit" intrinsic value and operational rights on
listed threatened and endangered species. Had the Act only accommodated
anthropocentric reasoning, Callicott argues, it would be a different policy
than the one we currently have. Therefore, he concludes, Norton's hypothesis
is not valid: Intrinsic value of nature arguments *do* make a practical difference
in environmental policy formulation and environmental decision making.

In Chapter 10, Paul B. Thompson focuses on how the CH has led Norton
toward a more explicit philosophical pragmatism in the years following the
publication of *Toward Unity*. Thompson considers the ways in which Norton's
engagement with the ideas of Dewey, Peirce, and the rest of the pragmatist
thinkers shaped his subsequent embrace of adaptive management and overall
approach to environmental philosophy since the early 1990s. Thompson then
builds a convergence argument of his own by tracing some of the connections between pragmatism and agrarian thought, illustrating how this general

philosophical orientation influenced land-use policy via the administrations of Thomas Jefferson and Theodore Roosevelt. Contrary to Thompson, Eric Katz (Chapter 11) argues that the CH departs from pragmatism in its rendering of philosophical ideas as meaningless in the face of common policy goals posited to exist among environmentalists. Katz also believes that the convergence thesis is refuted by the case of ecological restoration policy. Only anthropocentrists, he argues, will support restoration efforts; nonanthropocentrists will condemn them because restoration only creates "artifacts"; that is, landscapes diminished by the imposition of human intention and technology (and, more broadly, culture) on natural systems.

Andrew Light (Chapter 12) provides another spin on the relationship between pragmatism and Norton's convergence argument, suggesting that the latter has an important role to play in the development of environmental ethics into, as Light puts it, a more "public environmental philosophy" able to translate the disparate and often arcane moral languages of philosophers into a lexicon more hospitable to the justification of shared public policy goals. Light suggests that the CH is most powerful when conceived as a "thin" or methodologically pragmatic tool for environmental coalition building and problem solving, and he counsels against tethering it and the wider pragmatist approach in environmental ethics to any particular substantive arguments made by Peirce, Dewey, and the other "historical pragmatists."

Although Chapters 1–12 are certainly not written from the philosopher's mountaintop inasmuch as they are concerned with engaging practical implications of environmental ethics for policy argument, the final two chapters in Part III come directly from the policy trenches. The authors are not environmental philosophers, but rather environmental law and policy scholars with extensive experience and expertise in environmental policy and politics. In Chapter 13, Donald Brown reflects on the failure of environmental ethics to make inroads into environmental policy making, suggesting that this is due in part to the abstract nature of much environmental ethical analysis—especially its neglect of the economic, scientific, and legal issues that are contested in particular policy disputes. Brown argues for a more applied environmental ethics that can address these concerns and offers the case of the ethical evaluation of climate change policy as an illustration of the potential of concrete ethical analysis in environmental decision making. He concludes that Norton's convergence thesis is "more frequently right than wrong" in the climate policy example, though Brown emphasizes that the primary ethical conflict there is not anthropocentrism versus nonanthropocentrism, but rather tensions between anthropocentric ethical principles (e.g., rights-based and utility-based ethical considerations).

Science policy scholar Daniel Sarewitz makes a similar point in his "open letter" to Norton in Chapter 14. Arguing that nonanthropocentric rationales in environmental policy are politically impotent, Sarewitz suggests that, rather than devoting so much energy to the anthropocentric-nonanthropocentric dispute, we should acknowledge that the business of environmental policy making is more about the political struggle between various human interests; for example, aesthetic and cultural values of nature versus survival-based welfare values. The real challenge for normative convergence in environmental policy, Sarewitz believes, concerns the political task of aligning the major anthropocentric interests in resource conservation and biodiversity protection so that these outcomes are achieved, not building policy bridges with the nonanthropocentrists. It is an important point, especially given that environmental philosophers have strangely devoted comparatively little attention to understanding the moral and political motivations of those pressing anti-environmental agendas.[36]

In the concluding chapter of this book, "Convergence and Divergence: The Convergence Hypothesis Twenty Years Later," Bryan Norton replies to many of the criticisms raised in the preceding chapters while also providing deeper historical and intellectual context for his convergence argument. Although Norton hopes that the emergence of a less-dualistic form of environmentalism will ultimately reduce the need for the CH (which is premised on the value dualisms of environmentalists), he continues to think that it will remain a useful device for directing attention to areas of common ground and policy action and away from divisive and irresolvable philosophical contests over moral foundations and ideological purity in environmentalism.

Nature in Common? Environmental Ethics and the Contested Foundations of Environmental Policy provides a wide-ranging and philosophically balanced treatment of the dispute over the moral foundations of environmental ethics and the role of anthropocentric and nonanthropocentric values in shaping and supporting the environmental policy agenda. Although we can expect the debate over the practical consequences of environmental ethics, and Norton's convergence hypothesis in particular, to continue, the ideas and arguments in the following pages sharpen and expand our understanding of these vital issues. The chapters collected in this volume also signal, perhaps, the rise of a more engaged model of philosophical inquiry in environmental ethics, a particularly timely development given the growing concern that the field has not fulfilled its potential as a normative discourse for environmental policy making.[37] Hopefully, then, this book will encourage environmental philosophers to devote more serious attention to the complex intersection of environmental values and policy outcomes, a line of inquiry that can only render the concepts and arguments of environmental ethics more legible and relevant to intelligent environmental decision making.

11

The Convergence Hypothesis Debate in Environmental Ethics

The First Wave

BRIAN K. STEVERSON

Contextualism and Norton's Convergence Hypothesis

Introduction

A s a prominent voice in environmental philosophy for more than two decades, Bryan Norton has labored to show that the intractable axiological debate between "anthropocentrists" and "nonanthropocentrists"—which has served to frame most discussions of environmental ethics—often distracts attention away from the fact that when it comes to practical principles of environmental management, the two opposing approaches for the most part converge.[1] His argument has been that because the nonanthropocentric position involves highly questionable metaphysical and epistemological commitments, and because nothing of normative importance contained in nonanthropocentric theories is lost in dispensing with these commitments, environmentalists would be better served by adopting what he has called a "weak anthropocentric" standpoint. More recently, Norton has also been in the forefront of efforts to develop the conceptual apparatus for an approach to environmental management that is capable of accommodating both socioeconomic and environmental perspectives without requiring extraordinary sacrifices from the supporters of either position. In a number of writings, he has worked to articulate and defend an approach to environmental management that adopts as its mandate the maintenance of ecological "health" and that is

From Brian K. Steverson, "Contextualism and Norton's Convergence Hypothesis," *Environmental Ethics* 17 (1995): 135–150. Reprinted with permission.

loosely modeled on the paradigm of medical science. Because social and economic systems can be viewed as being contextually embedded in larger environmental systems, Norton holds that such an approach is capable of integrating socioeconomic concerns with environmental concerns, in that the maintenance of the health of the environmental context in which socioeconomic activity takes place is necessary if such practices are to continue to exist and flourish. These two intellectual activities converge in *Toward Unity among Environmentalists*, where he argues that despite divergences regarding ultimate values and justifications, "a consensus on the broad outlines of an intelligent policy" is possible among "environmentalists of different stripes" once their concerns are placed within a framework of environmental management centered on the maintenance of ecological health.[2]

A prime example of Norton's position can be found in a chapter devoted to interspecific ethics,[3] where he continues his program of reconciliation by arguing that when analyzed in detail, deep ecology—the paradigmatic example of a nonanthropocentric approach to environmental ethics—would not, in general, issue policy positions different from those advanced by "long-sighted anthropocentrists." Norton's conclusion is that "introducing the idea that other species have intrinsic value, that humans should be 'fair' to all other species, provides no operationally recognizable constraints on human behavior that are not already implicit in the generalized, cross-temporal obligations to protect a healthy, complex, and autonomously functioning system for the benefit of future generations of humans."[4]

Norton's position is that this policy convergence takes the form of a bilateral commitment to the standpoint that all species should be protected as long as the socioeconomic costs of doing so are bearable, a point of view that has been labeled the "safe minimum standard" (SMS) criterion.[5] I argue that even if one grants the premise with regard to practical policy formation that deep ecologists are committed to or would accept the SMS criterion, the possibility of convergence between deep ecology and long-sighted anthropocentrism is minimal, or even nonexistent. This is because the overall methodological framework for policy formation within which Norton places the concerns of long-sighted anthropocentrism—a framework that he refers to as "contextualism"—is unlikely to generate an overall approach to policy formation that accommodates the axiological intuitions of deep ecologists since it allows for the disappearance of species even when the costs of preserving them are bearable. I concede that, in the presence of scientific ignorance about the structure and functioning of ecological systems, the contextualist approach might commit environmental management to something at least as strong as the SMS criterion. Nevertheless, I argue that given the directive for ecological science set by contextualism, if ecological science does at some future time develop the required body of knowledge, then the most reasonable decision criterion for environmental management will be one that is considerably weaker than the SMS criterion, and too weak to capture the axiological intuitions of deep ecologists.

The Convergence Argument

The controversial nature of Norton's claim about convergence lies in the fact that the basic value assumptions that underlie anthropocentric approaches on the one hand and the deep ecology movement on the other stand in rather stark contrast to one another. Consequently, proponents of approaches based on ascriptions of intrinsic value to nonhuman species may be hesitant to concede Norton's point regarding policy formation because they perceive it also to be a concession on the more basic axiological commitment. Put another way, their intuition about the inherent value of all nonhuman species, which is expressed as a philosophical claim about intrinsic value, might appear to them to be incompatible with anthropocentric-based policies, which, at least prima facie, subordinate the value of nonhuman species to that of humans.

What Norton tries to show in *Toward Unity among Environmentalists* is that in agreeing to the kind of preservationist policy that emerges from the long-sighted anthropocentric approach, deep ecologists need not, in effect, abandon their initial intuitions about the value of nonhuman species. Rather, what they are abandoning is a particular philosophical framework for translating those intuitions into axiological claims. As Norton notes, when forced to develop precise policy positions, deep ecologists, as a consequence of their commitment to "unqualified egalitarianism," find themselves in situations of undecidable conflicts when faced with circumstances requiring (some) killing or exploitation.[6] Naess himself was aware of this problem and included in his original articulation of the principle of biospherical egalitarianism the qualification that such a principle was an ideal, and that "any realistic praxis necessitates some killing, exploitation, and suppression."[7] This qualification, however, as Norton points out, creates the possibility that a de facto hierarchy of value will supplant the ideal of biospherical egalitarianism, and, more seriously, that such a hierarchy will in effect "map onto the phylogenetic scale in a predictably anthropocentric pattern" an outcome that is self-defeating for the deep ecologist position.[8] For Norton, this consideration reveals the problem with the deep ecologists' approach to generating principles of policy: Its axiological framework is too individualistic. In committing themselves to the nonhierarchical ideal that *all individual* organisms are of *equal* inherent value, deep ecologists find themselves bereft of a methodology that allows them to escape the dilemmas posed by axiological conflicts. Further, the implicit metaphysical atomism contained in this individualistic axiology directly clashes with the professed metaphysics of deep ecologists, namely holism.

According to Norton, when the deep ecologists' intuitions about the value of nonhuman species are placed in a contextualist framework consistent with their own holistic commitments in which individuals are recognized as part of larger systematic wholes, the difficulties that emerge from an individualistic perspective (i.e., irresolvable conflicts) are avoided due to the fact that the continued "health" of larger, ecological wholes—a concern for any "realistic praxis"—may require that some individuals be "killed, exploited, or suppressed." Such ecological necessity does not entail that particular individuals are being treated in an "unfair" or "unjust" way because contextualism embodies an approach to environmental management based on the principle of "interspecific impartiality," that is, the view that restraints on species populations and their activities, *humans included,* are to be based on standards of ecological health, not on strictly anthropocentric standards. As Norton notes, this principle of interspecific impartiality requires that "humans are morally justified in culling elk only if the humans are willing, similarly and impartially, to limit their own populations when they exceed their carrying capacity."[9]

Norton's conclusion, understood contextually rather than atomistically, is that the deep ecologists' intuitions about the inherent value of nonhuman species are not threatened by an anthropocentric approach in that "No long-term human values can be protected without protecting the context in which they evolved [a diverse natural environment]."[10] Instead, what one comes to expect is convergence: human interests and nonhuman interests converge. Placed within the proper epistemological-axiological framework, the deep ecologist's call for the preservation of species will be identical to the demands of mainstream environmentalists that species be protected provided that the costs of doing so are bearable. The SMS approach rests on the presumption that all species are of value and that the burden of proof lies with those who would diminish this value to show that the socioeconomic costs of preserving species is prohibitive. As such, the concerns of such avowed nonanthropocentrists as the deep ecologists converge with those of anthropocentric mainstream environmentalists when one arrives at the point of general policy formation.

In this context, I am not interested in exploring the validity of Norton's convergence hypothesis itself, although, of course, such a critical assessment is necessary. Norton grants the hypothesis a dual status. It is both "a very general empirical hypothesis" and "an article of environmentalists' faith."[11] Whether it can stand as an empirical hypothesis and whether it ought to be a committed guide for environmental management are important questions to consider, though not ones I wish to pursue here other than to argue that in the case of species preservation, deep ecologists might be more than a little suspicious about the possibility of convergence. Also, I am not interested in reviewing Norton's argument that deep ecologists would be driven to a decision criterion similar to the SMS criterion. It must be conceded, however, that Norton's claim is at least plausible. Deep ecologists must be able to translate their normative claims into reasonably specific positions regarding action, both individual and collective. One would expect that in order to preserve their belief in the intrinsic value of nonhuman nature, deep ecologists would opt for a decision criterion that minimizes as far as possible the extent to which such value can be allowed to disappear or diminish. The SMS criterion is, prima facie, an appropriate candidate in that it represents an attempt to maximize the preservation of species by requiring that only *prohibitive* costs count as legitimate reasons for engaging in activities that threaten species diversity. An important point of dispute will of course be the question, "What counts as *prohibitive?*" Nonetheless, supposing that this issue could be settled to the satisfaction of deep ecologists and long-sighted anthropocentrists (which might prove to be quite a difficult task), it is quite plausible to believe that deep ecologists would be comfortable with the SMS criterion and convergence would be achieved.

Apart from whether or not the SMS criterion is the most plausible decision criterion for deep ecologists to consent to, the question I wish to explore is whether the SMS criterion is the most reasonable decision criterion for contextually framed, long-sighted anthropocentrism to accept. If it is not, then the convergence question has to be restated in terms of the decision criterion that the contextually based environmental manager *would* commit to. Understood this way, I think it becomes clear that no such policy convergence would occur and, in this specific context, that Norton's convergence hypothesis is not supported. Demonstrating this point requires an exploration of what Norton means by *contextualism.*

Contextualism

In a number of articles and in *Toward Unity among Environmentalists,* Norton develops the methodological framework for policy formation that he refers to as the contextualist approach.[12] Contextualism is a synthesis of a pared-down version of the traditional organicist metaphor and hierarchy theory, a contemporary approach to systems ecology. As Norton puts it, "Expressed metaphorically, contextualism is organicism—the biota is a living system which has an internal, self-perpetuating organization—but organicism minus teleology."[13] The "minus teleology" qualification is intended to demystify organicism by stripping it of any connotations of *intentional* activity on the part of ecological systems. What is left is a "methodological/metaphorical" version of organicism that Norton refers to as "minimal holism."[14] This version of organicism focuses on the autopoietic, or autogenic, capacity of ecosystems manifested through the many homeostatic and homeorhetic responses that they exhibit in reaction to internal disturbances and environmental changes. Although not developed in *Why Preserve Natural Variety?* as a part of contextualism, Norton provides in his earlier book a concise explanation of the nature of autopoietic ecological systems.[15] In the course of refining the traditional diversity-stability hypothesis in the light of contemporary ecological thought, Norton notes that the concepts of diversity and stability in an ecological context are "multiply ambiguous." Traditionally, diversity has been understood as "within-habitat diversity," and stability has been interpreted either as constancy, an ecosystem's capacity for withstanding structural disturbances, or as resiliency, an ecosystem's ability to "bounce back" from disturbances and resume a predisturbance state. It is the connection between the two concepts so understood that has failed to be empirically supported. To solve this difficulty, Norton offers an alternative way of formulating the hypothesis that involves different interpretations of the two constituent concepts. Instead of within-habitat diversity, Norton suggests that attention be focused on "total diversity," or the variety and relative abundance of species occupying all of the habitats that compose a given geographical region. Because ecosystemic boundaries are not fixed and are permeable, the species makeup of any given ecosystem is subject to natural fluctuations due to species immigration and emigration. By focusing on total diversity, these natural fluctuations—the downturns of which might otherwise be taken as signs of ecosystemic "illness"—can be accommodated without alarm since the entire pool of potential colonizers is accounted for, and a more realistic picture of the dynamic character of ecosystems is generated.

Regarding ecosystemic stability, Norton appropriately points out that it is an agreed-upon ecological fact that ecosystems change structurally over time. The idea of ecological succession—that ecosystems develop through stages—captures this inherent ecosystemic dynamism. As he indicates, however, constancy and resiliency are static concepts, applicable to ecosystems only as systems "frozen in time." To equate ecosystemic stability with constancy or resiliency is to deny the dynamic character of ecosystems by implying that a stable ecosystem is one that seeks to maintain some fixed structural state. What ecologists have come to realize is that ecosystems display a number of "normal" states to which they return after disturbances. A disturbance that exceeds a certain threshold causes a system to adjust to a new structural state, whereas disturbances below that threshold are followed by a return to the predisturbance state. This multiplicity of postdisturbance states is typical of both stable and unstable ecosystems. Drawing on Margalef's analysis of ecosystemic maturity, Norton argues that the difference between stable and unstable ecosystems lies in the fact that the future states of the former are largely the result of internal forces and not external environmental inputs, whereas the future states of the latter are due largely to such external forces.[16] *Stability* is defined in terms of a system's autogenic capabilities; so understood, it has a dynamic character, better reflecting the actual development of ecosystems. Ulanowicz has even called this capacity of ecosystems—the ability to "creatively" adjust to changes in circumstances—the defining feature of healthy ecosystems.[17]

Given these interpretations of diversity and stability, Norton recasts the diversity-stability hypothesis as the view that total diversity, because it represents the potential for intense competition for available niche space in regional ecosystems, leads to the development of autogenic ecosystems:

The proposed version of the diversity-stability hypothesis claims that, when ecosystems develop under such intense competition [present in an area with a large amount of total diversity], they will attain, both more quickly and to a greater degree, the characteristics associated with dynamic stability. Systems in which competition for niche space is intense will develop a high degree of complexity, interrelatedness, and niche specialization. These characteristics lead to greater degrees of autogenic determination: alterations of the system become increasingly determined by features internal to it.[18]

To fill out contextualism, Norton overlays this view of ecological systems as autopoietic with a template for understanding the complexity and internal organization of ecological structure drawn from hierarchy theory.[19]

According to hierarchy theorists, natural systems exhibit complexity because they embody processes that occur at different rates of speed; generally speaking, larger systems (such as a community) change more slowly than the microhabitats and individual organisms that compose them, just as the organism changes more slowly than the cells that compose it. Further, the community survives after individuals die and, while changes in the community affect (constrain) the activities of the individuals that compose it, the individuals themselves are unlikely to affect the larger system because the individual is likely to die before the slow-changing system in which it is embedded will be significantly altered by its activities.[20]

This hierarchical nesting of "subsystems" or "holons"—organ/organism, organism/population, population/microhabitat, microhabitat/ecosystem, ecosystem/bioregion, and so on, as they are called—allows one to model intrasystemic complexity by choosing from a range of temporal and spatial scales based on the particular goal of the investigation. As noted by Norton, although "higher" holons form the relatively stable environment in which "lower" holons operate, and they are relatively immune to the destabilizing activities of lower holons, that is not to say that higher holons are entirely immune to the effects of lower holons:

> As a part, the holon affects the whole, but scale is very important—the "choices" of one element will not significantly alter the whole—but if that part's activities represent a trend among its peers, then the larger and slower-changing system will reflect these changes on its larger and slower scale. One cell turning malignant will not affect an organism significantly unless it represents a trend toward malignancy. If such a trend is instituted, then the organism might eventually be destroyed by that trend in its parts.[21]

For Norton, this fusion of autopoietic function and multiscalar hierarchical structure represents the framework within which environmental management is to take place and provides a method by which to construct "an ecologically sound concept of dynamic health for ecological systems."[22] The "distinctive character" of contextual management is a focus "not so much on individual actions as on their collective effects on the larger system and their effects on trends across more distant time,"[23] with a goal of avoiding those activities that disrupt the autopoietic behavior of ecological systems by accelerating the rate of change in the larger holons.

Concerning the preservation of biodiversity, the general implication of contextualist management is that the accelerated rate of human-caused extinctions threatens ecosystemic health because, as a trend, it threatens to accelerate the rate of change in those larger systems that environ species populations (e.g., communities and bioregions). More specifically, relying on Norton's recommendation that the scale of resolution most proper to questions of species preservation is that of total diversity, the concern for contextualist environmental management is that the global trend of reduction in total diversity threatens to disrupt the "normal" rate of ecological change in bioregions. Consequently, the environmental manager will ultimately be concerned with activities that accelerate the "natural" pace of change in the species profile of bioregions. Activities that affect the pace in a fashion that causes it to diverge from its "normal" rate are to be deemed unacceptable because they will have the effect of deleteriously impacting the larger organizational levels of regional ecological systems.

In Norton's opinion, such a contextualist approach to environmental management produces a baseline recommendation that a species be preserved unless the costs of doing so are prohibitive or, alternatively, that a species be preserved as long as the costs are bearable. Norton describes the merits of the SMS criterion in this way:

It sets as its goal to save all species, but accepts that efforts to save species must be politically and ecologically viable, and that choices will have to be made as to how preservation dollars will be spent. The SMS criterion states the common sense position: In the extreme case, costs might override the strong presumption in favor of preservation, but the burden of proof always rests on those who would degrade a resource or destroy a species.[24]

Norton acknowledges in *Why Preserve Natural Variety?* that he adopts the SMS criterion because "it embodies the central assumption that all species have value," and he puts the burden of proof on those who would diminish or destroy such value to show that such a loss is unavoidable or necessary to satisfy some other equally stringent moral obligation.[25] It is clear from his later writings that his endorsement of the SMS criterion is also based on his belief that it is the most reasonable approach to protecting large-scale ecosystemic processes, inasmuch as protecting such processes is dependent on the maintenance of total diversity, and that it represents a presumptive commitment to protecting as many species as possible.[26]

Contextualism, Decision Criteria, and Convergence

As mentioned earlier, setting aside questions about the acceptability of the SMS criterion from the perspective of deep ecology, the other half of the convergence hypothesis can be questioned. Would long-sighted or weak anthropocentrism, understood within a contextualist framework, result in the SMS criterion? My position is that it would not. The problem is that contextualism provides inadequate support for the presumption that species can be allowed to diminish in abundance or go extinct (locally, regionally, or globally) only in those cases where the costs of preservation are prohibitive. In other words, there is room within contextualism for the environmental manager to adopt a decision criterion that lowers the acceptability standard for species loss below the "bearability" level; species losses may be acceptable even if the costs of preservation are bearable, or are not prohibitive.

The focus of the contextualist approach to environmental management is clearly on systemic issues. Specifically, in terms of biodiversity preservation, the goal is "to protect *total diversity at the landscape level of ecological organization*."[27] Interpreted in the light of hierarchy theory, the positing of such a goal entails that concern be directed at monitoring phenomena at the level of the lower holons that may accelerate the normal pace of changes in total diversity at the level of the "landscape" holon. In particular, the environmental manager is to be on the alert for developing trends in the decline of species populations that might, if unabated, accelerate changes in total diversity. As such, the contextualist is concerned with declines in the abundance of individual species only if such declines represent or have the capacity to initiate a trend in species loss.

The implication seems to be that the loss or decline of an individual species is not, in and of itself, an issue of concern. As hierarchy theorists admit, the activities of lower-level holons tend not to affect the higher-level processes unless such activities "represent a trend among its peers." If so, then the loss or decline of an individual species ought not to be cause for alarm unless one has good reason to think that such a loss or decline has the potential to initiate, or in fact is already part of, a regional trend in species decline and loss. Is it plausible to believe that in fact there may be instances in which the loss or substantial decline of an individual species or small set of species does not represent or does not have the potential to initiate "trends in its peers"? Or is such a scenario inherently implausible because every species loss or decline either represents the beginning of such a trend or has the potential to initiate one? I argue that such a scenario is indeed quite plausible.

As mentioned earlier, it is the nature of ecosystems, as autopoietic systems, to display the capacity for "creative" responses to environmental changes and internal disturbances, such as fluctuations in species abundance and demographics. If so, then it makes sense to assume that ecosystems have tolerance levels. Due to their structural and functional complexity, within certain parameters they may perhaps withstand the loss or decline of individual species and still maintain their autopoietic capacity at higher levels of organization. That ecosystems persist structurally over very long time periods seems to underscore the fact that as self-organizing systems they have "built-in" tolerances to environmental changes. The concept of ecosystemic threshold, mentioned earlier in the context of the definition of ecosystemic autopoiesis, is indicative of this inherent tolerance. Using the analogy of medicine, which Norton finds to be an appropriate metaphor for the approach of a contextualist environmental manager, the existence of one malignant cell does not seriously impact the health of the organism unless it represents a trend in malignancy. Additionally, the loss of any particular cell, or assemblage of cells, may not be cause for alarm if the organism's ability to maintain itself is not diminished. In either case, what is evidenced is the ability of an organism (a particular type of autopoietic system) to tolerate the loss or diminishment of some particular component. If so, then calls for invasive procedures to remove the malignant cell or avoid the loss of cells are medically unnecessary. Applied to species preservation, if the decline or loss of an individual species poses no threat to the "health" of the larger system, then calls for intervention to prevent further decline or to prevent the local (or global) extinction of such species, though not prohibited, are ecologically "unnecessary."

When the decline or loss of some individual species poses no threat to the autopoietic capacities of the larger systems, the socioeconomic costs required to reverse the decline or save the species from extinction take on greater significance than they do in cases where one is faced with a developing trend in species impoverishment. Once the ecological necessity of preserving an individual species no longer holds, one can plausibly argue that since society can avoid the socioeconomic costs that would be incurred if attempts were made to save the species, and in doing so create no or little risk to ecosystemic health, then, in accordance with the management goal of balancing environmental and socioeconomic concerns, the most reasonable *management* decision is to allow the species to continue to decline or go extinct. Because, as quoted above, Norton defends the view that questions about how to spend resources, financial and otherwise, are essential to decisions about species preservation, it is reasonable to assume that the contextualist manager could, in specific cases, decide to allow certain species to decline or go extinct (locally or globally) even though the costs of preservation are bearable. Notice that this same conclusion is reached if one considers cases in which certain socioeconomic benefits are derived from activities that impact the abundance of certain species, but where such impact does not represent an ecologically dangerous trend. In either case, the existence of certain species becomes a barterable commodity that can be exchanged for other benefits or to avoid certain costs. If so, then contextualism entails a much weaker decision criterion than the SMS criterion. Most likely, the actual decision criterion would be to avoid *trends* in species decline or loss unless the costs of doing so are prohibitive, which clearly marks a move away from assigning presumptive protection to species on an individual basis.

Of course, even this weaker decision criterion contains a presumptive commitment to preserving *many* species; a failure to do so would represent a trend in species decline or loss since species are interrelated. Nevertheless, this commitment, given the quantitative vagueness of *many,* is far different from a presumptive commitment to preserve *all* species if possible, and quite different from a commitment to preserve *as many species as possible.*[28] These differences follow from the fact that it is plausible to believe that ecosystems are structured so as to be capable of "tolerating" significant changes in the composition and amount of total diversity. Norton acknowledges as much when he remarks that: "Diversity must be understood dynamically, in terms of healthy processes, rather than merely as maintenance of current elements of the system."[29] If existing species patterns are not the *ultimate* object of concern for the contextualist environmental manager, then the goal of preserving *all* species or *as many as possible* is no longer operative. Noticeable changes in the "current elements" of any particular ecosystem become allowable not only in cases where preventive costs are prohibitive but also in cases where such costs are bearable.

When the implications of contextualist environmental management are spelled out in this way, the possibility that deep ecology and long-sighted anthropocentrism would converge at the level of policy formation seems less likely, bordering on the nonexistent. Norton's criticism of deep ecology's axiological individualism turns out to be a double-edged sword. True, unqualified egalitarianism leads to irresolvable policy conflicts; however, thoroughgoing contextualism, despite its apparent ability to achieve consistent policy formation, fails to provide adequate support for the preservation of individual species. It fails to do so because it turns the focus of environmental preservation away from individual species and toward ecosystemic processes. This shift in focus is mirrored by a shift in normative goals. Unlike the deep ecologist, who will be committed to preserving as many species as possible—and who will try to define "possible" in such a way as to maximize the amount of species diversity preserved without requiring extraordinary socioeconomic sacrifices—the contextualist environmental manager will be committed to the much weaker normative goal of avoiding trends in species loss. These different normative goals are not easily translatable into equivalent decision criteria. The intractability of the debate at the normative level is not relieved at the level of policy formation. The optimism expressed for the convergence hypothesis seems to wane when the issue of devising a single comprehensive decision criterion by which to develop practical policy is addressed, at least as regards species preservation.

Conclusion

There is an obvious and potentially powerful response to my argument that deserves consideration. It could be argued that my criticism of Norton's convergence hypothesis rests on a false assumption, namely, that we are in a position to predict which lower-level phenomena will or will not accelerate processes at higher systemic levels. Such an assumption, it can be argued, is simply false; we do not have at our disposal the requisite knowledge of ecological structures to make such predictions. As ecologists have come to recognize, ecosystems are so complex that simple linear explanations of ecological phenomena and their interrelatedness are grossly unrealistic. The fact that higher-level systemic processes occur over such long periods of time makes it terribly difficult, if not outright impossible, to accumulate the kind of data necessary to generate reasonably comprehensive principles of ecosystemic functioning and to test theories and models. Because of the short temporal scale of the studies that have been undertaken, the available data is at best "uncertain." Consequently, cases in which species can be "sacrificed" because of their "ecological unimportance" are in the best of circumstances only hypothetical, since the kind of ecological knowledge required in such cases is itself nonexistent. In the presence of ecological ignorance, the contextualist manager must be committed to the stronger version of the SMS criterion. Because we are not in a position to determine whether the loss of any particular species will initiate a trend, all species should be protected if the socioeconomic costs of doing so are bearable.

The appropriate response to this objection depends on the strength of the epistemological claim embedded in it. First, it is obviously true that we are far from the kind of ecological enlightenment necessary to make such cases a *real* possibility, and as long as that situation remains unchanged, my argument is at best a theoretical one. As a result, Norton can easily respond that such a theoretical problem is not worrisome because it has no impact on policy formation. At that level, the SMS criterion *will* be the most reasonable such criterion for the contextualist manager to adopt, and if it is also the most reasonable criterion for deep ecologists to adopt, then the convergence hypothesis holds for species preservation. However, some questions must be answered: Is our present ecological ignorance simply a contingent phenomenon, or are ecological structures so complex that it is inconceivable we will ever come to acquire sufficient knowledge to generate causal principles linking phenomena in lower holons with processes in higher ones? Are we suffering from temporary or permanent ecological blindness?

If ecological science continues to develop and ecologists begin to generate a body of principled knowledge capable of grounding predictive hypotheses, then the ability to predict the impact of lower-level phenomena on higher-level systemic processes may become a *real* possibility. If so, however, the appropriateness of the SMS criterion for contextualist environmental management will only be temporary. At some future point, the weaker version of the SMS criterion will become more reasonable. Convergence, if it is realized, will be a simple historical fact, not a principled position.

Furthermore, Norton and others who defend an approach to environmental management based on the metaphor of medical science operate with an overall framework that *requires* the availability of such ecological knowledge.[30] As Norton remarks, "Scientific contextualism places a heavy burden on scientific models to help us determine which activities may have long-delayed, but potentially catastrophic, consequences."[31] With regard to modeling environmental management on medical science, Norton writes, "Just as medical research must fulfill both a criterion of methodological rigor *and* a criterion of relevance—usefulness in healing patients—conservation biologists are likewise obligated to characterize ecological systems in ways that are not only accurate, but useful in protection and recovery programs."[32]

Norton acknowledges that the application of ecological principles of "diagnosis" and "treatment" to environmental management continues to be difficult because there is no adequate characterization of the "physiology" of ecological systems, which is primarily the result of difficulties in resolving "scale issues"; nevertheless, if environmental management is to be guided by the mandate "Protect ecosystemic health," then it must have at its disposal a body of knowledge that allows it to engage in diagnostic, curative, and preventive ecological "medicine."[33] With regard to a contextual hierarchical approach to environmental management, Norton holds out the hope that "hierarchy theory, or some other model of complex systems, may someday furnish mathematical ratios of change across systems of differing levels."[34] Without this type of knowledge, managing lower-level holons so as to avoid impacting the rate of change in higher-level holons seems to be little more than guesswork. In the presence of such knowledge, the possibility that we can determine when species decline or loss is ecologically benign becomes quite real.

Conversely, if a sufficiently detailed and comprehensive body of ecological knowledge is an impossibility, then environmental *management* becomes a practical impossibility in the same way that managing human health would have been impossible without the tremendous advances made by medical science. This kind of "argument from ignorance" is one that Norton uses quite extensively to criticize the traditional economic approach to valuing species. In *Toward Unity among Environmentalists*, he sums up the problem this way:

> Given the magnitude of the problems afflicting aggregative methods of valuing species, it is not surprising that Moralists ridicule the economists' attempts. Economists are very far from having, even for one well-known species, a complete accounting of all its present and future values. Given that many endangered species, especially in the tropics, have neither been named or studied, the Aggregator offers an approach to valuing species that is at best theoretical.[35]

If contextualism is plagued by a similar inherent inability to specify the ecological value of species, then Norton's criticism of the aggregator's approach applies to contextualism as well. Although it may represent a sound theoretical approach to environmental management, without the knowledge and techniques necessary to generate predictive hypotheses about the effects of species loss, contextualism will be an unfeasible approach to policy formation.

Thus, on the one hand, if ecological science is capable of developing the kind of clinical knowledge necessary to make contextualism work as a form of environmental management, then it is both conceptually and pragmatically unlikely that Norton's convergence hypothesis will hold with regard to species preservation. On the other hand, if clinical ecology is a conceptual impossibility, then contextualist environmental management will suffer a similar fate as a practical approach to environmental decision making. Because Norton is committed to a defense of contextualism, the latter position on ecological knowledge is not an option for him. Consequently, from the perspective of contextualism, the matter of policy convergence remains problematic. Because forming environmental policy is a matter of unifying diverse environmental perspectives, contextualism may prove to be an inadequate framework within which to attempt to derive environmental management policy that incorporates some of the more demanding normative, environmental claims, like those of deep ecology.

3   BRYAN G. NORTON

Convergence and Contextualism

Some Clarifications and a Reply to Steverson

Introduction

B rian Steverson has recently criticized my convergence hypothesis, arguing that it fails when articulated in conjunction with my contextualist
methodology because contextualism does not support the strong intuitions of deep ecologists in favor of species preservation.[1] The convergence
hypothesis, which I have offered as an alternative to the traditionally divisive characterization of environmentalists as split between "shallow" anthropocentric resource managers and "deep" nonanthropocentric environmental
radicals, states that "provided anthropocentrists consider the full breadth of
human values as they unfold into the indefinite future, and provided nonanthropocentrists endorse a consistent and coherent version of the view that
nature has intrinsic value, all sides may be able to endorse a common policy
direction."[2] The centerpiece of Steverson's argument is a proof that a contextualist such as myself—when emphasizing ecological systems and processes
as understood from many local perspectives—would be more willing than a
deep ecologist/nonanthropocentrist to sacrifice a species in some situations.
This policy divergence in certain situations—situations that he characterizes
only as "theoretical"[3]—is cited as evidence that the flexibility of contextualism dooms convergence.

From Bryan Norton, "Convergence and Contextualism: Some Clarifications and a Reply to
Steverson," *Environmental Ethics* 19 (1997): 87–100. Reprinted with permission.

I am indebted to Steverson for a concise and mostly accurate summary of my positions on convergence and contextualism, including changes in their emphasis over the years. Further, I agree that deep ecologists should accept the safe minimum standard criterion, according to which there is a strong presumption in favor of saving a threatened resource, provided the social costs are bearable.[4] Steverson and I also agree that advocates of the safe minimum standard criterion should directly address the question of what costs are bearable, and what costs are prohibitive. Even in these areas of agreement, however, clarification of an important ambiguity in the deep ecologists' intuitions is necessary.

What Exactly Is the Intuition of the Deep Ecologists?

Because the deep ecologists' position is put forward simply as an intuition,[5] we must be very clear what that intuition says; however, Steverson himself characterizes it in at least two, apparently nonequivalent, forms. When he is not criticizing contextualism for its failure to provide adequate protection for species, Steverson refers to the deep ecologists' intuition as a belief that "nonhuman nature" has intrinsic value: "One would expect that in order to preserve their belief in the intrinsic value of nonhuman nature, deep ecologists would opt for a decision criterion that minimizes as far as possible the extent to which such value can be allowed to disappear or diminish."[6] At other points in Steverson's work, and especially when he is criticizing contextualism for not being adequately protective of species, he says that deep ecologists have an "intuition about the inherent value of all species."[7] It is not clear to me whether Steverson believes that these assertions are equivalent (that "nonhuman nature" and "all species" are synonyms) or whether, as one would naturally assume, the first is a general intuition and the reference to all species is a nonequivalent version of this general intuition because it is more specific.

This semantic ambiguity is crucial, because if the two phrases are synonyms, then it is impossible for there to be a divergence between policies to protect species and policies to protect nature—by definition, these would be identical goals. If, conversely, the general intuition includes elements of nature—such as intact ecosystems—as having intrinsic value, then there could be conflicts between species preservation and ecosystem preservation and restoration. The scientific jury is still out on the importance of species, *qua species,* a subject to which I return below. I hold that deep ecologists, especially if they are inclined to accept the safe minimum standard criterion, should (at least for now) leave open the question whether species is to be *the one and only* unit of nature to which intrinsic value applies. At any rate, it seems a mistake to resolve this important question by intuitively supported definition. Indeed, the negotiability of such questions seems the essential outcome of the "unless costs are unbearable" clause in the safe minimum standard criterion. If deep ecologists accepted the safe minimum standard criterion, they would presumably join contextualists in weighing the scientific and value arguments regarding the actual importance of individual species, both in general and in specific situations.[8] Alternatively, if intrinsically valuable "nature" is *defined as* "the current stock of species," then the criterion has very different implications, emphasizing species at the expense of ecosystem processes in all cases. The problem for Steverson, however, is that the sensible, flexible interpretation of the deep ecologists' intuitions regarding intrinsic value is not sufficient to support his central critical arguments. Agreement to use the safe minimum standard criterion may not, therefore, resolve the related but apparently independent question of whether we should in all cases make species protection our first priority, unless it does so arbitrarily, by definition.

This definitional question, whether we should in all cases consider saving nature to be equivalent to saving the totality of species, has consequences for real-world conservation conflicts. In 1992 *Science* magazine reported that the important efforts of the state of Florida to reestablish the pulse regimen of water flow in the Everglades could further endanger the snail kite, a species that survives there by preying upon a single species of snails.[9] The question was whether the kite, greatly reduced in numbers, could survive the draining of a holding area that had become their main feeding grounds. An official of the Fish and Wildlife Service believed that the endangered kite populations might be harmed and filed a "jeopardy opinion," halting plans to restore the Everglades' hydrology. It is debatable whether the kite case indeed represented a conflict between ecosystem management and species management, and the dispute has subsequently been resolved,[10] but the fact that such a conflict could arise reveals the importance of the ambiguity in the intuition that Steverson attributes to deep ecologists. If deep ecologists believe that species *and only species* have intrinsic value, they may be forced to oppose important actions to repair damaged ecosystems, with the paradoxical result that failure to save processes could on a longer scale lead to a loss of even more species.

The Problem of Conservation Targets

Steverson accepts my argument that, even with the assumptions of Arne Naess and other deep ecologists, it is impossible to apply, straightforwardly in practice, the principle of biospecies egalitarianism at the individual level;

thus, he recommends that deep ecologists accept my appeal for a more "holistic" approach and that they join me in accepting the weaker standard of "biospecies impartiality."[11] Biospecies impartiality is applied not at the individual level but at the species level. Driven by a recognition that deep ecologists must formulate *some* specific policy recommendation on species protection, and convinced by this argument, Steverson concludes that deep ecologists would probably embrace the safe minimum standard criterion as I formulate it. Nevertheless, Steverson's argument is confusing because the dichotomy of individualism versus holism represents, in the present policy context, only two-thirds of a trichotomy: the issue is not simply whether to protect individuals or species, but whether to protect individuals, species, or ecosystems/processes!

It appears to me that Steverson has not sufficiently distinguished three separable problems. The first problem is that of *conservation targets*: What should be the object of most conservation efforts—genes, populations, species, ecosystems, or something else?[12] A second problem, which becomes unavoidable if one endorses the cost-accounting approach that constitutes safe minimum standard reasoning, is that of *defining prohibitive costs in a nonarbitrary manner*: At what point, and based on what types of evidence, might a society conclude that a species, a population, or an ecosystem might be allowed to disappear or decline? Steverson mainly addresses a third, more theoretical problem, *determining which objects in nature have ultimate value,* which he associates with having intrinsic value.[13]

Choosing the correct conservation targets seems to me to be more a matter of good science than of having good intuitions regarding what has intrinsic value. For example, suppose we refrain from restoring the pulse flow of the Everglades to save the kite, only to find that the populations of their prey snail gradually disappear over decades because more and more populations of their host plant are lost during every drought and fail to replace themselves. How should we balance impacts on these different scales? Note that, in some situations, almost anything we might do puts some species at risk either directly or indirectly, and it is not clear how a general intuition that all species have intrinsic value can resolve real management decisions in such situations.

My current views on the importance of the Endangered Species Act—that we should retain the Act, continuing to protect all species as long as the costs are bearable—are summarized in another publication.[14] I conclude that, given current knowledge, we should retain the Endangered Species Act, but that we should begin to experiment—as some amendments from supporters propose—with pilot programs and experiments that attempt to protect "clusters" or "communities" of species. I have taken it as obvious, based on my reading of biology and ecology, that species are important *and* that ecosystem processes are important; however, I doubt that the question of which is *most important* in particular contexts can be resolved with intuitions regarding what objects in nature have intrinsic value. If there are cases in which actions to protect species and actions to protect ecosystems/habitats are in conflict, then I think we face soul-searching investigations that may require the best scientific and philosophical minds to resolve the issues. Nevertheless, I hope that scientific information, such as the importance of a given species to ecological processes, whether the species is indigenous to the system or not, and other empirical questions will at least be relevant to the resolution of these difficult issues. If I were, in some contexts, to advocate protecting ecological processes at the cost of increasing risk for some identified and protected species, it would be on the grounds of scientific understanding of the case and based on a hypothesis about what policy is likely to be most effective; I do not see how Steverson's intuitions about intrinsic value help to resolve these practical questions.

Scientific Uncertainty and Prohibitive Social Costs

The general intuition of deep ecologists also does not do much to clarify what we should count as a "prohibitive cost," whatever our philosophical beliefs. In this section, I explore the inevitably intertwined questions of how to define prohibitive costs and the problem of choosing policies in a context of partial knowledge about consequences of human activities. I treat these two questions together because uncertainty and lack of knowledge are inevitable, often dominant, aspects of every real-world decision situation, and it is in such situations that some reasonable working definition of bearable versus prohibitive costs of protection efforts will be hammered out.

I am unable to respond directly to Steverson's views on the problem of prohibitive costs because I find his views confusing. Having assumed that deep ecologists know that species are the object of ultimate value in every case, one would think that Steverson could address questions of strategy quite straightforwardly—that he would consider no cost to be prohibitive when dealing with the protection of an object of ultimate value. However, his endorsement of the safe minimum standard criterion, which itself makes preservation negotiable according to cost, already indicates that Steverson does not want to use intuitions regarding ultimate value as a direct determinant of policy in all cases. So what *do* Steverson and the deep ecologists say about the complicated questions of strategy and tactics that face conservation biologists, ecological engineers, and restoration ecologists in situations representing real conflicts?

Assume for the moment that the Everglades case really is one that sets efforts to save the kite at odds with protecting the health of the Everglades ecosystem, and ask: What strategy should be followed by someone who believes species are of ultimate value? If the kite is of ultimate value, apparently we should set the "prohibitive cost" value of the species very high (hence, Steverson's implication that the deep ecologists are more steadfast in defense of species). However, to save the kite in this case may be to threaten several other species over the coming decades. At this point, it seems unlikely that an intuition of the ultimate value of all species will help resolve the conflict. Nor does an intuition seem likely to resolve the equally interesting case that results if we modify the story to say that no other endangered species exist in the Everglades, thereby pitting a species against an ecosystem simpliciter. The only thing to do in these cases is to step from behind the facade of intuitionism, set aside generalizations about ultimate values, and look at the real-world situation. In the real-world situation, it is often necessary to emphasize ecosystem-level processes over species because of what we know and do not know about the organization of ecological communities and about interspecific relationships. Contextualism advocates addressing the question of conservation targets, especially whether to emphasize species or ecosystem processes, on a case-by-case basis. In each case, one applies what is known— both generally about species-species and species-ecosystem interactions, and about specific species and local ecosystems—to seek a policy that will protect as much as possible in the particular, local situation.

Because the contextualist approach places so much emphasis on knowledge and its role in determining prohibitive costs, it is necessary to respond to Steverson's central argument—that contextualists face a destructive dilemma regarding knowledge. Steverson considers the contextualist method to be a commitment to minimal holism and a belief that the goal should be to protect total diversity at the landscape level.[15] He argues that it "turns the focus of environmental preservation away from individual species and toward ecosystematic processes,"[16] and that a contextualist should adopt the "much weaker normative goal of avoiding trends in species loss."[17] He supports this claim by discussing my idea that ecosystems can be viewed from the inside as autopoietic, self-organizing systems, and my associated approach to policy, in which I recommend that we seek to protect the "health" of ecological systems and processes.

In particular, based on his interpretation of contextualism, Steverson correctly attributes to me the view that built-in redundancies in natural systems entail that there are "thresholds" in nature. From this view, he incorrectly infers that I believe "that the loss or decline of an individual species is not, in and of itself, an issue of concern."[18] It is essential to recognize that the latter view is derived from the former on the assumption that decision makers would in crucial cases, in which I am willing to dispatch species, have *full knowledge of the consequences of the loss of the species in question*. But, of course, as Steverson recognizes, such knowledge involves a counterfactual assumption. In *this* world, constrained as we are by our ignorance, questions of strategy often outweigh "ultimate values," simply because we do not know how to protect all the ultimate values that are threatened. Again, it seems that general intuitions of ultimate, or intrinsic, value are not directly relevant to the question of setting the level of prohibitive costs.

However, what of the charge that I as a contextualist am impaled on the horns of a dilemma? According to this dilemma, which again assumes the possibility of complete knowledge of consequences of species losses, I must either (a) admit that there *could* be sufficient knowledge regarding the consequences of the loss of a species to determine when a species is redundant (in which case, I will surely discard any redundant species on the grounds that it will not cause cascading losses) or (b) admit that there *could not* be sufficient knowledge of the consequences of the loss of a species and its consequences for other species. In the latter case, Steverson argues that I could not possibly manage contextually because the goal of contextual management—to protect ecosystemic health and integrity—requires that "it must have at its disposal a body of knowledge that allows it to engage in diagnostic, curative, and preventive ecological 'medicine.'"[19] Steverson concludes that "without the knowledge and techniques necessary to generate predictive hypotheses about the effects of species loss, contextualism will be an unfeasible approach to policy formation."[20] Notice here that the prosecution of Steverson's dilemma against contextualists *assumes* that it is species loss—and only species loss—that should concern contextual managers. Notice also that this assumption is simply the embodiment of the less-flexible, definitional resolution of the question discussed above—whether species should always be the dominant priority in nature protection. Below I show that without this definitional assumption, the sting of the second horn of Steverson's dilemma loses its force.

I find the first horn of the dilemma simply irrelevant—it assumes the impossible hypothetical that we could know with reasonable certainty that a species is redundant. Steverson has not recognized how difficult it is to have "full knowledge" of the extent of vulnerabilities in ecological systems and the likelihood that a given species may support many other species. In fact, the complete knowledge scenario has been proven to be impossible in principle because assessing the contributory value of a species—the value a species has in providing resources or habitat for other species—requires knowing inherently unpredictable events, such as the way an ecosystem will be reconstituted after a severe natural disturbance.[21]

If we examine the real-world situation, however, recognizing the dominance of uncertainty and ignorance in all "to save or not to save" situations,

Steverson's case is so improbable as to be ludicrous. The case that worries Steverson is one in which a contextualist might conclude with sufficient certainty that an extinction will cause no cascading impacts on other species or ecological systems and in which the contextualist judges that it is *safe* to dispatch a species. But such a case could not occur in a situation so permeated with uncertainty as our present situations always are. What is not unlikely is that we might encounter cases in which, despite the usual reasons to prefer species preservation over extinction, conflicting demands and alternative priorities might lead us to reluctantly sacrifice a species *despite acknowledgment of a significant risk entailed by the loss*. These are the relevant and difficult cases in which, given what (little) we know, other commitments and concerns force us reluctantly to accept the risk—the size of which is unknown—of taking the irreversible step of causing an extinction and hence risking the onset of cascading effects and further losses of species. In these cases, what is important is some sense of the scale of possible negative impacts of a decision, a healthy respect for the dangers of irreversibility, and a willingness to view complex problems on multiple scales and levels.

While Steverson correctly notes that I insist on counting "total diversity" as the target (which includes diversity of habitat as an important element), he does not mention my use of what might be called "Whittaker's Law," which is relevant here. R. H. Whittaker argues that, while we cannot claim straightforwardly that diversity begets stability, it does seem unquestionable that diversity begets more diversity, and that losses of diversity tend to cause more losses.[22] In other words, any loss of species increases the likelihood of further losses, justifying the general presupposition in favor of resource protection that is embodied in the safe minimum standard criterion. Whittaker's Law has not, to my knowledge, been challenged by biologists.[23] It seems to me that this law, coupled with a realistic assessment of the scientific uncertainties involved in predicting short- and long-term effects of species losses on other species and ecosystem processes, provides an adequate support for the safe minimum standard rule—which is currently applied in U.S. official policy—that there should be a presumption in favor of saving each and every species, provided that the cost of saving that species is bearable. Scientific uncertainty (some elements of which are explained later in this section) combined with the presumption created by Whittaker's Law, seems to me to render irrelevant the case in which a contextualist too quickly dispenses with "redundant" species. The hypothetical case on which it is based simply cannot occur in any world similar to ours.

In contrast, the second horn of the "dilemma" seems to me to be unproblematic for a contextualist, as can be seen by paying more attention to the multiscalar aspects of biodiversity protection. As I have just argued, it is hard to dispute our ignorance and uncertainty regarding the impact of economic and management policies on particular species, and especially difficult to conclude with confidence that any given species is redundant. Contextualism, however, emphasizes ecosystem-level characteristics that are associated with the larger-resolution characteristics of the system itself. Good contextual management may not require knowledge of all interspecific dependencies at the smaller, species level of resolution in order to make, and act effectively in response to, judgments regarding trends in the health or integrity of communities and ecosystems. Suppose that, while we know little about the interspecific interactions of species in a given system, we do know that (a) recent studies have shown a rapid decline in populations of several readily observable and valued species (although no cause for the declines is known); (b) other studies show that the system is suffering rapid invasion by aggressive and opportunistic exotics; (c) toxicological studies show increasing loadings of toxic pollutants in the system; and (d) observable changes are occurring in the means by which energy is transported and distributed through the system. I submit that, in this case, it would make perfectly good sense to hypothesize that the system is under stress, that its ecological integrity is declining, and that its health is threatened, *even in the absence of much reliable information regarding which species depend upon other species in that system.*

A key aspect of contextualism is the recognition that there are emergent characteristics of ecological systems (that are not reducible to characteristics of their component individuals or species). Contextualists may therefore suggest that in some or most situations we would be well advised to aim at policies perpetuating ecological health, and allow species to perpetuate themselves within a healthy system, rather than concentrating exclusively on species. Since the ecosystem health and integrity movement is premised squarely on setting management goals in terms of ecosystem-level characteristics, it is therefore possible for me to adopt the following position, which qualifies, and then embraces, the second horn of Steverson's dilemma: while we do not, and probably cannot, have sufficient knowledge to predict the impacts of proposed policies on the survivability of all other species, we may be able to recognize ecosystematic trends that are good indicators of ecosystematic health. If so, then it is possible to manage "contextually" by applying less fine-grained models and criteria that measure ecosystem-level characteristics. Indeed, one of the advantages of contextualism is that it reduces the information demands of good management by focusing not so much on the detail of interspecific interactions within the system, but rather on observable system-level characteristics.

Note also that this argument does not require one or another answer to the question of what has ultimate value. One might, for example, follow Steverson in believing that protection of species is the ultimate value, but nevertheless believe that, given current levels of knowledge, we will be more successful (in general or in some specific cases) if we protect ecosystems and habitats and let species fend for themselves. Again, it proves to be important to distinguish the practical problem of conservation targets and strategies from intuitions about ultimate value.

It may be useful to summarize briefly some of the scientific results that make me so cautious in applying universal principles to resolve complex real-world cases such as priority conflicts among different species and ecosystems. Some very good scientists and dedicated conservationists believe that we should concentrate on species protection; other experts favor a habitat emphasis. In their arguments for these differing positions, they often mix theoretical, empirical, and practical reasons, but their discussion is mainly strategic and not based on a priori intuitions. It is an unquestioned advantage of the species-by-species approach that species are observable and countable entities, which goes a long way toward simplifying the statement and pursuit of conservation goals. Nevertheless, other experts place more emphasis on habitat.[24] We know that extensive fragmentation of habitat causes loss of species and that it is the most serious cause of species endangerment and extinction worldwide. We know that some species are "keystones" in their ecosystem and play important roles in maintaining the structure of the landscape; their loss would set in motion changes that would no doubt stress many other species. The alligator, for instance, is a keystone species in many southern ecosystems because its abandoned wallows sustain other wildlife through periodic droughts. Other species, such as the northern spotted owl, can be argued to be "indicator" species—those that would be the most likely to decline as their habitat is fragmented. In the latter case, much has been made of the fact that the owl is an indicator of ecological integrity, suggesting that its protection is part of a larger ecosystem plan, which it is.

If these scientific considerations are taken to suggest that we might favor some species more than others, and that we might sacrifice some species to protect ecosystems but not others, it is also possible to cite contrary evidence. For example, Linda Brubaker, by sampling pollen from ancient lake beds, has shown that interspecific associations that determine community structure are ephemeral over middle (ecological) and long (geological) time scales and that species persist much longer than associations of plants.[25] In addition, there is the interesting (and apparently applicable, if true) hypothesis that species that are redundant in one stable state may be especially important in reestablishing a new equilibrium after a major disturbance or regime shift. These considerations might be thought to recommend a policy that saves species while worrying less about ecosystems. Thus, I doubt there is a general answer to the question: "Are species important or are ecosystems important?" Neither is there likely to be a general answer to the question of what counts as a prohibitive cost in the protection of a species. The best we can do is to examine the facts of a given situation, factor in what we know about species persistence in general, and make the best decision possible in the particular context at hand. That is, the best that we can do is to act contextually.

Convergence: A Hypothesis

I now turn to some clarifications regarding the convergence hypothesis. I would not be surprised if a deep ecologist who persists in the views that (a) all and only species have intrinsic value *and* that (b) he or she knows this intuitively (without empirical evidence or support) defended policies that in some instances diverge from contextualism. Contextualism seeks relevant scientific and other empirical information to guide policy. Anyone who insists that general policy goals (such as placing higher priority on species than on processes in every situation) are intuitive and beyond evidence would eventually hold divergent policy recommendations from the contextualist who advocates an experimental, open, and adaptive approach to setting management goals. Nevertheless, this situation does not call *convergence* into question; rather, it provides a perfect example of what the convergence hypothesis is intended to avoid. Reliance on intuitions and ideology in setting conservation goals narrows the range of policy actions that are examined, and opportunities for unification behind specific policies are lost. The convergence hypothesis is about what would happen if intuitionists and ideologues shifted their attention from abstractions to how we can resolve real and difficult cases.

The convergence hypothesis is a general, empirical hypothesis *about policy*—it claims that policies designed to protect the biological bequest to future generations will overlap significantly with policies that would follow from a clearly specified and coherent belief that nonhuman nature has intrinsic value. In a stronger version of the hypothesis, defended in *Toward Unity among Environmentalists*,[26] I have claimed that, given the present state of knowledge and concerns for other species, policies that score high on the safe minimum standard criterion, applied from an anthropocentric, contextualist perspective, will *do as much good in protecting the moral commitment of deep ecologists as any other possible policy that could be undertaken given what we know now*. Again, it is taken as a given that the current situation includes both uncertainty and ignorance, and that management is based on a sincere interest in saving important aspects of nature. One of the constraints on achieving "rational" policy, from any perspective, is lack of knowledge. The point is to move toward better policy *given that we act in ignorance and uncertainty*, not to intuit what we would do in imaginary worlds, in which uncertainty and ignorance are somehow conquered.

I do not know if the convergence hypothesis is false in Steverson's imaginary, probably impossible, world. I only know that it is false in the real world and that it is false in any world that resembles the real world in most ways relevant to policy choices. The convergence hypothesis is a contingent truth; a very general empirical hypothesis that shapes solutions sought by adaptive managers in particular situations. It is supported by facts, both directly and indirectly; it could be falsified, but it has not been so far.

Notice that it would be remarkable if it were to turn out that there is *no* convergence between what is good for humans and for other species. Is it at all surprising to claim that human activities that threaten other species are likely to pose threats to human beings? The evolutionary kinship of all the species has been a theme in biology since Darwin. Leopold, Carson, and many other environmentalists all operate on the expectation that caring in detail for human well-being broadly understood usually converges with the well-being of other species.[27] We share our evolutionary history with other species, especially those that are closely related to us, and it is hardly surprising that we share many of their vulnerabilities.

The convergence hypothesis implies, as noted above, important and falsifiable predictions. For example, amphibians around the world are disappearing at an alarming rate. Suppose we learn the cause(s) of this demise with some confidence. The convergence hypothesis predicts that, once that complex of causal processes is understood, those processes that threaten amphibians are more likely than random to eventually have negative impacts on humans. If in ten years we understand that a complex of processes is causing amphibians to disappear, the convergence hypothesis predicts that more of these processes will be harmful to humans than will be benign.

The convergence hypothesis does not, of course, claim that the interests of humans and interests of other species *never* diverge, but only that they *usually* converge. Hence, if our knowledge base regarding a given species and its interactions with other species is weak, as it usually is, the presumption is to assume that the species should be saved. The burden is shifted under the safe minimum standard criterion to anyone who argues that the costs of saving *any* species are unbearable—and this shift brings us back to the difficult questions: What counts as "prohibitive social costs" of saving a species? How are we to set conservation priorities? I challenge Steverson, the deep ecologists, and everyone else in environmental ethics to address these real-world problems on a local, contextual basis and join the search for adaptive solutions and sustainable human institutions, cultures, and lifestyles in each local area. If we do not accomplish that task, nature has no chance; if we do, however, I doubt we will find the path by general intuitions from beyond experience, but rather from experience, respect for diversity, social learning through participation in the decentralization of institutions, and the reversal of landscape homogenization. What is needed are many local sciences of the integrity of many places, as well as the particularity of their species, of their natural history, and so forth. In the process of many experiments, given a management approach guided by the overall goal of minimizing human impacts on important processes and to save species whenever possible, we may learn how important species really are, and what the costs of losing a species are as compared with losing an important process. By pursuing convergent goals and experimenting in areas where local viewpoints differ, we can learn which strategies to choose in various situations and therefore improve our ability to minimize anthropogenic impacts at all levels and scales. As Dewey argued, this sort of social learning is more likely to occur in an open and democratic process in which science works for the public good.[28] But I doubt that intuitive pronouncements, asserted to be known without empirical evidence, will have a significant role in this process.

4

LAURA WESTRA

Why Norton's Approach Is Insufficient for Environmental Ethics

The environment is man's first right
We should not allow it to suffer blight
The air we breathe we must not poison
They who do should be sent to prison
Our streams must remain clean all season
Polluting them is clearly treason
The land is life for man and flora,
Fauna and all: should wear that aura,
Protected from the greed and folly
Of man and companies unholy.

—KEN SARO-WIWA[1]

The Ecological Point of View and the Canadian "Fish Wars"

On 10 March 1995, a story appeared on the front page of Canada's national newspaper, *The Globe and Mail:* "Four warning bursts of machine gun fire across the bow brought the Spanish trawler Estai to a halt after a four-hour chase through the foggy Atlantic." The problem was overfishing beyond the 200-mile limit in the Grand Banks off the coast of Newfoundland. When increased national quotas and the use internationally of complex modern fishing technologies reduced the availability of fish in the North Atlantic,[2] the Spanish fishers pushed their trawlers beyond the legal 200-mile limit, thus coming too close to the already depleted waters surrounding the Canadian mainland. Use of gunpowder in defense of fish stocks is almost unprecedented in Canadian history, but Clyde Wells, then Newfoundland's premier, explained his action. He argued that the Canadians in many fishing villages have not only watched their communities slowly die as European vessels fished large amounts of cod and flounder from 1988 to 1993

From Laura Westra, "Why Norton's Approach Is Insufficient for Environmental Ethics," *Environmental Ethics* 19 (1997): 279–297. Reprinted with permission.

and caused the disappearance of the cod in 1992, but they have also seen Spanish vessels take as much as 50,000 tons of turbot over the last three years, in spite of their own 16,300-ton limit (and the Spaniards' own legal limit of only 3,400 tons).

Is this simply a controversy between two nations, a dispute to be settled through dialogue, diplomacy, and negotiations? This view of the problem misses the major point of the controversy, captured in the wording on a placard waved in a Newfoundland fishing village by one of the six thousand demonstrators against Spain: "This is a World Fishery, not a Spanish One."[3] The "turbot battle" was eventually settled through an international deal between then Canadian fisheries' minister Brian Tobin and the European Community's representatives. It was clearly a *world* issue in the eyes of the Newfoundland fishers, who had already seen the results of the collapse of the cod stocks and the resulting disappearance of their economy and traditional lifestyles. Canada and all other countries must learn to curb their overall economic goals, and even reduce them from previous years' expectations, if they are not prepared to face complete extinctions not only of specific fish but also of traditional lifestyles.

The quest for increased profits based on increased quotas, even if they are sought to support traditional lifestyles, is not necessarily desirable. For instance, although natives in the Amazon claim to be living harmoniously with nature (and they are indeed less disruptive to natural processes than commercially exploitive foreign practices in the area), their goals and those of conservation biology do not necessarily mesh.[4] The problem is that native hunters, for instance, may pursue a species to extinction and then move on to exploit another "resource" beyond its capacity to recover.

From the scientific perspective of the ecosystem approach (and of complex systems theory), there is no guaranteed "safe," commercial, sustainable catch, but there is *also* no clear linear causality showing the connection between the overfishing of resources such as cod and their extinction.[5] Such factors as climatic changes, increases in ultraviolet rays because of ozone depletion, increased pollution and dumping in the oceans, and toxic rain may all be contributing causes. Hence, it is not acceptable to argue that because some practice was followed in past years, on the basis of earlier quotas, the *same* guidelines should be followed in the future and that continued increases in fishing quotas cannot be supported on the available scientific evidence. For instance, new fishing technologies may need to be abandoned, such as gill nets, which Carl Walters calls "one of the more destructive and wasteful fishing gears ever invented."[6]

Further, neither Canada nor any other country can simply focus on the economic aspects of a natural "resource" as its only value; the value of natural ecosystems far transcends this narrow view. Plants and animals all play important parts in the ecosystems in which they live and they fulfill specific functions that would no longer be present if they were extinct, or even if their numbers were not sufficient to support their ecosystemic function. For instance, in a discussion of ecosystems and sustainability in fisheries, Monica Hammer, Ann Mari Jansson, and Bengt-Owe Jansson state, "Whereas species diversity is a property at the population level, the *functional diversity*, what the organisms do and the variety of responses to environmental changes, especially the diverse space and time scales to which organisms react to each other and the environment, is a *property of the ecosystem*."[7] To limit oneself to dealing with the areas in which *our* interests lie (e.g., areas of ecosystem health, viewed and treated as instrumentally valuable) is to ignore the larger picture and the life-support and benchmark functions of the wild, in landscapes of appropriate geographical size (biomes). Hence, the primary concern must focus on the wild (core areas), even when sustainability is the question at issue. Sustainability is here understood as undiminished function capacity, supported by the undiminished structural systems of wild areas of appropriate size.[8] To put it plainly, sustainable agriculture, forestry, and fisheries make little sense unless the sustainability of wild ecosystems is addressed first, at least in the long term that is anticipated and in fact *required* by most North American and global regulations and treaties, all of which include future generations in their reach. Some will argue that as we do not have a precise reference point or baseline for ecosystem integrity, we do not need anything to which we ought "to conform" or "to return" environmentally. But we do not need to know the specific composition or the detailed structure of a landscape in order to know when it no longer functions. Because of all-pervasive pollution and environmental degradation, we cannot be assured that any area is "as it should be," meaning that the changes that have occurred (including biodiversity losses) are purely due to its natural trajectory and to nonanthropogenic stresses. But we do know when a system has collapsed, that is, when it has lost all its natural capacity to function appropriately for its scale and geographical location. Reed Noss writes:

> Ecosystems remain viable only when their processes—nutrient cycling, energy flow, hydrology, disturbance-recovery regimes, predator-prey dynamics, etc.—continue to operate within their natural range of variability. . . . Furthermore, the integrity of aquatic ecosystems is directly linked to the condition of the landscape around them.[9]

In a general sense, neither specific systemic processes nor "predator/prey dynamics" can remain unaffected when either naturally occurring predators or prey are eliminated from a system. We also know that when whole areas, or whole countries, are so affected, they no longer function in support of humans.

Because ecological sustainability must remain primary,[10] I argue that (1) as many others have noted, current evaluations of technology (and of the business enterprises that depend on these technologies) are insufficient for public policy if they are only based on cost-benefit analyses; and that (2) even the necessary introduction of traditional moral theories and of respect for democratic institutions and practices is not sufficient to acknowledge the required ecological component of public policy decisions (as the "fish wars" indicate) in spite of the free, informed citizen choices that prevailed at the time.

In the next section, I examine the limits of "economic evaluations" based purely on human preferences. I then turn to a major stumbling block one encounters when proposing a biocentric, holistic approach—that is, the belief that nonanthropocentric theories fail when they are used in support of environmental choices. Some view all holistic theories as lacking, from both a philosophical and a practical point of view. I argue, instead, that they are superior on both theoretical and practical grounds, using an example that deals with natural systems and populations (the "fish wars"), and that we need to go far beyond both economic and even traditional (intrahuman) moral evaluations in order to achieve sound environmental policy.

The Limits of Economic Evaluation and Anthropocentrism

Although the use of firearms to protect the natural world was new to Canada in March 1995, illegal protests and even violence had occurred elsewhere. For example, in 1994, protesters from Canada and the United States made their way to British Columbia, threatened violence, and chained themselves to trees to subvert corporate activities and prevent the logging of old-growth forests in Clayoquot Sound. In taking this action, protesters were appealing to international law and to regulative bodies beyond those of the countries involved in the dispute. This tactic was unprecedented—comparable, for instance, to protests by native groups, whether in Canada or in the United States, intended to support the rights to certain lifestyles (and the beliefs that support them). I have argued this point in detail elsewhere.[11]

One wonders, however, whether an appeal to traditional, anthropocentric moral doctrines is sufficient not only to address but also to prevent such problems from developing in the face of increasing environmental disintegration and degradation and the mounting scarcity of "resources" as populations increase. Many have addressed the need to ensure that cost-benefit analyses and economic evaluations of technology are made to focus prominently on ethical considerations beyond aggregate utilities and majority preferences.[12] I believe that the anthropocentric/nonanthropocentric distinction presents a false dichotomy in several senses, and that it is no more than a red herring, advanced by those concerned with defending the status quo. Accordingly, they are led to propose a somewhat modified, "greened" revamping of the same hazardous, uncritically accepted practices to which all life on Earth has been subjected, as I argue in the next section.

Utilities and preferences are normally understood (in philosophical and political theory) as reflecting the wishes, and maybe the (descriptively) perceived "good" of a society, as do appeals to rights, justice, fairness, and due process. The question, however, is whether ethical considerations based on moral doctrines designed primarily for intraspecific interaction—that is, designed to guide our interpersonal behavior—are in fact sufficient and clearly necessary to ensure that our activities conform to an inclusive and enlightened morality. Recent global change affecting our resource base everywhere *proves* the inadequacy of calculations that depend solely on economics, so that evaluations founded on moral doctrines and upholding both "natural" and "civil" rights indeed appear mandatory. Would that approach have been sufficient in the case of the Newfoundland fishers and the North Atlantic fish stocks? The fishers' earlier arguments, even before the decline of the cod population, could have been supported from the standpoint of human ethics and anthropocentrism. They were concerned with (1) sustainable development (Newfoundland is probably the poorest province in Canada) and increased financial security for themselves and their families; (2) aggregate utility, not for their "preference wants" but for their basic needs; (3) their local/national "visions" specific to the place they inhabited;[13] and (4) their democratic right to free choice.

Although their grounds appeared prima facie to be unimpeachable and could be defended not only from a moral but also from a legal point of view; in our present worldwide environmental situation, all four points need reexamination in the light of what Don Scherer calls our "upstream/downstream" world.[14] The underlying notion of human rights is also questionable, in view of McGinn's argument about "technological maximality" and the hazards that approach engenders. The combination of (1) "absolute" human rights (that is, of human rights viewed as primary even when they support nonessential, nonbasic preferences), (2) greatly increased numbers of such "rightholders," and (3) the well-entrenched drive to newer/bigger and more, that is, to "technological maximality," jointly engenders threats that are not present in any separate individual action. As shown in the previous section, Goodland argues for the primacy of ecological sustainability; McGinn proposes "contextualized" theories of rights.[15] Either of these positions could have been helpful in responding to the mounting environmental problems that eventually led to the Canadian "fish wars," since they both recommend that the scientific information be available to policy makers and the general public, and that the "rights" of fishers to increasing quotas and the access to more complex fishing technologies be jointly evaluated.[16]

While both these arguments focus primarily on human beings, they are anthropocentric in an enlightened and morally sensitive way. This sort of anthropocentrism (at least on the part of McGinn) may be close to what Bryan Norton calls "weak anthropocentrism."[17] However, Goodland's argument hinges also on the basic role of natural systems' integrity, in regard to general life support (for both humankind and nonhuman nature).[18] McGinn acknowledges the existence of the ecological impasse to which we are brought by present individualism and by preference-based, largely unrestricted choices, but he believes that it might be sufficient to shift the emphasis to *community* concerns, hence to contextualize present theories of rights.[19]

Could the communitarian emphasis have prevented the crash of the fisheries, which led to violence in the normally peaceful fishing industry? It seems that it would not have been enough. Returning for a moment to the arguments to which the fishers might have appealed, at least one of the strongest is already communitarian, for one of their concerns was the support of communitarian values and traditional lifestyles. Yet, in this typical case, even subordinating *individual* rights to aggregate community/national ones was not enough, unless the "community" that would have been accepted as primary could have been, minimally, the international global community or—as I argue in the next section—the community of life.

In contrast, neither the Canadian nor the Spanish fishing communities would have raised the question of other international community rights or the need to reexamine or contextualize their own, as McGinn suggests. Even Mark Sagoff's position, if adopted, might have been insufficient to prevent the violent conflict that arose.[20] He would have suggested that the Canadian government should have supported its *citizen* values, incorporating their local beliefs and practices, rather than the *consumer* (and *producer*) values of increased availability of reasonably priced fish and profit maximization. But Newfoundlanders are a proud people who love both their land and their traditional lifestyles. In their case, their continued dependence on successful local fisheries represents far more than the preference of either a consumer or a producer. It is instead the embodiment of a national, or specifically "place-based vision" of what a traditional "good life" should be. Therefore, one could argue that it was "citizen values," rather than consumer values, that motivated their continued quest for increased quotas for cod and eventually turbot.

The same argument could be applied to the Spanish fishermen and *their* "traditional" village values on the other side of the ocean. Thus, even if the motives of *all* fishermen were not purely economic, the problem of the commons would persist, or of the "common pool," as Eric Freyfogle puts it: "According to many economists, the solution to the tragedy of the common pool is to divide the common asset and distribute shares or parts to individual users."[21]

Returning to the "fish wars," if we continued our present practices without restraints other than a different allocation of the quotas, and all the North Atlantic fish stocks crashed, we might be able to develop some alternative source of protein, but it would do nothing to restore the fishers' communities or lifestyles. Conversely, we might instead turn to aquaculture as a comparable source of food, and a socially adequate source of comparable employment. Nevertheless, aquaculture is also environmentally hazardous, as it releases nutrients and wastes into ecosystems, thus disrupting their natural processes. The introduction of transgenic fish also affects natural populations, thus biodiversity, and often releases antibiotics into the system and into the food chain.[22]

The basic problem for us anywhere, not just for Canadian fisheries, is sustainability.

William Rees, for instance, proposes adopting an "ecological worldview," in contrast with the prevailing established "expansionist worldview," which represents "the dominant social paradigm."[23] As Leopold did before him, Rees recognizes that we are not independent of, and separate from, an "environment," but, as in Goodland's work, ecological sustainability is foundational, so that it makes perfectly good sense to abandon our present unsustainable and indefensible worldview. Rees and Wackernagel write: "By contrast, an ecological economic perspective would see the human economy as an inextricably integrated, completely contained, and wholly dependent subsystem of the ecosphere."[24]

This position is supported by Rees's research in the Vancouver-Lower Fraser Valley region of British Columbia, Canada, but can be easily generalized for all urban, affluent Northwest centers. His findings show that "assuming an average Canadian diet and current management practices," the local "regional population support(s) its consumers' lifestyles" by importing "the productive capacity of at least 23 times as much land as it occupies." To put this point in a more general way, "the ecological footprints of individual regions are much larger than the land areas they physically occupy."[25]

When we continue to import others' carrying capacity, we are "running an unaccounted ecological deficit," and "our populations are appropriating carrying capacity from elsewhere or from future generations."[26] The same can be said about "sinks" for our resource appropriation and waste disposal. Our approach in northwestern nations such as Canada has been one of neocolonialism with regard to less-developed countries, and one of ruthless exploitation (through "environmental racism") toward minorities and the disempowered in our own countries.[27]

Crises could have been avoided only through policies and practices consistent with an "ecological worldview," one going beyond competing aggregate preferences of various human groups. In the next section, I discuss what such a worldview might require. I argue that the radical change called for by the current emergencies can only be supported through an ecocentric or biocentric viewpoint, whether or not our concern is primarily directed toward human beings.

A radically changed approach is required, starting from ecocentrism, as well as a major shift in burden-of-proof theories and standards. Robert Ulanowicz argues that, even in highly funded, uncontroversial research, such as research into cancer causes, a holistic approach would be far more fruitful than the present reductionist method, with an exclusive focus on genes or viruses.[28] Holism can make a large difference in issues concerned with the interface between humans and the environment. In addition, in accordance with an ecocentric perspective, all untried and potentially hazardous substances are "guilty" until proven "innocent" beyond a doubt. Even then, given the uncertainties endemic to the scientific method, the precautionary principle still needs to be applied.[29]

The shift in the burden of proof, here suggested, is already part of the language of the Great Lakes Water Quality Agreement, through its emphasis on "zero discharge," and on "sunset" and "sunrise" chemical controls.[30] These substances can be viewed minimally as not contributing to the natural evolutionary processes of ecosystems, thus as naturally inimical to the mandated respect for ecosystem integrity. In essence, I argue that an ecosystem can be said to possess integrity when it is an "unmanaged" ecosystem, although not necessarily a pristine one. This aspect of integrity is most significant; it is the aspect that differentiates integrity from ecosystem health, which is compatible with support/manipulation instead.[31] Hence, exotic, potentially hazardous substances and processes are judged to be inappropriate, or "guilty," in order to prevent their introduction into natural systems. As McGinn argues, meaningful changes in our evaluation of technology cannot take place unless we are willing to question our assumptions about rights and the role of democracy.[32]

Beyond the Anthropocentrism/ Nonanthropocentrism Debate

The conclusion reached in the previous section indicates that to ameliorate presently accepted technology-dependent lifestyles or redress present inequities, it is preferable to change our approach and accept the primacy of ecological integrity—as many national and international laws and regulations already do, at least in their language—rather than expect real change from "end-of-pipe" solutions. Insofar as ecocentrism is akin to deep ecology's platform, however, such a position is in direct conflict with a position such as Bryan Norton's: "As academics, spokespersons for deep ecology have been able to avoid adopting policies on difficult, real world cases such as elk destroying their wolf-free ranges, feral goats destroying indigenous vegetation on fragile lands, or park facilities overwhelmed by human visitors."[33]

To the contrary, a truly holistic position, such as the one supporting the primacy of integrity, has clear-cut, though not necessarily popular, answers for all such questions, as can be seen from our approach to the "fish wars." In every case, when there is human interference giving rise to problems in the wild, it is not only acceptable but also mandatory to interfere again temporarily to redress the difficulty, and with the clear goal of withdrawing when the system's evolutionary path has been restored, according to the best scientific information available and under the guidance of the precautionary principle.[34] The goal in the case mentioned is one of restoration, when the area affected is wild. That is to say, although the present goal is to restore natural function and systemic health, the ultimate goal is to withdraw all support and manipulation so that some restored systems can return to a state of integrity or of unmanaged evolutionary processes once again—hence, the present call for the establishment of marine fisheries reserves.[35]

This approach does not mean that we must discontinue altogether human-centered practices everywhere. It simply indicates that we must recognize the necessity of (1) leaving appropriately sized areas wild and unmanipulated on both land and seas (the sizes required need to be established in dialogue with conservation biology and aquatic ecosystem science); and (2) limiting our intrusive practices upon the rest of the Earth to whatever will not have an adverse impact on integrity/core/wild areas.[36] Conservation biology, entomology, ecology, and biology all contribute to the necessary dialogue to establish the scales appropriate to either one or the other of these approaches in different landscapes, globally. As I have argued elsewhere,[37] the ultimate goal of the principle of integrity is to protect and restore both structural and functional aspects of ecological integrity, and doing so requires that large areas be kept wild.[38] It also demands that we be prepared to "embrace the challenge of complexity," as Kay and Schneider argue, that one be willing to abandon the misconception that all systems can and should be managed.[39] Instead, management and controls should be confined to human individuals and societies, except when needed briefly for restoration purposes in core and buffer areas in natural landscapes.

By way of contrast, I noted in the case of Canadian fisheries the dismal failure of the presumption to manage nature. Educated guesses about how far we can push the safety factor with our quotas—particularly when these are manipulated by economic and political interests (both of which are notoriously shortsighted) and supported by uneducated democratic preferences and "values"—are simply insufficient to protect either the fish species or the local survival needs of affected humans. Norton has argued that: "Long-sighted anthropocentrists and ecocentrists tend to adopt more and more similar policies as scientific evidence is gathered because both value systems—and several others as well—point toward the common-denominator objective of protecting ecological contexts."[40]

Norton is not alone in this belief; Gary Varner, for instance, appears to concur.[41] But in his effort to continue his ongoing campaign against the supporters of intrinsic natural value, Norton appeals to two concepts, which, as I show, are also problematic, either practically or theoretically. Norton refers to a rare, if not nonexistent, ethic—that of the "long-sighted anthropocentrist." Where does one find such a position? Not among politicians and policy makers, to be sure: The hard pressure of political correctness with regard to other issues tends to relegate green concerns to the back burner, although some examples can be cited, such as the Endangered Species Act and some policies on radwaste disposal, both of which take a "long-sighted" approach. What about large multinational corporations? These are somewhat vulnerable to public opinion, but even more vulnerable to shareholders' displeasure and internal and external competition. It is hard to find much "long-sightedness" in those boardrooms, beyond public relations campaigns to calm the public's "irrationality" and their fears. If one were to encounter that rara avis, "long-sighted anthropocentrists," how would one distinguish them from their ecocentrist counterparts?

Norton describes their salient characteristics: They would appreciate "scientific evidence," and thus be disposed to share with the ecocentrist the "objective of protecting ecological contexts."[42] But this characterization is only trivially true. That is, they would be willing to follow that path if and only if they were convinced that no other path would support their interests equally well. Such beliefs and sentiments are indeed shared by politicians, industry giants, and many others; they are easy to voice because they remain vague and unspecific.

Serious questions can be raised, for instance: *How far* would the weak/long-sighted anthropocentrist go to protect such systems? For *what* would they understand that protection to be necessary? For the weak/long-sighted anthropocentrist, continued exploitation, variously defined, might be a convincing candidate. However, given science's imprecision and the "challenge of complexity," and thus the impossibility of finding a guaranteed point of "safe" pollution/exploitation, particularly in the face of cumulative and synergistic stresses, how easy it would be to convince the weak/long-sighted anthropo-

centrist that his or her interest would be amply served by an ecologically untenable position. Newfoundland's fishers had every interest in the continued
thriving of the fish species upon which they depended, in a far more immediate and vital way than any politician; yet they could not make the connection,
even in their own interest.

One could object that scientific uncertainty would also work against the
ecocentrist's approach. The differences between the two approaches are significant and they can be captured in two main points. First, the ecocentrists
start from the primacy and value of wilderness; hence, they begin by questioning any intrusive or risky practices and shift the burden of proof to the
would-be risk imposers. Their criteria becomes progressively more stringent
when the proposed technology and economic activity is intended for human
settlements and cities or for areas of ecosystem health (sustainable agriculture of forestry areas, for instance). Most technological intrusion would be
excluded from wild, core areas, as required in order to protect their role and
function.[43]

Second, given the primary value of preserving or restoring natural, evolutionary function in certain designated areas, and the necessity to ensure this
function through human activities compatible with this goal, the nonanthropocentric holists would use the precautionary principle to decide on all economic and technological issues. The precautionary principle (Principle 15 of
the Rio Declaration on Environment and Development) states:

> In order to protect the environment, the precautionary approach shall
> be widely applied by States, according to their capabilities. Where there
> are threats of serious or irreversible damage, lack of full scientific
> certainty shall not be used as a reason for postponing cost-effective
> measures to prevent environmental damage.[44]

Finally, how will the weak/long-sighted anthropocentrist vote and act
when environmental protection conflicts with local jobs or other legitimate
human aspirations without relying entirely on the example I have proposed?
This question, it seems to me, is the "litmus test" for the convergence of ends
that Norton envisions between his weak/long-sighted anthropocentrist and the
ecocentrists, despite Norton's assertion that his position "recognizes the crucial
role of creative, self-organizing systems in support of economic, recreational,
aesthetic and spiritual values."[45] As I have shown in the "fish war" example,
even such recognition may not be enough.

Yet, in some sense, Norton is right: there is a commonality between the
two positions, but this commonality only emerges when we subordinate
"human economic, recreational, aesthetic and spiritual values," whatever these
might be, to the imperative of survival. This imperative represents the common

denominator we share with the rest of life. When we recognize the primacy of that commonality and the ways in which ecological integrity supports it for all, globally, then we are ecocentrists, or biocentric holists (the term I have chosen), because our anthropocentrism has been so weakened as to be non-existent, dissolved into the reality of our presence first and foremost, as part of the biota of natural systems.[46]

Some will argue perhaps that it is not necessary to argue for intrinsic value for other nonhuman animals and other individuals and wholes; rather, it is sufficient to recognize that we are a part of the biota of natural systems and that we share our habitat with the rest of life. Those who support this position will view weak/long-sighted anthropocentrism as theoretically/philo-sophically defensible; all others, based on ecocentrism or biocentrism, will not find it acceptable. Norton has certainly held this position consistently through the years.[47] The polarization of the two positions is well docu-mented in the environmental ethics literature.[48] But this polarization—to say the least—remains misguided.

The weaker anthropocentrism becomes, the less defensible it is *as such*— that is, as a variant of anthropocentrism. But why should we weaken anthro-pocentrism in the first place? Norton's answer, if I understand him correctly, is because humankind has more than economic interests. These other "inter-ests" represent "values" that mitigate the crassest forms of purely economic anthropocentrism, thus making the position more acceptable. Norton defines his position as follows: "A value theory is weakly anthropocentric if all value countenanced by it is explained by reference to some felt prefer-ences of a human individual or by reference to its bearing upon the ideals which exist as elements in a world view essential to determinations of con-sidered preferences."[49]

This position is therefore *weak* from the standpoint of moral theory as well: It is open to all the charges to which utilitarianism is open, in its weak-est formulation. Based upon Norton's position, all we can offer to any group of individuals or policy makers intent upon advancing their common inter-ests, which might be strongly anthropocentric, is our plea for the support of "values," explained by reference to some "felt or considered preferences of a human individual."[50] Whether or not these are aggregate rather than individ-ual preferences, and whether they even embody some ideal, the answer is still the same: The result can be purely utilitarian in a time-limited sense (al-though Rawls's position might mitigate it to some extent). Choices based on preference-satisfaction are often blind to other individual rights and to justice considerations. They can also be "culturally relative" (for example, for some cultures, female genital mutilation is part of a "moral" family-oriented ideal); hence, many such preferences may not be universally defensible from a moral standpoint.

The example of the "fish wars," where *citizen* as well as *consumer* preferences were involved, shows how useless such a position would have been from the standpoint of reaching an environmentally fair and ecologically sound solution. Any position that presents a choice between "considered preferences A" and "considered preferences B" offers no ground, other than a counting of heads, efficiency, or (for a policy maker) perhaps political expediency, for the ultimate result. Hence, the proponents of such a position must bear the responsibility for their stance even if, in their individual case, their choice might have been just as sound and prudent as one reached on ecocentric grounds.

The problem is one envisioned by Plato, that is, of knowing the road to Larissa without knowing why. In other words, even reaching a right decision on wrong principles may not be sufficient if the principles are such that they would permit a morally bad decision on another occasion. The issue is not exclusively a matter of personal moral purity; it also involves responsibility for consequences to which others, even human innocents now and in the future, may be subjected through our choices and our choice of principles.

Norton rejects all defenses of intrinsic value in nonhuman nature, whether holistic or individualistic,[51] although he aims his attack primarily at Callicott's own position and his interpretation of the land ethic of Aldo Leopold.[52] Leaving aside for the moment individual grounds for intrinsic value in nonhuman animals, a holistic perspective supports respect for all parts of natural systems, as well as the wholes within which they function. We ourselves are parts, at least physically, of these structures. They also respect system functions, that is, the process they engender, which involve their biotic and abiotic parts, a necessity when we wish to defend the survival of any species.[53]

An ecocentric position such as the biocentric holism recommended by the principle of integrity recognizes (1) the interrelationship between human and nonhuman nature and their "connaturality"[54] and kinship,[55] hence (2) the intrinsic value of natural/evolutionary processes,[56] and (3) the foundational value of life-support systems for ecological sustainability.[57] It also acknowledges that (4) ecological sustainability is primary, as it alone supports economic and social sustainability.[58] Therefore (5) at the most basic level—that is, at the *life* level—the dichotomy between anthropocentrism and nonanthropocentrism is a false one. I believe it is false *not* because anthropocentrism is the only defensible theory, but rather because "preferences" sometimes address want-interests as well as need-interests and because at the basic survival level *only*, we have no interests that are completely separate from those of all other life, so that their "values" and our "values" coincide.[59]

Hence, the argument proposed here is not that humans have interests that are defensible because they are intrinsically valuable beings unlike anything else, but because humans and nonhumans *share* an interest, a need for a safe habitat, and—whether or not it is consciously acknowledged—the value of survival conditions persists and includes the valuable contributions of all participants in ecosystemic processes. This view does not render all life equal, but it shows that all living things are possessed of value singly and collectively, for themselves and for all else. Rather than relying on "preference satisfaction" indicators, a position that has been found morally lacking in risk assessment and technology assessment,[60] my approach defends the general (human and nonhuman) value of integrity and health for various habitats, in appropriate proportions.[61]

Norton prefers to isolate another common regulatory and legislative strand, which, like the appeals to ecological integrity, can also be found in many documents: the issue and rights of future generations (of humans, if I understand him correctly). If he is looking for a publicly accepted legislative priority, he is correct. If, however, Norton is seeking a moral basis that is less hard to defend, or less controversial than "intrinsic value" for nonhumans, then the "future generations" emphasis he has chosen is both controversial and debated, and even harder to sell to the man or woman in the street as a possible preference than ecological life support, with all its prudential implications.[62]

In conclusion, pace Norton, there is no clear, obvious, and philosophically defensible difference between the concepts and values that sustain the argument of the weak/long-sighted anthropocentrist, and those that support the intrinsic value beliefs of the ecocentrist, nor is ecocentrism as vacuous and "exotic" as Norton claims.[63] In practice, Norton claims holistic/intrinsic value arguments are impotent. But, when dealing with agencies and government bodies (such as Environment Canada or the Great Lakes International Joint Commission) or major organizations such as the International Union for Conservation of Nature (IUCN), it is no easier to attempt to support environmental action by appealing to the *details* of philosophical debates regarding future generations, than it is to appeal to intrinsic value arguments. At the level of scientific evidence and with the support of ecology, the intrinsic value arguments are not only easier to use, particularly for wholes and processes (though, admittedly, less so for individual animals, unless endangered), but by the very same arguments culled from ecology, they are a necessary and integral part of the arguments of "future generations" that Norton prefers. In order to accept a determinant role for duties to future generations, we must understand why we need to respect the life-support function of systemic processes. In other words, if the consequences of unrestrained technological and economic activities were simply various changes in the natural environment requiring changes in preferences and the exercise of our ingenuity and our technological abilities, we would have little or no reason to moderate our activities in respect for the future, as some argue.[64]

It is only because of the mounting evidence showing the life-support function of systemic processes and the role of their component parts that we must accept that it is not the deprivation of this or that resource that we may inflict on the future, but the limitation of the very basis for any life at all. It goes without saying that neither ecology nor biology can make absolute pronouncements about these issues. However, the evidence (mentioned in our discussion of agricultural and fishing practices) appears to be on the side of the defense of naturally evolving entities. We affect, severely, the health of all human and nonhuman animals through anthropogenic stress to ecosystems leading to nonevolutionary changes.[65]

Warming trends represent *indirect* global changes that affect reproduction, hence individuals as well as species. Recent research has shown that *direct impacts* extending to reproductive function and well beyond it can be traced to certain features of our technological lifestyles and the corporate activities that foster and support them. The groundbreaking research of Theo Colborn and others has shown how human-made chemicals, long known to be hazardous and carcinogenic, and also many others that were thought to be biologically inert affect the reproductive organs and related capacities of most species from fish to birds to mammals, including humans.

As "hormone mimics," they also alter significantly our behavior, intellectual capacities, and parenting abilities.[66] The results of Colborn's research present a clear indictment of the way we interact with corporations and industry. After cataloging a litany of horrors resulting from even minute exposures to polychlorinated biphenyls (PCBs) affecting vulnerable persons, women of reproductive age, infants, fetuses, and children, Colborn says of the move to produce PCBs: "Confident of their safety as well as their utility, the Swann Chemical Company, which would soon become part of Monsanto Chemical Company in 1935, quickly moved them into production and onto the market."[67]

In essence, it is the corporations, the large businesses that have the resources to research, test, and market these complex and novel products and processes. Even in democratic nations, however, we have no institutional or collective mechanism to oversee these industrial giants, acquire information about them (impossible because of "trade secrets" laws), or debate their activities, let alone impose limits on them. Even the tiniest molecule of a PCB compound is not biodegradable; moreover, it is durable, it travels, and it persists. Hence, it has a range of negative effects: "Researchers studying declining seal populations have found that seventy parts per million of PCBs is enough to cause serious problems for females, including suppressed immune systems and deformities of the uterus and of the fallopian tubes."[68]

PCBs are not the only chemicals with far-reaching, transgenerational effects. In addition to dichlorodiphenyltrichloroethane (DDT), "PCBs (209 compounds), . . . 75 dioxins, and . . . 135 furans" were invented by chemists in laboratories "to kill insects threatening crops and to give manufacturers new materials such as plastics." Inadvertently, however, the chemical engineers had also created chemicals that jeopardize fertility and the unborn. Even worse, we have unknowingly spread them far and wide across the face of the Earth.[69]

As long as our quietism permits the continuation of present practices, and because governments do not appear to be eager to mandate controls given the present unemployment and slow economies, emphasis is on deregulation rather than on tighter controls.

In that case, although Colborn and her collaborators propose principles of mitigation and change based on the "Wingspread Consensus Statement"[70] within the present political and institutional system, it may be hard to achieve acceptance of and compliance with her recommendations, right as they are. The tobacco industry resisted regulation and controls for a very long time, although there were clear, unambiguous links between their products and the number of deaths they caused.[71]

I argue that we need to understand and accept this responsibility and recognize our obligation to respect life-support systems from a biocentric standpoint in order to support the changes indicated by the existence of these hazards. From Norton's point of view, in order to introduce arguments about future generations, we also need to understand the many ways that we may have negative impacts upon them. For this task, simple interhuman considerations will not suffice: We need to expand our consciousness, our understanding, and our respect as required to include these processes and causal links. The holistic position would thus extend Norton's argument to all future generations, to human and nonhuman life.

5

BEN A. MINTEER AND ROBERT E. MANNING

Convergence in Environmental Values

An Empirical and Conceptual Defense

Introduction

Must our disagreements about the moral status of nature prevent us from supporting the same environmental policies? This question is at the core of Bryan Norton's convergence hypothesis, first discussed in an early paper in *Environmental Ethics* and later developed in his book *Toward Unity among Environmentalists* as well as in several more recent publications.[1] Stated simply, Norton's claim is that individuals who rely on a sufficiently broad and temporally extended range of human values (a position he originally termed "weak anthropocentrism") and nonanthropocentrists who embrace a consistent notion of the intrinsic value of nature will both tend to endorse similar policies in particular situations. This overlapping of human and nonhuman concerns is to be expected, since in order to adequately sustain a broad range of human values over time, the ecological contexts on which these goods depend must also be sustained—a goal accomplished through the formulation of long-sighted, multivalue environmental policy. If this sort of common ground exists among individuals of varying ethical stripes, then Norton believes environmental philosophers (and environmentalists generally) might consequently agree to set aside many of our increasingly worn contests

From Ben A. Minteer and Robert E. Manning, "Convergence in Environmental Values: An Empirical and Conceptual Defense," *Ethics, Place, and Environment* 3 (2000): 47–60; available at http://www.informaworld.com. Reprinted with permission.

over the philosophical bearing of various environmental commitments. Once this happens, attention could be turned toward more concrete (and therefore more useful) analyses of the location and character of environmental values in actual policy discussions. The theory of convergence thus comports well with Norton's general pragmatic approach to environmental ethics, a stance that has found him calling for a practical environmental philosophy focused not on speculative metaphysical arguments about nonhuman nature, but on the complex and interpenetrating moral underpinnings of actual environmental policies and practices.[2]

Given the traditional emphasis of environmental philosophers on the founding and vigorous defense of general and universal moral principles (the very habits that Norton is attempting to leave behind), the convergence hypothesis has, not surprisingly, met with less than universal support in environmental ethical circles. In particular, J. Baird Callicott, Laura Westra, and Brian Steverson have come out in strong opposition to Norton's thesis.[3] As we explain below, we take it to be significant that none of these critics attempt to engage the convergence hypothesis at an empirical level—the realm in which Norton clearly believes his thesis is to be either validated or rejected. Elsewhere we have argued that environmental philosophers can learn much from such experimental approaches toward environmental values.[4] This need is especially great with respect to notions like convergence because, in their objections, Norton's critics have tended to revert to their own precast environmental ideologies, taking issue with Norton's own philosophical proclivities rather than considering the practical questions he raises about the relationship between concrete public environmental values and policy judgments.

Of course, Norton's epistemological and ontological claims are fair game, and we do not seek to discourage critical analyses of the serious philosophical concerns at stake here. We simply suggest that more attention needs to be paid to the examination of the idea of value convergence on environmental policy from an empirical standpoint. This sort of analysis could provide a useful service for environmental philosophical discussions, and might contribute to the ongoing development of a more practical and effective style of environmental ethical inquiry. If it can be demonstrated that public ethical diversity toward the natural world does not preclude a high level of agreement on common policy goals (at least in particular cases), then we would argue that environmental philosophers should refrain from dismissing arguments like the convergence hypothesis out of hand, especially if such dismissals are made simply because the convergence model refuses to be blindly monistic in its countenance of a range of moral programs.

In this chapter, we therefore attempt to provide an empirical exploration and defense of a general convergence framework. First, we briefly rehearse and consider the various critiques of convergence, and show that while his critics attempt to draw out perceived philosophical flaws in Norton's thesis, they do indeed avoid the important practical question about convergence on real matters of environmental policy. We then present and discuss an empirical study of environmental ethics, values, and attitudes toward forest policy (carried out in the context of Vermont's Green Mountain National Forest) that leads us to endorse a reading of Norton's thesis as an accurate model of public environmentalism, at least in the Vermont case. We conclude by discussing how these data lead us to question a number of the dispositions and the practices of environmental philosophy. In particular, we suggest that the unmistakable pessimism in the attitudes of Norton's critics toward the ability of the public to arrive at sound environmental policy without sole recourse to a nonanthropocentric foundation is unwarranted. Further, we propose that this stance is detrimental to the development of a more inclusive public environmental philosophy.

The Convergence Hypothesis in Environmental Philosophy

As his declaration of the convergence hypothesis as "dead wrong" attests, Callicott has been one of the most strident critics of Norton's thesis in the field.[5] It is clear in his critique of Norton's project, however, that Callicott has mostly been concerned with what he sees as the theoretical shortcomings of the convergence argument, rather than the more practical question of whether Norton's proposal is an accurate portrayal of how people actually go about supporting certain types of environmental policy. In other words, and not unexpectedly, Callicott appears less interested in the empirical bearing of convergence than he is in the axiological and ontological problems he finds in Norton's own weak anthropocentrism:

> If all environmental values are anthropocentric and instrumental, then they have to compete head-to-head with the economic values derived from converting rain forests to pulp, savannahs to cattle pasture, and so on. Environmentalists, in other words, must show that preserving biological diversity is of greater instrumental value to present and future generations than lucrative timber extraction, agricultural conversion, hydroelectric empoundment, mining, and so on. For this simple reason, a persuasive philosophical case for the intrinsic value of nonhuman natural entities would make a huge practical difference.[6]

Here Callicott is objecting to a specific move Norton makes following the argument for convergence; namely, since both nonanthropocentric and weak

anthropocentric projects can be expected to support similar policies in particular cases, environmental philosophers (and others) might therefore be
better off embracing something like Norton's contextualism. Norton's justification is that such a position is ultimately less problematic than the endorsement of intrinsic value theory, a stance he holds to be both practically and
metaphysically troubling.[7] Since Callicott is one of the preeminent nonanthropocentrists in the field, however, it is not surprising that he cannot bring
himself to accept Norton's invitation to the anthropocentric camp. This leaves
Callicott little choice but to assert the "practical" necessity of intrinsic value
for environmental protection and to deny that such a position is rendered a
"pernicious redundancy" by the conclusions of Norton's convergence hypothesis.[8] Callicott therefore concludes that convergence between human-based
and nonanthropocentric positions is highly unlikely since Norton's contextualism will always lack the moral force necessary to defeat consumerist values
in environmental policy contests.

Laura Westra (Chapter 4) takes a similar tack in her appraisal of Norton's
approach. In claiming that there is little to commend the appeal to human
values in the formulation of strong environmental policy, she goes on to suggest that Norton's weak anthropocentrist is nothing more than a convenient
fiction: "Norton refers to a rare, if not nonexistent, ethic—that of the 'long-
sighted anthropocentrist.' Where does one find such a position?"[9] We are
puzzled by Westra's incredulity here, since our experience, and that of scores
of other researchers into public environmentalism, has been that environmental values oriented to future generations consistently draw strong support
from a broad segment of the public.[10] But moving on, we can see that Westra,
much like Callicott, believes that since Norton does not advance an unswerv-
ing articulation of intrinsic value (like the "principle of integrity" that figures
in Westra's own "biocentric holism"), his prediction of convergence is, in most
cases, simply wishful thinking. Westra does concede that convergence between human and nonhuman considerations in some sense exists at the base
level of survival (since it would be difficult to imagine how civilization could
flourish after nature's total demise), but this is essentially an uncontroversial
and philosophically trivial claim. At the end of the day, it seems clear that
Westra thinks that Norton's weak anthropocentrists will, more often than
not, part company with ecocentrists because of the profoundly different
policy directions she believes these philosophical commitments necessarily
entail.

Also like Callicott, Westra effectively fails to engage the empirical merit
of Norton's claim. Even though she couches her arguments against convergence in a real-world example involving a Canadian contest over fishing
rights, she ends up considering how Norton's position might have panned out

in the specifics of the case—how it would have been if weak anthropocentric appeals were made—rather than discussing the degree to which participants in this setting actually employed arguments resembling Norton's contextualism. Following this hypothetical reasoning, Westra proceeds to reject the weak anthropocentric approach based on her conclusion that it would have been unable to support the cause of protecting ecological integrity in the fisheries example. Such a strategy might tell us much about Westra's nonanthropocentrism and why she finds it more attractive than any alternative anthropocentric posture, but it unfortunately does not get us any closer to understanding whether such theoretical contests may actually collapse in real policy agreements. Westra can only turn to speculative predictions about what policies the fishing communities would arrive at if they argued from a contextualist standpoint, reading these conclusions through the lens of her own philosophical commitments instead of drawing them from the real claims and decisions made by the citizens involved. Nowhere in her critique does she provide anything approaching falsification of the convergence hypothesis.

Brian Steverson (Chapter 2) is up front about his neglect of the empirical status of the convergence argument, although of Norton's critics he alone seems to recognize the need for such a discussion in the literature. Stating that he is not interested in exploring the validity of Norton's convergence hypothesis itself, Steverson nevertheless does conclude that this sort of analysis is required; indeed, he believes that whether convergence can hold as an empirical hypothesis and also serve as a guide in decision making about management and policy are "important questions to consider."[11] But again, like Callicott and Westra, Steverson chooses to direct his entire critical attention to Norton's anthropocentrism, specifically the logical implications of Norton's contextualist position within the convergence framework. Arguing that this approach would not be adequate for the protection of individual species in particular cases because Norton's contextualist manager would allow extinction if it did not threaten larger ecological processes, Steverson concludes that such a stance obviously runs counter to the practical judgments and normative intuitions of nonanthropocentrists. As a result, he believes that we should not expect to find convergence between these camps at the level of policy formation. In fact, according to Steverson, the possibility is nearly "nonexistent."[12]

Norton has, in our view, persuasively replied to Steverson's arguments (see Chapter 3), and interested readers should refer to his defense of contextualism therein. Here, we would only like to observe that a significant part of Norton's response devolves on the empirical question of the validity of convergence, a subject he believes is avoided with Steverson's appeal to nonanthropocentric intuitions and his reliance on a hypothetical critique of contextualism and the convergence thesis. As Norton writes, "The convergence hypothesis is a general, empirical hypothesis *about policy* . . . I do not know if [it] is false in Steverson's imaginary, probably impossible, world. . . . It is supported by facts, both directly and indirectly; it could be falsified, but it has not been so far."[13]

The Empirical Evasion

By now it should be clear that it is not our purpose here to explore the meta-ethical questions that arise in the particular anthropocentric/nonanthropocentric division held within the convergence debate, although they are important and merit critical attention. Hopefully, our discussion has revealed that there are (at least) two distinct paths of inquiry pertaining to the convergence argument. The first concerns matters of ontological and epistemological import and the consequences for philosophical practice that follow from Norton's hypothesis. These are the issues that Callicott, Westra, and Steverson are obviously concerned with. It is the reason they fall back on strong arguments for the necessity of nonanthropocentrism and intrinsic value theory, and why they assert the improbability of convergence based on an inflated view of the philosophical determination of public policy choices.

The second path of inquiry—the primary concern of our chapter—addresses the empirical validity of Norton's prediction of convergence of differing ethical stances on similar environmental policies. On this point, as mentioned above, his critics have little to say. Callicott simply assumes that an unshakeable commitment to intrinsic value—one held prior to inquiry into the varying contexts of specific environmental problems—makes a practical difference in discussions over policy options. Westra, despite her promising setup of a real-world case involving fisheries management, retreats to hypotheticals and ideological criticisms of the weaknesses of the anthropocentric claims in Norton's framework. And Steverson openly discards the empirical question altogether, preferring to address the faults he finds in the contextualist position and its divergence from the "intuitions" of nonanthropocentrists.

By taking aim at Norton's anthropocentrism rather than attempting to refute the empirical claims of the convergence hypothesis through falsification, we feel that his critics have essentially backed away from the real-world problems and questions to which environmental philosophy was originally intended to speak. Callicott, Westra, and Steverson seem to be saying that Norton's understanding of convergence is somehow philosophically wrong and should therefore be swept aside, regardless of whether it might actually hold in particular cases. For Norton's critics, the moral justification of environmental practice and policy is delivered through their universal nonanthropocentric principles (i.e., Callicott's ecocentric reading of Leopold's "land ethic" and Westra's "principle of integrity"), under which all cases and situations must ultimately be subsumed. What concerns us here is that the biophysical and cultural settings in which actual public moral inquiry occurs is, for these theorists, essentially deemed irrelevant to ethical judgment. As Callicott puts it, "providing theoretical grounds for according intrinsic value to nature . . . [is] the principle, the defining project of environmental ethics."[14] Once this philosophical foundation is laid, the task is then to "institutionalize" this eco-centric ethic in natural resource management and policy arenas.[15]

Our fear is that Callicott's move threatens to undercut real democratic debate about the appropriateness of such foundations as universal ethical prescriptions for human-nature relationships, and that the turn to ontological arguments (i.e., the single-minded desire to fashion a "master principle" that supports the moral standing of nonhuman nature) draws attention away from the empirical contexts of specific environmental problems. In taking this route, we believe Norton's critics miss the potential resources located within normatively diverse human value experiences that might be up to the task of promoting strong environmental protection. Westra, for example, also appears to subscribe to a foundational view of moral judgment and decision making, as evidenced by her remark that "Even reaching a right decision on wrong principles may not be sufficient if the principles are such that they would permit a morally bad decision on another occasion."[16] Implicit here is that only those justifications that rely on a narrow set of nonanthropocentric claims articulated prior to moral deliberation will be able to meet the demands of protective environmental attitudes. In other words, to the extent that ethical debate over the multiple values at play in specific decision-making contexts does not reduce these goods to a nonanthropocentric principle defined in advance, it can produce only second-rate, weedy justifications for environmental policy, or possibly the philosophical equivalent of "dumb luck."

We do not think that there is much to be gained by these approaches to moral argument in environmental philosophy. Since one of us has written elsewhere about the virtues of an alternative, pragmatic approach toward ethical justification regarding nature that draws upon Dewey's moral contextualism, we do not rehearse the specifics of this sort of project here.[17] Rather, our present purpose is simply to suggest that stances like Callicott's, Westra's, and Steverson's seem to discount the relevance of actual public opinion for the business of supporting our environmental commitments through management and policy actions. Indeed, there seems to be an open dismissal of the legitimacy of citizens' environmental philosophies by Norton's nonanthropocentric critics. This refusal to engage the specific claims in the convergence hypothesis reveals an antiempirical sentiment that we feel is counterproductive to the practical policy goals of environmental ethics. Accordingly, we turn our discussion toward one example of an empirical study that we think illuminates the usefulness of Norton's convergence hypothesis—the Vermont public's general environmental commitments and their specific attitudes toward Green Mountain National Forest policy. Specifically, we believe our research in this arena addresses the main question raised in Norton's thesis; that is, does public value pluralism regarding nature necessarily prevent practical agreement at the level of sustainable environmental policy? If the Vermont data we report on below are at all accurate, the answer to this question would appear to be a resounding "No."

An Empirical Test

To empirically measure public environmental ethics, values, and forest policy attitudes, we adopted a mail survey technique commonly used in social scientific research. Specifically, we administered a study questionnaire to a representative sample of 1,500 Vermont households, as drawn from telephone directories covering the state. The questionnaire was administered in the spring of 1995 following procedures recommended by Dillman.[18] There were 272 questionnaires returned as undeliverable, reducing our sample size to 1,228, and 612 were completed and returned, yielding a response rate of 50 percent.

Because our study was designed to measure the Vermont public's support for a range of environmental ethical positions, we needed to construct a typology of philosophical claims about human-nature relationships. We did this through an analysis and synthesis of a wide selection of philosophical and historical literature in environmental thought.[19] The resulting typology of seventeen environmental ethics, grouped in five thematic categories, is presented in Table 5.1. Since we were interested in developing an extensive (though by no means exhaustive) list of potential environmental ethics, our study identified an additional number of moral stances that fell outside the weak anthropocentric and biocentric/ecocentric positions that Norton sets up in his convergence framework, although biocentric and weak anthropocentric positions are clearly included in our analysis. If the notion of convergence can hold among the positions captured within our broader philosophical net, then we think that Norton's thesis is even more persuasive and of greater practical import. Furthermore, this extended typology resonates with our approach to a set of metaphilosophical issues in environmental ethics. Specifically, we believe that a contextual and situation-centered understanding of ethical judgments is a more appropriate model of moral experience; a stance that suggests individuals are (and should be) less ideological and categorical in their views of what actions are "right" regarding nature.[20] If this is so, then our investigations into public environmentalism need to adopt an unabashedly experimental spirit, employing materials and tools that are shaped, but not entirely determined, by well-known theoretical debates in environmental philosophy.

To test public support for these ethical positions regarding nature, we composed a battery of sixty-four statements designed to measure agreement with each of the seventeen environmental ethics included in our typology. Study participants were directed to indicate whether they agreed or disagreed with each statement by means of an eleven-point Likert-type scale. Summary results of respondents' mean scores for these seventeen ethics are presented in Figure 5.1.

In addition to this examination of citizens' support for specific environmental ethical claims, we also investigated the more general types of values that nature (in this case, Vermont's Green Mountain National Forest) might provide for the public. These were drawn from several conceptual classifications of the

TABLE 5.1   ENVIRONMENTAL ETHICS TYPOLOGY

Environmental Ethics	Representative Statement
Anti-environment	
(1) Physical threat	(1) Nature can be dangerous to human survival
(2) Spiritual evil	(2) Nature can be spiritually evil
Benign Indifference	
(3) Storehouse of raw materials	(3) Nature is a storehouse of raw materials that should be used by humans as needed
(4) Religious dualism	(4) Humans were created as more important than the rest of nature
(5) Intellectual dualism	(5) Because humans can think, they are more important than the rest of nature
Utilitarian Conservation	
(6) Old humanitarianism	(6) Cruelty toward animals makes people less human
(7) Efficiency	(7) The supply of goods and services provided by nature is limited
(8) Quality of life	(8) Nature adds to the quality of our lives (for example, outdoor recreation, natural beauty)
(9) Ecological survival	(9) Human survival depends on nature and natural processes
Stewardship	
(10) Religious/spiritual duty	(10) It is our religious responsibility to take care of nature
(11) Future generations	(11) Nature will be important to future generations
(12) God's creation	(12) Nature is God's creation
(13) Life-based/mysticism	(13) All living things are sacred
Radical Environmentalism	
(14) Humanitarianism	(14) Animals should be free from needless pain and suffering
(15) Organicism/animism	(15) All living things are interconnected
(16) Pantheism	(16) All living things have a spirit
(17) Natural rights	(17) All living things have a moral right to exist

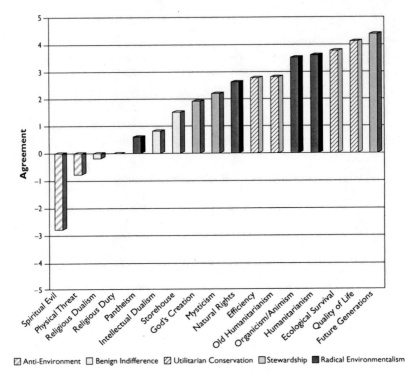

Figure 5.1   Environmental Ethics

potential social values supported by the environment.[21] Respondents' support for these eleven human values of nature was measured by means of a six-point scale, ranging from "not at all important" to "extremely important." Results of this investigation are reported in Table 5.2.

As we have discussed in more detail elsewhere, our study of public environmental ethics reveals a strong moral pluralism embraced by Vermont citizens.[22] Even a quick glance at the results presented in Figure 5.1 suggests not only that respondents subscribed to a diverse mix of moral claims about nature (from utilitarian views to radical environmental stances) but also that a considerable number of these positions drew high levels of agreement from the study sample. We can see that the "future generations" ethic (a claim that is the centerpiece to Norton's contextualism) and the "organicism/animism" and "natural rights" ethics (elements common to much biocentric and ecocentric theory) all enjoy a substantial level of public support. This pluralism in public environmental commitments is further bolstered by the results of the human values of nature analysis reported in Table 5.2. A number of these values produced high average importance ratings, especially aesthetic, ecological, recreational, and educational values. Significantly, economic values were at the bottom of the heap, suggesting, contra Callicott, that nonconsumptive human-based environmental values are not always held hostage to commercial values in public opinion.

Turning to the question of support for environmental policy, we constructed a series of statements concerning various ecosystem-based goals and objectives for managing Vermont's Green Mountain National Forest.[23] Support for these items was recorded on a five-point agreement scale, ranging from strong disagreement to strong agreement with the policy items. These statements, along with respondents' average agreement scores, are presented in Table 5.3. Taken as a whole, these statements effectively map out the sort of "long-sighted" and multivalue environmental policies described by Norton in the convergence hypothesis.

TABLE 5.2   HUMAN VALUES OF NATURE

Value	Statement	Average Importance Rating*
Aesthetic	The opportunity to enjoy the beauty of nature	4.97
Ecological	The opportunity to protect nature in order to ensure human well-being and survival	4.95
Recreation	The opportunity to camp, hike, and participate in other recreation activities in nature	4.83
Education	The opportunity to learn more about nature	4.68
Moral/ethical	The opportunity to exercise a moral and ethical obligation to respect and protect nature and other living things	4.53
Historical/cultural	The opportunity to see and experience nature as our ancestors did	4.4
Therapeutic	The opportunity to maintain or regain physical health or mental well-being through contact with nature	4.35
Scientific	The opportunity for scientists to study nature and ecology	4.3
Intellectual	The opportunity to think creatively and be inspired by nature	3.93
Spiritual	The opportunity to get closer to God or obtain other spiritual meaning through contact with nature	3.81
Economic	The opportunity to get timber, minerals, and other natural resources from nature	2.98

* 1 = Not at all important; 6 = Extremely important.

TABLE 5.3 FOREST POLICY ATTITUDES

| Statement | Level of Agreement (%) | | | | | |
	Strongly Agree	Agree	Uncertain / No Opinion	Disagree	Strongly Disagree	Mean Score*
(1) Greater protection should be given to fish and wildlife habitats on the Green Mountain National Forest	42.8	37.3	11.7	7.4	0.8	1.86
(2) Greater efforts should be made to protect the remaining undisturbed forests on the Green Mountain National Forest	47.8	32.0	11.2	7.4	1.5	1.83
(3) Management of the Green Mountain National Forest should emphasize a wide range of benefits and issues rather than timber and wood products alone	36.1	50.9	7.5	4.3	1.2	1.84
(4) Management of the Green Mountain National Forest should focus on the forest as a whole and not on its individual parts (such as bears and trees)	21.9	54.1	8.6	13.0	2.4	2.2
(5) Logging on the Green Mountain National Forest should not be allowed to disrupt the habitats of animals such as bears	26.4	45.9	13.4	11.8	2.5	2.18
(6) The Green Mountain National Forest should be managed to protect basic ecological processes and not to favor individual plant or animal species	13.1	46.2	20.0	17.1	3.5	2.52
(7) The Green Mountain National Forest should be managed to meet human needs and desires as long as the basic ecological integrity of the forest is protected	12.1	59.1	13.4	11.9	3.5	2.36

TABLE 5.3 (continued)

	Level of Agreement (%)					
Statement	Strongly Agree	Agree	Uncertain / No Opinion	Disagree	Strongly Disagree	Mean Score*
(8) Human and economic uses of the Green Mountain National Forest should be managed so that they are sustainable over the long run	28.8	60.9	7.3	2.0	1.0	1.86
(9) The Green Mountain National Forest should be managed as a complete ecosystem and not as a series of towns or other political jurisdictions	31.5	51.1	11.7	5.2	0.5	1.92
(10) The Green Mountain National Forest should be managed to protect the natural diversity of plant and animal life	33	57.8	6.5	2.3	0.3	1.79
(11) The Green Mountain National Forest should be managed to meet the needs of this generation while maintaining the options for future generations to meet their needs	25.7	56.4	9.7	6.5	1.7	2.02

* 1 = Strongly agree; 5 = Strongly disagree.

As the results suggest, our Vermont sample overwhelmingly supported this kind of sustainable forest policy. Specifically, respondents endorsed a holistic model of environmental management, strongly agreeing with the importance of protecting species diversity, wildlife habitat, and the overall ecological and social sustainability of the Green Mountain National Forest.

Discussion and Conclusions

How do our study results bear on the question of convergence? Based on our findings, we can conclude that, at least in the case of the Vermont citizenry and the Green Mountain National Forest, a convergence model is empirically valid for the understanding of the integration of ethical pluralism at the level of sound environmental policy. Our sample visibly subscribed to a wide range of environmental ethics and human values of nature, including traditionally identified anthropocentric and biocentric positions. Rather than discouraging agreement in attitudes toward sustainable forest management, however, this philosophical diversity seems to have converged on an ecosystem-based policy regime in the manner predicted by Norton. As mentioned above, we believe that his hypothesis is even more persuasive in light of our data because it holds not among narrower camps of environmentalists, but among the broader Vermont public. While ours is but one empirical study offered in support of Norton's thesis, and is obviously constrained by demographic and situational parameters, we believe that our results nevertheless provide support for his convergence hypothesis. Moreover, we think that our findings provide a firm response to Norton's philosophical critics. According to their predictions (which again we would suggest stem from their commitment to a priori, moral foundations), the potential for public convergence on common policy goals ranged from the "highly unlikely" to the "nearly nonexistent." It should be clear from our analysis, however, that Norton's detractors have taken an overly cynical view of the likelihood of convergence on specific environmental policy regimes. We would therefore suggest that contributors like Callicott, Westra, and Steverson be much more cautious when making empirical predictions about the actual policy preferences and environmental values of the general public.

One of the more intriguing facets of Norton's project is, we believe, its applicability to interdisciplinary and transdisciplinary discussions outside the walls of environmental philosophy. Because of its inclusive ethos and empirical spirit, we consider the notion of convergence to be a valuable tool for inspiring and guiding collaborative, multidimensional studies of human-nature relationships. Along these lines, we are heartened by the growing number of nature-culture analyses that complement the virtues of the general pragmatic approach in environmental ethics. In particular, several researchers laboring in the environmental history arena appear to be charting a parallel course in their localized, place-based studies of environmental values.

Indeed, the histories provided by Robert McCullough and Richard Judd, which examine the regional beginnings of the American conservation impulse, mark an emerging contextual trend in several fields of environmental thought.[24] By tracing the neglected story of New England communal landscape norms and management, these authors construct intricate portraits of the region's complex and evolving moral geography, demonstrating the weaknesses of the dogmatic utilitarian narratives commonly ascribed to this place and its people throughout the nineteenth century. Importantly, their work shows how conventional accounts miss the nuanced aesthetic and ethical sensibilities exhibited in New Englanders' civic management of their forests, fields, and waters; worldviews that, even though decidedly human centered, would spark the popular beginnings of the conservation movement and visibly outline a nascent stewardship ethic of care for the natural world. This sort of historical attention given to the local context of environmental sentiments, by empirically documenting the practical moral resources present in community traditions, reinforces and embellishes the core philosophical project of environmental pragmatism. We would like to think that such sympathetic multidisciplinary research into environmental values can make a number of valuable contributions to the study of public attitudes toward nature, with environmental philosophers closely working alongside not only historians but also sociologists, political theorists, anthropologists, economists, geographers, and others interested in the interpretation of the elaborate cultural web of human-environment relationships.

Finally, our findings lead us to draw a few conclusions about the practice of environmental philosophy and its relationship to public life. Specifically, we would argue that our study's support of the convergence hypothesis underscores the nonideological character of most citizens' environmental commitments. In the main, despite holding a number of dramatically different moral commitments about the philosophical value of nature, the sample of the Vermont public queried in this study arrived at policy-oriented common ground in their goal of managing the Green Mountain National Forest in a sustainable, multivalue manner. This makes us question some of the assumptions prevalent in environmental philosophy, especially the notion that adequate environmental protection is unattainable absent the guarantees provided by some sort of universal, nonanthropocentric master principle. For example, as his remarks excerpted earlier illustrate, Callicott is worried that the convergence argument will force a "head-to-head" competition between economic and environmental values, a contest he seeks to avoid through an appeal to ecocentric considerations—values he presumably feels are able to trump all other goods in discussions about environmental policy.

What concerns us in this sort of pessimism toward the virtues of citizen environmental debate is the extent to which such an attitude acts to forestall the development of a truly public philosophy of the environment, one characterized by an open interchange between professional philosophical argument and everyday public discourse. Instead, since Callicott states that he is interested in giving the "right" reasons for environmental protection—those foundational intrinsic value arguments that get their moral weight from philosophical purity rather than from public debate and discussion—the citizenry is effectively left out of the serious moral project of environmentalism.[25] And even though Callicott clearly wants to assert the practicality of an intrinsic value stance, he views Norton's project as "antiphilosophical," an old canard about pragmatists and a riposte that only underscores his aversion to empirical discussions about public environmental values and their relationship to policy.[26]

As the political theorist Benjamin Barber observes, the consequence of such positions is often the construction of a barrier to a fully democratic conversation about the environment as a fount of common values:

Nowadays, rather than developing a discussion on behalf of the civic good, environmentalists often feel compelled to engage defensively in strident, unlistening polemics focused as much on their own moral self-righteousness as on the common good, or on, say, the rights of hikers and bird-watchers deployed as counterweight to the rights of snowmobilers and loggers. In the face of adversarial interest politics, the public good that might bring together loggers and bird-watchers in a community of concern about sustainable environments goes missing.[27]

We see Norton's convergence hypothesis, in its quest for "unity among environmentalists," as an attempt to avoid these ideological tendencies in debates over the appropriate course of human-nature relationships. Further, his thesis properly turns philosophical attention to the interpretation and evaluation of specific matters of environmental policy, the domain in which environmental values are effectively harnessed and administered through the institutional realm. In light of this, it seems clear that rather than dispelling the value diversity in public environmentalism through appeals to a priori or intuitively defended moral foundations, environmental philosophers might better draw upon citizens' value pluralism in a practical engagement of the alternatives available within policy and problem-solving discussions. It is our belief that this sort of pragmatic approach will go a long way toward building strong and lasting public constituencies for meaningful environmental stewardship. If, conversely, a majority of ethicists prefer to vociferously defend some version of nonanthropocentrism as the only valid mission of moral inquiry into human-nature relationships, and therefore as the only correct ethical stance when it comes to environmental protection, then we are unfortunately less sanguine about the likelihood that Barber's discussion of the environment as a common good will be realized. Regardless, we hope that the results of our study have demonstrated the relevance of public-attitudes research for discussions in environmental philosophy, and that they will encourage further empirical investigations into the thick moral context of human-nature relationships.

ACKNOWLEDGMENTS

We thank Bryan Norton and Bob Pepperman Taylor for their thoughtful suggestions and criticisms, as well as two anonymous referees for *Ethics, Place and Environment* for their helpful recommendations made for an earlier version of this chapter. We also owe a debt of gratitude to Bill Valliere for his methodological assistance over the course of this study. Finally, we would like to acknowledge the support of the USDA Forest Service North Central and Pacific Southwest Forest Experiment Stations and the McIntire-Stennis Forestry Research Program.

MIKAEL STENMARK

The Relevance of Environmental Ethical Theories for Policy Making

Introduction

An issue of great importance is whether differences in ethical theory have any relevance for the practical issues of environmental management and policy making. Bryan G. Norton has been one of the key advocates of the view that the difference in value commitments has little relevance when it comes to concrete decisions about growth, pollution control, biological diversity, and so on. In his book *Toward Unity among Environmentalists,* he offers an extended argument for this conclusion. The central hypothesis of the book is that "environmentalists are evolving toward a consensus in policy even though they remain divided regarding basic values."[1] He calls this the "convergence hypothesis." Norton tries to vindicate this hypothesis by taking us through four regions of the current policy debate (issues of growth, pollution control, biological diversity, and land-use policy). His conclusion, if generalized, is that introducing the idea that other species have intrinsic value and that humans should be "fair" to all other species provides no operationally recognizable constraints on human behavior that are not already implicit in the generalized, cross-temporal obligations to protect a healthy, complex, and autonomously functioning system for the benefit of future generations of humans.[2]

From Mikael Stenmark, "The Relevance of Environmental Ethical Theories for Policy Making," *Environmental Ethics* 24 (2002): 135–148. Reprinted with permission.

Many nonanthropocentrists disagree, however, claiming that divergence in basic values makes all the difference when it comes to environmental policy making. Paul Taylor, for example, writes: "It makes a practical difference in the way we treat the natural environment whether we accept an anthropocentric or a biocentric system of ethics."[3] Likewise, Holmes Rolston III is convinced that "A model in which nature has no value apart from human preferences will imply different conduct from one where nature projects all values."[4] Finally, J. Baird Callicott's direct reply to Norton is that "Norton's 'convergence hypothesis' . . . is dead wrong."[5]

Who is right? Can Norton's convergence hypothesis be sustained or is Callicott right that it is dead wrong? More specifically, what differences (if any) could or should divergence in basic values make for environmental management and policy making? My aim in this chapter is to offer an answer to this issue, which I call the *theory-policy issue*. I explain that there are good reasons to reject Norton's position if it is taken to imply that the value differences between anthropocentrists and nonanthropocentrists are of little relevance at the level of policy making. I also state more explicitly what these differences amount to on the policy level.

The chapter is arranged as follows: First, I distinguish between some of the main versions of anthropocentrism and nonanthropocentrism. Second, I identify the different goals that the advocates of these ethical theories set up for environmental policy making. Third, I discuss three important policy areas (human population, wilderness preservation, and wildlife management) and show that differences in basic values generate divergent policies.

Versions of Anthropocentrism and Nonanthropocentrism

Anthropocentrism and nonanthropocentrism come in a variety of different forms. It is therefore necessary that we stipulate what versions of them we intend to compare. We should also find formulations that make the step from ethical theory to policy fairly easy. We can then specify the view that people's behavior toward nature should ultimately be evaluated solely on the basis of how it affects human beings, whereas nonanthropocentrism is the idea that people's behavior toward nature should be evaluated also on the basis of how it affects other living beings or ecosystems. The reason anthropocentrists give for why we should take into account only humans is that they maintain that humans are the only ones who have intrinsic value or moral standing. Correspondingly, the reason nonanthropocentrists give for taking into account not merely humans is that they claim that other living things or natural objects also have intrinsic value or moral standing.

Furthermore, two important versions of anthropocentrism need to be distinguished. *Traditional anthropocentrism* is the position that people's behavior toward nature should be evaluated solely on the basis of how it affects now-living human beings, whereas *intergenerational anthropocentrism* is the view that people's behavior toward nature should be evaluated on the basis of how it affects both present and future human generations. (Norton's claim is thus, more exactly, that nonanthropocentrism provides no operationally recognizable constraints on human behavior that are not already implicit in intergenerational anthropocentrism.) But two versions of nonanthropocentrism must also be distinguished. *Biocentrism* is the view that people's behavior toward nature should be evaluated on the basis of how it affects living beings (including humans) and only them. Hence, at least some living things besides humans have intrinsic value or moral standing, but since species or ecosystems are not living things per se, they lack such a value or standing. Ecocentrists, however, deny this view. Thus, *ecocentrism* (or the land ethic) is the view that people's behavior toward nature should be evaluated also on the basis of how it affects species and ecosystems and not merely living beings.

These views show that anthropocentrists, biocentrists, and ecocentrists disagree, first, about which natural things have intrinsic value or moral standing. They offer different answers to the question concerning the kinds of things in nature we can treat morally rightly or wrongly and thus we must take into account our moral evaluations. I call this disagreement the *moral standing issue*. However, we need more information to be able to detect whether these ethical theories support different environmental policies. Second, to state the point differently, environmentalists disagree about whether the natural things we can treat morally rightly or wrongly have the same moral standing or equal moral worth. They offer different answers to the question of what degree of moral significance the objects of moral standing have. These differences are possible because moral standing does not entail equal moral significance. I call this issue the *moral significance issue*. Callicott, for example, claims:

> The land ethic manifestly does not accord equal moral worth to each and every member of the biotic community; the moral worth of individuals (including, take note, human individuals) is relative, to be assessed in accordance with the particular relation of each to the collective entity which Leopold called "land."[6]

Taylor, however, maintains that "every species counts as having the same value in the sense that, regardless of what species a living thing belongs to, it is deemed to be prima facie deserving of equal concern and consideration on the part of moral agents."[7] Callicott's ethic is thus an example of a value-differentiated nonanthropocentrism, whereas Taylor's is an example of a value-undifferentiated nonanthropocentrism. Accordingly, we can expect that an ecocentrism that contains the idea that the moral significance of human beings is much higher than that of species and ecosystems will be much closer to intergenerational anthropocentrism when it comes to policy issues than a form of ecocentrism that treats human beings as plain members and citizens of the biotic community and thus maintains that the moral significance of species and ecosystems is higher than that of human beings.

The problem is that the options—when it comes to the question about moral significance—are almost innumerable, although we know, for instance, that ecocentrists typically accord a higher moral worth to biological wholes than biocentrists, who tend to emphasize biological individuals. However, it will suffice for our purpose to differentiate between a weak and a strong version of biocentrism and ecocentrism. What I take to be characteristic of the *strong version* is that its advocates accord almost equal, equal, or higher moral significance to some other nonhuman natural things, which are taken to have moral standing. Thus, Callicott's statement, "In every case the effect upon ecological systems is the decisive factor in the determination of the ethical quality of actions," illustrates strong ecocentrism.[8] Examples of strong biocentrism include Regan's view that "all animals are equal, when the notion of 'animal' and 'equality' are properly understood, 'animal' referring to all (terrestrial, at least) moral agents and patients, and 'equality' referring to their equal possession of inherent value,"[9] and Taylor's view that contains a "total rejection of the idea that human beings are superior to other living things [including plants]."[10]

What is common for the *weak version*, conversely, is that its defenders accord in general (though not always) a higher moral significance to humans than the other natural things that are taken to have moral standing. On these grounds, Rolston is an example of an advocate of weak ecocentrism. In contrast to Callicott, who takes the effect of decisions upon ecological systems to be the decisive factor, Rolston writes, "*an* important ethical constraint in environmental decisions is concern for the integrity, stability and beauty of biotic communities."[11] In other words, the effect upon ecological systems is important, but not necessarily the most important constraint on human behavior. Rolston thinks, for instance, that it "has been necessary in the course of human history to sacrifice most of the wildlands, converting them to rural and urban settlements, and this is both good and ecological."[12] A Swedish professor of ethics, Carl-Henric Grenholm, has defended a weak version of biocentrism. He claims that "a human being has a unique moral standing. His or her intrinsic value carries greater weight than the intrinsic value of other living creatures. . . . In a conflict between the well-being of humans and that of animals, the well-being of humans has in general a greater weight than that of animals."[13]

Notice also that we can, in a similar way, distinguish between weak and strong versions of intergenerational anthropocentrism. We can say that those anthropocentrists who maintain that future human generations have almost equal, equal, or higher moral significance than now-living human generations are defenders of strong intergenerational anthropocentrism, whereas those who deny this are defenders of the weak version. Thus, Andrew C. Kadak's statement that "no generation should (needlessly), now or in the future, deprive its successors of the opportunity to enjoy a quality of life equivalent to its own," is an example of the strong version.[14] A defender of the weak version is arguably James P. Sterba, who writes that "a right to life applied to future generations would be a right of a person whom we can definitely expect to exist to receive the goods and resources necessary to satisfy their basic needs or to noninterference with their attempts to acquire the goods and resources necessary to satisfy their basic needs."[15] Thus, the weak and the strong versions offer different principles of intergenerational equity.

The Goal of Environmental Management and Policy Making

The question we need to answer is whether differences in basic values have an impact on the choice of environmental policies. This question can now be restated as follows: *Does nonanthropocentrism (either in its strong or weak biocentric version or in its strong or weak ecocentric version) support different environmental policies than intergenerational anthropocentrism?*

A problem we immediately face is that while we can find a number of documents where the policies of intergenerational anthropocentrism are explicitly stated, such as the World Commission's *Our Common Future* and the United Nations' *Agenda 21*, similar documents expressing the policies of biocentrism and ecocentrism are harder to find. What we typically have to settle for are the examples philosophers sometimes give of what practical implications they attribute to their biocentric or ecocentric theories. Let us, however, proceed in this way and, with the help of the distinctions drawn in the last section, see if we can systematize their accounts and perhaps also derive additional practical consequences from their basic value commitments.

Let us first, however, focus on the *goal* of environmental policy making. According to the World Commission, the purpose of environmental protection and management is "to begin managing environmental resources to ensure both sustainable human progress and human survival."[16] We can read in the chairman's foreword that the report's "message is directed toward people, whose well-being is the ultimate goal of all environmental and development policies."[17] This statement fits nicely with what is also stated in the first principle of the Rio Declaration, namely, "Human beings are at the centre of concerns for sustainable development." The goal of intergenerational anthropocentric policy making is, thus, *to ensure that the natural resources are used in an efficient and a farsighted way so that the needs of present and future human generations can be satisfied.* The goal is to create an ecologically sustainable development.

What is the purpose of environmental protection according to biocentrists? This purpose is seldom stated explicitly, but we get a good hint when, for instance, Regan writes, "the overarching goal of wildlife management should not be to insure maximum sustainable yield; it should be to protect wild animals from those who would violate their rights."[18] Contrary to what the World Commission claims, it is not merely the well-being of humans, but also of animals (and Taylor would add, plants) that is the ultimate goal of all environmental and development policies. The objective is to formulate a policy program that is also fair to other living things. The goal of biocentric policy making would then be *to ensure that humans in their treatment of nature do not violate the rights of other living things to be left alone and to flourish.*

It is perhaps not so difficult to formulate what ecocentrists think is the purpose of environmentalist Leopold's famous words: "A thing is right when it tends to preserve the integrity, stability, and beauty of the biotic community. It is wrong when it tends otherwise."[19] Hence, the goal of ecocentric policy making seems to be *to insure that humans in their use of nature do not violate the integrity and stability of the biotic community and its individual members.* That is, in Rolston's terminology, to ensure that we do not get engaged in "superkilling."[20] A decisive, or at least an important, factor to take into account in formulating a policy program is therefore the effect the policies have on the health and flourishing of species and ecosystems. Wetlands, rain forests, and endangered species are at the center of concern, and they are of concern whether or not it benefits the human community.

In other words, the goals for environmental policy making that anthropocentrists, biocentrists, and ecocentrists envision are not the same, but what about the *means?* Are the specific policies that are required to reach these different goals nevertheless the same? In the following text, I demonstrate that anthropocentrism, biocentrism, and ecocentrism support divergent policies to a significant extent, which perhaps is not surprising once we become aware that the advocates of these views offer different accounts of what the goal of environmental protection and management should be.

Human Population Policies

In many parts of the world, the population is growing at rates that cannot be sustained by available environmental resources and in such a way that the productive potential of the ecosystems is threatened both in the short run and the long run. Urgent steps are therefore needed to limit extreme rates of population growth. The World Commission agrees on this point, but also notes that the issue is not just the size of the population, but how the number of people relates to available resources. An additional person in an industrial country consumes far more and places much greater pressure on natural resources than an additional person in the third world. Therefore, the World Commission argues that governments need to develop long-term population policies because "sustainable development can only be pursued if population size and growth are in harmony with the changing productive potential of the ecosystem."[21] Furthermore, the "critical issues are the balance between population size and available resources and the rate of population growth in relation to the capacity of the economy to provide for the basic needs of the population, not just today but for generations."[22] That is to say, our responsibility toward other people and future human generations requires what we can call a "stabilization policy": *We must ensure that the size of the population stabilizes at a level compatible with the productive capacity of the supporting ecosystems.* Not until it is stabilized can the objective of "ensuring a sustainable level of population" be achieved.[23]

What a sustainable level of population is in more absolute numbers is merely suggested. It is perhaps that the global population stabilizes at 7.7 billion by 2060.[24] This level would occur if the replacement level were reached in 2010 (that is, when slightly more than two children on average per couple are born). But for the anthropocentrists, of course, the issue is always related to how much we can improve agricultural productivity and efficiency within the framework set by the carrying capacity of the supporting ecosystems. The "challenge" is "to keep pace with demand, while retaining the essential ecological integrity of production systems."[25]

What about the nonanthropocentrists? Can we find any hints about what population policies they advocate? Yes, and there are good reasons to believe that they typically differ from the intergenerational anthropocentric policies. Rolston maintains, for instance, that "conserving the Earth is more important than having *more* people." It is even "more important than the needs, or even the welfare, of *existing* people."[26] Arne Naess tells us that one of the key principles of deep ecology is that "The flourishing of human life and cultures is compatible with a substantial decrease of the human population. The flourishing of nonhuman life requires such a decrease."[27] Furthermore, in response to an answer given by a United Nations study to the question "Given the present world-wide industrial and agricultural capacity, technological development, and resource exploitation, how many people could be supported on Earth today with the standard of living of the average American?" Naess writes:

The authors think that 500 million would not result in a uniform, stagnant world and refer to the seventeenth century. Agreed, but the question raised refers only to humans. How about other living beings? If their life quality is not to be lowered through human dominance, for instance agriculture, are not 500 million too many? Or: are cultural diversity, development of the sciences and arts, and of course basic needs of humans not served by, let us say, 100 million?[28]

Likewise, Callicott suggests that as "omnivores, the population of human beings should, perhaps, be roughly twice that of bears, allowing for differences of size. A global population of more than four billion persons and showing no signs of an orderly decline . . . is at present a global disaster . . . for the biotic community."[29]

I do not think, however, that nonanthropocentrists give a homogeneous answer to the question of what an optimal human population would be. In part, their answer is related to an issue within human ethics: Should we maximize the number of people with a minimal standard of living or should we limit the number of people and strive to have a high standard of living? It also depends on whether we have in mind the weak or the strong versions of biocentrism and ecocentrism. Nevertheless, in all the examples just given, other living things are assumed to have such a high moral significance that a self-limitation of the human population is taken to be morally mandatory. These nonanthropocentrists support, in contrast to the World Commission, a "limitation population policy": *We must ensure that the size of the population is reduced to a level that is compatible with a respect for other living things and/or the integrity of species and ecosystems.* Many of them even think that a substantial decrease in the size of the human population is morally required. It is less clear, however, what strategies the nonanthropocentrists think we should use to implement the limitation policy. I do not think that most nonanthropocentrists share William Aiken's radical view that "massive human diebacks would be good. It is our duty to cause them. It is our species' duty, relative to the whole, to eliminate 90 percent of our numbers,"[30] at least not if "eliminate" means shooting people. Rather, Irvine and Ponton list a number of what I believe are more reasonable options available to the nonanthropocentrists:

There could be payments for periods of non-pregnancy and non-birth (a kind of no claims bonus); tax benefits for families with fewer than two children; sterilization bonuses; withdrawal of maternity and similar benefits after a second child; larger pensions for people with fewer than two children; free, easily available family planning; more funds for research into means of contraception, especially for men; an end to fertility research and treatment; a more realistic approach to abortion; the banning of surrogate motherhood and similar practices; and the promotion of equal opportunities for women in all areas of life.[31]

Nonanthropocentrists nevertheless need to be more explicit about how they think we should implement the limitation policy. However—and this is what is relevant for my argument—it is clear that nonanthropocentrism and intergenerational anthropocentrism support different population policies.

Wilderness Preservation Policies

An issue closely related to the population problem concerns how much of nature ought to be left wild or unexplored. If the population is allowed to continue to grow, then those areas of nature not presently used by humans must be transformed into agricultural landscapes to satisfy people's needs.

According to the authors of *Our Common Future* and *Agenda 21,* the question of the size of the wilderness is understood as an issue about the conservation of living natural resources. The objective is to conserve "a representative sample of Earth's ecosystems," that is "an indispensable prerequisite for sustainable development," and they add, "our failure to do so will not be forgiven by future generations."[32] They write that now nearly 4 percent of the Earth's land area is protected, but add that probably the total expanse of protected areas needs to be at least tripled.[33] This expansion would amount to, in toto, roughly 12 percent. It is not clear, however, if they think that it is a *duty* we have toward future generations to protect areas of roughly this size. They at least maintain that we have a duty toward future generations not to exploit all areas of wilderness. But let us assume that a representative sample of Earth's ecosystems would amount to 12 percent of all the land on the planet and that it is our duty to future generations to ensure that such areas are set aside and protected.

Can we find a consensus in policy on this issue even though differences in basic values remain between anthropocentrists and nonanthropocentrists? To some extent, as I show below, the answer is yes. Rolston, who has been classified as a weak ecocentrist, writes, "I do not say that there is no further cultural development needed, only that we do not need further cultural development that sacrifices nature for culture, that enlarges the sphere of culture at the price of diminishing the sphere of nature."[34] He thinks that we have a duty to protect the wilderness that remains (although this is a duty toward ecosystems and not to future people). Hence, the weak ecocentric "wilderness preservation policy" is *to ensure that the remaining areas of wilderness stay wild and nonexploited.*

What nevertheless makes it difficult to compare Rolston and the World Commission is that Rolston estimates that 90 to 95 percent of the land is already modified by humans, whereas the commission obviously thinks that at least 15 percent (if not more) still remains wild.[35] However, since Rolston takes the objective to be ensuring that the remaining areas of wilderness stay wild, the wilderness preservation policy suggested by the commission seems to converge with Rolston's, namely, that *we must ensure that roughly 12 percent of the landscape remains wild.* No difference in the short run would, therefore, exist between intergenerational anthropocentrism and weak ecocentrism.

Nevertheless, they do diverge in the long run. The justification of this wilderness preservation policy given by the commission is that species and natural ecosystems make many important contributions to human welfare; in particular, they contain useful genetic material.[36] But, of course, these wilderness areas can only provide important genetic material for future generations if *they* (in contrast to us) are allowed to *use* these areas. Nothing, it seems, would therefore require that this 12 percent of the landscape remain wild or untouched also in the future. Rolston, however, thinks enough is enough. Any further exploitation of the wilderness would only further upset an already unbalanced situation.[37] Independently of whatever use present or future generations may make of these wilderness areas, they ought to be left alone—now and forever. Thus, the intergenerational anthropocentric wilderness policy is actually that we must ensure that 12 percent of the landscape remains wild *for future human generations to use,* whereas the weak ecocentric wilderness policy is that we must ensure that 12 percent of the landscape remains wild *for plants and animals to use.*

Is it reasonable to think that advocates of strong ecocentrism would be satisfied with this wilderness preservation policy? Certainly not, because according to Callicott, the effect upon ecological systems is the decisive factor in the determination of the ethical quality of actions. The well-being of the biotic community, and not of the human community, ought to be at the center of concern for environmental policy making. It is therefore likely that a strong ecocentric ethic would imply that humans should live in such a way that much less of the natural ecosystems would be modified for human purposes than is actually the case. Thus, Bill Devall and George Sessions write that "we should live with minimum rather than maximum impact on other species and on the Earth in general,"[38] and Callicott tells us, "The land ethic . . . requires a shrinkage, if at all possible, of the domestic sphere."[39]

But is shrinkage of the domestic sphere possible or, phrased differently, could we successfully restore cultivated land if we wanted to? Rolston argues that it is possible to restore, for instance, a prairie that has been not too badly overgrazed:

> Revegetating after strip mining cannot properly be called rehabilitation . . . because there is in fact nothing left to rehabilitate. But one

can rehabilitate a prairie that has been not too badly overgrazed. Over-grazing allows many introduced weeds to outcompete the natives; perhaps all one has to do is pull the weeds and let nature do the rest. . . . Overgrazing allows some native plants to outcompete other natives, those that once reproduced in the shade of the taller grasses. So perhaps, after the taller grasses return, one will have to dig some holes, put in some seeds that have been gathered from elsewhere, cover them up, go home, and let nature do the rest. . . . The natural-ness returns.[40]

Let us therefore grant that once we put the parts back in place, nature can heal itself. Thus, shrinkage of the domestic sphere seems to be possible and, according to strong ecocentrism, it is also a part of our duty toward eco-systems and other species. However, depending on what degree of moral sig-nificance is given to natural ecosystems and other species in contrast to human beings, strong ecocentrists may disagree about exactly how much al-ready "occupied land" we ought to return to the other members of the biotic community.

Nevertheless, we can certainly assume that their basic values lead them to an environmental protection program that not only contains the wildlife preservation policy but also a restoration policy, that is, a "wildlife restoration policy" that states: *We should rehabilitate those (or, at least, parts of those) areas of the land that can still be restored to pristine nature.* We ought to back off from these occupied areas for the sake of the wildlife, so that they can once more live there and the land can heal itself. Notice also that this policy may not necessarily require extensive human intervention in the ecosystems be-cause the ecocentrists also endorse the population limitation policy, which is typically taken to imply a significant reduction of the number of human be-ings in the future. Thus, nature itself can be assumed to take care of most of the rehabilitation work.

Wildlife Management Policies

Let us move on to a third and final area for environmental policy making, namely, wildlife management, and on this issue compare principally biocen-trism and anthropocentrism. The focus of biocentrists is not so much on bio-logical wholes such as wetlands and rain forests as on the individual inhabit-ants of the land. According to a strong biocentrist such as Regan, environmental policy making is about defending "wild animals in the possession of their rights, providing them with the opportunity to live their own life, by their own lights, as best they can."[41] Hence, wildlife management should be designed to protect wild animals against humans. We ought to let wildlife be and let the members of these other species carve out their own destiny. Likewise, Taylor explains that the biocentric rule of noninterference "means that we must not try to manipulate, control, modify, or 'manage' natural ecosystems or otherwise intervene in their normal functioning."[42] If, for instance, the extinction of the members of a species population is due to entirely natural causes, we are morally prohibited from trying to stop the natural sequence of events from taking place in order to save it, even if that species would provide us with important genetic material.

This prohibition means that the general directive for wildlife management consists of a "hands-off policy": *We must ensure that wildlife is left alone and that human interventions in it are severely restricted.* Furthermore, strong biocentrism generates a "hunting and fishing policy" that tells us *to ensure that hunting, trapping, and fishing are severely restricted or even prohibited.* Regan maintains that what hunters "do is wrong because they are parties to a practice that treats animals as if they were a naturally recurring renewable resource."[43] Taylor writes that besides "breaking the Rule of Fidelity, hunting, trapping, and fishing also, of course, involve gross violations of the Rules of Nonmaleficence and Noninterference."[44]

But these strong biocentric policies seem to come in direct conflict with intergenerational anthropocentrism as it is developed in *Our Common Future* and *Agenda 21.* No argument can be found in these documents for a comprehensive hands-off policy. Rather, the objective is to begin "managing environmental resources to ensure both sustainable human progress and human survival."[45] We must promote a more efficient, long-term natural resource use. In other words, in this particular case, we must learn to use animals and plants in a more efficient and long-range way. If, for instance, a species population is threatened by natural extinction and we know that it can provide present or future generations with important genetic material, then we should try to save this species (unless the costs are unbearably high).

Thus, the whole idea of managing environmental resources to ensure both sustainable human progress and human survival is the very opposite of Regan's idea. The commission's viewpoint is that we must have a program for wildlife management that takes into account the idea that animals *are* naturally recurring renewable resources. We therefore need policies that regulate hunting, trapping, and fishing in such a way that no animal species (or at least those with high instrumental value) are threatened by extinction. The challenge is to do so while at the same making sure that these practices become more efficient in feeding the growing population. What is needed is a hunting and fishing practice that is more efficient and ecologically sustainable. The World Commission writes: "Landings [of fish] have increased by 1 million tons per year over the past few years; by the end of the century, a catch of around 100 million tons should be possible."[46] The problem is, however, that the catch is well short of the projected demand and there are indications that freshwater fish stocks are fully exploited and damaged by pollution. One piece of advice the commission gives to solve this problem is to suggest a further development of aquaculture or fish farming because it "can help meet future [human] needs."[47] The intergenerational anthropocentric hunting and fishing policy is, therefore, not to prohibit or severely limit hunting, trapping, and fishing, but *to insure the improvement of these activities,* both when it comes to efficiency and ecological sustainability. Once again, differences in basic values lead to different policies.

Conclusion

I have addressed the issue of whether differences in ethical theory have any relevance for the practical issues of environmental management and policy making. I have called this issue the theory-policy issue. Norton's answer, expressed as a convergence hypothesis, is that environmentalists are evolving toward a consensus in policy even though they remain divided regarding basic values. I have argued that there are good reasons for rejecting Norton's position, at least if it is taken to imply that the value differences between intergenerational anthropocentrists and nonanthropocentrists are of little relevance when it comes to policy making. I have done so by (1) distinguishing between different forms of anthropocentrism and nonanthropocentrism, (2) contrasting the different goals that anthropocentrists, biocentrists, and ecocentrists set up for environmental policy making, and (3) identifying three important policy areas (population growth, wilderness preservation, and wildlife management) where differences in basic values generate divergent policies.

III

Expanding the Discussion:
The Convergence
Hypothesis Debate Today

Converging versus Reconstituting Environmental Ethics

Enlightening Anthropocentrism

Bryan Norton propounds a "convergence hypothesis." He also predicts that convergence is taking place between the anthropocentrists and the nonanthropocentrists. Further, he promotes this. Anthropocentrism, also called "homocentrism," or "human chauvinism," is "the view that the earth and all its nonhuman contents exist or are available for man's benefit and to serve his interests and, hence, that man is entitled to manipulate the world and its systems as he wants, that is, in his interests."[1] As Norton writes, "The thesis of anthropocentrism . . . [is that] only humans are the locus of intrinsic value, and the value of all other objects derives from their contribution to human values."[2]

Nonanthropocentrism, variously including "biocentrism," "ecocentrism," and "deep ecology," is the contrasting view that there are intrinsic values in nature, whether at the level of individuals or collectives, species, ecosystems, products, or processes, which at times constrain such human entitlements and interests. Natural things can and ought to count morally for what they are in themselves.[3] The convergence claim is that "environmentalists are evolving toward a consensus in policy, even though they remain divided regarding basic values."[4]

If the claim is that anthropocentrists and biocentrists have some common ground, no one will deny great confluence of interests. They both want clean air and water. We ought not to foul our own nest. Further, what is good for a whole range of human values is also good for nature itself, and this becomes truer the longer the time scale. But the argument only starts there; it argues that this common ground, upon thinking and acting on it, enlarges until the domain is all common ground. "The convergence hypothesis asserts that, if one takes the full range of human values—present and future—into account, one will choose a set of policies that can also be accepted by an advocate of a consistent and reasonable nonanthropocentrism."[5] Thus, we get the global claim of "a unifying vision . . . shared by environmentalists of all stripes."[6] Such convergence will not be true for all those who may call themselves environmentalists; those who conserve forests for maximum timber, water, and game production will still disagree with those who want maximum wilderness preservation. But it will be true of all those reasonable anthropocentric environmentalists willing to be enlightened toward those policies that Norton desires, who will be meeting en route those whom Norton judges to be reasonable and consistent nonanthropocentrists, presumably mellowing out regarding attention to human desires and needs.

Norton must greatly approve of such projects as the huge Millennium Ecosystem Assessment, whose summary report, *Living beyond our Means: Natural Assets and Human Well-Being*, reveals their basic orientation: "At the heart of this assessment is a stark warning. Human activity is putting such strain on the natural functions of Earth that the ability of the planet's ecosystems to sustain future generations can no longer be taken for granted."[7] The several technical and accompanying volumes say it again and again: *Our Human Planet: Summary for Decision-Makers*,[8] *Ecosystems and Human Well-Being: Health Synthesis*,[9] *Ecosystems and Human Well-Being: Opportunities and Challenges for Business and Industry*,[10] *Ecosystems and Human Well-Being: Wetlands and Water Synthesis*,[11] and *Ecosystems and Human Well-Being: A Framework for Assessment.*[12]

Human well-being is a mantra through them all. A basic framework is to classify ecosystem services into four categories: (1) supporting services that result directly from ecosystem functioning, such as nutrient cycling and primary production; (2) provisioning services, the products obtained directly, such as food, freshwater, and fuel wood; (3) regulating services, such as climate regulation, erosion control, and control of pests and diseases, often viewed as "free" services; and (4) cultural services, nonmaterial benefits such as cultural heritage values, sense of place, and spiritual and inspirational values. No one can object to our prudent attention to our life-support system (the focus of the first three) or, for that matter, to the cultural services. I have regularly championed these myself.

But what starts to ring hollow are the numerous services for just our human well-being. Justice here is for "just us" humans. This Promethean force-fitting of every possible conservation good into something good for us in our place goes sour, analogously to the way that force-fitting the conservation of goods for the many peoples of the world into goods for us Americans, or the conservation of goods for Americans into what is good for me and my family goes sour. The goods sought curve back in on ourselves, and no matter how much we enlarge the circle with increasing enlightenment, eventually the curve comes back to us and reveals the underlying motivation as self-interest, something less than fully moral.

Someone who wanted to be unkind, perhaps inaccurate, might say that Norton has found the best reasons to be difficult and pragmatically retreated to a less-demanding position. Most classical ethics is focused on humans. If one believes in any ethics at all, one must believe in promoting human welfare; everybody wishes to promote his or her own welfare. The natural world is regarded as a resource in almost all policy debates, as well as by most applied scientists, so why not swim with the stream and go with the flow? All you need to do is shift the rudder a little in a different direction; soften the anthropocentrism, but keep it.

Maybe, but maybe one ought to be suspicious of an anthropocentric ethic that is so sure such an ethic will always tell us the right thing to do. This is parallel to the suspicion one has of an ethic that tells Americans (or the British or the Israelis) to act in their enlightened self-interest and they will always do the right thing. In that light, the presumption from classical ethics is not that humans acting in their enlightened self-interest will do the right thing. The presumption is the other way around: ethical agents need a self-transcending vision of the values (goods, rights, utilities) that ought to be protected. Tribalism, even tribalism writ large, is not vision enough.

But the deeper reason such a complaint would be inaccurate (and unkind) is that Norton does not make his anthropomorphism easy or classical at all. He demands a radically transcending vision, first of the individual self on behalf of the larger goods of the human community, and, equally radically, of what is good for the human community.

Norton finds wide-ranging possible goods from biodiversity. Spiders build finely spun and surprisingly strong webs; whales communicate underwater; boa constrictors go long periods of time without food, camels without water. Humans might learn something from such species. Some species are r-selected, some k-selected (differing reproductive strategies). "This contrast provides a powerful metaphor for human population policy."[13] Norton is likely right enough often enough that saving species as resources, rivets in our ecosystems, indicator species, Rosetta stones, recreational species, and study species makes good anthropocentric sense in setting national policy. But will these arguments do enough work?

An anthropocentrist might first suppose that a healthy and productive life in harmony with nature is quite possible without wolves on the landscape.

But this is not so. When Norton, as "an anthropocentric advocate of wolf protection," considers wolf policy (in Norway, presumably similarly in Montana), he argues that legislation is needed to force the sheepherders to accept the wolves; and, accompanying that, they need to be persuaded to see that the wolves are good for them. "I would argue that in this case the local people should . . . be pushed to change somewhat in the direction of wolf protection." Otherwise, those sheepherders will "have sacrificed their birthright of wildness for a few sheep."[14]

"Too often, local communities have acted on the basis of short-term interests, only to learn that they have irretrievably deprived their children of something of great value."[15] People should want wolves on the landscape lest future generations "feel profoundly the loss of wilderness experiences."[16] The wolves are gone; what a pity—my grandchildren cannot have a real wilderness experience. They will never shiver in their sleeping bags when the wolves howl. So what are wolves good for? Making my grandchildren shiver. The "something of great value" is not the wolves; intrinsically they are of no value at all. The something of great value is the tingle in our grandchildren. We would not give a damn about sacrificing the wolves were it not that sacrificing them sacrifices our grandchildren's birthright to stand in their awe.

But notice that the anthropocentrism, however resolutely insisted on, is becoming less and less anthropocentric in focus. We start out thinking that we will be winners if we gain our interests at the expense of others. But then we learn that many of our interests are not a zero-sum game, not in the human-human parliament of interests. Next, we learn that again in the human-nature parliament of interests. Then we learn that many of our interests are not at all what we first thought they were. Once we wanted sheep to sell in markets; now we want to tingle when wolves howl. We win by ever moving the goalposts further out until the playing field is not human interests but the infinite creativity of natural history on Earth. Maybe we are winning, but we are also doing a lot of renouncing. I was mistaken about those sheep; the wolves are what I really want.

Given his convictions about how anthropocentrism can be enlightened, stretched, wolves to spiders, I fear that it might become pointless to offer Norton any more examples of direct caring for nature; he is going to cut all the evidence to fit his paradigm. "In the long run, what is good for our species will also be good for other species, taken as species,"[17] and vice versa. So I next give him the example of the Delhi Sands flower-loving fly standing in the way of building a hospital in California, also blocking an industrial development with twenty thousand jobs.[18] A California state senator exclaims: "I'm for people, not for flies."

I predict Norton will say something inspirational about people's birthright to hear these needle-mouthed flies buzz (they are bizarre and interesting flies). Whatever case I give him, he is going to say that we have entwined destinies with these creative natural processes and all the resulting created products, rare flies included. Then he will fall back to our self-centered human interests in preserving whatever we have entwined destinies with. But, against Norton, I am doubting that entwined destinies with odd flies is going to be as politically persuasive as the respect for a unique species with a clever form of life defending a good of its own.

I too claim that no species among the five or ten million on Earth is worthless; each has a good of its kind; each is a good kind. But it is going to be quite a stretch to show that each and every one of them is some good to us. Norton himself backs off from his good-for-our-species, good-for-all-species claim above: "The convergence hypothesis does not, of course, claim that the interests of humans and interests of other species *never* diverge, but only that they *usually* converge."[19] Usually they do, but often they do not. In fact, I think many of them are of little or no use *to us*. I do not lament that; the other way around, I am quite pleased that this is so. I do not want to live on a planet where my own species arrogantly claims that none of the other millions of species is of any account except as resources in our larder. If there is often divergence, we will need some nonanthropocentric convictions to save such species.

Nonanthropocentric Enlightening

Convergence suggests that the sides more or less equally move toward each other and meet in the middle, like compromise. Examining Arne Naess's wolf policies in Norway, Norton finds "a tendency to find compromise positions that may be acceptable to both anthropocentrists and nonanthropocentrists" and this, he thinks, "tends to confirm the convergence hypothesis."[20] So the farmers accept some wolves, and the deep ecologists agree to reimbursing the farmers' losses and to the removal of problem wolves in agricultural areas. Nevertheless, Norton does not really equate convergence with compromise. Convergence is not compromise because when it happens each side has dynamically altered its convictions, perhaps not its deeper metaphysical position, but its convictions about what action this requires in practice. They are now not compromising, because in a compromise each side gets only part of what it wants and gives up the rest. Now each side gets entirely what it wants; they turn out (despite their differing underlying principles) to want identically the same practice.

The anthropocentrists are getting more and more enlightened in the direction of accepting what the nonanthropocentrists wanted in the first place. Is it likewise true that the nonanthropocentrists are becoming increasingly enlightened in the direction of what the anthropocentrists wanted when this convergence started? It is more difficult to find examples of this. It is not difficult, on the political scene, to find nonanthropocentrists agreeing to compromises. Politicians must work in a parliament, with pulling and hauling among interest groups. So the nonanthropocentrists (who also believe that nature is of value to people) will have to collect all the support they can from whatever quarter they can, enlightening the anthropocentrists as much as they can, and compromising when they can get only half a loaf. But increasingly, with convergence, the nonanthropocentrists get more and more of the loaf. With convergence, the goalposts are moving, but mostly for the anthropocentrist toward the nonanthropocentrists. With compromise, nonanthropocentrists may settle for less than they want, but this is not convergence.

Looking back across human history, conflicts of interests are perennial, especially in political life. One might expect they are forever with us. But if Norton is right on environmental interests, so long as there is a little more enlightenment each year, there will be less contesting and more convergence on policy, until finally there is no disagreement at all and there is consensus. That might not happen because in each generation a whole new set of anthropocentrists will be born who have to be so educated. The reeducation rate might be slower than the rebirth rate, so that the perennial problem continues into the indefinite future. I would be delighted if Norton were right. It might not happen until long after I am gone, but should it happen, I hope my great grandchildren are delighted. Meanwhile, what is misleading about the "convergence" metaphor here is that it is really the anthropocentrists who are increasingly pulled and hauled over to the nonanthropocentrists' policy: nature preservation, with more and more of these intangible benefits; wolves and wilderness are really good for your character.

What is happening is not that anthropocentrists and nonanthropocentrists are mutually enlightening each other and converging, but that the nonanthropocentrists are doing the enlightening. If they were not on the scene with their arguments, these anthropocentrists would not be moving toward these higher-level conservationist directions. Aldo Leopold finds an A/B cleavage in attitudes toward nature conservation. (Though Leopold does not flag his A/B cleavage this way, I utilize it here as a convenient mnemonic: A=anthropocentric, B=biocentric). The A side sees land, water, and forests as commodity, the B side as community. The cleavage continues with game versus wildlife, acre-feet of water versus rivers in ecosystems, timber versus forests, owning land versus sense of place, and humans as conquerors versus humans as citizens. Leopold argues: "A thing is right when it tends to preserve the integrity, stability, and beauty of the biotic community."[21] It seems that we start out A (anthropocentric) and become increasingly B (biocentric).

No, says Norton, this shift is still in our enlightened self-interest, so it is a sort of bioanthropocentric convergence. True, the revised view is not commodity but now ecosystem oriented, with human and plant-animal goods entwined. We used to think of water in the river as a commodity, but now we think of it as our bloodstream—still our health is involved. Protection of the health (Leopold's integrity and stability) of these landscape-level processes should be the central goal of biodiversity policy because it is the same as the protection of human health.

But, meanwhile, is not Leopold's integrity of the biotic community pulling these anthropocentrists as far as they have come in the land-health direction? "That land is community is the basic concept of ecology, but that land is to be loved and respected is an extension of ethics."[22] Without Leopold's nonanthropocentric love and respect for land, which Norton considers "an unfortunate interpretation of Aldo Leopold's land ethic,"[23] these anthropocentrists would never have become so enlightened.

Consider animal experimentation. For more than a decade, the University of Pennsylvania Head Injury Clinic conducted a series of experiments using primates upon whom they deliberately inflicted massive head injuries in order to simulate the sort of injuries humans experience in sports injuries and automobile crashes. Scientists could study such injuries and also practice innovative brain surgery. The research was federally funded at a million dollars annually through the National Institutes of Health. When the nature of these experiments was revealed, then U.S. Department of Health and Human Services Secretary Margaret Heckler terminated the government funding.[24]

On Norton's account, since there is not any intrinsic value in animal welfare, what policy we set depends on whether the experiments benefit our human welfare. Norton seeks long-term horizons and, in the long term, there are likely to be such benefits. On the animal welfare account, these benefits have to be traded off against decades of intense animal suffering, a disvalue that outweighs any promised human benefits. Anthropocentrists and nonanthropocentrists do not agree on policy.

To get convergence here, Norton will have to find some way to convince the anthropocentric researchers and their supporters that it is in the best interests of humans not to do such experiments. A National Institutes of Health spokesman initially praised the laboratory but, with continuing protests, an investigation found the laboratory to be unsanitary, deficient in surgical techniques, and poor in record keeping, and the researchers were inadequately supervised. So, why not clean up the lab and continue? Possibly because such experiments make the researchers sadistic, make us humans callous to animal pain, or because humans need to appreciate the great apes as relatives, or some such argument.

But, of course, if there is no value present in these monkeys, baboons, and apes, and therefore no disvalue in the animal suffering, then one ought to be callous to it. Perhaps the great apes are ancient relatives, but since value only appears with humans ("only the humans are valuing agents"[25]), there is no reason to count the primates at all. In fact, the real force driving those who insisted on the change of policy was that this is unethical treatment of these animals, not simply that it does not well serve our human interests. One effectively has to stop being anthropocentric to stop such experiments.

Ducks feed on spent shot that fall into their ponds, needing grit for their gizzards, and afterward die slowly from lead poisoning. Two to three million ducks and geese were dying this way each year. This had little effect on the total duck population, since ducks reproduce amply. Steel shot are a little more expensive, wear the bore a little faster, and were unfamiliar to hunters, who must adjust for the weight difference. Weapons manufacturers and hunters resisted steel shot for decades; federal agencies increasingly required their use for waterfowl hunting.[26] If one is anthropocentrist, why count the duck suffering, since ducks have no intrinsic value on their own sakes? Nonanthropocentrists disagree; duck suffering is a bad thing.

Perhaps one can enlighten these anthropocentrist hunters; they would get concerned if the lead shot were reducing waterfowl populations, or if some humans also ingested lead shot perhaps embedded in the flesh of the eaten ducks. Perhaps some hunters feel bad about the needlessly killed ducks. But most of these lead-poisoned ducks die out of sight and out of mind. Why feel bad about it, if the ducks do not count morally? The ducks need to count to stop lead shot. Those nonanthropocentrists concerned about suffering waterfowl were the drivers in this policy change, even if they managed to convince anthropocentric hunters only so far as some supposed better self-interest.

Consider the case of Royal Chitwan National Park in Nepal, a primary sanctuary for Bengal tigers and half a dozen other extremely endangered species. This region in lowland Nepal (the Terai) was too malarious to live in year-round until the 1950s; it was formerly a hunting preserve, hunted in the dry season. Following a mosquito eradication campaign in midcentury, Nepalis began to move into the region. The migrants cleared the forests and started cultivating crops, also poaching animals. In 1973, to increase protection, the hunting preserve was designated a national park. Nepalis were surrounding it. The population of the Terai was 36,000 in 1950; in less than a decade, it was one million. With one of the highest birthrates in the world, and with the influx continuing, the population in 1991 was 8.6 million—90 percent of them poor, 50 percent of them desperately poor.[27]

People cannot live in the park or cut grasses, graze cattle and buffalo, or timber the park at will. They are allowed to cut thatch grasses several days a year, and 30 percent of park income from tourists is given to Village Development Committees. The Royal Nepalese Army is responsible for preventing poaching, grazing, cutting grasses, pilfering timber, and permanent habitation of the land. They also do what they can to improve the lot of the people. Probably the park would not survive the local social pressures except for the tourist income, which the national government much desires. Probably, however, the park would not have come into existence and been maintained except for the nonanthropocentric concerns of groups such as the World Wildlife Fund to save the endangered species there.

I have argued that we should continue to give the tigers priority over the people inside this park, a relatively small portion of the lowland inhabitable land.[28] I could not justify such efforts to protect the tigers if I did not believe that they have intrinsic value, if I did not believe that species lines are morally considerable, or if I thought that the values of tigers were only those that bring income to the nation. Norton will have to find anthropocentric reasons to save the tigers. Some are not far to seek: tourist income, a biodiversity reserve, some national pride in the tigers. But enough anthropocentric benefit to justify keeping tens of thousands of persons hungry in order to save the tiger could be hard to find. Nepalis have, I suppose, a "birthright" to hear tigers roar (like the Norwegians and Montanans and their wolves).

Norton advocates "adaptive management," which is both ecologically sound and community-based, a process that can "guide a community toward shared goals" to create an environmental policy that protects many or most of the values that are articulated by community members, and to do so democratically.[29] He wants to be "contextual" and "pragmatic," helping communities "to refine goals through iterative discussions among stakeholders."[30] His challenge is to "environmental ethics to address these real-world problems on a local, contextual basis and join the search for adaptive solutions and sustainable human institutions, cultures, and lifestyles in each local area. If we do not accomplish that task, nature has no chance."[31] Alas, however, if Nepal were to become a functioning democracy (otherwise, much to be desired), and these nine million Terai people set policy by voting their "pragmatic" and "contextual" stakeholder preferences, the tigers would likely be voted out, repeatedly.

Norton and I would agree that this is a pity, but (since he wants a procedure that produces effective on-the-ground policy) he should realize that his enlightened anthropocentrism is not going to save the tigers in Nepal. The incidence of conflicts has been escalating for the last half century and shows little sign of slacking off. Norton thinks that accounts of duties to endangered species are too thin to introduce into policy, but introducing a birthright to hear tigers roar is hardly going to prove any thicker for forming policy in lowland Nepal. He may find himself shuddering while tigers roar only to find that they roar no longer because their forests have been cut. Only if there are effective advocates who care for the tigers and other endangered species placing some check on local desires (and enlightening them too when they can) do the tigers have a chance.

Norton and I will also agree that if this were an ideal world, there are ways in which Nepal could have its millions of humans in the Terai and its tiger sanctuary as well (massive aid, economic development, or whatever). We both will look for win-win strategies, if we can find them. I also concede that some strategies I might find morally desirable are not politically possible; hence I might compromise. Meanwhile, on present policy in the real world and in this park, the tigers are being given priority over poor people, and I approve. One of my arguments for this is that sacrificing the park provides no long-term solution to the human problem; human problems have to be fixed where they arise, in unjust and malfunctional social structures.

But that complements my main nonanthropocentric motivation: that tigers as a species ought not to be sacrificed on the altar of human mistakes, regardless of what persons made mistakes and where in the complex chains of events. Fixing those mistakes is something I also desire; otherwise, maybe the tigers cannot be saved forever, and that will be good for people. Norton might hold out that saving the tigers is valuable because it gives humans an opportunity to fix these mistakes. But such remote humanistic reasons will never save the tigers today. For that, policy makers will also need the enlightening that nonanthropocentrists can provide.

When we get to the convergence, what do we have—anthropocentrism, biocentrism, ecocentrism, something polyglot? Sometimes Norton will just say that he does not have to answer metaphysical questions. He is agnostic about all these deeper issues, just a pragmatist who wants to get the conservation job done, and functional anthropocentrism will work fine—at least it will work fine if we can enlighten it sufficiently. There are many different ways of justifying wise environmental principles and policies.

Norton teaches in a School of Public Policy, and if I worked there, I might myself have gotten diluted (or become more inclusive) and come around to his position. If he and I were on the floor of the Georgia legislature, defending the Georgia wetlands, or the floor of the U.S. Congress defending the Endangered Species Act, his position would be my fallback position. I would be trying to transform those legislators into becoming more enlightened environmentalists. I would stoop to conquer. But afterward I would be sorry I had to stoop to conquer. I might congratulate myself on my political insight or on my psychological analysis of the way average citizens think, but I would think I had fallen back from philosophical high ground. (A day or two later, I might be apologizing to ordinary people, as well as to Georgia legislators, for selling them short as though they were never able to occupy any high moral ground respecting God's good creation.)

Norton allows that what we have is many worldviews, anthropocentrists and nonanthropocentrists of all stripes, but he also steadily claims that all we need is anthropocentrism. He tells us, with considerable enthusiasm, "why I am not a nonanthropocentrist."[32] The problem, as he sees it, is not the anthropocentrism ipso facto, but that anthropocentrists have been shortsighted and gross about what their interests really are. He needs resolute but "weak anthropocentrism."[33] The problem, as I see it, is that without the nonanthropocentrists making their strong stand and weakening his anthropocentrism, the anthropocentrists will never see how shortsighted and narrow-sighted they are. The anthropocentrists need the nonanthropocentrists as their educators.

At times Norton seems to think that nobody's worldviews change; only their policy gets more enlightened: "Environmentalists . . . have not accepted a common and shared worldview, and those who look for unity in the explanations and rhetoric of environmentalists will be disappointed. I will pursue a different strategy and look first for the common ground, the shared policy goals and objectives that might characterize the unity of environmentalists."[34] So, Norton remains an anthropocentrist, though becoming a weaker one; Paul Taylor remains a biocentrist; and I remain a true believer in intrinsic value in nature. The result: "diverging worldviews, converging policies."[35]

At times, however, it seems as if worldviews change. Perhaps Norton will want to say they get enlightened about what their larger, longer-range interests are. But on my account, we can better frame what is going on by saying that their goals get reconstituted; their sense of personal identity gets reconstituted. The more comprehensive their field of identity, the less and less plausible it is to speak of this as anthropocentric group self-interest.

Norton thinks his convergence hypothesis "is a falsifiable hypothesis about real-world policies."[36] In real-world policies, as everyone knows, resource-based anthropocentrists (like James Watt) disagree with nonanthropocentrists (like Edward Abbey), so Norton has to appeal to less-polar anthropocentrists and nonanthropocentrists. These too often disagree (sustainable foresters versus wilderness advocates in the Pacific Northwest), so Norton has to suppose still more enlightened anthropocentrists—those who think our birthright to owls overrides clear-cutting and replanting. Those in this projected dialogue about increasing convergence become less obviously those in fact contending in real-world politics. Some such persons can actually be found in the world (Norton is one of them), but finding such a minority is not much evidence for the hypothesis in real-world politics. One needs evidence that such persons are increasing in number or that the strength of these most enlightened convictions can determine and set policy equally well as do strong convictions about intrinsic value in nature.

Even if Norton were right that the various schools of environmentalism all come out desiring the same policy, it is still important to clarify motives. An ethicist wants the best reasons for action, not simply those that are good enough. Perhaps a political pragmatist will be satisfied to get the policy right, no matter who the supporters are and what their motives, as long as they are conserving the environment: John saves the whales because he respects and admires their skills; Jack saves the whales because he runs the tour boat and makes money taking John and others to see them. Susan cares for her aging mother because she loves her; Sally cares lest she be cut out of her mother's will.

Behaviors converge, but we are more impressed with John's motive than Jack's; we admire Susan's behavior and are depressed by Sally's. When mother becomes incompetent and can no longer change her will, when tourists no longer come because the whales are sparse, behaviors will change. Perhaps we can enlighten Jack; he too will come to admire the whales, and continue to operate his tour boat. Maybe even Sally, taking turns with Susan caring for their mother, will come to admire her resolution and courage in prospect of death, and will both love her and desire the inheritance. But to be at all secure in conservation policy, we need transformations of values driving behavior, not simply convergence of behavior. Perhaps Norton's enlarging anthropocentrism can effect such transformations. He next advocates "transformative value."

Transformative Value

Consider Norton's account of sand dollars on a Florida beach, which, since it is autobiographical, must be a real-world case. He chooses, admirably, to place his memorable encounter with a little girl collecting sand dollars on a Florida beach as an introduction to his *Toward Unity among Environmentalists*. The sand dollar is featured on the book jacket. I share Norton's hope that she and her mother can find better ways of valuing sand dollars than to toss them into Clorox to kill and bleach them, make ornaments to sell, and sell the extras for a nickel each at the local craft store. But when he tries to give a rationale, to imagine what might be said to such a utilitarian mentality, he finds himself stuttering, unable to escape his "environmentalists' dilemma."[37]

Perhaps he and the little girl and her mother, who was nearby "strip mining sand dollars"[38] can have a conversation and there will be convergence. So Norton says: They are alive and I interact with them with "character-building transformative value."[39] I get an enlarged sense of my place in the world. And you could, too. The little girl replies, at first: I know they are alive, that's why we throw them into Clorox, to kill them. But I want to make them into dried shells for the ornaments my mother makes, and I value them for that. The mother adds that she has won prizes for her artistry with the shells—for her a transformative experience building her sense of self-worth. So far, the conversation will be just Norton's interactive experience against those of the collectors. His interactive acts lead to his behavior. Their interactive acts lead to another. Different spokes for different folks. Norton ended his conversation on the beach, "in ideological impasse," in a "dilemma in values." "I fell silent, stymied." This dilemma with sand dollars, he muses, is a "microcosm" of the human relation to the whole biosphere.[40]

Nothing will change until Norton can appeal to a better appreciation of what is actually there. He might bring the two exploiters around to his view ("convergence" on the "transformative value" of respecting the sand dollars for what they are in themselves, living creatures with a good of their own), but only by pulling the girl and her mother far into the orbit of respecting intrinsic value in living organisms, as he himself has learned to do. He shifts their goalposts, as his goalposts have been shifted.

No, Norton may reply, the goalposts have always been the same—to maximize human well-being—all that has changed is strategy. Once, the girl and her mother found a sense of self-worth collecting the shells and making lovely ornaments. Now they are more enlightened to the sand dollar for what it is in itself, but this feeds into a more enlightened sense of self-worth in respecting all things, great and small. So they join Norton is wishing to conserve the sand dollars, and feel proud of themselves in a new way. They now have new, more enlightened virtues.

Norton dislikes any hint of correspondence theories of truth. Following C. S. Peirce and John Dewey, he "re-focuses discussions of truth and objectivity from a search for 'correspondence' to an 'external world' (the 'conform' approach) to a more forward-looking ('transform') approach." "A pragmatist, transform approach to inquiry such as Dewey's may provide a way around the 'fact-value' gulf."[41] First we might have thought that what is in our interest (exploiting the sand dollars) differs in such cases from what we take an interest in (the welfare of the sand dollars). But now it seems that whatever we take a beneficial interest in (the welfare of the sand dollars) is in our beneficial interests (transforming us). Usually we think we can sometimes distinguish between what we take an interest in (the well-being of the sand dollars) and what is in our interests (getting to be better persons). But no more.

Meanwhile, Norton's behavior belies his logic. What Norton himself clearly feels "is this sense of respect for sand dollars as living creatures,"[42] for value present there that ought not to be sacrificed for a nickel. He gets transformed, yes; but he gets transformed because his knowledge "conforms" (God forbid that we should say "corresponds") to facts of the matter about the living sand dollar. Something "matters" to the sand dollars; that is the problem with killing them so trivially. Norton hit reality when he encountered the sand dollars, something that "matters" to him, and he lamented the little girl making a resource of them; but he has yet to face up to the epistemic crisis that contact with sand dollars entails.

Celebrating Creativity

More recently, Norton "values nature for the creativity of its processes." As he writes, "It is possible to recognize a deeper source of value in nature, what might be called 'nature's creativity.'" And further: "It may be possible to find, in a celebration of nature's infinite creativity, a universal value" that we all can share. "What is valued in common by persons with diverse relationships to nature is its creativity."[43] Amen! We can learn to respect the sand dollar as a product of this creative process. So our goal is to celebrate this infinite creativity; and we can and ought to conserve it. I too rejoice in this continuing creativity, and I rejoice that Norton has found it. Had I been along on his beach walk, he and I together would have urged the girl and her mother to celebrate nature's creativity.

But Norton quickly cautions, though this is "a deeper source of value in nature," do not think that this means we are locating any values in nature!! "Nature's creativity is valued both in the present and for the future because it is the very basis of human opportunity." As he puts it, "These creative processes, we can further say, are valued by humans because a creative and building nature provides options and opportunities to fulfill human values whatever these human values are."[44] So we are still figuring what is in it for us; we really do not care about creativity past or present, except for what it means for the human prospect.

Norton had earlier put it this way: "If one separates the question of the warranted assertibility of environmentalists' goals from the question of where values in nature are located, the search for an objective realm of value realism can be seen to be unnecessary."[45] We do not need to know whether nature in itself is valuable in the processes or products of this infinite creativity. All human environmentalists need to do is to assert their goal, which is "to maintain a non-declining set of opportunities based on possible uses of the environment for future members of their community."[46] It is "just us," after all.

So I was too quick with my "Amen!" I had jumped to the conclusion that Norton had found value in nature's creativity and was celebrating that. If I now try to say that celebrating this infinite creativity seems to exceed whatever human utilities are forthcoming from it, and that this infinite creativity does not sound like an anthropocentric goalpost anymore, Norton will pull back and start celebrating human transformation (these "environmentalists' goals") in the presence of such infinite creativity (denying that it is "an objective of realm of value realism"). Preserve whatever might have a chance of transforming your life. You need to be part of this larger whole, and such an environmental ethic can translate into a more promising environmental policy. Get more inclusive; fit yourself into the bigger picture. Celebrate creativity; it is good for your soul and you will get a "creativity high" (this is analogous to helping others in order to get a "helper's high").[47] My problem is that I do not think it is high moral ground to celebrate something else in your own self-interests, no matter how enlightened those interests (analogously to helping others in order to get a kick out of it).

So Norton and I both try to persuade the girl and her mother to save the sand dollars. If we succeed, he thinks he has brought both through a transformative experience; the three of them are all enlightened anthropocentrists. But I do not think they and I have converged on anything halfway between anthropocentrism and biocentrism. I think they have been converted to my worldview that there is an ecosystemic nature that creatively generates a richness of biodiversity and biocomplexity on Earth, which humans ought to respect. Only Norton cannot bring himself around to admit this; that would be too upsetting to his anthropocentric epistemology.

I suppose that if, in further expansion of his discoveries, he comes to find an infinite Creator in, with, and under this infinite creativity, he will urge praising God because that too is good for us. Get yourself an abundant life. He does not think humans generally are able to face the universe without asking: "What's in it for us?" Or if some among them can, they do not need to.

"Introducing the idea that other species have intrinsic value, that humans should be 'fair' to all other species, provides no operationally recognizable constraints on human behavior that are not already implicit in the generalized, cross-temporal obligations to protect a healthy, complex and autonomously functioning ecosystem for the benefit of future generations of humans."[48] Continuing, introducing the idea that there is infinite creativity to be celebrated in nature provides no operationally recognizable constraints on human behavior that are not already implicit in protecting healthy ecosystems in order that humans can flourish by celebrating such creativity. Well, stretch it this far, and maybe it is not operationally different for the super-super-enlightened, but it has gone far astray logically, stretching self-interest to the breaking point—which probably also means that it will not in fact do all that well operationally either. In fact, Norton says to the little girl: Put most of the sand dollars back.[49] I say to her: Put them all back.

Well, no, Norton will reply. You were not listening when I championed "transformative value." This ethic can be transforming. The enlightened environmentalist wants photosynthesis in place, freshwater in streams, a stable climate—*and spiritual inspiration*, transformative encounter with sand dollars. Nature preservation is justified because it leads to the fostering of multiple levels of values in human life and culture worth preserving. True, we can all agree about the basic, vital, lower-order values. But the convergence is toward nobler, higher-order values, equally vital to human well-being, and these are not reducible to the familiar anthropocentric array of demand or preference values.

This is a metamorphic transformation, maybe analogously radical to a caterpillar becoming a butterfly. Norton once explored Henry David Thoreau's use of insect analogies, wondering if humans, like butterflies, can be transformed from the "larval" stage, mostly consuming the world, to a "perfect" state in which consumption is less important, and in which freedom and contemplation are the ends of life. There is a "dynamic dualism in which the animal and the spiritual self remain in tension, but in which the 'maturity' of the individual—transcendence of economic demands as imposed by society—emerges through personal growth based on observation of nature."[50] So there is transformation from bodily growth, consumption, to personal growth, spiritually. It does seem as though the goalposts have changed, or have they, since we are still seeking to win: only the sort of growth we seek has shifted from physical to spiritual?

Norton insists, right through to the end of his book searching for unity among environmentalists: "Moralists among environmental ethicists have erred in looking for a value in living things that is *independent* of human valuing. They have therefore forgotten a most elementary point about valuing anything. Valuing always occurs from the viewpoint of a conscious valuer. . . . Only the humans are valuing agents."[51] Maybe there is much transformation of people and what they choose to value, but this nowhere leaves him well placed to celebrate this creativity that nature has expressed in the nonconscious sand dollars, much less nature's global "infinite creativity." Are we to conclude: Well, there is infinite creativity out there, *independent* of us humans, but it is of no value until we conscious humans come along and evaluate it as beneficial to, *transformative* of, our human character? "The creative force is outside us," but we keep "the original idea of anthropocentrism—that all value will be perceived from the viewpoint of conscious [human] beings—intact."[52]

Maybe Norton can keep this subtlety clear in his mind (infinite creativity out there; all value in here, in my transformation), but my mind is not subtle enough to keep that difference intact in my head for long. I doubt whether the citizens he wishes to persuade toward better environmental decisions will see that difference either. I can make good sense of the idea that we humans are the only species that can become consciously aware of this infinite creativity; we alone can celebrate it. I might say that we humans are at the "apex" of creation, the most valuable species—as far as we know. Human culture is now the leading story on the planet. But that does not justify any conclusions about humans being the solitary locus of value.

Norton also dislikes too much human self-centering; he fears its arrogance. Once we needed the rhetoric of the nonanthropocentrists, he says. That helped us reframe our picture of ourselves in the world. Now that we recognize our finitude, we no longer need such rhetoric:

The attack on human arrogance, which was mounted as a response to anthropocentrism, was well motivated but badly directed. One need not posit interests contrary to human ones in order to recognize our finitude. If the target is arrogance, a scientifically informed contextualism that sees us as one animal species existing derivatively, even parasitically, as part of a larger, awesomely wonderful whole should cut us down to size.[53]

That is what those wolves are good for: making my grandchildren shiver, cutting them down to size. That is how nature serves our interests, cutting us down and forcing us to confront this awesomely wonderful whole. I myself have argued that the encounter with nature "protects us from pride."[54] Norton seems right on target until we start to wonder if seeing nature as valueless until we (the only valuing agents) get cut down to size keeps ourselves at the center of it after all by cutting nature (with its infinite creativity) down to our size.

Norton's convergence at this point has become rather similar to Peter Wenz's environmental synergism: "*Environmental synergists believe that synergy exists between respect for people and respect for nature. Overall and in the long run, simultaneous respect for people and nature improves outcomes for both. . . . Respect for nature promotes respect for people, so the best way to serve people as a group is to care about nature for itself.*"[55] Wenz, too, can push this argument way past intelligent exploitation of nature to a thoroughgoing caring for nature, still finding the major push our own postenlightened self-interest. He concludes: "*People as a group get more from the environment by caring about nature for its own sake, which limits attempts to dominate nature, than by trying to manipulate it for maximal human advantage.*"[56] This is a kind of backfire argument: You anthropocentrists should care for nature lest you get too pushy. Caring for nature is good for us; it cuts down our covetousness. If you want the most out of nature, less is more. That too sounds right—until we ask whether there is anything in nature on its "own sake" worth caring for, anything of value that justifies such care. Here, Wenz will answer yes. Norton will reply: Do not ask; all you need to know is that caring for nature is good for you.

Why do Americans want their national parks and wilderness areas? Because they can recreate there, of course. The outdoor experience enriches their lives. That is true enough, and it is where we must begin; it may be as far as we get on the floor of Congress. But it is only a beginning when we are in the field, whether as hikers on the trail or park managers. We find ourselves enlarging our vision. Norton will say: We find ourselves transformed, and that enriches us. But is this the best way to phrase it?

Roger DiSilvestro finds something radically novel about humans setting aside for protection their wildland parks:

Territorial boundaries are ancient; they are artifacts dating from a primordial world. They are, in essence, established for the exploitation of the earth. . . . Only in the past century has humanity begun to set the protection of wildlands as a broad social goal, creating national parks, national forests, wildlife refuges, even protected wilderness areas. This is something truly new under the sun, and every protected wild place is a monument to humanity's uniqueness. The greatest qualitative difference between us and nonhuman animals is not that we can change and modify our environment. Practically every living creature does that. . . . But we are the first living things, as far as we know, to make a choice about the extent to which we will apply our abilities to influence the environment. We not only *can* do, but we can choose *not to do.* Thus, what is unique about the boundaries we place around parks and other sanctuaries is that these boundaries are created to protect a region from our own actions. . . . No longer can we think of ourselves as masters of the natural world. Rather, we are partners with it.[57]

Norton might concur, provided that we recognize how we are still partners with nature, not masters but beneficiaries of setting such boundaries, gaining a new vision of ourselves in so doing. But this is a curious kind of anthropocentrism, which resolves to let wildlife be, to place wildness in sanctuaries protected from human mastery and control. Maybe the human uniqueness is that we are the one species that can care enough about other species to draw back and set some territories that are not our own, where we only visit and celebrate the wildness there. Parks are for people, the anthropocentrists will say. Yes, but here the park boundaries set sanctuaries, to protect wildlife *from* people as much as *for* people.

Winning and Losing

Since I have been pushing Norton further and further toward nonanthropocentric goals, and lamenting his refusal to renounce his ever-weakening anthropocentrism, I must conclude by conceding that when I think about winners and losers, I sometimes myself move closer toward his convergence hypothesis.[58] The issue whether those who do the right thing are losers is as old as Socrates, with his puzzling claim that: "No evil can come to a good man."[59] Doing the wrong thing ruins the soul, the worst result imaginable. Doing the right thing ennobles character. Yes, but can we translate this into environmental ethics?

Environmental virtue ethicists think so. An inclusive moral virtue, well-rounded excellence of character, requires that we be properly sensitive to the flow of nature through us and its bearing on our habits of life. Otherwise, life lacks propriety; we do not know our place under the sun. Norton has said the same thing. Wallace Stegner epitomizes this memorably: "Something will have gone out of us as a people if we ever let the remaining wilderness be destroyed. . . . That wild country . . . can be a means of reassuring ourselves of our sanity as creatures, a part of the geography of hope."[60] Walt Whitman found this out: "Now I see the secret of the making of the best persons, It is to grow in the open air, and to eat and sleep with the earth."[61] So, for the sake of our own identities, of being who we are where we are, of being at home in the world, of being the best persons, we need to maintain the integrities of the fauna and flora on our landscapes. This is not as much getting cut down to size as being lifted up to our noblest self-understanding.

I advocate this enthusiastically. But these wild others cannot be seen simply as a source of personal transformation. We must make the model at least an ellipse with two foci: human virtue and natural value. "In an environmental virtue ethics, human excellence and nature's excellence are necessarily entwined."[62] Yet "An environmental virtue ethics may start from a concern for human interests, but it cannot remain there."[63] To be truly virtuous, one must respect values in nature for their own sake, and not simply as tributary to human flourishing. An enriched humanity results with values in persons (the anthropocentric ones) and values in nature (nonanthropocentric ones) compounded—but only if the loci of value are not confounded. It seems cheap and philistine to say that excellence of human character is all that we seek when we preserve endangered species. Excellence of human character does indeed result, but only when human virtue cherishes, celebrates the value found in nature.

Winning, interpreted as becoming more virtuous, requires getting your goals right. My ancestors lost in the Civil War; they lost their slaves, they lost the war. But then again they did not really lose. Without this loss, "the South would not be anywhere close to the prosperous society that exists today, where whites and blacks have more genuine and more productive relationships, trade flourishes, people are autonomous, human rights defended, and so on. The South may have lost the war, but it did not really lose, because the war was wrong. When the right thing was done, things turned out win-win in the long term."[64] But I would not have said to the slave-owning whites: Free your slaves because you will get a benefit from it.

For us men, granting equality to women has been a similar experience. I would not have thought, as a man, that I should treat women equally in order to increase my opportunities.

Can we extend such reasoning to environmental ethics? Consider the Pacific Northwest. There will be some losers, in the sense that some loggers will have to change jobs. They will, meanwhile, come to reside in a community that is stable in its relationship to the forests in which it is embedded, and that makes them winners. They once lived in a community with a world-view that saw the great forests of the Northwest as a resource to be taken possession of, exploited. But that is not an appropriate worldview; it sees nature as commodity for human gratification, and nothing else. The idea of winning is to consume, the more the better. When the goalposts are moved, these "losers" at the exploitation game will come to live in a community with a new worldview, that of a sustainable relationship with the forested land-scape, and that is a new idea of "winning." "What they really lose is what it is a good thing to lose: an exploitative attitude toward forests. What they gain is a good thing to gain: a land ethic."[65] I can say: Get a land ethic; it's good for you—but with misgivings analogous to those above about whites freeing slaves, or men treating women more equitably.

If someone protests that this is cheating, redefining winning by moving the goalposts, I reply that the analogy is bad. "If such a person is wrong, the goal posts, since they are misperceived, will have to be moved. That is not cheating to win, that is facing up to the truth: what was before thought to be winning is losing."[66] But we do want to make sure we know where those goal-posts are and what winning means for all concerned. This is not so much converging anthropocentrists and nonanthropocentrists—any more than whites and blacks converging on freeing the slaves, or men and women con-verging on equality. This is reconstituting an ethic where the anthropocen-trists, like "us whites" and "us men," get the focus off themselves and focus on the inclusive conservation of values outside no less than inside them and their gang.

Can and should humans ever lose? The world is a complicated place and there is no simple answer. The answer is first yes and later no; sometimes yes, sometimes no; in some ways and places yes, in others no; superficially yes and at depth no; yes for self-aggrandizing humans, no for communitarian humans, not if their sense of moral community becomes inclusive of life on Earth.

> We have a great deal to gain by doing the right thing; and, even when it seems that we lose by doing it, we typically do not; not if we get our goal posts in the right place, not if we can refocus our goals off the nar-row self and enlarge them into the community we inhabit. There is al-ways a deeper, philosophical sense in which it seems impossible to lose; that is all the more incentive to do the right thing.[67]

I applaud Norton when he enlarges the sense of human community and the deeper senses in which we humans can win. I applaud his celebrating nature's infinite creativity. I remain disappointed that he cannot yet reach a genuinely inclusive ethic, unable to count anything unless he can figure out a way to covet it for human opportunity. As long as he still looks at Earth and says, "All this can be yours," he has not yet been cut down to size. He is still in the larval stage and not yet transformed into a spiritual butterfly. He does not yet have the goalposts in the right place. Actually, if I were to psychoanalyze him, I think he has crossed over unconsciously into more inclusive territory and cannot yet face up to this undertow flowing beneath his rational consciousness. He is both more virtuous and being carried out further than he realizes.

But rather than psychoanalyze Norton, let me rationalize my own inner struggles.[68] Do I think that in seeking such virtues, celebrating and conserving nature, humans are always, if subtly, acting in their own (now enlightened) self-interest? Here I twist and turn, torn between the natural world I seek to enjoy and the classic self-defeating character of self-interest. These fauna and flora have a good of their own, they are located in a good place, they are desired for their own sake; and appreciating them is my flourishing. That is a win-win situation. Oppositely, losing them is losing the quality of life that comes based on them, as well as their being lost in their own right; that is a lose-lose situation. We win when we assume responsibility for heritages that are greater than we are. Some things have to be won together.

Humans can and ought to inherit the Earth; we become rich with this inheritance, as and only as we oversee a richness of planetary biodiversity that embraces and transcends us. We are not choosing this inheritance for our happiness, but our happiness is bound up with it. Having moved the goalposts to where they now are, we are in significant part constituted by our ecology. There are essential cultural ingredients to happiness, but they now are conjoined with this ecological "birthright," to use Norton's term. Repudiating the natural world in which we reside, repudiating our ecology, is itself unsatisfying. Not choosing these ecological goods in order to gain authentic happiness, therefore, is a logical, empirical, psychological impossibility. So, in the end, Norton and I may be converging after all.

8

DOUGLAS MacLEAN

Environmental Ethics and Future Generations

In a number of influential books and articles published over the past twenty-five years, Bryan Norton has described and defended themes in environmental philosophy that deservedly command the attention of philosophers and policy makers alike. His views emphasize common sense over extremism, pragmatism over other ideologies, and the importance of philosophers not only to *apply* their ethical theories to real problems but to do so in a way that gives *practical* advice to those who must make important decisions and want to do the right thing. This last theme invites some controversy, which I discuss in the last section of this chapter.

One of the traits I admire most in Norton's writings, and from which I have been well and usefully instructed, is a perspective that looks both to the past and to the future. He traces many of the philosophical views he wishes to reject to the Cartesian tradition of epistemology and metaphysics, which the kind of pragmatism he shares with Dewey and Rorty is keen to overcome. He also traces divisions within environmental philosophy to the origins of the environmental movement in America more generally, especially to the contrasts and the often colorful debates among such figures as Gifford Pinchot, John Muir, and Norton's own hero, Aldo Leopold.[1]

Yet another of Norton's themes, which looks both to the past and to the future, is what he calls "contextualism." This is the idea that we must understand our relationship to and our responsibilities for nature in a historical context in which we recognize that our current state of ecological fragility coupled with our technological powers must shape our sense of responsibility to future generations.

Looking to the future more specifically, Norton has argued that different periods and themes in the environmental movement can be understood in large measure by the time scales of the issues that have been their concern. He defends a "tri-scalar model" of temporal horizons, which shows how different ways of looking at issues are more appropriate for different temporal scales, and he uses this model to argue for integrating normative principles that are usually taken to divide the environmental community between conservationists and preservationists, anthropocentrists and ecocentrists, economists and philosophers, and in other ways.[2]

Although time scales play an important role in Norton's philosophical views, his specific discussion of intergenerational ethics is brief and sketchy. One of my goals in this chapter is to begin to fill in some parts of this complicated picture. Norton's own most general principle is that we should view our interactions with others, in Edmund Burke's famous words, as "a partnership not only between those who are living, but between those who are living, those who are dead and those who are to be born."[3] That is to say, our values must in part be understood in terms of our relationship to the world in which we live, including its history and its future.

But how do we make that idea practical, as Norton insists we must try to do? He suggests that we could apply John Rawls's technique for justifying principles of justice to this problem. Rawls's idea is that we can think of principles of justice for organizing the basic structure of society as those principles that rational individuals concerned primarily with furthering their own interests would choose from behind a veil of ignorance that shields them from knowledge of their specific circumstances.[4] Norton's suggestion is that we can extend this device of the veil of ignorance that characterizes parties in the "original position" to include knowledge of the generation in which one will live.

As it turns out, Rawls explicitly refused to extend his conception of the original position in this way.[5] Instead, he opted to restrict membership in the original position to members of the present generation and let the intergenerational implications of his theory of justice be determined by the interest of members of the present generation in saving for their children and grandchildren. Rawls's savings principle is thus compatible with arguments for discounting future costs and benefits that are familiar in the economics literature, for surely a person's natural interest in saving for his heirs decreases over time and probably does not extend for more than two or three generations at most. This way of thinking may not help us adequately to cope with the kinds of longer-term environmental issues with which Norton and others are concerned, but there are some deeper problems involved in trying to extend the idea of the original position to include members of future generations. Rawls was surely aware of these difficulties, for he claimed that the question of justice between generations "subjects any ethical theory to severe if not impossible tests."[6]

My argument in this chapter has four parts. First, I characterize in a very general way the kind of impersonal ethical issues that are involved in thinking about environmental values and responsibilities to future generations. Then I discuss the issue of discounting future costs and benefits in evaluating alternative environmental policies. That argument leads to a discussion of what is called the nonidentity problem and the difficulties of extending Rawls's framework to the intergenerational case. I conclude with some remarks about the relation between these issues and the debate within environmental philosophy about anthropocentrism.

Impersonal Ethical Responsibilities

The philosophical issues at the heart of both environmental ethics and intergenerational ethics have emerged as a subject of serious philosophical discussion only in recent decades. Each raises difficult normative issues. Of course, not all normative issues are ethical. The grounds of rational belief, matters of correct English grammar, and rules of etiquette are all normative issues, because they raise questions about what we ought to do, but most of them are not ethical issues. Ethical issues involve not only what we ought to do, but what we can be held responsible for doing or blamed or punished for not doing. One might feel bad or embarrassed to discover that he has formed some important belief on the basis of poor evidence, that he has failed to master the grammar of a language in which he wishes to be fluent, or that he ate his salad with the wrong fork at a formal dinner; but it would not be reasonable to feel shame for such failings. Blame, punishment, and shame are reasonable only when they are warranted by avoidable failures of responsibility. If humanity as a whole neglects or fails to meet its responsibilities for nature or for future generations, no other creature could blame or punish us, but shame would surely be appropriate. Environmental responsibilities and responsibilities with respect to future generations are both ethical issues for this reason.

But if these are ethical issues, they are also unusual. They involve the kind of responsibility for which it makes sense to talk about duties or obligations, in the most general sense in which we use these concepts in ethics, but it is not clear that there is any person to whom or object to which we owe these duties. This is a puzzling feature about this kind of ethical responsibility. The history of moral philosophy, at least in the modern era, has been primarily concerned with what people owe to each other, that is to say, with the

set of rights, claims, and obligations that determine the norms of our interpersonal relationships. A renewed recent interest in the moral virtues also
connects our ethical thinking to the personal concerns of the ancient philosophers about the ideals that govern how a human being ought to live. This
new kind of responsibility is *impersonal*. It may be related to ethical virtues,
but these are not easily interpreted as duties we owe to ourselves, nor are they
duties we owe to anyone else. Yet they cannot be dismissed; they are parts
(even if not yet central parts) of the subject of moral philosophy.

Another feature of the way we have come to think about values, at least in
the modern era, has to do explicitly with how we think about nature or the
environment. One legacy of the Enlightenment, in which science emerged as
a secular discipline that has proven to be enormously successful in enabling
us to control our lives and the world around us, is that many people came to
believe that the world or the environment outside human experience had only
instrumental value, to the extent that it provided the means for promoting
human well-being. Some people still believe this, but the idea that people
value nature not simply as a set of resources to be exploited for maximum human benefit over time must now be taken seriously. Our attitudes toward
nature include awe and respect, and for many people nature is symbolic in
one way or another. These attitudes imply norms for actions and policies that
are appropriate expressions of our relationship to the natural world. Some
environmental philosophers and others thus find it natural to talk about our
responsibility to nature. This does not mean that we must understand ethical
norms in a nonanthropocentric way, as a number of these writers have insisted. It does mean, however, that we must try to comprehend why people
find it reasonable to value nature in noninstrumental ways.

Before the 1960s, one can find in the English-language philosophical literature almost no discussion of responsibilities to future generations. When
the topic first appeared, perhaps in response to the threat of nuclear war or
the thought of massive environmental destruction, it was treated as an extension of the scope of interpersonal ethics, to include those people and societies
who would be affected by our actions but had no voice to press their claims
and concerns. As I have already suggested and explain further below, this apparently natural way of thinking about obligations to future generations has
some deeper problems and may be incoherent. But no ethical theory would
be found plausible today if it implied that we had no responsibilities with respect to the future of humanity. The best way to understand these responsibilities, I argue, is impersonally. But I approach this issue obliquely, beginning with more familiar ways of thinking about our responsibility for the
consequences of our actions as they extend into the further future.

Environmental and intergenerational ethics are today closely linked by
the problems of global warming and climate change. The question of what

actions, costs, and sacrifices, if any, we ought to take upon ourselves for the sake of preserving the environment and well-being of future generations has risen to the top of the political agenda in most countries. I turn now to discuss this issue.

Intergenerational Ethics: Discounting and Climate Change

One of the difficulties of comparing the costs and benefits of different policies (or actions) involves time. The uncertainty of the future effects of our actions is one problem, but the time at which a future effect is realized can itself be relevant to how we understand its value. The value of money, as well as the value of commodities, is partly a function of time. Thus, when economists evaluate the costs and benefits of different actions, they apply a discount rate for time. The discount rate allows them to compute a present value for costs and benefits that occur at different times, which makes them comparable. Many economists also accept an assumption of pure time preference, which means that not only the value of money and commodities should be discounted as a function of time for reasons of economic efficiency, but also that equivalent changes in the well-being of people should be valued more highly in the present than in the future. These are very different ideas, and a discussion of the ethics of discounting must examine them separately. My purpose here is not to settle questions about what the discount rate should be. Rather, it is to show where and how ethical issues arise in thinking about what should be discounted and at what rate.[7]

Efficiency Reasons for Discounting

Suppose a person has a choice either to spend $78.35 today or to invest that money at a 5 percent rate of interest. This investment would yield $100 in five years. At 5 percent interest, $78.35 is the present value of $100 five years from now. If she is rational and chooses to spend the money today (and granting some other assumptions about her), then we can infer that she values $78.35 now more than $100 in five years. The opportunity cost of spending the money today is what the money could earn if invested, which is a function of time. This is as true of public spending as it is of private trade-offs of consumption versus savings. We should discount the value of money over time by its opportunity cost, which in this example is 5 percent per year. Discounting as a way of accounting for opportunity costs is a matter of economic efficiency.

A different reason for discounting, which is also based on considerations of efficiency, rests on two empirical assumptions about the future. The first assumption is that *the economy will continue to grow in the future*, just as it has grown in the past. Economic growth means that the average wealth per person increases over time. The second assumption is about the *decreasing marginal utility* of the value of resources or commodities. The first car a family purchases may lead to a large benefit for them; a second car will give them some additional benefit, but less than the first. The assumption of decreasing marginal utility says that a given amount of money will benefit a poorer person more than the same amount of money will benefit a richer person. Another way to put this assumption is that the better off people become (in terms of well-being), the less efficient they are in converting additional resources to further increases in well-being. Most economists (as well as others who think about this issue) accept this assumption as a general truth.

The assumption of economic growth implies that people who live in the future will be better-off than we are. They will have more commodities or resources than we do, and their level of well-being will be higher than ours.[8] The assumption about the decreasing marginal utility of additional resources implies that people living today will benefit more than people in the future from the same increments in resources or wealth. Saving for future generations thus involves a redistribution of wealth from those who are worse-off to those who are better-off. In order to maximize the value of resources, therefore, we should discount future costs and benefits. This too is an argument based on efficiency. Discounting is justified as a way of maximizing the value of commodities or resources over time. The empirical assumptions behind the argument may be controversial, but the logic of the argument is hard to resist.

Some experts deny that the economy will continue to grow in the future. They may believe that global climate change or some other event will have catastrophic implications that will bring economic growth to a halt or will cause the global economy to shrink. If these pessimists are right, then one implication might be that the discount rate due to increased productivity should be set at zero, or it should be negative. I am not an economist, so I do not address this issue here.

By calling these arguments "efficiency-based reasons" for discounting future costs and benefits, I mean to indicate that in at least one important respect, they are not based on controversial ethical assumptions. In particular, they are neutral with respect to how we should value the well-being of future generations compared to the well-being of members of the present generation. To see this, it is sufficient to notice that efficiency-based reasons for discounting are compatible with utilitarianism, which claims that an action or policy is right if and only if, among the feasible alternatives, it maximizes the total or aggregate happiness or well-being. Because utilitarianism focuses only on aggregate well-being, it is insensitive to how well-being is distributed among individuals or groups. It is insensitive to inequalities in well-being per se, but given the assumption of diminishing marginal utility, utilitarianism is not in-sensitive to the distribution of commodities or resources over time. For reasons of efficiency, it supports policies that redistribute from those who are better-off to those who are worse-off.

Efficiency-based reasons for discounting do not discount the well-being of future generations. Thus, a critic of discounting future costs and benefits who claims that discounting is simply a way of cheating our children misses the mark if he objects to all discounting of future costs and benefits. This criticism does not apply to opportunity costs or to productivity reasons for discounting.

Of course, these arguments leave unsettled what choice a person ought to make about consuming today or saving for the future; and they leave unsettled what decision a society or government ought to make, even when it knows the preferences of individuals regarding their own savings rates. These arguments also leave unsettled what kinds of things have opportunity costs, for which money is a reasonable surrogate value. They leave other issues unsettled as well. It is with some of these issues that ethical questions about discounting arise.

Before turning to these other issues, however, it may be worth illustrating just how important the choice of a discount rate is for evaluating policy proposals that will have significant future impacts. Where time horizons are large enough, small changes in the discount rate can overwhelm most other aspects of a cost-benefit analysis. This effect is well illustrated in a recent debate about the urgency of nations to act now in order to reduce the future impact of climate change. The British economist Nicholas Stern produced a report for the British government in 2006 that argues that the best estimate of the correct discount rate to apply to the future costs of climate change is around 1.4 percent per year.[9] Stern concludes that his analysis supports our taking strong measures immediately to reduce these costs to future generations. Working with the same scientific data, a number of American (and other) economists argue that the discount rate we ought to apply to the costs of climate change is around 6 percent.[10] These economists argue that the case for immediate action is a lot less urgent. As the discount rate increases, the case for deferring consumption or increasing savings weakens.

The effects of climate change will last a very long time, and economists are trying to evaluate these effects far into the future. In one critical review of the Stern report, Martin Weitzman comments: "In fact, it is not an exaggeration to say that the biggest uncertainty of all in the economics of climate change is the uncertainty about which interest rate to use for discounting. In one form or another, this little secret is known to insiders in the economics of climate change, but it needs to be more widely appreciated by economists at large."[11] As Weitzman notes, very much hinges on what discount rate is chosen. "The disagreement over [a 1.4 percent or a 6 percent] interest rate to use for discounting is equivalent here in its impact to a disagreement about the estimated damage costs of global warming a hundred years hence of *two orders of magnitude*. Bingo!"[12]

Ethical Reasons for Discounting

Issues of uncertainty affect in many ways how we think about the future consequences of our current policies and practices. I want to mention here just one of these issues, which is tied specifically to how we think about our responsibilities with respect to future generations. This is the possibility that future generations will never come into existence. Some catastrophe—for example, a nuclear war or a giant asteroid striking the Earth—could lead to the extinction of the human race.

If we are concerned about the long-term effects of climate change, for example, then of course we cannot discount these effects by the risk that climate change itself could lead to the extinction of the human race. That would be as absurd as the story of the boy who, convicted of murdering his parents, pleads for leniency in sentencing on grounds that he is an orphan. But we might take seriously the prospect that other things will cause the extinction of the human race. If we discount for this reason, we are discounting the well-being of future generations of people because of the uncertainty that they will exist. Stern incorporates this kind of uncertainty in his analysis. He estimates the chance of something causing the extinction of the human race to be one in a thousand per year. Thus, he adds a 0.1 percent per year discount for uncertainty.

This discount rate also adds up over time. It implies, for example, that the chance of humanity surviving on Earth another seven hundred years is just 50 percent. Stern's estimate of the risk of extinction seems rather high to me, but I have no expertise upon which to challenge it. Note, however, that even though his discount rate for climate change reflects this uncertainty assumption, his critics still claim that his discount rate is too low.

DISTRIBUTIVE JUSTICE
Turning to some other ethically motivated reasons for discounting, we can begin by noticing that because the productivity argument for discounting that I describe above is compatible with utilitarianism, it is also susceptible to philosophical arguments against that ethical theory. Utilitarianism, as I have claimed, looks only at aggregate well-being and is insensitive to how well-being

is distributed. It can therefore prescribe policies that many people regard as objectionable on grounds of fairness or distributive justice.

If there were a way to redistribute well-being (not resources or wealth, but well-being) from those who are worse-off to those who are better-off, such that the total aggregate well-being remained the same, then a strict utilitarian could have no objection to this redistribution. Utilitarianism can also prescribe policies that impose extreme sacrifices on a small group of people for the sake of producing small benefits for a much larger population, thereby increasing total well-being. Many philosophers find these implications sufficient grounds for rejecting utilitarianism. As Rawls famously put it, by focusing only on aggregate well-being, "Utilitarianism does not take seriously the distinction between persons."[13] These critics believe that it is unfair to impose large sacrifices on some people merely as a means for increasing total well-being.

There are several ways to block this implication of utilitarianism and to introduce sensitivity to concerns of distributive justice into a theory that evaluates alternatives in terms of their consequences. One way to do this is to replace equality in the consideration of well-being with a principle that explicitly gives greater weight to the well-being of those who are worse-off.[14] Assuming that people in the future will be better-off than we are today, the argument from distributive justice is a reason for discounting the *well-being* of future generations in evaluating the costs and benefits of our actions.

Notice that this reason for discounting is different from efficiency-based reasons for claiming that the value of commodities or resources is a function of time or wealth. Commodities and resources have value only as means to well-being, and consumption is the process that converts commodities or resources into well-being. Ethical-based reasons for discounting claim that the value of well-being itself should be seen as a function of time. One reason for discounting future well-being, as we have just described, is based on egalitarian assumptions and a concern for distributive justice.

It turns out that this reason plays an important role in explaining the different discount rates that Stern and his critics choose to apply to the costs of climate change. Stern is egalitarian (or nearly so) in how he accounts for the social value of changes in the well-being of present and future generations. He writes, "[Our] argument . . . and that of many other economists and philosophers who have examined these long-run, ethical issues, is that [a positive time discount rate] is relevant only to account for the exogenous possibility of extinction."[15]

I discuss time preference below, but the implications of Stern's egalitarianism from the perspective of distributive justice can be disturbing. Partha Dasgupta estimates that, given Stern's assumptions, the present generation should save 97.5 percent of its income for future generations to mitigate the costs of climate change. This is, as I have noted, because these costs will extend for a very long time, and there will be many generations of people who will live in the future and be affected by them. Dasgupta concludes that to accept Stern's conclusion "would be to claim that the current generation in the model economy ought literally to starve itself so that future generations are able to enjoy ever increasing consumption levels."[16] He makes an ethical judgment that this amount of sacrifice is too great to impose on any individual or group. There ought to be a limit to how much any generation must be required to sacrifice in order to achieve the best consequences overall. Dasgupta takes this judgment to be a reason to increase the discount rate applied to the costs and benefits of climate change. He writes: "The moral is this: we should be very circumspect before accepting numerical values for parameters for which we have little *a priori* feel. . . . [Discount] values of 2–4 [percent] for [changes in well-being] yield more ethically satisfactory consequences."[17] He points out that setting the discount rate for well-being at 3 percent implies that the current generation would be required to save or invest 25 percent of its net output. This is considerably more than the current savings rate in most developed countries, but it seems neither unreasonable nor terribly disruptive. It would be nice to have a principle to decide how much sacrifice it is reasonable to impose, but in the absence of such a principle, Dasgupta's proposal strikes me as intuitively plausible. The philosophical point, however, is simply to show how discounting for well-being can be an instrument for reducing the sacrifice demanded from those who are worse-off as a means for maximizing well-being overall. To discount for this reason is to reject strict utilitarianism. The justification would have to be based on principles of distributive justice.

TIME PREFERENCE

Economists often aim to be neutral with respect to ethical theories, so very few of them appeal explicitly to principles of distributive justice to justify a discount rate. Many economists, however, do appeal to *time preference* as a reason for discounting. Time preference is not based on considerations of economic efficiency, nor does it appeal to uncertainty. It claims simply that future costs and benefits should count for less than present costs and benefits, or that the well-being of future generations should be valued less than the well-being of the present generation in our social decisions.

Some economists acknowledge that time preference is an ethical issue, and they reject it. Roy Harrod claimed that, "[P]ure time preference [is] a polite expression for rapacity and the conquest of reason by passion."[18] His ethical sympathies were basically utilitarian, and he could see no reason why the ethical value of the consequences of our actions should vary with the distance, in time or space, of those who will be affected by them. Some other economists see the issue as Harrod saw it but reject his conclusion. Kenneth Arrow, for example, says, "I take the problem of discounting for projects with payoffs in the far future . . . to be largely ethical."[19] Arrow claims that strict utilitarianism requires an unreasonable degree of sacrifice on the present generation, and he defends time preference as a constraint on the unpalatable consequences of utilitarianism. But unlike Dasgupta, who suggests that discounting can express a different and conflicting ethical principle of distributive justice, Arrow apparently accepts utilitarianism as an ethical theory but sees the need to restrict the demands of ethics by allowing some agent-relative considerations, or "a principle of self-regard," to help guide our actions. Thus, he concludes that "it is not necessarily obligatory to fully comply with impersonally moral obligation."[20]

The conflict between Harrod and Arrow is clearly a philosophical one, but most economists who recommend a discount rate do not try to settle this conflict on philosophical grounds. They tend to avoid committing themselves to any nontrivial ethical principles, and yet many of them endorse a discount rate for reasons of time preference. This fact needs to be explained.

We might begin to explain it by examining the implications of time preference. On one interpretation, time preference means that otherwise identical states of affairs have less value or count for less if they occur later rather than earlier. On this objective interpretation, time preference is an implausible ethical principle. Why should the mere timing of events matter to their value? Time preference interpreted in this way would imply that the death in 2010 of a thirty-year-old is worse than the death in 2020 of an otherwise identical thirty-year-old. It would mean that the loss of one hundred Union soldiers killed in the Battle of Gettysburg in 1863 is much worse than the loss of one hundred American soldiers killed at Iwo Jima in 1945, simply because the American Civil War occurred much earlier than World War II.

Economists like Arrow and Dasgupta who defend a discount rate partly on ethical grounds do not interpret time preference in this implausible way. They rely instead on an agent-centered or relativistic interpretation. Their aim is to constrain the implications of pure utilitarianism, which can require unlimited sacrifices of the present generation in order to produce benefits that will affect countless future generations. They interpret time preference, therefore, as something that is to be applied from the temporally relative perspective of the present, just as a principle of self-regard that can limit sacrifice is a principle that is applied from an agent-relative perspective. On this interpretation, time preference does not apply to the value of events in the past, which our actions cannot affect.[21] Rather, it applies from a time-relative perspective to events that are in the (relative) future.

Arrow's preferred principle, in fact, is more narrowly tailored to prevent excessive sacrifice in the present. He defends a principle that applies a discount rate to the value of future states but then decreases until the rate falls to zero. The implication of this kind of principle is that future costs and benefits should count for less than present costs and benefits in evaluating alternative policies, but at some point in the future this effect disappears, so that costs and benefits in the further future do not count for less than costs and benefits in a nearer future. Arrow's proposal would avoid the implication that with even a small discount rate, foreseeable effects in the distant future count for nothing.

Should we accept time preference interpreted in this subjective or relativistic way? The ethical intuitions that favor time preference are intuitions that depart from utilitarianism. We should make explicit, therefore, some of the ethical assumptions of utilitarianism that we reject if we accept time preference. One assumption is about the *impartiality* of ethical judgments. Utilitarianism accepts Bentham's maxim that: "Each counts for one, and none for more than one."[22] Time preference claims that the well-being of people living now counts for more than the well-being of future people. So time rejects the Benthamite principle of impartiality.

Another utilitarian assumption that time preference rejects is *neutrality*, which claims that ethical value is not relative to a point of view. Time preference makes value relative to the present, and this has some disturbing consequences. To illustrate the issue, consider an individual trying to decide what is best for herself, now and in the future. If she applies time preference to her thinking about her alternatives, then she will give less value to her future states than to her present state. We have rejected the objective interpretation of time preference. Surely she does not think that her own happiness at a later time will be less important to her overall well-being than her happiness at an earlier time (holding everything else as equal as possible in trying to make such comparisons). If her time preference is for the present relative to the future, however, and if she knows that later times will someday be present, then she faces a different problem. As time passes, she will take up different temporal perspectives, and the value of events or states at different times will change. Thus, she may make a decision that is best from her present perspective, while having to acknowledge now that it will not be best from some future perspective. She may determine one policy to be best while knowing that she will later correctly judge it to have been the worse alternative for her. John Broome calls attention to this implication of time preference and correctly concludes that it "implies a strange dissociation in your judgments. It is hard to reconcile it with being a properly integrated person."[23]

The analogous problem for social decisions involves intergenerational conflict. When economists talk about time preference, they often make simplifying assumptions that allow them to consider generations as discrete and separate entities. In reality, however, our world always contains members of overlapping generations. If different time perspectives are appropriate for members of different generations, then at any time we take to be the "present," the time preferences of representatives of different generations may be irreconcilable. My interests might lead me to discount the welfare effects that we expect to result in thirty years from a policy we are considering today, but the interests of a child today might suggest that these welfare effects should not be discounted. If we consider the people alive today all to be members of the present generation, however, then we are excluding from fair consideration the interests of members of future generations. Time preference fails to give equal representation to these interests in decisions that will affect them. It is for this reason that economists like F. P. Ramsey dismissed time preference as "a practice which is ethically indefensible and arises merely from the weakness of the imagination."[24]

Resolving Issues about Discounting

Ethical-based reasons for discounting future costs and benefits are reasons for discounting the well-being of future people relative to the well-being of people in the present. Leaving issues of uncertainty aside, we have discussed two kinds of ethical-based reasons: one rests on claims of distributive justice, and the other appeals to time preference. Now, if these reasons are ethical-based, as I have claimed, then they will have to be assessed and justified on philosophical grounds. John Broome recognizes this fact and concludes that economics should therefore be regarded as a branch of ethics. He is fully aware that such a claim will rankle many economists. This, he says, is because "economists don't like to engage in ethical theory. As you know, economists are self-effacing people, who don't like to throw their weight about, and they hate the idea of imposing their ethical views on other people."[25] This attempt to avoid ethical argument exposes a serious flaw in the way many economists think about discounting.

The flaw can be traced to some mistaken ideas that many economists hold about the nature of democracy and the role of experts within a democratic system. It is evident in the debate between Stern and his critics. Stern, as we have seen, accepts some version of strict utilitarianism, which he takes as his reason for rejecting time preference and choosing a low discount rate. He says little in his long report in defense of utilitarianism, but it is clear enough that this is his view. In order to defend time preference and a larger discount rate, his critics must reject this ethical view, but they tend not to take on this philosophical burden explicitly.

William Nordhaus, for example, approaches the issue as follows:

[Stern] argues that fundamental ethics require intergenerational neutrality as represented by a near-zero time discount rate. The logic behind [Stern's] social welfare function is not as universal as [he] would have us believe. It stems from the British utilitarian tradition with all the controversies and baggage that accompany that philosophical stance. Quite another ethical stance would be to hold that each generation should leave at least as much total societal capital (tangible, natural, human, and technological) as it inherited. This would admit a wide array of time discount rates. A third alternative would be a Rawlsian perspective that societies should maximize the economic well-being of the poorest generation. The ethical implication of this policy would be that current consumption should *increase* sharply to reflect the projected future improvements in productivity. Yet another approach would be a precautionary (minimax) principle in which societies maximize the minimum consumption along the riskiest path; this might involve stockpiling vaccines, grain, oil, and water in contemplation of possible plagues and famines. Yet further perspectives would consider ecological values in addition to anthropocentric values. The morals of major religions—present and future—might clash with the utilitarian calculus of Ramsey growth theories.[26]

Having described these alternative ethical stances, Nordhaus makes a point of refusing to discuss or to attempt to justify any of them. He simply states that, "[A]lternative perspectives provide vastly different prescriptions about desirable climate change policies."[27] Then he shows how different assumptions plug into economic climate-change models to yield different long-term outcomes. Finally, he asks:

What should the prudent reader conclude from all this? There are many perspectives through which to view the future costs and benefits of policies to slow global warming. These perspectives differ in terms of normative assumptions, national interests, estimated behavioral structures, scientific data and modeling, risk aversion, and the prospects of future learning. No sensible policymaker would base the globe's future on a single model, a single set of computer runs, or a single national or ethical perspective.[28]

Of course, it is very important to try to predict how different assumptions, behaviors, or policies will affect climate change and its future costs. But Nordhaus here lumps ethical and normative issues together with empirical assumptions. It is not for the economist to determine which scientific assumptions are most likely to be correct; his job is only to try to predict the economic outcomes that result from different assumptions that have been suggested. Apparently, Nordhaus believes the same is true for ethical or normative assumptions. It is not for the economist (or the policy maker!) to choose ethical assumptions. His criticism of Stern, in the end, is not for having adopted an incorrect or unjustifiable ethical stance, but for committing himself to an ethical position at all.

But then how *should* we decide among ethical principles or normative assumptions? Weitzman gives a standard economist's answer when he criticizes Stern's "*cri de coeur*" of rejecting time preference and "relying mostly on *a priori* philosopher-king judgments about the immorality of treating future generations differently from current generations—instead of trying to [determine] what possibly more-representative members of society . . . might be revealing from their behavior is *their* implicit rate of pure time preference."[29] This is how the economist who refuses to engage in philosophical discussion proposes to address normative ethical questions.

> An enormously important part of the "discipline" of economics is supposed to be that economists understand the difference between their own personal preferences for apples over oranges and the preferences of others for apples over oranges. Inferring society's revealed-preference value of [time preference] is not an easy task in any event . . . but at least a good-faith effort at such an inference might have gone some way towards convincing the public that the economists doing the studies are not drawing conclusions primarily from imposing their own value judgments on the rest of the world.[30]

But we must ask: Why should we look to society's revealed time preference value in choosing a discount rate for government climate-change policies? Society's revealed time preference value is the aggregate of the revealed time preferences of individuals ("the preferences of others for apples over oranges"), which can be discovered empirically. But an ethical question can be raised about the normative weight we ought to give to these facts. Individuals express time preference for many reasons, including impatience, weakness of will, and, as Ramsey claims, failure of imagination. Figuring out how to discount costs and benefits for time is, as Weitzman points out, a very difficult thing to do, and many individuals would welcome expert advice about what it is reasonable to discount and by how much. We consider it entirely appropriate for a doctor to advise her patient about a complex medical decision that he may face; we consider it entirely appropriate for a financial planner to advise her clients about better and worse ways of planning for their retirements; and we consider it entirely appropriate for other experts, such as lawyers, accountants, engineers, physical therapists, kitchen designers, and so on, to advise their clients with respect to various normative questions that we face in life. In fact, we would consider it a dereliction of professional responsibility for experts to refuse to advise people in appropriate situations about what they ought to do. Why is the situation different with respect to economists and the normative ethical questions that they recognize as essential parts of economic decisions?

One might think that economists believe they should defer to other experts, perhaps philosophers, to resolve normative ethical questions. But Weitzman's remarks clearly illustrate that this is not what they think. They believe that individuals should be left alone to resolve difficult ethical issues like the correct rate of time preference to apply to climate-change policy. By keeping their own views to themselves, these economists abandon their responsibility as experts to engage in discussion and argument about the essential normative and ethical dimensions of important economic decisions.

This fault, I believe, can be traced to two assumptions about the nature of democratic societies and the role of economic experts in a democracy. The first assumption is the principle of citizens' sovereignty, which claims that in a democratic society the ultimate authority to make decisions rests with the citizens. The values and preferences of citizens should, in the end, determine public policy. The second assumption is that within a society that rests on citizens' sovereignty, the role of an economic expert should be to advise policy makers on the science of economics. Where economic choice rests on or expresses preferences, then the economists should measure and report citizens' preferences. They should leave their own preferences at the doorstep.

Both of these assumptions are mistaken, or at least overly simplistic. A democracy that respects citizens' sovereignty has at least two tasks: One is to find the means for expressing and interpreting the will of the citizens. But the other, equally important task is to inform citizens so that their will and preferences will be reasonable and, to the extent feasible, the result of sound judgment. This is why the democratic process of electing representatives, for example, involves not only elections, which could more efficiently be replaced by opinion polls or surveys, but also campaigns. The purpose of a campaign is to inform citizens in order to allow them to reach reasonable judgments about the views and values of candidates for office. And the process of political campaigns (however flawed it may be in practice) is an essential part of a democratic electoral system. It is only in the light of such a process that we believe elections are a reasonable or justifiable way to select representatives.

With respect to difficult policy choices, citizens need to be aware of the relevant facts. Unless they are informed in this way, their preferences would count normatively for very little. Consent has little moral force if it is not informed. And where decisions require making choices among different and possibly competing ethical principles, then here too citizens must be informed. But being informed about ethical principles does not mean being informed only about facts; even less does it mean being informed only about the preferences of others. Our preferences about ethical principles, if they are to have any moral force, must be based on reasons and arguments. The responsibility of economic experts in a democratic society, therefore, includes not only recording and measuring the preferences of citizens but also giving reasons and arguments for ethical principles so that citizens may make informed judgments about them. This is a responsibility that many economic experts have self-consciously abdicated.

This brings us to the second assumption, about the role of economic experts in advising policy makers. Neither economists nor philosophers have the power or authority to determine which ethical principles will guide our laws and policies. That responsibility is left to the political process. All any of us can do is offer reasons and arguments for our ethical principles and allow others to reach their own judgments about them. When an economist defers to "more-representative members of society" or warns against "imposing our own value judgments on the rest of the world," he suggests that it would be arrogant to argue for or accept a possibly controversial ethical principle. I am arguing that this is precisely what we must do in matters as complicated and ethically laden as selecting a discount rate for determining climate-change policies. Broome is one philosopher/economist who correctly understands and calls attention to this issue:

> There is no arrogance in offering your judgments and arguments to the public. That is what an intellectual ought to do. The arrogance is on the other foot. The arrogant thing is to imagine that you yourself actually embody the democratic process. It is to imagine you have the job of bringing together the judgments of the people, and on the basis of them determining what the society does. That is how an economist thinks when she declines to offer ethical arguments and instead tries to pick up values from the public. She claims humility in declining to form judgments of her own, but actually she is arrogantly supposing she is not merely one thinker among all the others who are engaged in debate. She imagines she stands above the debate, as the arbiter who gathers in other people's judgments, and decides on the basis of them what society will actually do.[31]

Stern has at least made his position about time preference clear. It is important to show the implications of his view, as Dasgupta tries to do, and to show how his assumptions interact with other economic assumptions to yield predictions about future costs and benefits, as Nordhaus and others have done. But if other economists want to reject Stern's view, then they should lay their cards on the table and offer us their reasons and arguments for choosing a different rate of time preference and a different discount rate. The fact that the public—Weitzman's "more representative members of society"—shows a time preference rate in its economic behavior is not by itself a compelling reason to adopt that rate of time preference in climate-change policies. We ought to be discussing these issues explicitly, on their merits, in the hope that we can reach a consensus. That is how a democratic process ought to work.

The Nonidentity Problem and Impersonal Ethics

One of the problems with selecting a discount rate by choosing the time preference that people reveal in their economic behavior is that future generations and their interests are not represented in this process. How should we address this issue? It would seem to be a straightforward matter of distributive justice, or an extension of democratic principles, to ensure that people who will bear significant effects from our climate-change policies have some voice in choosing those policies. Of course, future generations do not exist when the policies are chosen, but they can be represented indirectly by trustees of their interests.[32]

It turns out, however, that this suggestion has problems, which I believe must force us to abandon it. The proposal regards our responsibilities with respect to future generations as matters of distributive justice, or as rights that future people have against us, or as what we owe to people who will exist in the future and whose well-being we can affect. All of these ways of interpreting the proposal assimilate these responsibilities to the more familiar set of rights and duties that largely define interpersonal ethics. These rights and duties, in turn, are based largely on *person-affecting principles*, that is, on ways that we might benefit or harm other people by our actions.

Consider now actions that *cause* another person to exist. It is not unreasonable to claim that such actions cannot also benefit or harm the persons they cause to exist.[33] I will assume that this claim is true. We thus interpret person-affecting principles to mean that only people who do or would in any case exist are capable of being benefited or harmed by an action. An example can help to bring out the implications of this assumption.[34] Consider first a woman who knows that she is pregnant. Suppose she also knows that if, strictly for pleasure, she engages in a certain unnecessary activity, she will almost certainly cause serious harm to the fetus that she is carrying. But she decides to engage in it anyway, and as expected, she causes harm to the fetus. The child she later bears has a serious impairment. We would certainly say that what this woman did was ethically wrong. Her action harmed her child, even though the child was not yet born at the time of the action.

Consider next a situation in which a woman has not yet conceived, but she is interested in having a child. She engages for pleasure in a certain unnecessary activity, and she knows that if she conceives a child during the period she is involved in this activity, that child will almost certainly be born with a serious impairment. She also knows that if she stops this activity and waits a month to conceive, her child will most likely be normal. Now suppose she decides to conceive a child without stopping her impairment-causing activity and the child is born with a serious impairment. We would certainly want to say that she acted in an ethically irresponsible way, just as the first woman has, but we cannot explain the wrongness of her actions by saying that she harmed *this* child. Had she stopped her reckless behavior and waited to conceive, she would have given birth to a different child. Due to an unremarkable but true fact about reproduction, her alternative means that the impaired child would never have existed and a different child would have existed instead. If a couple could conceive at one time, or at some different time, then their choice will determine which of two genetically distinct and thus nonidentical possible children they will conceive. Had your biological parents waited a year, or even a month, to have a child, it is not true that you would have been a year (or a month) younger than you are. You would never have existed, and the child they would have conceived would have been a different individual, no more identical to you than is your sibling. The woman who conceives a child while engaging in unnecessary risky activity may have done something just as wrong as the woman who engages in the activity while pregnant, but we cannot explain our ethical judgment of the first woman's action by claiming that she harmed her child. How, then, should we explain what she has done wrong? This is the nonidentity problem.

The debate over climate-change policy is about whether we should adopt strong and costly policies now to avoid or mitigate the future costs of our actions, or whether we should apply higher discount rates to future costs, which would prescribe less-drastic actions now in favor of a more gradual approach to changing behavior. Now, it is certainly true that the way we resolve this issue will have profound effects on our society and perhaps more globally as well. The course of society and history under these alternative choices will certainly be different, and this difference will affect many aspects of life, including patterns of marriage and reproduction. This may seem an irrelevant or sophistical point, but it has important implications for how we make sense of our ethical responsibilities. If our actions today affect the well-being of future people who would have existed no matter what we did, then we can talk about our ethical relationship to them in terms of benefits and harms, rights, and justice. But if we are dealing with nonidentity situations, as we most likely are when thinking about the effects of climate change, then we cannot explain our ethical responsibilities to future generations by appealing to these person-affecting principles and concepts. We have to find a different way to understand them. This is the reason for thinking that most of the serious issues about our ethical responsibilities with respect to future generations are matters of impersonal ethics, in the same sense that our responsibilities with respect to nature and the environment are matters of impersonal ethics. We will not be able to understand or explain them in terms of what we owe *to* other people or objects.[35]

A better way to understand issues of impersonal ethics is in terms of the more general reasons we have to value things in the ways we do and to adopt certain attitudes toward the world and our place in it, which of course includes appreciating how our temporal position (including our mortality) helps to shape our ethical values and attitudes. I cannot develop a theory of impersonal ethics here, but its contours will not be unfamiliar. Someone who has no concern for the well-being of future generations reveals an attitude similar to that of someone who views nature or the environment strictly as providing the means for his own pleasure or happiness. These attitudes are narrowly self-interested. They suggest that we think of well-being hedonistically or strictly in terms of our experiences. But these are not the attitudes we tend to find most natural or that we most admire in ourselves and others when we think about the lives we ought to live and our responsibilities for other people and the world around us. Most people find reasons to appreciate and value many things, not only for the experiences that these things make possible but also for properties or traits in those things. Our normative attitudes are directed to a significant extent to things outside our own experiences. We admire people who dedicate themselves to making the world a better place in ways that may transcend what they will ever experience. This is the kind of attitude that motivates people to want to preserve natural beauty or cultural artifacts for future generations. An ethically responsible and virtuous person learns to appreciate and identify himself as occupying a small part in a much grander scheme of things.[36]

Of course, this is only the starting point of an ethical discussion that needs to be included in the justification of public policies. The reasons that explain our attitudes and policies to others need to be articulated and made both plausible and compelling. They need to be related to practical principles, including principles of time preference, which a consensus of the public can endorse as expressing our values, our concerns, and our sense of responsibility for the world and its future. There is no escaping philosophy and moral theory in deliberating about these matters. If economic experts have an important role to play, then they must join this debate.

Anthropocentrists and Their Critics

I have criticized economists for trying to avoid engaging with philosophical issues in thinking about environmental values and future generations. I have said nothing about the tendency of many economists to evaluate costs and benefits only in terms of human well-being or the means for changing levels of human well-being. This brings us to the issue of anthropocentrism, which divides not only economists from some environmental philosophers but also anthropocentric philosophers like Norton from some of his philosophical critics.

One of the longest-running debates in the short history of environmental philosophy is whether all values can be understood in anthropocentric terms or require instead a shift to a broader perspective that recognizes intrinsic ethical value in nonhuman and even nonsentient things. Economists are sometimes portrayed as being narrowly anthropocentric because they see intrinsic value only in human experiences, which are supposed to be the objects of human preferences. According to this view, if a rational person has a preference for preserving some bit of nature, it is because she believes the use of this bit of nature or the mere awareness of its existence somehow produces positive experiences in her.

Norton and others like him (including many professional economists) take a broader perspective on the object of preferences. They believe that people can value plants, species, bits of nature, and the like, as ends or in their own right, without seeing them as contributing directly to their personal happiness or well-being. These views are also characterized as anthropocentric, however, because they still regard normative questions about what we ought to do in terms of what maximizes the satisfaction of human preferences. Those who reject anthropocentrism claim that we should recognize intrinsic value in bits of nature other than human experience. This value is supposed to make normative claims on us in ways that are independent of our preferences. A more enlightened ethical perspective would recognize and respond appropriately to this kind of intrinsic value.

Now, all sides in this debate see it as potentially a narrow philosophical dispute that turns on metaphysical views that have little to do with matters like climate-change policies and their impact on future generations. However, the debate is kept alive among environmental philosophers because the parties on both sides believe the issue has consequences. Norton wants environmental philosophy to be practical, as he says, and not just applied. He believes that his expansive anthropocentrism can appeal to economists and policy makers while at the same time capturing most of the concerns of environmental philosophers who want to remain faithful to Aldo Leopold's call for a shift in worldview from a narrow economic perspective to one that appreciates the world in the holistic manner of ecology. The "deep" environmentalists who reject anthropocentrism see themselves in the vanguard of an intellectual revolution that is necessary in order to get people to act more responsibly as citizens of the planet and trustees for future generations.

We should be cautious about the claims we make for the practical implications of different metaphysical views. Disputes between anthropocentrists and their critics raise philosophical issues that may have little to do with supporting attitudes that are compatible with environmental protection. Those who are concerned primarily with changing environmental policies are well advised to put their money behind environmental activists and political organizations, not associations of practical or environmental philosophy. These remarks may put me at odds with Norton, but as the preceding arguments in this chapter should make clear, I share his sympathy for engaging with the work of economists. My criticisms of the views of some economists are based on philosophical reasons, but it also seems to me that mainstream economists who have been at work for decades analyzing and pricing the benefits of environmental protection, and incorporating these benefits into cost-benefit analyses, are contributing at least as much to the environmental movement as philosophers who reject anthropocentrism.

My view thus puts me more at odds with some of Norton's critics. Consider, for example, J. Baird Callicott's forthright advocacy of an "evolutionary and ecological worldview" that dismisses Norton's defense of pragmatism and convergence of different perspectives as "environmental antiphilosophy."[37] Callicott is driven by his conviction that philosophy can and should change the world:

> Granted, we may not have the leisure to wait for a majority to come over to a new worldview and a new nonanthropocentric, holistic environmental ethic. We environmentalists have to reach people where they are, intellectually speaking, right now. So we might persuade Jews, Christians, and Muslims to support the environmental policy agenda by appeal to such concepts as God, creation, and stewardship; we might persuade humanists by appeal to collective enlightened human self-interest; and so on. But that is no argument for insisting, as Norton seems to do, that environmental philosophers should stop exploring the real reasons, the best reasons, why we ought to value other forms of life, ecosystems, and the biosphere as a whole.[38]

These real and best reasons, of course, are that bits of nature have intrinsic ethical value. But someone who has a more philosophical and less-evangelical temperament than Callicott might wonder about the ethical status of this kind of intrinsic value as supporting reasons for action.

Let us begin with the observation that, on this planet at least, human beings are the only creatures capable of valuing or acting for reasons. This implies that any reasons for acting must be able to "reach people where they
are." They must appeal to interests and concerns that make sense to rational
human beings as reasons for caring or holding the different attitudes that
lead us to act. In this trivial sense, ethics must be anthropocentric. If nonanthropocentrism denies this claim, then it has no role to play in ethical
thought.

Following this line of argument a bit further, we are also all familiar with
reasons for valuing as ends things other than our own experiences. Philosophers have argued for centuries that our lives are better and richer when we
care about some things outside our own experience for their own sakes or as
ends.[39] To value anything other than our own experiences only as the means
to having pleasant or desirable experiences is both shallow and self-defeating.
Any person who had this kind of attitude would be robbed of many of the
kinds of experiences and pleasures that for most people make life more
meaningful and rewarding. If anthropocentrism denies that we value anything outside our own experiences as ends, then we should reject anthropocentrism. But this is hardly an unorthodox or revolutionary thing to say.

I have argued above that we should regard our responsibilities with respect to the environment and future generations as parts of impersonal ethics. This means that we need to understand the reasons why we should value
bits of nature and the existence and well-being of future generations. These
reasons are not primarily about how to enhance our own well-being or about
the requirements we recognize in our interactions with other humans. In exploring these reasons, nothing excludes us from claiming that our own lives
are better, richer, or deeper if we act from a perspective in which these things
matter for their own sakes. The reasons for valuing things in one way or another need not rest on metaphysical claims about intrinsic value.

All the difficult work in defending these values remains to be done. This
is the work of spelling out and making compelling the (human) reasons for
valuing and adopting certain attitudes toward nature and future generations,
including the reasons for keeping in mind a perspective from which we see
our own existence as a small part in a much larger scheme of things. How will
these attitudes make our lives richer and more meaningful? And if they do,
then how do lives that are richer and more meaningful in this sense relate to
ideas of human well-being, happiness, or flourishing?

In articulating these reasons and making them compelling, appeals to
intrinsic value have no important role to play. First, as Bernard Williams has
emphasized, arguments about whether things that are not subjects of experience have intrinsic value (or interests of their own) has no ethical point unless we can see how this value makes claims on us.[40] If living things have

value simply in virtue of belonging to a species, then the HIV virus is one such thing, and the implications for our reasons for acting remain unclear.

More important, however, all claims about intrinsic value are philosophically controversial, and there is no practical or theoretical advantage for environmentalists to take a stand on these metaphysical questions. Nonanthropocentrists like Callicott sometimes describe their opponents as being committed to the view that only human beings have intrinsic ethical value. These nonanthropocentrists claim instead that living things and systems other than human beings also have intrinsic value. What makes all such claims controversial is that they are relics of what Williams calls "the enchanted world" of religion and prescientific ways of thinking.[41] If we are truly to take seriously the lessons of evolution and ecology, as most ecocentric environmental philosophers insist that we must, then we should realize that neither human beings nor the Earth itself have any particular cosmic significance. This is bad news for anthropocentrists who may cling to the idea that human beings have some kind of special cosmic status. But it is also bad news for those who want to spread cosmic significance more broadly on Earth. It is an illusion to think that we can discover intrinsic value, in ourselves or in our surroundings, and that this discovery will tell us how we should act. We live in a world toward which we have a wide range of reactions and attitudes. We can reflect upon them and modify them to varying degrees as we try to live happier, richer, and more meaningful lives. Our reasons for protecting the environment and passing on a better world to future generations should be seen in this light. Controversial metaphysical claims about intrinsic value will not help us either in making sense of these reasons or in making them effective.

ACKNOWLEDGMENTS

For comments and discussions of these issues, I am grateful to Geoffrey Brennan, John Broome, Tom Hill, and Ben Minteer.

J. BAIRD CALLICOTT

The Convergence Hypothesis Falsified

Implicit Intrinsic Value, Operational Rights,
and De Facto *Standing in*
the Endangered Species Act

Introduction

S tated plainly, the convergence hypothesis alleges that anthropocentric instrumental values and nonanthropocentric intrinsic values eventually lead to the same public policies. Also stated plainly, anthropocentrism is the doctrine that only human beings have intrinsic value and all nonhuman natural entities have only instrumental value—that is, they have value if and only if they serve in some way as means to human ends. The human ends served may be very broad indeed; they may be psychological and spiritual as well as material and consumptive. And they may be long; they may include the ends of future generations. Thus, to value and preserve the Grand Canyon as a scenic and recreational resource for human enjoyment in perpetuity is no less anthropocentrically instrumental than to value it as the potential site of a reservoir.

If the convergence hypothesis is true, then environmental ethicists do not need to persuade the public to value nonhuman natural entities nonanthropocentrically in order to win popular support for policies designed to conserve or preserve those nonhuman natural entities. Thus, if the convergence hypothesis is true, for the pragmatic purposes of policy making, nonanthropocentric intrinsic values are otiose. And the time and effort that environmental philosophers have spent constructing nonanthropocentric environmental ethics has been but an intellectual exercise of no practical consequence.

If the convergence hypothesis is a genuine hypothesis, not a philosophical dogma, it should be verifiable, that is, we should be able to test its truth empirically, and either confirm it or falsify it. How would we test its truth? If we can identify a public policy that is clearly based on nonanthropocentric intrinsic values, and it would not be the same policy had it been based exclusively on anthropocentric instrumental values, then the convergence hypothesis will be unequivocally falsified. There is one such public policy—the U.S. Endangered Species Act of 1973. Therefore, the convergence hypothesis is false.

The Concepts of Instrumental and Intrinsic Value and the Question of Their Allocation

Section 2(a)(3) of the Endangered Species Act of 1973 (ESA) explicitly identifies the following values of threatened and endangered species: aesthetic, ecological, educational, historical, recreational, and scientific.[1] The order in which these values are stated appears to be alphabetical, not ordinal. In the literature of academic environmental philosophy and ethics—which emerged at about the same time, the mid-1970s—values are classified dichotomously as (A) instrumental or (B) intrinsic. The value of something as a means to an end other than itself is instrumental. The value of something for itself, for its own sake, as an end in itself, is intrinsic. Classically, Western philosophy and law invested only human beings with intrinsic value and regarded everything else as only instrumentally valuable, in service of human ends. Contemporary environmental philosophy and ethics challenge the anthropocentrism of classical Western philosophy and law and reopen the question of just how instrumental and intrinsic value should be allocated. The convergence hypothesis, in turn, challenges the practicality of this philosophical exercise.

Instrumental and intrinsic values are not mutually exclusive. Some entities have both. Employees, for example, are of instrumental value to their employers, and of intrinsic value—if not to their employers, at least to themselves. Public recognition of the intrinsic value of employees is manifest in laws guaranteeing a minimum wage, occupational health and safety, and other protections of employees against the purely economic forces determining the labor market. Most of us hope to be of some use to others (family, friends, associates, employers) and to be responsible, contributing members of society. But when age or infirmity reduces our instrumental value (for others and for society) to a degree approaching zero, we expect others and society to acknowledge our intrinsic value. If anthropocentric intrinsic value were not publicly recognized and legally institutionalized, we would simply dispose of one another—when that time comes—as we discard things that are of value solely instrumentally, such as broken tools, junk cars, and withered houseplants. Hence, we can think of an entity's intrinsic value as the value that remains when all its instrumental value has been subtracted.

Granting that human beings have intrinsic value, do nonhuman *species* also have some? I argue here that the ESA *implicitly* allocates some intrinsic value to listed species and awards them the *operational* equivalent of legal rights and *de facto* standing to sue in federal district courts. I argue that the ESA would do none of these things—contrary to the convergence hypothesis— if it were, in fact, based solely on anthropocentric instrumental values. I begin by reviewing the explicit, evidently instrumental values of the ESA and how they are conventionally quantified.

Instrumental Anthropocentric Values Appropriately Quantified by Means of a Monetary Metric

Taken together, the values of endangered species *explicitly stated* in the ESA appear to be largely of the anthropocentric instrumental kind. Indeed, delivering the majority opinion in *Tennessee Valley Authority v. Hiram Hill et al.*, Chief Justice Warren Burger, in sampling and summarizing the legislative history of the ESA just prior to enactment in 1973, emphasizes the utility of threatened and endangered species: "Congress was concerned about the unknown *uses* that endangered species might . . . have." He quotes expert testimony declaring that "it is in the best interests of mankind to minimize the losses of genetic variations. The reason is simple: they are potential *resources*."[2] If the values of endangered species are exclusively of the instrumental (or utilitarian) kind, they may be quantified in a monetary metric in order to compare them with other things that have instrumental value—such as livestock pasture, farmland, and shopping malls—for purposes of making rational choices between competing instrumental values.[3]

Some environmental philosophers have objected to quantifying the value of nonhuman species (and other aspects of the natural environment) in the monetary metric because that would "reduce" such values as aesthetic, ecological, educational, historical, recreational, and scientific values to "economic" value.[4] From the point of view of contemporary economics, such objections are unfounded. Human beings instrumentally value many things in many ways. A car may be instrumentally valued as a means of transportation, an object of aesthetic delight, and a symbol of status. To aggregate the several and quite diverse values represented by cars we need a common metric. Money is a convenient metric for the diverse values bundled in things like cars because it is quantitative and fungible. A car's market price is the sum of its several and quite diverse kinds of value expressed in a monetary metric. Its price is not an additional "economic" value of a car; rather, its price is the quantification of its transportation, aesthetic, and status-symbol values. Thus, from the point of view of environmental economics, to quantify the—presumably instrumental—aesthetic, ecological, educational, historical, recreational, and scientific values of endangered species in monetary terms is not to reduce these values to some other value: economic value. Rather, it is to express them in the same metric in which other competing instrumental values are expressed for purposes of comparison and rational choice.[5] (Discomfort with quantifying the values of endangered species in a monetary metric may suggest, instead, a feeling that the values of endangered species are not solely of the instrumental kind, but that endangered species may also be intrinsically valuable.)

In his latest book, *Sustainability*, Norton seems to equivocate about the existence of a unique kind of "economic" value. He calls "Economism" the doctrine "that all important environmental values can be understood as economic values." This suggests that there is a distinct class of "economic" values, rather than that the discipline of economics only attempts to quantify various anthropocentric instrumental values—important anthropocentric, instrumental *environmental* values among them—in a common metric. However, Norton seems to concede that economics is an exercise in facilitating "trade-offs" among our anthropocentric instrumental values, so that we can make "good investments in environmental protection—and making these by comparison to other investments the society might make in education, infrastructure, and so forth." But in order for those trade-offs to be made intelligently, the competing anthropocentric instrumental values at stake must be quantified in a common metric. The bulk of his discussion of "Economism" is devoted to the difficulty of accurately quantifying, in the monetary metric, those anthropocentric instrumental environmental values that are not actually traded in markets, and for which there are not any direct shadow prices (discussed later in this chapter). An example that Norton provides is "an increase in visibility in a national park." From this discussion, one could infer that the problem is purely technical and that, as environmental economics matures, we can expect that methods of more accurately and reliably quantifying anthropocentric instrumental environmental values in the monetary metric will be forthcoming. In which case, from all Norton says about the matter, it would seem to be appropriate, when finally economists are able to do it well, to quantify *all* important anthropocentric instrumental environmental values in the monetary metric for purposes of making trade-offs between them and other, competing anthropocentric instrumental values—such as hydroelectric power, lumber, beef, and the like—that can often be obtained only by sacrificing environmental values.

Commodities such as lumber derived from natural capital are traded in markets and thus have a price. Recreation is sometimes a bundle of commodities and services for sale at a price. Take for example a "canned hunt" on a private parcel of land, in which, for a price, a paying customer gets guided to a confined game animal, the ego-affirming experience of killing it, and the animal itself partly mounted as a trophy and partly butchered for meat.[6] The value of a wooded property clear-cut for lumber can thus be compared with its value preserved for canned hunts—because both register an unambiguous signal in a common monetary metric. Nonconsumptive forms of recreation involving endangered species, for which there is no actual market, such as searching the piney woods of East Texas for red-cockaded woodpeckers, also register a clear signal in the same metric—the amount of money people spend on transportation, food, and lodging pursuing this form of recreation. In addition to such so-called "implicit pricing methods," the aesthetic, ecological, educational, historical, and scientific values of the red-cockaded woodpecker—for which there is no market to determine their price—are expressible in the monetary metric by other, indirect methods, such as "contingent valuation."[7]

Some endangered species are keystone species—"a species whose ecological impact is large and disproportionately large relative to its abundance."[8] For example, when the southern subspecies of sea otter was commercially hunted to near extinction for its fur, the underwater kelp "forests" on the continental shelf off the West Coast of the United States began to disappear—because their holdfasts were being eaten by irrupting populations of sea urchins—with cascading ecological effects. Sea otters prey on shellfish, sea urchins included. When sea otter populations rebounded, the number of sea urchins was reduced and the kelp forests regrew, and once again provided a habitat for many other animal species.[9] Because sea otters indirectly benefit other species and are vital to the persistence of kelp-dominated aquatic communities, their ecological value is greater than the commodity value of their fur, measured on the monetary metric.

Today, we are more aware of the instrumental value of ecosystem services than in 1973.[10] However, although the southern sea otter may well be essential to the provision of ecosystem services, few threatened and endangered species are. As David Ehrenfeld notes, "the species whose members are the fewest in number, the rarest, the most narrowly distributed—in short, the ones most likely to become extinct—are obviously the ones least likely to be missed by the biosphere. Many of these species were never common or ecologically influential; by no stretch of the imagination can we make them out to be vital cogs in the ecological machine."[11] The red-cockaded woodpecker, for example, is not a keystone species, nor does it play any other vital role in its ecosystem. The very fact that it is endangered by lumbering suggests that the red-cockaded woodpecker's instrumental value compares poorly with the competing instrumental values, quantified on the monetary metric, of the forests where it lives when they are clear-cut for timber.

But what about future generations; how palpably will they miss the red-cockaded woodpecker, should it be rendered extinct by wholesale destruction of its habitat? We can answer that question by posing another: How palpably does the current generation miss the extinct Carolina parakeet—arguably a far more charismatic bird? I miss it; I lament its extinction. Doubtless, Norton does too, and probably so do tens of thousands of environmentalists. But just as probably, the vast majority of the more than six billion members of the present generation have never heard of the Carolina parakeet and, if informed of its previous tenure on Earth and its extinction only about a century ago, could not care less.

The ESA Operationally Provides Legal Rights for Listed Species and Implicitly Recognizes Their Intrinsic Value

As stated in Section 2(a)(1), the intent of the ESA is clearly to temper "growth and development" by "adequate concern" for species "in danger of or threatened with extinction" leading to "conservation" of them. But, as noted, the explicitly stated instrumental values identified in Section 2(a)(3), when quantified in the monetary metric, would not appear to be robust enough to achieve conservation of such species in competition with economic growth and development even when their market values are "corrected" by environmental economists deploying the full arsenal of their valuation techniques. Nor would adding the existence-value preferences of a tiny minority of biologically well-informed members of future human generations make much difference to the outcome of a red-cockaded woodpecker valuation exercise. The Act thus provides *operational* legal rights for listed species, effectively exempting their conservation from purely anthropocentric utilitarian—and thus purely economic—considerations.

Christopher D. Stone identifies three criteria that, when met, "operationally" confer legal rights on some entity, irrespective of whether the discourse of rights is used: (1) legal action may be commenced on its behalf; (2) in granting legal relief, the court must take injury to it into account, not only to some third party; and (3) relief must run to the benefit of it, not only to some third party.[12]

As to Stone's first criterion, Section 11(c) of the Act provides for "the several district courts of the United States" to have "jurisdiction over any actions arising under this Act." Section 11(g)(1) provides that "any person may commence a civil suit" (A) against any other private person, the United States, or any agency thereof who is alleged to be in violation of the Act or any regulation issued under its authority; (B) to compel the secretary of the interior to apply the provisions of the Act; or (C) against the secretary for alleged failure to apply the provisions of the Act.

The federal courts of the United States are established by Article III of the Constitution to adjudicate "cases" and "controversies." Article III nowhere mentions "standing," but in the virtually Talmudic tradition of U.S. case law and precedent, the concept of standing has devolved from the Article III circumscription of the jurisdiction of federal courts to "cases" and "controversies." "To satisfy Article III-standing requirements, a [would-be] plaintiff must show that (1) it has suffered 'injury in fact' that is (a) 'concrete and particularized' and (b) actual or imminent, not conjectural or hypothetical; (2) the injury is fairly traceable to the challenged action of the defendant; and (3) it is likely, as opposed to merely speculative, that the injury will be redressed by a favorable decision."[13]

The ESA does not require the person bringing suit on behalf of a listed species in a U.S. district court to allege that *he* or *she* has been personally injured—"in fact" or otherwise. So in providing that "any person" may bring suit on behalf of a listed species, the ESA confers *de facto* standing on the listed species. The citizen who brings the suit is, in effect, representing the aggrieved species. This provision was noted with approval by Justice Burger, writing for the majority, in *TVA v. Hill*: "Citizen . . . involvement was encouraged by the Act, with provisions allowing interested persons to . . . bring civil suits in United States district courts to force compliance with any provision of the Act"—*interested* persons, not injured persons. Further, because the "citizen-suit" provision of the ESA confers *de facto* standing on the injured species, the U.S. District Court, Northern District of California, took the next logical step and observed that *de facto* standing had been sometimes conflated with *de jure* standing: "Some courts have permitted suits to go forward *under the citizen suit provisions of the ESA* with fish and wildlife species named as the plaintiffs."[14] (I indicate these suits by name in the next section.)

As to Stone's criteria (2) and (3), Section 4(a)(1) specifies injury (in fact) to threatened and endangered species from (A) "destruction, modification, or curtailment of its habitat or range" or (B) "overutilization for commercial, recreational, scientific, or educational purposes" as warrant for granting it legal relief. And Section 4(d) directs the secretary of the interior to "issue such regulations as he deems necessary and advisable to provide for the conservation of such [listed endangered] species." Especially in the mandate in Section 4(b)(2) to conserve the "critical habitat" of endangered species, relief of injury to listed endangered species clearly runs primarily to their benefit.

When these criteria are met, an entity acquires "a legally recognized worth and dignity in its own right, and not merely to serve as means to benefit 'us' (whoever the contemporary group of rights holders may be)," according to Stone.[15] In other words, legal rights recognize and are based on the intrinsic value of the entities to which such rights are accorded. In short then, the ESA *operationally* (*sensu* Stone) confers legal rights on listed threatened and endangered species and thus *implicitly* recognizes their intrinsic value and awards them *de facto* (occasionally construed as *de jure*) standing.

How Stone's Innovative Legal Theory May Have Insinuated Itself into Law

The ESA was the culmination—and one might say the crowning achievement—of an emergent "environmental movement" that had gained force over the previous decade (the 1960s) in response to a perceived "environmental crisis." Several works were instrumental in creating the impression of an environmental crisis and galvanizing an environmental movement—most notably *The Quiet Crisis* by Stewart Udall, secretary of the interior in the Kennedy administration; and *Silent Spring* by Rachel Carson, an eminent marine biologist and gifted author.[16] A third book emerged as the bible—in the words of one historian—of the nascent environmental movement: *A Sand County Almanac* by Aldo Leopold, a forester turned game manager turned wildlife ecologist. The capstone essay in *Sand County* was titled "The Land Ethic,"[17] in which Leopold suggested that species should have rights based on their intrinsic value. As to species rights, he avers:

> One basic weakness of a conservation system based wholly on economic motives is that most members of the land community have no economic value. Wildflowers and songbirds are examples. . . . Yet these creatures are members of the biotic community and . . . they are entitled to continuance.
>
> When one of these non-economic categories is threatened, and if we happen to love it, we invent subterfuges to give it economic importance. At the beginning of the [20th] century songbirds were supposed to be disappearing. Ornithologists jumped to the rescue with some distinctly shaky evidence to the effect that insects would eat us up if birds failed to control them. The evidence had to be economic in order to be valid.
>
> It is painful to read these circumlocutions today. We have no land ethic yet, but we have at least drawn nearer the point of admitting that birds should continue as a matter of *biotic right*, regardless of the presence or absence of economic advantage to us.[18]

Leopold then goes on to insist that "predators [too] are members of the biotic community and that [therefore] *no special interest has the right* to exterminate them for the sake of a benefit, real or fancied, to itself."[19] And as to intrinsic value, Leopold writes: "It is inconceivable to me that an ethical relation to land can exist without love, respect, and admiration for land, and a high regard for its value. By value I of course mean something far broader than mere economic value; I mean *value in the philosophical sense.*"[20] Because, as noted, all anthropocentric instrumental values are appropriately quantified by economists in the monetary metric, by contrasting "value in the philosophical sense," with "economic value," Leopold could only mean by the former what contemporary environmental philosophers call "intrinsic value."[21]

Nor was Leopold the first famous environmentalist to suggest that having rights was not an exclusively human prerogative. In *A Thousand Mile Walk to the Gulf*, John Muir wrote, "How narrow we selfish, conceited creatures are in our sympathies! How blind to the *rights* of all the rest of creation!"[22] Unlike Leopold, however, Muir provided no theoretical support for expanding the realm of rights holders. Nevertheless, just as the context makes clear that Leopold is thinking of rights for nonhuman *species*—not for individual nonhuman beings nor for less-circumscribed entities, such as mountains or ecosystems—so the context suggests that the entities Muir regarded as candidates for rights are also species. His exclamation comes in the midst of a disparaging discussion of the low regard that many people, whom Muir met in his trek through southern Georgia and northern Florida, had for the alligator.

So before Stone had theorized the underpinnings of operational legal rights for natural objects, the idea of rights for threatened species, based on their intrinsic value, had become familiar in the environmental movement, because the matter had been broached by Muir and elaborated by Leopold. The critical migration of the idea of rights for natural objects—more especially, rights for threatened species, as Leopold more narrowly envisioned it—from mere legal theory to (cryptic) federal law may have been facilitated by the Supreme Court. Stone had written his paper, "Should Trees Have Standing?" specifically to influence the Court in a pending case, *Sierra Club v. Rogers C. B. Morton.*[23] And while the Court ultimately ruled that the Sierra Club lacked standing to sue to save the Mineral King Valley in the Sierra Nevada Mountains from ski-resort development by Walt Disney Enterprises, Justice William O. Douglas warmly endorsed Stone's theory in the very first paragraph of his dissenting opinion:

The critical question of "standing" would be simplified and also put neatly into focus if we fashioned a federal rule that allowed environmental issues to be litigated before federal agencies or federal courts in the name of the inanimate object about to be despoiled, defaced, or invaded by roads and bulldozers and where injury is the subject of public outrage. Contemporary public concern for protecting nature's ecological equilibrium should lead to the conferral of standing upon environmental objects to sue for their own preservation. See Stone, Should Trees Have Standing? Toward Legal Rights for Natural Objects, 45 S. Cal. L. Rev. 450 (1972). This suit would therefore more properly be labeled as *Mineral King v. Morton*.[24]

Perhaps not inconsequentially, Douglas cited, in his last paragraph, Aldo Leopold's "The Land Ethic." Also subconsciously influencing Douglas's thinking might have been his knowledge that Muir—the first to float the concept of rights for nonhuman species—was the founder of the Sierra Club, the plaintiff in the Mineral King case. That a Supreme Court justice, albeit in the minority, took Stone's "operational"-legal-rights-for natural-objects theory seriously may have legitimated it among those who make and dispense federal laws.

In any event, Congress enacted the ESA the next year. And five years after that, the Supreme Court allowed Hiram Hill to sue the Tennessee Valley Authority on behalf of the snail darter. Rogers C. B. Morton of *Sierra Club v. Morton* was secretary of the interior in the Nixon administration. Hiram ("Hank") Hill was a student of the University of Tennessee law professor Zygmunt J. B. Plater, who successfully argued the famous Tellico Dam case before the Supreme Court. The choice to file the case in Hank Hill's name appears to have been a symbolic assertion of the citizen-suit provision of the ESA, for certainly Hill would not "in fact" be injured "individually, concretely, particularly, and materially" by the willful extinction of the snail darter.

To repeat: The ESA does *not* provide intrinsic value, legal rights, and standing for listed species; rather, it provides *implicit* intrinsic value, *operational* legal rights, and *de facto* standing for listed species. It was, however, a short step from *de facto* standing to presumed *de jure* standing for listed species. After the *TVA v. Hill* decision in 1978, the state of Hawai'i was sued by a bird in 1979: *Palila v. Hawaii Department of Land and Natural Resources*.[25] It was a somewhat longer (ten-year) step from presumed *de jure* standing for listed species to affirmed *de jure* standing for them. Upon review in 1988, the Ninth Circuit Court of Appeals appeared unequivocally to grant standing to the injured species. The court wrote that the Palila had "earned the right to be capitalized since it is a party to these proceedings," and that it has "legal status and wings its way into federal court as a plaintiff in its own right."[26] After that decision, a number of other suits were brought in the name of injured species as plaintiffs: the northern spotted owl, the Mount Graham red squirrel, the Hawaiian crow, the marbled murrelet, the Florida key deer, the hawksbill sea turtle, the loggerhead turtle, the coho salmon, and, most expansively, the cetacean community.[27] Some of these cases are discussed in more detail in the penultimate section of this chapter. And the standing saga for listed species has taken many a twisted turn in the nearly twenty years that have elapsed since the *Palila* case was ultimately decided.

Why Intrinsic Value Should Not Be Quantified in the Monetary Metric

Dispute rages in the large literature on intrinsic value in environmental philosophy about its ontological status.[28] Is intrinsic value—as its name would suggest—an objective property of something that has intrinsic value, like its length or weight? Or is intrinsic value subjectively conferred, like something being loved or hated? In 1973, did the U.S. Congress implicitly ratify a new moral *discovery* that endangered species have intrinsic value—analogous to a new scientific discovery, such as the discovery of new forms of life near volcanic vents on the ocean's floor? Or did the Congress implicitly *grant* endangered species intrinsic value—as it might grant amnesty and guest-worker status to undocumented foreign nationals living in the United States? There is an even larger literature in legal philosophy on the ontological status of rights.[29] Are rights natural and real or are they artificial and conventional? While these questions are philosophically interesting and important, their answers make no practical difference. Whether endangered species literally *have* intrinsic value (like birds have feathers and plants have chlorophyll) or they *are valued* intrinsically (like X is a target only when Y aims at it), and whether their rights are natural or artificial, the practical consequences are the same. On this head, Bryan Norton and I are in complete agreement. But whatever its ontological status, having intrinsic value *or* being valued intrinsically—or not—makes a huge practical difference.

The locus classicus of the concept of intrinsic value is found in the immensely influential moral philosophy of Immanuel Kant, who wrote:

> [E]verything has either a *price* or a *dignity*. Whatever has a price can be replaced by something else as its equivalent; on the other hand, whatever is above all price, and therefore admits of no equivalent, has a dignity. That which is related to general human inclinations and needs has a *market price*. That which, without supposing any need, accords with a certain taste, i.e., with pleasure in the mere purposeless play of our faculties has an *affective price*. But that which constitutes the condition under which alone something can be an end in

itself does not have a mere relative worth, i.e., a price, but an intrinsic worth, a *dignity*.[30]

The distinction that Kant draws between a market price and an affective price is roughly the same distinction that economists make between a market price and a shadow price. Things that people want (the objects of "human inclinations") and need are traded in markets—thus, they have a market price. By things that accord with certain tastes and involve pleasure in the mere purposeless play of our faculties, Kant means objects of aesthetic experience. Some of these—works of art—also have a market price. But those that do not—for example, many environmental amenities, such as wild and scenic rivers and clear view sheds—have, according to Kant, an affective price. They have a value, that is, which can be expressed in the monetary metric. But it is inappropriate, Kant thinks, to price things that have intrinsic value; it is wrong to value them in monetary terms.

Two schools of thought have dominated Western moral culture since the late eighteenth century—utilitarianism and Kantianism. In the former, the aim of public policy should be to achieve "the greatest happiness of the greatest number" (of human beings)—"happiness" then being understood to consist in a greater balance of pleasure over pain.[31] Later utilitarians substituted "welfare" for happiness and defined welfare in terms of "preference satisfaction."[32] Preferences are treated as in themselves neither good nor bad and they are aggregated among preference-satisfying individuals, who are regarded as counting equally. Thus, a preference for the music of Beethoven is not better than a preference for the "music" of LL Cool J. Nor are those who prefer Beethoven given more weight in welfare calculations than those who prefer LL Cool J. The "rational" aim of each private person is to maximize his or her own welfare and the aim of public policy is to maximize aggregate welfare, from the point of view of the contemporary utilitarian school.

However, aggregate preference satisfaction or total welfare may, in some circumstances, be maximized at an extreme cost to a few individuals. John Rawls's example is slavery.[33] The aggregate welfare of a preindustrial slave-owning society may be greater than that of a preindustrial egalitarian society. Ancient Athenian society is a case in point. Without slaves to do all the physical work, the privileged Athenian intelligentsia would have lacked the leisure to create the ancient Greek science, philosophy, literature, and art that we still enjoy two and a half millennia later. Thus, in such circumstances, no self-consistent utilitarian argument can be deployed against the institution of slavery. Amartya Sen's example is torture.[34] It seems to me that the most graphic example is gladiator shows. Thousands of Romans took great pleasure in watching a few people compelled to fight to the death in the Colosseum and similar arenas.[35] The modest but significant welfare gain of a gladiatorial spectator multiplied by fifty thousand (the seating capacity of the Colosseum) might well outweigh the extreme welfare loss of a few vanquished gladiatorial contestants. The Kantian conceptual constellation of intrinsic value, dignity, and rights counters the potentially repugnant outcome of the unbridled utilitarian welfare calculus.

According to Kant, rationality is the sole intrinsic-value-conferring property.[36] And, although he held open the possibility that there may be other rational beings in the universe, human beings were the only rational beings of which Kant was aware. Thus, human beings and various aspects of human being were, until recently, the only entities accorded intrinsic value, dignity, and rights in Western moral culture. The clearest and most unambiguous effect of the recognition of the intrinsic value, dignity, and rights of human beings is to make a market in human beings illegal and to prohibit such things as gladiator shows in which the lives of some human beings are sacrificed for the entertainment of others.[37] As to aspects of human being, legally prohibiting prostitution and some mind-altering drugs suggests that sex and chemically unaltered states of human consciousness are also accorded—by whom I explain below—a dignity and intrinsic value.[38] With the advent of organ-transplant techniques, a market in human organs is now prohibited in the United States and many other Western countries.[39]

Proposals to accord intrinsic value, dignity, and rights to various nonhuman beings dominate the animal-liberation, animal-rights, and environmental-ethics literatures. To argue that some nonhuman animals (such as primates and cetaceans) are rational and thus should be accorded intrinsic value, dignity, and rights least departs from the original Kantian paradigm.[40] To argue that some other intrinsic-value-conferring property should be substituted for rationality preserves the structure of Kant's ethic but alters its content, to one degree or another. Salient among the various substitutes that have been proposed are being a "subject of a life," being "sentient," being a "teleological center of life," having a good of one's own, and having interests.[41] Some of these proposals have had limited success in making their way into public policy. While there are still robust markets in animals—everything from livestock markets to puppy mills to the zoo trade—the increasing body of law governing the humane treatment and care of animals in agriculture, biomedical research, zoos, and rodeos suggests that pleas for animal liberation and animal rights have had some measurable effect on public policy.[42] The ESA is outstanding in this regard for two reasons. First, it accords listed species robust legal rights, as here noted, albeit only "operationally," not formally or explicitly. Second, the theoretical justification of such rights is not as well developed as the theoretical justification of animal rights.[43] There has been no success in translating into law or regulation the claim that *individual* plants and other subsentient organisms—except for specimens of listed endangered species—have intrinsic value.

It should be immediately clear why the ethical concept of intrinsic value should not be conflated with the economic concept of existence value, as some economists propose.[44] Existence value is a personal preference. Some people would, for example, prefer that black-footed ferrets remain in existence rather than suffer extinction.[45] This kind of preference, as any other, may be expressed in the monetary metric, either by contingent valuation (asking respondents how much they would be willing to pay to keep black-footed ferrets in existence) or by estimating what fraction of the total monetary support donated to such organizations as the Nature Conservancy and Defenders of Wildlife might be fairly allocated to the conservation of black-footed ferrets.[46] To accord something intrinsic value, conversely, is to declare that it has a dignity and that it should not be subject to pricing of any kind, shadow or otherwise.

There is another, more intuitive, way of highlighting the difference between intrinsic and existence value. In modern Western moral culture, human beings are recognized to have intrinsic value. But for each of us, only our respective family members, friends, neighbors, colleagues, and acquaintances have measurable existence value. How much would you be willing to pay to assure the existence of your next-door neighbor? I would be willing to pay all the money I could get my hands on to preserve my son (my only child) if his existence were threatened or endangered. Understandably, most readers of this chapter would be willing to pay only much less to assure the existence of *my* son. And when one factors in consideration of all the people in the world, the existence value that I can honestly set on individual human beings to whom I am unrelated and with whom I am unacquainted shrinks to infinitesimal amounts. (I can get my hands on only so much money and there are more than six billion human beings in existence. So what honest answer could I give if I were asked how much I would be willing to pay to preserve the existence of, say, an individual Swede whom I have never met?) In contrast, all human beings have intrinsic value and all have it equally in modern Western moral culture, as reflected in the concept of universal human rights (which was formally endorsed by the United Nations in 1948) and the U.S. Constitution's Fourteenth Amendment ideals of equal protection under the law and equal legal liability for violating laws protecting human beings.[47] But the existence value of any given human being varies wildly with circumstance. For example, the existence value of the scion of a very wealthy family may approach a billion dollars; that of a street urchin in Rio de Janeiro may approach zero. To conflate existence and intrinsic value is to think like a kidnapper, rather than as a member of Kant's idyllic "Kingdom of Ends."[48]

The Dual Democracy of Value
Objectification: The Market
and the Legislature

The domain in which our utilitarian values are appropriately expressed is the market. As noted, the market is not perfectly efficient, in part because all the things we value instrumentally are not routinely bought and sold and thus do not have actual prices. And, also as noted, to partially correct such imperfections of the market, the things we value instrumentally that are not traded are valued by industrious economists in the monetary metric—shadow priced—less directly, for purposes of comparison and rational choice. The market, despite its imperfections, is, on the whole, quite democratic. People "vote," as it were, with their dollars (or units of other currency) for such things as McDonald's fast food and Coca Cola. Those things for which people do not "vote" in the market soon disappear. Infamous examples are Edsel automobiles and Beta videotape cassette players. When we look around ourselves, we can literally see the democratic common denominator of aggregated individual preferences—massaged, of course, in myriad ways by advertising—in contemporary society: the world of fast-food chain stores, strip malls, gas-guzzling SUVs, cell phones, light beer, Wal-Mart superstores, and so forth.

According to Mark Sagoff, the appropriate democratic domain for the expression of our nonutilitarian values is the legislature—in the United States, the bicameral Congress at the federal level of government, often similarly bicameral legislatures at the state level, city councils at the municipal level of government.[49] Both our instrumental and intrinsic values are arguably subjective. Certainly, preferences—such as the preference for Coca Cola over Royal Crown Cola—are incontestably subjective. The market and its surrogates, however, serve in a way to objectify preferences. Aggregate consumer preferences are quite literally objectified in the form of the fast-food chain stores, strip malls, gas-guzzling SUVs, cell phones, light beer, Wal-Mart superstores, and so forth that we see everywhere around us. It would seem that the belief that some things have intrinsic value while others do not is also subjective. Certainly, differences of opinion about what has intrinsic value and what does not are easy to find, but difficult to resolve by any evidentiary hearing or peer review, as disputed findings of fact and scientific discoveries are resolved. Some people—members of People for the Ethical Treatment of Animals, for example—believe that many kinds of individual animals have intrinsic value (and ought to have rights to life, liberty, and the pursuit of happiness), while other people (who are still in the great majority) do not. Analogous to the way the market objectifies preferences, we may think of legislatures as objectifying noninstrumental values. Thus, in contemporary Western democratic societies, the intrinsic value accorded human beings and certain aspects of human being is legislatively objectified by laws prohibiting murder, slavery, other forms of human trafficking, prostitution, selling human organs, and selling (indeed, even possessing) mind-altering drugs. Many other non-utilitarian values that are objectified by legislation (or are so fundamental as to be institutionalized in the U.S. Constitution) orbit the intrinsic value of human beings—freedom of speech and religion, for example, property rights, and the right to privacy.

That preferences are not the same as those values that transcend preferences is indicated by the different way each is objectified. Preferences are objectified through aggregate choice. Intrinsic value and the transcendent values surrounding it (freedom of speech and religion, property rights, and the right to privacy) are objectified through public debate. Legalized segregation and racial discrimination in the South were not abandoned because they were no longer preferred by a majority of Americans. (Indeed, the persistence of *de facto* segregation and racial discrimination suggests that they are still preferred by a majority of Americans.) Rather, we democratically decide to objectify—through legislation (and sometimes subsequent judicial interpretation)—intrinsic value and its transcendent satellite values on the basis of principle and argument from principle, irrespective of our preferences and often in defiance of them.[50] The wider extension of intrinsic value by legislation—to human fetuses, for example—is the subject of intense and often acrimonious public debate. Quite remarkably, the ESA objectifies the intrinsic value of listed endangered species. Listed endangered species are in effect awarded legal rights and their intrinsic value is implicitly recognized by the democratically elected Congress of the United States. In that special sense, the intrinsic value of listed endangered species has become objective.

Congress immediately responded to the *TVA v. Hill* decision by amending the ESA—with Section 7(e)—to create a cabinet-level Endangered Species Committee (irreverently known as the "God Squad") invested with the very power that the Supreme Court abjured. The committee consists of the secretary of the interior, who serves as chair, the secretaries of agriculture and the army, the administrators of the Environmental Protection Agency and the National Oceanic and Atmospheric Administration, the chairman of the Council of Economic Advisors, and one person from each affected state, nominated by the governors of such states and appointed by the president.

Legislatively objectified intrinsic value shifts the burden of proof on to competing instrumental values. For example, the burden of proof rests with a state or federal government that is threatening the liberty of an intrinsically valuable human being by prosecuting him or her on charges of larceny. Conversely, a landowner can dispose of specimens of nonlisted plants and many kinds of nonlisted wildlife and fish—the intrinsic value of which has not been legislatively objectified—on his or her property in accordance with his or her preferences (provided they are not protected by game laws and similar statutes). But because the intrinsic value of listed endangered species has been objectified by the Act, any application for an exemption to the ESA's provisions is certainly not regarded as *prima facie* worthy of granting, unless the Fish and Wildlife Service can prove that it should not be granted. On the contrary, the applicant for an exemption must demonstratively meet very stringent, multiple criteria. Among these are—as specified in Section 7(h)(2)—the necessity to show that "the benefits of any such action [that would violate any provisions of the Act] clearly outweigh the benefits of alternative courses of action consistent with conserving the species or its critical habitat." Moreover, the benefits at stake must not be merely private profit; the applicant must also demonstrate that "such action is in the public interest." The God Squad has only convened three times and approved an exemption only once.[51] Warwick Fox has identified and clearly explained the burden-of-proof shifting effect of legislatively objectifying intrinsic value.[52]

Is the Endangered Species Act Endangered?

The ESA has not been popular among political "conservatives" for whom any expansion of the class of rights holders (except to human embryos) is anathema and for whom the property rights of traditional rights holders is paramount.[53] In the 1995 *Babbitt v. Sweet Home* decision, the Supreme Court upheld the interpretation of "harm" in the ESA to include critical habitat destruction, an interpretation that had been in place as an Interior Department regulation since 1975.[54] Thus, if a private property owner logs the critical habitat of the northern spotted owl or the marbled murrelet, that would constitute a prohibited "take" under the provisions of the Act.

For that reason, the ESA is perennially a target of ultraconservative activists who argue that enforcement of the ESA prohibitions on "taking" a listed species through destruction of its habitat is equivalent to a different kind of "taking"—the taking of private property, as in eminent domain.[55] Therefore, just as in an eminent domain taking, they argue, the Fifth Amendment of the Constitution requires the government to render "just compensation" to property owners for effectively appropriating their land.[56] Of course, among the ultraconservative amalgam of shibboleths are also "smaller government" and tax and spending cuts; and so proposals to compensate aggrieved property owners are not accompanied by proposals to fund compensation through taxation.[57] The ultimate effect would be to undermine the ability of responsible agencies to enforce the takings prohibitions of the ESA against private property owners.

Thus, when ultraconservatives controlled the Congress as well as the presidency, we should not have been surprised to see the ESA under assault. HR 3824, a bill to amend the ESA, was passed by the House in 2005 and sent to the Senate, which, fortunately, took no action on it. In the now-popular Orwellian fashion of green-washing antienvironmental policy and legislation with innocuous, even progressive-sounding labels, the bill was titled "Threatened and Endangered Species Recovery Act of 2005." In addition to compensating property owners for putative opportunity losses from the existing budget allocation of the Department of Interior, it would direct the secretary to list new species "sparingly," thus empowering the secretary, a political appointee, to decide which data represents the "best scientific data available," and would amend that phrase to read "best scientific and commercial data available." Worst of all, perhaps, it flatly repeals the authority of the secretary to designate critical habitat. Its sponsor, Richard Pombo, was defeated in his reelection bid in 2006—thanks in part to a concerted effort by environmental groups—as were many of his ultraconservative Republican colleagues. Thus, with Congress currently controlled by Democrats, the ESA is safe for the time being from ultraconservative congressional attack.

The ESA, however, has also come under ultraconservative judicial assault. When the favorable judgment of *Palila v. Hawiian Department of Land and Natural Resources* was upheld in 1988, the appellate court appeared to grant standing to a listed species to sue "in its own right."[58] In a subsequent case, *Marbled Murrelet v. Pacific Lumber*, defendants challenged the standing of the named species.[59] Relying on the appellate court's 1988 *Palila* ruling, the district court allowed suit to be brought in the name of the injured species and expressly granted it standing. Quoting the 1988 *Palila* judgment, the court specifically ruled that "as a protected species under the ESA, the marbled murrelet has standing to sue 'in its own right.'"[60] In *Loggerhead Turtle v. County Council of Volusia County, Florida*, the standing of the turtle was also challenged by the defendant along with the standing of Shirley Reynolds and Rita Alexander, who joined the turtle as plaintiffs.[61] The district court declined to rule on the challenge to Reynolds and Alexander's standing, and accepted jurisdiction for the case solely on the strength of the turtle's standing, citing *Marbled Murrelet v. Pacific Lumber* as precedent to do so. On appeal, the defendant abandoned the claim that the turtle should not be granted standing because it was not human, but pressed the claim against its standing because, the defendant alleged, the turtle was not injured in fact by Volusia County and that a decision in favor of the species against the county would not redress its injuries even if it were.[62] The appellate court disagreed and ruled that the turtle had standing.[63]

In these and other suits brought in the name of endangered species (see note 34) the scale was small. This or that single species (Palila, 'Alala, spotted owl, etc.) sued this or that public or private party (a county, corporation, state department of natural resources, the current secretary of the interior) for relief. Thus, they ran pretty much under the judicial radar and could be ignored as amusing anomalies. But in 2003, a suit was brought on a global scale in the name not of a single species, but of a whole taxonomic order against the president of the United States (and his secretary of defense)—*The Cetacean Community v. Bush.*[64] The cetaceans sought relief from the U.S. Navy's use of Surveillance Towed Array Sensor System Low Frequency Active Sonar, which injures them, in fact, in various ways. The District Court of Hawaii agreed with the defendants that the cetaceans lacked standing. The cetaceans appealed and the Ninth Circuit Court of Appeals upheld the district court's ruling. But how could this ruling be consistent with the ruling by the same court of appeals in the *Palila* case?—a point argued by the cetaceans.

With sleight of hand dexterity, the three-judge panel (Judges Hug, Alarcón, and Fletcher) of the 2004 Ninth Circuit hearing the cetacean case decided that the three-judge panel (Judges O'Scannlain, Shroeder, and Noonan) of the 1988 Ninth Circuit hearing the *Palila* case used "nonbinding dicta" when they wrote that the Hawaiian honeycreeper, "had legal status and winged its way into federal court as a plaintiff in its own right."[65] As the 2004 panel noted, "A statement is dictum when it is 'made during the course of delivering a judicial opinion but . . . is unnecessary to the decision in the case and [is] therefore not precedential.'"[66] Because the Palila's standing had not been challenged, the statements about the legal status of the honeycreeper and its being a plaintiff in its own right did not address points at issue and so could be rendered moot as *dicta*. Then shouldn't the *Palila* decision be overruled for lack of a plaintiff with standing to sue? No, because the species was joined as plaintiff by the Sierra Club, the National Audubon Society, the Hawaii Audubon Society, and Alan C. Ziegler, "whose standing had always been clear"—despite *Sierra Club v. Morton*, we must suppose.[67] However in the *Cetacean* case, the cetaceans were not joined by conventional plaintiffs and their standing was the central bone of contention in the case.

In *Cetacean Community v. Bush*, the appellate court reasoned that the language of the ESA forecloses any interpretation of the meaning of a "person," who may bring suit, to include the injured species itself. Section 3(13) defines "person" to mean "an individual, corporation, partnership, trust, association, or any other private entity; or any officer, employee, agent, department, or instrumentality of the Federal Government, or any State, municipality, or political subdivision of a State; or any other entity subject to the jurisdiction of the United States." Even though the latter clause appears to be so broad as to plausibly include listed species, the court contended that it does not because Section 3 also provides separate definitions of threatened and endangered "species," and of "fish and wildlife." "It is obvious from the scheme of the statute, as well as the statute's explicit definitions of its terms, that animals are the protected rather than the protectors. . . . [Thus, a]nimals are not authorized to sue in their own names to protect themselves."[68]

Interestingly, in *Cetacean Community v. Bush*, Judge Fletcher noted that there is nothing in the Constitution to prevent threatened and endangered species from being plaintiffs in their own right. Indeed, he quotes Stone, who, in defense of his own proposal to grant standing to trees and other environmental entities, wrote, "The world of the lawyer is peopled with inanimate rights holders: trusts, corporations, joint ventures, municipalities, Subchapter R partnerships, and nation-states, to mention but a few."[69] And, thus, if the ESA had specifically included them under its definition of "person," they could, constitutionally, sue in their own names. Accordingly, Katherine Burke has suggested the possibility of amending the ESA to permit them to do so statutorially.[70]

However, even though after *Cetacean Community v. Bush,* threatened and endangered species cannot sue in their own names and in their own right, it makes no practical difference. Being wild and mute, the only way they could sue is by a representative proxy. They may no longer be recognized to have actual legal rights and *de jure* standing, but they still do have operational legal rights (*sensu* Stone) and *de facto* standing. If a threatened or endangered species retained standing to sue as its own protector, it must necessarily be represented by a lawyer, just as any other "incompetent" plaintiff must be. But since any human "person," as defined by the Act, has standing to sue as its protector, regardless of injury ("in fact") to himself or herself, the practical effect is the same—it has a protector able to litigate on its behalf, for injury ("in fact") to it, and the remedies of a favorable judgment run to its benefit.

Out of the frying pan and into the fire. A 1992 Supreme Court decision, *Lujan v. Defenders*, threatens to undercut even the operational (or *de facto*) standing and legal rights of threatened and endangered species by questioning the constitutionality of the ESA's citizen-suit provision.

Defenders of Wildlife and other environmental organizations sued the secretary of the interior to abandon a revised regulation—promulgated in 1983 by the Reagan administration—exempting federally funded activities abroad from the provisions of the ESA.[71] The district court granted Secretary Hodel's motion to dismiss for lack of standing. Defenders of Wildlife appealed to the Eighth Circuit Court, which reversed the decision of the district court.[72] After all, the ESA Section 11(g)(1)—the "citizen-suit" provision—plainly states that "any person may commence a civil suit" against the secretary of the interior to compel enforcement of the provisions of the Act. On further appeal by the secretary, the case then went to the Supreme Court. Defenders of Wildlife alleged, on appeal, that two members, more particularly, of the organization—Joyce Kelly and Amy Skilbred, both conservation scientists—would be liable to injury by the new regulation. Putatively, Kelly's interest in making future observations of the Nile crocodile and Skilbred's in making future observations of the Asian elephant would be variously harmed. Opining for the majority, Justice Scalia argued that their alleged injuries do not rise to the level of standing as rooted in Article III of the Constitution and elaborated in numerous precedent cases. Scalia, however, did not leave it at that. He questioned the constitutionality of the ESA Section 11(g)(1):

> Vindicating the *public* interest (including the public interest in government observance of the Constitution and laws) is the function of Congress and the Chief Executive. The question presented here is whether the public interest in proper administration of the laws (specifically, in agencies' observance of a particular, statutorily prescribed procedure) can be converted into an individual right by a statute [the ESA] that denominates it as such, and that permits all citizens (or, for that matter, a subclass of citizens who suffer no distinctive concrete harm) to sue. If the concrete injury requirement has the separation-of-powers significance we have always said, the answer must be obvious.[73]

Ironically—as in *TVA v. Hill*, which affirmed and reinforced the ESA, and also in *Lujan v. Defenders*—the decision was based on judicial restraint. In the former case, the Court refused to presume to calculate the "incalculable" value of an endangered species and weigh it against the benefits of a nearly completed dam. In the latter, the Court refused to protect the public interest, claiming that the Constitution only "established courts to adjudicate cases and controversies as to claims of infringement of individual rights whether by unlawful action of private persons or by the exertion of unauthorized administrative power."[74] In sharp contrast, *TVA v. Hill* expressly states the following separation-of-powers doctrine: "Once Congress, exercising its delegated powers, has decided the order of priorities in a given area, it is for the Executive to administer the laws and *for the courts to enforce them when enforcement is sought*."[75] The question of citizen-suit provisions in general and the constitutional separation of powers is reviewed by Robert B. June and Stephen M. Johnson.[76]

According to the argument of this chapter, the operational legal rights and *de facto* standing of listed species turns on the citizen-suit provision of the ESA. If Scalia's opinion were precedential, the citizen-suit provision of the ESA would have been invalidated. However, because the issue in *Lujan v. Defenders* was whether Kelly and Skilbred had standing to sue, not whether the citizen-suit provision was constitutional, Scalia's attack on it is clearly *dicta*—ominous *dicta*, but nonbinding *dicta*, nonetheless.

Fortunately, when the ESA's citizen-suit provision came before the Supreme Court in 1997 as the issue in contention, it did so in a way that so attracted ultraconservative support that its constitutionality was expressly affirmed—by Justice Scalia, no less, opining for the Court's unanimous judgment. In *Bennett v. Spear*, lower courts had ruled that the plaintiffs lacked standing under ESA's citizen-suit provision, essentially because they were not environmentalists suing on behalf of endangered species—the "zone of interest" sought to be protected by the Act—but irrigation districts and ranchers.[77] The would-be plaintiffs claimed that the federal agencies involved had not given due consideration to "economic impact" as the Act also requires.[78] Scalia first revisits the standing requirements rooted in Article III of the Constitution, as talmudically evolved through many precedent cases, including both *Sierra Club v. Morton* and *Lujan v. Defenders*—which, if anything, narrowed them. In addition, the courts may further restrict standing by imposing "prudential limitations."[79] According to Scalia, constitutional limitations are both "immutable" and an "irreducible . . . minimum," but prudential limitations may be "modified or abrogated by Congress." Accordingly, "The first question in this case [*Bennett v. Spear*] is whether the ESA's citizen suit provision . . . negates the zone of interests test (or perhaps more accurately expands it). We think it does." The parenthetical remark is cryptic and ambiguous, but, as we shall see, it seems to mean that Congress can in fact relax the irreducible constitutional minimum required for standing and expand the class of those who have constitutional standing as well as negate the additional prudential requirements imposed by jurists. Scalia notes that the citizen-suit "provision says that 'any person may commence a civil suit'" and comments that it is "an authorization of remarkable breadth when compared with the language Congress ordinarily uses." Then he goes on to say that:

Our readiness to take the term "any person" at face value is greatly augmented by two interrelated considerations: that the overall subject matter of this legislation is the environment (a matter in which it is common to think all persons have an interest) and that the obvious purpose of the particular provision in question is to encourage enforcement by so called "private attorneys general." . . . Given these factors, we think the conclusion of expanded standing follows *a fortiori* from our decision in *Trafficante v. Metropolitan Life Ins. Co.*, 409

U.S. 205 (1972), which held that standing was expanded to the full extent permitted under Article III by a provision of the Civil Rights Act of 1968 that authorized "[a]ny person who claims to have been injured by a discriminatory housing practice" to sue for violations of the Act. There also we relied on textual evidence of a statutory scheme to rely on private litigation to ensure compliance with the Act. The statutory language here is even clearer, and the subject of the legislation makes the intent to permit enforcement by every man even more plausible.[80]

Given Scalia's very stringent interpretation of Article III standing requirements in *Lujan v. Defenders*, which is reiterated in *Friends of the Earth v. Laidlaw*, it is very hard not to think that the ESA's citizen-suit provision expands standing not just "to the full extent permitted under Article III," but well beyond what is permitted under Article III as talmudically interpreted. Indeed, that is just what Scalia wrote in the *dicta* of his *Lujan v. Defenders* opinion. Fortunately, the more recent *Bennett v. Spear* decision not only contradicts but lays to rest those *dicta*. Because it was a victory for plaintiffs seeking to redress economic grievances, not to protect endangered species, it may appear to be a battle lost for the cause of species preservation—just what one would expect from a decision crafted by Justice Scalia.[81] While it may indeed be a battle lost for the cause of species preservation, it also appears to be a more far-reaching victory for the crucial and controversial citizen-suit provision of the Act, on which turns the operational rights and *de facto* standing of listed species. Not only does *Bennett v. Spear* confirm the constitutionality of the citizen-suit provision, by creating a more equal balance between environmental and economic interests, it may, according to Deanne Barney, relieve pressure on Congress to dismember the Act.

Conclusion

While the overt language of the ESA itself and that of *TVA v. Hill* is free of references to "rights," and "intrinsic value," noninstrumental rhetoric occasionally bubbles to the surface in the latter. For example, "It is conceivable that the welfare of an endangered species may weigh more heavily upon the public conscience, as expressed by the final will of Congress, than the write-off of those millions of dollars already expended . . . for Tellico in excess of its present salvageable value."[82] The loss of a potential natural resource, something of mere instrumental option value—something especially of as little potential utility as the snail darter—can be regrettable, but hardly a matter of "conscience." Nor can an entity that has no intrinsic value have a "welfare" of its own. And while the expert testimony before Congress quoted in *TVA v. Hill* focuses on the "incalculable" utility of threatened and endangered species, such rationales are characterized as "the most narrow possible point of view"—the noninstrumental, intrinsic-value point of view presumably being the more expansive one.[83] Further, while *TVA v. Hill* concludes, as noted, that "Congress was concerned about the unknown uses that endangered species might . . . have," it also goes on immediately to conclude that Congress was also concerned "about the unforeseeable place such creatures may have in the chain of life on this planet."[84] That may simply express a risk-averse instrumental concern for poorly understood ecological services parallel to a risk-averse instrumental concern for potential ecological goods— that is, natural resources. But it may, conversely, express a noninstrumental concern for the intrinsic value of biodiversity and ecological integrity. If *TVA v. Hill* is the high point of jurisprudence concerning the ESA, *Lujan v. Defenders* is the low point. In the latter, there is no hint of concern of any sort for endangered species and Justice Scalia can barely conceal his contempt for the concerns for them evinced by Joyce Kelly and Amy Skilbred.

In a 2003 decision by the U.S. Court of Appeals for the District of Columbia, *Rancho Viejo v. Norton* (a case much discussed in the Senate Judiciary Committee hearing for the nomination of John Roberts as chief justice of the United States), the possibility that Congress intended to confer intrinsic value on endangered species was noted: "Is the ESA's true purpose to preserve the economic potential of species whose commercial value we cannot now foresee, or did Congress regard species protection as a moral imperative? . . . For courts to insist on making these kinds of determinations a prerequisite for upholding the validity of congressional legislation is a recipe for judicial intervention in the political process."[85] The majority presumed that Congress regarded species protection as a nonanthropocentric moral imperative. Judge Roberts dissented.

To quote once again the words of Christopher Stone, when legislation such as the ESA creates "a legally recognized worth and dignity in its own right [for an entity], and not merely to serve as means to benefit 'us' (whoever the contemporary group of rights holders may be)," then the contemporary group of rights holders may come to resent it. ESA in effect created a legally recognized worth and dignity in its own right for each listed species by stealth—because the discourse of intrinsic value, dignity, and rights does not appear in the Act. But when first tested in the courts, *TVA v. Hill* showed the effects to be the same. I am not sure what all it means to be "politically conservative," but it seems that at least part of what it means is to resist and when possible to roll back attempts to expand the group of rights holders. A contemporary example would be the conservative resistance to expand marriage rights to gay and lesbian couples. A counterexample might be the conservative zeal to expand the group of rights holders to include human embryos and fetuses. But a more cynical interpretation would view that as only a ruse to roll back the recently won reproductive-freedom rights of women and to restore the patriarchal rights men once enjoyed in controlling women's sexuality. With John Roberts, who dissented in *Rancho Viejo v. Norton,* now and for many years to come serving as chief justice of the United States and Samuel A. Alito joining him as associate justice, we should not be surprised to discover that an ultraconservative judiciary would try to roll back the rights of listed endangered species "operationally" provided them by the ESA.

Whatever the future of the ESA, it clearly falsifies the convergence hypothesis. Upon analysis, the ESA is nonanthropocentric. It awards listed species implicit intrinsic value, *de facto* legal standing, and operational legal rights. Indeed, it is so clearly nonanthropocentric that a number of cases were litigated under the Act, some successfully, in the name of the listed species under threat by an action or inaction of some public or private entity or person. That is, some lawyers and judges construed the ESA to provide *de jure* standing to some listed species as legal persons. Legal protection for endangered species based on their purely anthropocentric instrumental value would provide altogether weaker protection. Perennial conservative attempts to gut the ESA by making endangered species preservation compete with other anthropocentric instrumental values dramatizes what would be the case if the ESA were, in fact, based on purely instrumental values. An ESA based on purely anthropocentric instrumental values would require the value of endangered species to be quantified on the monetary metric and be subjected to comparison with other anthropocentric instrumental values in Benefit-Cost Analysis (BCA) exercises. Jurisprudential interpretation of the actual ESA, implicitly based as it is on nonanthropocentric intrinsic value, going back to *TVA v. Hill,* exempts listed species from monetary valuation and BCA-driven trade-offs. In short, an ESA based on purely anthropocentric instrumental values would not converge on the same policies and protections as the ESA we actually have, implicitly based on nonanthropocentric intrinsic value. Therefore, the convergence hypothesis is false.

ACKNOWLEDGMENTS

Research assistance for the preparation of this chapter was provided by graduate students Elyssa Back, Yale School of Management, and Megan Ceronsky, Yale Law School.

PAUL B. THOMPSON

Convergence in an Agrarian Key

Bryan Norton offered "the convergence hypothesis" as the central thesis in his 1991 book *Toward Unity among Environmentalists*. It was intended as a way to achieve the goal stated in the book's title, but it was articulated both as a conjecture about the implications of divergent positions in environmental philosophy and as an appeal to his fellow environmental philosophers. The conjecture held that the philosophical differences dividing ecocentric and anthropocentric perspectives in environmental ethics did not entail very many different policy prescriptions, and that such differences tended to disappear as the geographical or temporal scope of the policy prescription grew larger. The appeal enjoined philosophers to engage in a form of pragmatic pluralism when working with nonacademic audiences, and especially in connection with public policy. The intervening years have seen Norton move more forcefully toward a pragmatist position. But pragmatism, I have argued, has its roots in agrarian philosophies of the eighteenth and nineteenth centuries.[1] Since agrarian philosophy makes a more obvious and explicit linkage to nature and environment than classical pragmatism, it is worth examining how it might engage Norton's goals of convergence.

I argue that this engagement consists especially in tempering the complexities of classical pragmatism with a more readily accessible narrative about how nature frames and reinforces important moral habits, character traits, and virtues. I do not provide details of how this reinforcement occurs or what virtues are inculcated, but instead focus on the way that agrarian ideals and rhetoric actually have been influential in key public policy decisions in U.S. history. A better account of the details can be had by reading the pragmatists themselves, but I summarize the idea of "habit-taking" as I see it in the work of Charles Sanders Peirce, William James, and John Dewey. First, however, it is important to situate the entire topic within the framework of convergence, as well as the further development of Norton's thought.

From Environmental "isms" to Convergence

Toward Unity among Environmentalists portrayed environmental philosophers as deeply split along anthropocentric and ecocentric lines (details to follow), but in essence, Norton's appeal to his fellow philosophers urged them to temper their views when mounting criticisms of perspectives or rationales for environmental policy expressed by nonphilosophers. He argued that within contexts of political persuasion or practical decision making, the distinctions philosophers develop to parse their own positions were unlikely to make a material difference to the policy prescription that would ultimately be endorsed by environmentalists. What is more, he thought, the infighting among philosophers at best reinforced the perception that environmental ethics was of marginal value to the policy process, and at worst threatened to undermine the consensus needed for environmentalists to achieve commonly agreed-upon policy goals. Hence, an important epistemological assumption behind the convergence hypothesis held that policy disagreements among environmentalists were due to their "anthropocentric" or "ecocentric" commitments.

This philosophical divergence was stated in deceptively simple terms in Norton's 1991 book. On the one hand, a number of philosophers and environmental activists were said to promote pro-environment policy prescriptions because they had recognized how important they were for human flourishing. These *anthropocentrists* saw little need for revising what were said to be the central claims of mainstream ethical theory, claims that on the utilitarian side emphasized satisfying the preferences of individual human beings and on the neo-Kantian side emphasized respecting other human agents as "ends-in-themselves," possessing intrinsic value. On the other hand, *ecocentrists* were said to hold that at least some nonhuman entities possess the type of intrinsic value worthy of moral consideration. This was viewed as a straight-forward logical consequence of traditional ethical theory by Peter Singer, who argued that it was simply inconsistent to count satisfaction of human preferences and ignore the suffering of animals when tallying the consequences of a personal or policy action. In contrast, Holmes Rolston argued that what was needed was wholly new for ethics, a way to understand the permanence and integrity of nonsentient entities such as species, forests, or ecosystems.

Anthropocentrists were themselves divided between those who saw environmental ethics as an enlightened form of consequentialist optimization and those who saw intrinsic value (albeit for humans) in the preservation of endangered species or cherished places. Environmental economists dominated the former group, while Mark Sagoff has been the preeminent representative of the latter position. The ecocentric camp included Rolston and his followers, as well as deep ecologists, whose ideas had been inspired by Arne Naess and ecofeminists, who were arguing that nature had been subjected to the same forms of domination and marginalization that had afflicted women. Those like Singer, who saw sentience as the basis of any ethical claim, wore the mantle of ecocentrism less comfortably and quickly divided among themselves over the question of whether the moral standing of animals needed a more neo-Kantian formulation in animal rights. Norton's portrayal of the convergence hypothesis concealed all this complexity by appealing to three emblematic figures. John Muir was the paradigmatic ecocentrist, while Gifford Pinchot was anthropocentric, and their battle over Hetch Hetchy Valley in the early years of the twentieth century was offered as a model for policy decisions where the difference was more than cosmetic. Aldo Leopold was put forward as the model of convergence.

In many respects, all the diverse threads of environmental philosophy operant in 1991 have continued to develop along independent lines. Certainly, none of the individuals mentioned above have recanted their views. Yet the convergence hypothesis itself has changed significantly in the intervening decade and a half. On the one hand, as Phil Cafaro notes in a recent review essay, most environmental philosophers now recognize broad complementarities among the various strands,[2] even while they continue to mine the conceptual and philosophical veins with which they have greatest affinity. As such, the weak pluralism Norton called for seems to have been realized in the practice of environmental philosophers, if not in their specific doctrines. On the other hand, Norton's own views have moved more decisively in the direction of a pragmatism that he was beginning to articulate as early as 1988 in his reading of Leopold. Leopold's notion of community, he argued, was drawn from the philosophical pragmatism of C. S. Peirce, William James, and John Dewey. Norton presented evidence to suggest that Leopold encountered these ideas through contact with the work of the pragmatist political economist A. T. Hadley, who was the Yale University president during Leopold's time on the New Haven campus as a science and forestry student.[3] Norton's recent work continues to read Leopold as the crowning articulation of pragmatist philosophy within the domain of environmental ethics, though he has also taken pains to lay out a philosophically more detailed sketch of pragmatism that stresses not only the work of Peirce and Dewey, but also Otto Neurath and Jürgen Habermas.[4]

Pragmatism is a notoriously difficult philosophical approach to summarize. In the following section, I sketch my own version of some important elements in the work of Peirce, James, and Dewey, but do not attempt to retrace Norton's development of environmental pragmatism from *Sustainability: A Philosophy of Adaptive Ecosystem Management*. While I emphasize some elements that Norton does not, I believe that our respective understandings of pragmatism are entirely compatible.

From Convergence to Pragmatism

Broadly speaking, pragmatism is a philosophy that holds that the resolution to many long-standing philosophical dilemmas lies in the abandonment of foundationalist schemes that try to establish doctrines on a few fundamental principles and in resigning oneself to the likelihood that philosophical progress will involve immersing oneself in the domain of pragmatics. "Pragmatics" is sometimes defined as the implicit, unarticulated, and often subconscious presumptions, assumptions, and practices that support meaningful uses of language in a specific context. Within contemporary analytic philosophy of language, there is a presumption that the practices that constitute pragmatics can be specified in the form of rules. Among pragmatists, the presumption is that this network of linguistic practices has a more Darwinian or evolutionary structure, an order derived from chaos largely by the weight, endurance, repeatability, or sustainability of patterns that have been relatively successful in previous tests. To push the analogy further, the Darwinian account of why individual members in a species tend to exhibit a given phenotypic trait has nothing to do with following well-specified rules. Traits are stable to the extent that a phenotype's having them contributes to reproductive success of the genotype. Similarly, for pragmatists, the loose but serviceable fit between strict meaning and implicit assumptions that allows a claim to have truth conditions in a given context is largely a matter of averages, routines, and dominant tendencies that have enabled successful communication more frequently than not, rather than strict rules. Furthermore, pragmatists see a wide array of mental processes, including perception and belief formation and not just language, as governed by pragmatics in a similar fashion.

The term that Peirce, James, and Dewey use to indicate this flexible yet serviceable type of stability is *habit*, and processes of habit formation or, as Peirce put it, "habit taking," become central to pragmatist philosophy. It is important to recognize that all three saw these processes operating across a broad array of ontological substrates, not just genes or linguistic practices. In each case, habit formation involves a mechanism of reproduction, where the proclivity or tendency to respond in a given way can be replicated from one context or situation to another. Such mechanisms have a potential for variation, possibly random, so that any instance of replication will have degrees of similarity and difference with any other. The other key element is supplied by the environment, which provides some form of feedback so that some variations are more likely to be reproduced in subsequent instances than others. It was James who emphasized habit taking in psychology, where the mechanism of reproduction is a form of memory. "Learning" then becomes the gradual accumulation of tendencies to respond (in words or in conduct). Responses that elicit hoped-for results (successful communication or practice) are more likely to be replicated in subsequent situations than are responses that die the death of silence or physical pain. The American tourist who insists upon shouting ever more loudly (in English) to a French store clerk or cab driver is only reproducing a response that has worked in the past, but its failure to achieve any sign of recognition will eventually weaken the "programming" that underwrites this practice in its new context.

James was less preoccupied with language than were philosophers who came after him, and he focused on the accumulation of responses or experiences into more or less stable patterns that serve as the basis for many cognitive phenomena, including self and other. Here it is important to note that James saw such stability as the metaphysical basis for both a *concept* of oneself (or self-image)—a view he might have adapted from Hume—and also for the very experience of a unified perspective within experience, the so-called *cogito* or Cartesian subject. A cognitive subject was thus, for James, a fragile accumulation of stabilities within the "stream of consciousness," one that when healthy "grows by its edges" as it incorporates new forms of relatedness into its processes of association and reproduction. Peirce also had a strongly metaphysical understanding of the accumulative (but contingent) ordering that evolutionary processes achieve, but he saw them operating even in physics and chemistry. Rejecting determinism and embracing metaphysical chance, Peirce's view of the reproduction, variation, and selection nexus that constitutes habit taking extends to the material world. Going a step beyond Hume in another direction, Peirce argued that causal relations just *are* such stabilities existing in a fundamentally random universe. His view anticipates contemporary speculation that constants in the laws of physics may represent evolutionarily established moments of order, with the possibility that alternative worlds (inaccessible from ours) have evolved with different values for these constants.

Peirce and Dewey were more inclined to take pragmatism into ethics than was James, and both recognized the role of social reinforcers such as praise, ostracism, and approbation in creating the effective environment for taking on psychological habits. Both believed that it was impossible to make sense of individual habits without such an environment, yet both also believed that social reinforcing mechanisms could become dysfunctional, reinforcing behaviors and attitudes (e.g., habits) that prevent people from flourishing or that actually contribute to a breakdown in the social environment itself. As such, pragmatist ethics consists in seeking a balance between personal habits (perhaps construed as "values" or "virtues") and social habits or institutions (the norms, prejudices, and social rules that provide the reinforcers for personal conduct). This balance point cannot be specified in advance or in detail, in part because the moral discourse we use to specify and communicate is itself the product of prior habit-taking processes. When philosophers "do ethics," they are replicating sociolinguistic forms that have been associated with choice and with social control in the past. If these forms have resonance and communicative effect in the present, they will be incorporated into effective social norms.

Peirce and Dewey insisted that the precariousness of this situation is less worrying than it might initially appear, for while we do not privilege any single element in our existing set of institutions and proclivities, neither do we ever throw out the lot of them in some futile attempt to start over from "new" foundations. As such, ethics consists in taking a constantly critical and dialectical attitude to norms, institutions, or values, one that takes all challenges seriously and attempts to evolve better social and personal responses. We may not know that a response is "better" in advance of trying it, but the feedback gained from experimentation provides a basis for either reproducing the probe in new contexts or discarding it and moving on. Norton makes this point in *Sustainability* through frequent references to Neurath's boat, where carpenters on board during a long sea voyage eventually replace every plank and timber one by one, while the ship sails merrily above the ocean waves without incident.

From Pragmatism to Adaptive Management

Dewey, in particular, was most sensitive to the increasing importance of formal institutions within the environment of social reinforcers that establish personal habits. Most institutions are informal. Queuing for service is a good example. People learn to queue up based on seeing others do it, and from the negative reinforcement they get when they fail to follow suit. The ontological substrate for standing in line is thus just the collective memory, attitudes, and behavior of individuals. It is a norm because everybody conforms to it, serving its own social reproduction without the need for explicit, conscious effort to do so. Formal laws and public policy, however, exist because organizations such as legislatures, enforcement agencies, and courts of law employ people with the explicit purpose of ensuring that norms are established and enforced. And organizations such as schools, hospitals, and businesses have their own apparatus for creating, reproducing, and reinforcing institutions, as well.

Dewey recognized that both informal and especially formal institutions could continue to reproduce habits and patterns of reinforcement long after they had ceased to have value for any conceivable human purpose. He was particularly attentive to the way that schools were perpetuating patterns of reinforcement that had lost all usefulness, and that were, in fact, inculcating dysfunctional habits and norms in the population. Formal education is the preeminent social institution dedicated to reproducing the norms, attitudes, and mental routines that are needed not only for individuals to navigate the vicissitudes of daily life and career, but also for society as whole to develop well-functioning organizations (like governments) capable of developing and enforcing good public policies. As such, education took a central role in Dewey's thought and career, and various school institutions, such as curriculum or disciplines, were a natural target for his critical eye.

Within higher education, disciplines achieve a certain amount of independence from immediate social reinforcers. Formal mechanisms are created that launch practitioners on forms of inquiry that may have no short-term value for problem solving outside the academy. In this, schools provide both a place for experimentation into wholly new modes of discourse and thinking and also serve as a repository where modes of discourse and thinking are reproduced in an environment sheltered from the feedback mechanisms that would otherwise lead to their demise. Higher education exposes students to these new and old ideas, and at advanced levels continues to reproduce, refine, or develop them. In this it provides a route to what Dewey called "the method of intelligence," where trial and error selection of problem solving probes can develop into a more critically active and potentially effective mode of thinking. But the hothouse environment of the schools can also go wrong if academic disciplines become wholly detached from the problem environment of society as a whole.

Late in life, Dewey undertook a study of how the academic discipline with which he was most familiar (philosophy) had become bogged down in meaningless repetition of inquiries about the foundations of knowledge, a "quest for certainty." These inquiries had once contributed to the rise of modern science, but by the 1920s, they were, in Dewey's view, subsisting largely because the mechanisms for reproducing the discipline of philosophy—curriculum, publication in academic outlets, and recruitment of new faculty—had become isolated from any selection mechanism, any form of feedback that would allow unhelpful inquiries to be dropped and new ones to be initiated. Particularly problematic were a nexus of philosophical doctrines that revolved around the abstraction of the Cartesian subject, a self, soul, or psyche that was presumed to have a thinglike unity and integrity. Although Jamesian psychology had abandoned this view without loss (in Dewey's view), it persisted both because a number of philosophical doctrines deeply beloved in philosophy departments depended on either defending or rebutting it, keeping the discourse stuck in a closed loop, and because ethics in particular seemed limited to either Kantian or utilitarian conceptions of the right and the good that were grounded in human subjectivity. What is more, since the work philosophers did in universities was largely unconnected to matters such as whether buildings fall down, wars are won, or fortunes are made, there was little external reinforcement that could penetrate the shell that academic philosophy had built for itself.

As such, Dewey dedicated his last decades to a variety of philosophical projects that were intended to show how critical awareness and a willingness to experiment could yield an ethics capable of effecting change in public policy (*The Public and Its Problems*) or within the discipline of philosophy itself (*Reconstruction in Philosophy*). For present purposes, we can cut to 1991 and note the extent to which many of the "isms" that motivated Norton's original plea for convergence were still rooted in a metaphysics of the Cartesian subject. Certainly, the most obvious versions of anthropocentrism were committed to the idea that value has its root in the subjective experience of human beings. For utilitarians, experiences of pleasure, pain, or satisfaction of preferences were experiences *had* by Cartesian subjects. With no subject, there was no locus or grounding for value. Neo-Kantians like Sagoff are equally committed to the subject, whose autonomy is the basis for any defensible notion of intrinsic value. Animal liberationists of all stripes fit here as well, insisting that it is either the subject's experiences or the subjects themselves that are the only defensible place to locate value, and taking issue only with the limitation of subjectivity to the human species. And to the extent that other ecocentrists were wedded to the idea of intrinsic value, they were launched on a quest of finding some property or trait that links species, forests, or ecosystems to subjectivity in a manner that permits one to say that they "are" or at least are sufficiently like Cartesian subjects to warrant an attribution of intrinsic value.

In contrast to philosophical strategies that use the subject as the foundation for ethics, a pragmatist view would regard ethical commitments, norms and practices, rights, virtues, and values as temporary nodes of stability within a flux of experiences, habits, social institutions, and feedback from the natural world. Philosophy should examine any of these nodes, but to do so it must rely on the stability and accumulated wisdom or experience reflected in the larger network of fluctuating but relatively stable ethical practices. Along with this stability, we are constantly plagued by problems, felt needs, and elements of social controversy or contest that suggest all is not well. Since we cannot examine the entire network at any given time, we use intuition, science, and experiment to selectively tweak a given pattern of practice and try to gauge what happens as a result. If problems improve, we tend to incorporate the tweak more deeply into the network, but whether *that* will succeed is not totally at our disposal. The tweak may be at odds with some other habit of thought or action, or there may be institutions at work that will eventually quash it. When we become more fully aware that this is what our philosophical, ethical practice in environmental affairs is all about, we become environmental pragmatists. Norton calls this "adaptive management," acknowledging Leopold as the originator of this mode of philosophy in the domain of game management.

None of this means that an environmental pragmatist abandons the arguments that are familiar in other domains of ethics or environmental philosophy. It is still appropriate to argue that some policy is necessary in order to respect the rights of the poor, or that it is contrary to utilitarian goals of optimizing trade-offs between benefit and cost. These are institutionalized modes of communicating ethical problems and raising critical consciousness. But for a pragmatist, while these arguments may be the planks we stand on while trying to fix one set of problems, they can just as readily become the planks that need to be tweaked (or perhaps removed altogether) when in the context of another problem we become aware that they are the source of what we diagnose as problematic. We can expect that others will complain if we try to rip out planks in our ethical boat to no purpose, and the fact that they do is one of the forces that yields whatever stability and integrity our network of habits has in the first place. Their complaints are a problem, and one to which we must attend.

From Adaptive Management to Public Policy (by Way of Agrarianism)

One goal of convergence, however, was policy effectiveness, and one can question whether the philosophy of adaptive management sketched above really has it. On the one hand, the term "adaptive management" seems like it could apply to almost any method of natural resource policy formulation, even those that remain committed to the view that some environmental*ism* has given us a certain and incontrovertible account of which things matter in nature and why. It is a term that has been in wide use by people who have no knowledge and little interest in the pragmatist pedigree that Norton (and I) are attempting to tag onto it. On the other hand, this pragmatist pedigree has not shown remarkable ability to work itself into the nexus of philosophical doctrines and theories pursued by academic philosophers to any significant degree. After all, the vast majority of environmental philosophers continue to follow lines of inquiry deeply tied to the abstractions of the Cartesian subject, and many popularizers of environmental ideas are deeply attracted to the thought of subjects in nature, as well. Michael Pollan, for example, has pursued this thought in his wonderful book *The Ecology of Desire*.

Philosophical pragmatism is complex and complicated stuff. The ideas of Peirce, James, and Dewey may percolate into the common person's consciousness eventually, just as Descartes' ideas have been realized for the mass consciousness in films like *The Matrix*. But the whole point of environmental philosophy is that we may not have that long. There is thus a need for an articulation of this philosophy that has greater philosophical content (and also greater spiritual, emotional resonance) than adaptive management, and also more familiarity and accessibility than the arguments of Peirce, James, and Dewey, arguments that are in their details much more complex than the already too complex exposition they have been given above. I have argued that we might achieve this by returning to agrarian modes of moral discourse that were commonplace only a few decades ago, and that still continue to have meaning for many outside academic circles today. Agrarian thought stresses ways in which virtues and practices are formed and reinforced through interaction with the local environment in which human beings live. In its most obvious forms, it notes the way that farmers, hunters, and fisherman acquire habits of practice that are attuned to place-specific attributes such as soil type, drainage, patterns of drought and flooding, and specific flora and fauna that thrive at different seasons of the year. The essays that Leopold uses to describe a year on his Wisconsin "Sand County" farm provide an excellent example of this type of local knowledge, and the oft-quoted aphorism citing the "two spiritual dangers of not owning a farm" (thinking that food comes from the market or that heat comes from a furnace) indicates the link between this local knowledge and the habits naturally acquired in subsistence occupations.

In other contexts, I have waxed at length on agrarian philosophy's elements and heritage.[5] Montesquieu's political philosophy is grounded in a sophisticated account of the way that climate and geography shape political institutions. Elements of agrarian thought can be found in the writings of Kant, Hume, and Adam Smith. I do not re-rehearse that line of analysis here, but I do offer a suggestive portrayal of agrarian thought by way of illustrating its application in U.S. land-use policy. But it is also important to interject a note of caution. Hegel's philosophy of history made extravagant claims for the power of soil and climate to influence conceptions of community, freedom, self, and polity. It is, perhaps, the extravagance of such claims, especially when linked to doctrines of European expansion or racial superiority that contributed to a discrediting and subsequent decline of agrarian ideas. Yet even in the work of Thoreau and Emerson, many of the critical adjustments needed to tweak and correct these extravagances can be found. I have thus argued elsewhere that we can work with many elements of agrarian thought to formulate new and possibly more effective strategies in conservation policy, though we must not think that we can adopt agrarian philosophies from the eighteenth or nineteenth century without adaptation.[6]

It is more appropriate here to ask whether agrarian philosophy can meet the convergence hypothesis's test of influencing public policy, while remaining true to the more subtle and complex pragmatism articulated in Norton's version of adaptive management. My answer is that we cannot know before we try, but more pointedly, we can show that agrarian thought *has been* singularly influential in land-use or environmental policy in the American past. In that vein, I turn now to two extended examples of agrarian rationales that were utilized and articulated by American presidents Thomas Jefferson and Theodore Roosevelt, respectively. It is by way of this exegesis that some further exposition of agrarian philosophy can be offered, as well.

Agrarianism to Policy I: Jefferson and the Louisiana Purchase

The Louisiana Purchase added more than 500 million acres to the territory of the United States. It was a controversial move, and the terms of the controversy were complex. On the one hand, Jefferson, Madison, and those in his party were more disposed to build foreign relations with the French, from whom the purchase was obtained, while Federalists tended to evaluate the decision in terms of its likely impact on relations with England and Spain. On the other hand, the controversy focused on the domestic political future of the nation, and it was here that agrarianism's influence could be seen. Federalists such as Alexander Hamilton had been focused on establishing a wealthy and secure leadership elite much like England's House of Lords on the theory that wealth would isolate political leaders from the temptation to pursue pecuniary interests at the expense of the public good. In this connection, they had urged the creation of an industrial center in New Jersey and in concentrating future development of the nation along the eastern seaboard.[7]

Jefferson's preferences are clearly documented throughout his writings. He preferred a greater democracy and more diffuse distribution of power. Like the Federalists, he feared the potential of the mob, but Jefferson believed that the risks of mob rule could be significantly curtailed by avoiding the growth of industrial manufacturing and the wage labor associated with it. Jefferson believed that small farmers would be "the most virtuous citizens," not because he had a romantic vision of noble savages, but because he believed that small landholders who invest their time in improving lands for agricultural use are strongly motivated to ensure the stability and defense of their country. Both owners and workers in manufacturing industries had reasons to think in the short term, and could pull up stakes and move on, just as many Tory manufacturers had moved to Canada during the period of the Revolution. At about the same time that Jefferson executed the Louisiana Purchase, Hegel was giving lectures at Jena, arguing that nations where agricultural production was organized along the lines of small holder units were most conducive to the emergence of a collective national identity and virtues of patriotism.

Policy decisions, especially those executed on the scale of the 1803 treaty that produced the Louisiana Purchase, are seldom if ever based solely on any single philosophical rationale. Nevertheless, Jefferson's agrarian views are evident in the reasoning that supported westward expansion of the United States over the industrial development favored by Hamilton's Federalists. While the early nineteenth century geopolitics and contrasting views on postrevolutionary France were hardly absent from the debates, there are at least two clear agrarian arguments that favored Jefferson's decision. One was negative. The "mob rule" feared by Hamilton and associated with the French reign of terror was linked with cities and industrial workers who were not only vulnerable to the vicissitudes of economic boom and bust, but who also formed a ready source for street protest and violent uprising when employment was short. Jefferson argued that it was better to keep the working classes employed on the farm where their labors would at least ensure them something to eat, and where there would be less opportunity for spontaneous rioting. He made this argument initially in the 1781 *Notes on the State of Virginia* (not published until 1787), where he wrote, "It is better to carry provisions and materials to workmen [in Europe], than bring them to the provisions and materials, and with them their manners and principles. . . . The mobs of great cities add just so much to the support of pure government, as sores do to the strength of the human body."[8]

The corresponding positive agrarian theme is sounded in the oft-quoted *Notes* passage, "Those who labour in the earth are the chosen people of God,"[9] and in the almost as frequently quoted 1785 letter to John Jay, "Cultivators of the earth are the most valuable citizens."[10] The subject of the Jay letter was sea power, and the immediate point was to prove that the American states needed a navy to ensure that they would be able to transport raw commodities to Europe and bring back finished goods. As the previous *Notes* passage shows, Jefferson regarded this prospect as more attractive than bringing the factories to America, and there is little evidence that he had changed this view by the time he was supervising the Louisiana Purchase in 1803. But the positive rationale for adding more land (and more farmers) lay not (or at least not solely) in the fact that this would yield more commodities (more "provisions and materials") for trade with Europe. Jefferson believed that tying a person's economic interest to land also cultivated the basis for virtues of patriotism and citizenship. Unlike manufacturers and traders, who in the American Revolution emigrated to Canadian provinces in droves,[11] the farmers' tie to the land ensured a political loyalty that makes them "the most valuable citizens."

As a matter of public policy, such views would clearly incline Jefferson toward the Louisiana Purchase and away from developing America's manufacturing capability. As such, the argument that agrarian philosophy influenced this critical land-use decision is relatively straightforward. It is, perhaps, worth stressing the sense in which Jefferson's thinking was oriented toward habit taking as described above, rather than value optimization or in protecting intrinsic value through legal constraints. Jefferson was as sensitive to rights-oriented constraints as any man of his time. Yet the reasoning that supported the Louisiana Purchase over industrial development in New Jersey was somewhat more subtle. The Louisiana Purchase was not justified because Jefferson saw immediate use value for the new lands (though he certainly envisioned that they would be farmed) or because he wanted to protect their intrinsic value. Indeed, valuation in either of these contemporary senses was not critical to either of the two agrarian arguments sketched above. Jefferson was thinking about how different ways of deriving one's subsistence—factory work versus farming—would produce habits of virtue (in the form of patriotism) and habits of thought that would incline citizens toward more stable and long-run priorities.[12]

Agrarianism to Policy 2:
Theodore Roosevelt and Federal Lands

Although the Louisiana Purchase may have been the single most momentous land-use policy decision in American history, Theodore Roosevelt's development of national parks and forests is perhaps more directly relevant to twenty-first-century environmental policy. Although the U.S. National Forests were established a full decade before Roosevelt became president, it was he who made the most extensive use of presidential authority to set aside public lands under the U.S. Land Revision Act of 1891 until the administration of President Bill Clinton. Roosevelt set aside reserves totaling 194 million acres in the form of parks, forests, preserves, and wildlife refuges. Although these acts do not lend themselves to the kind of single-decision analysis developed above for the Louisiana Purchase, collectively they represent a very strong candidate for the basis of contemporary environmental policy, and especially for those land-use policies aimed at conservation and preservation of natural areas. Why did he do it?

The lore of environmental studies might incline one to interpret Roosevelt's conservation policies in utilitarian terms. This lore recounts the conflict between John Muir, founder of the Sierra Club, and Gifford Pinchot, founder of the U.S. Forest Service, over the fate of Hetch Hetchy Valley in the Yosemite area of California. According to the story, Muir saw Hetch Hetchy as a sacred place that should not be sacrificed for human use, while Pinchot applied anthropocentric use values to calculate that loss of the valley for a water project would yield greater value in utilitarian terms. This account of the conflict over Hetch Hetchy portrays Muir as the advocate of ecocentric intrinsic environmental values that form the basis for constraints on human use (something very much like "rights" for natural entities). Pinchot is the anthropocentric, utilitarian precursor for contemporary resource economics and its myriad ways of computing the value of natural resources. Since Pinchot had a prominence in the Roosevelt administration that no subsequent head of the U.S. Forest Service has begun to approach, it is plausible to think that Pinchot's reasoning was also Roosevelt's.

The lore rests on a series of conflicts between Muir and Pinchot that allegedly culminated with Hetch Hetchy, though the actual history of their relationship is contested.[13] Bryan Norton recounts the story in order to portray Aldo Leopold as the environmental pragmatist able to mediate between Muir's and Pinchot's ideological extremes.[14] Pinchot's biographer Char Miller puts Roosevelt in the gap between Muir and Pinchot: "Roosevelt drew upon the preservationist and utilitarian ideals of conservation for which they are considered the leading exponents, but was not doctrinaire in his application of either set of principles."[15] But Roosevelt should not be read simply as an arbiter of political compromise between two philosophically incompatible points of view. There is ample evidence to support an agrarian thread in his political philosophy.

Roosevelt was a naturalist and a prolific author. His books include numerous titles on native flora and fauna, as well as his better-known titles recounting his adventures as a big game hunter. There are, in addition, several volumes of hortatory essays in which Roosevelt holds forth on the role that living on the land without benefit of modern conveniences can play in developing proper habits of character and judgment. *The Strenuous Life* (1903) is a particularly apt example, but *Autobiography* may be the most revealing text for the way that Roosevelt intersperses the character-forming episodes of his own life with notes on politics and political leadership. Here, Roosevelt recounts a life balanced between intellectual pursuits (especially reading) and vigorous activities including riding and hunting. He describes himself as having won successes of the "commoner type," that are owed to the development of qualities found in an average man "who has no remarkable mental or physical abilities, but who gets just as much as possible in the way of work out of the aptitudes that he does possess."[16]

While much of *Autobiography* is devoted to Roosevelt's political career, he describes years that he spent in the West ("In Cowboy Land") between 1883 and 1889 as particularly important for his own character development. He writes, "I owe more than I can ever express to the West."[17] The chapter describes a series of personalities and adventures encountered while Roosevelt occupied himself with a ranching partnership. Many of these vignettes are tied to the development of individual personality traits or to interpersonal relationships of interdependence, reciprocity, and trust. He summarizes these years as follows: "I do not believe there ever was any life more attractive to a vigorous young fellow than life on a cattle ranch in those days. It was a fine, healthy life, too; it taught a man self-reliance, hardihood, and the value of instant decision—in short, the virtues that ought to come from life in the open country. I enjoyed the life to the full."[18]

In his speeches, Roosevelt extends the need to cultivate such virtues through hard work and training within the citizenry as a whole: "In the last analysis a healthy state can exist only when the men and women who make it up lead clean, vigorous, healthy lives; when the children are so trained that they shall endeavor not to shirk difficulties, but to overcome them; not to seek ease, but to know how to wrest triumph from toil and risk."[19]

These writings do not amount to the kind of theoretically calculated agrarian philosophy found in Jefferson, but while Jefferson's agrarian passages actually represent a fairly small percentage of his written work,[20] passages in which Roosevelt extols the role of outdoor pursuits, including both subsistence work and sporting activities, are spread throughout his writings. Furthermore, Roosevelt's more pointed policy prescriptions are also attentive to the cultivation of good habits, and to ways of ensuring that power and decision-making authority are entrusted to individuals of good character. One should not interpret these passages cynically or as mere platitudes. Roosevelt was not unaware of the potential for such a reading.[21] Rather, they testify to the way in which a regard to habits, judgment, and framing of action were as important to Roosevelt's policy making as were intrinsic values or utilitarian considerations.

Indeed, Char Miller's discussion of Roosevelt's conservation policy, and of the Hetch Hetchy episode in particular (it was not settled until after Roosevelt left office), emphasizes his ability to incorporate a complex mix of values and philosophical influences in his thinking. Roosevelt, who traveled with both Muir and Pinchot, was clearly weighing arguments of a preservationist sort and was also mindful of the use that water supplies and timber would have for utilitarian purposes. These considerations were not absent, nor were they "trumped" by the character and virtue arguments that I have associated with an agrarian style of thought. All were copresent. In Miller's account, Roosevelt's ultimate sympathy for the water project that spelled doom for

Hetch Hetchy rested on his judgment that a decision favoring Muir's point of view would simply have provoked outrage from the citizens of California. He wrote Muir advising that protecting natural beauties requires "a certain degree of friendliness toward them on the part of the people of the State in which they are situated."[22] This comment may reflect simple political realism—a form of vulgar pragmatism—but it may equally be grounded in agrarian appreciation of the need to cultivate both habits of aesthetic judgment as well as a political practice in which preservation is not pitted directly against material prosperity.

In sum, Roosevelt's belief in the value of hard work and other vigorous pursuits carried out in a relatively untamed environment predisposed him toward the array of environmental policies that have won him the praise of subsequent generations. He was not deaf to intrinsic value arguments, but he recognized that they would not carry the day against more utilitarian uses for natural resources. His frequent use of agrarian-style thinking in stressing the formation and maintenance of virtues should not be regarded as mere campaign rhetoric. Nor are the land-use policies for which he is remembered the only elements of his presidency that support this judgment. His administration also launched an effort to reinvigorate American agriculture and rural life based on principles drawn heavily from Jeffersonian agrarianism under the aegis of a Commission on Country Life chaired by Liberty Hyde Bailey.[23] A more fully developed environmental philosophy might replace the intrinsic value/utilitarian dichotomy with a triad in which Muir, Pinchot, and Bailey represent complementary orientations to environmental thinking, each of which is reflected equally in Roosevelt's land-use policy.

Concluding Thoughts

There are myriad additional connections that might be drawn in developing an agrarian pragmatism. One of the more intriguing possibilities emphasizes Bailey's role as a mediator between Dewey and Leopold. Paul Morgan and Scott Peters hint at this in a recent paper, noting that Bailey's thought on what we now call agroecology and the importance of establishing a moral relationship to land both preceded and influenced Leopold's, while Bailey's work also acknowledges a debt to the educational philosophy of Dewey.[24] It would also be useful to articulate the "ecological" character of pragmatism more explicitly, and to discuss how pragmatic conceptions of moral habits, social institutions, and their relationships of selection and reinforcement promote an environmental philosophy more deeply connected to the principles of ecology than any approach resting on modern philosophy's conception of a Cartesian subject. It would also be worthwhile to probe the connections between pragmatism and leading figures in mainstream environmental ethics.

Rolston, for example, teases out notions of self-replicating order in his development of intrinsic value,[25] while Sagoff relies heavily on Wilfrid Sellars's deeply pragmatist reading of Kant to develop his own conception of intrinsic value.[26] The potential for spelling out such connections may prove that the Cartesian subject is less important for the dominant environmental philosophies than my own analysis suggests. It is worth noting even these tentative and undeveloped linkages to illustrate pragmatism's emphasis on developing interwoven networks of ideas, as opposed to hierarchies with strict logical derivations or dependencies.

Yet the present context surely calls us away from further divergence, and back toward a consideration of Norton's convergence hypothesis and the implications of agrarian pragmatism in a public policy context. I have suggested a number of possible linkages and connections above that promote a particular reading of convergence and its relationship to environmental pragmatism. This reading begins with a fairly straightforward statement of the ambitions Norton originally articulated with respect to convergence as situated within the context of environmental philosophy circa 1991. I have argued that Norton probably overstated the prospects for merging the diverse strands of environmental philosophy into a coherent voice, but that philosophers have nonetheless become reconciled to the idea that complementarities exist among these views. What is more, the sense that diverging philosophical ideals would lead to such radically different environmental policy proposals as to split the global movement for environmental protection has certainly weakened. But I have also intimated that what may be of more enduring interest about the convergence hypothesis is the way that it foreshadowed Norton's growing interest in the philosophical orientations of American pragmatism. The connections to pragmatism began to be recognized with the appearance of Andrew Light and Eric Katz's *Environmental Pragmatism* (1996), but it is only with Norton's *Sustainability* (2005) that we have a full-blown statement of its epistemological principles.

Rather than summarizing Norton, I have offered a somewhat impressionistic account of pragmatic views on habits and habit taking. It is worth stressing, again, the sense in which Peirce, James, and Dewey saw this as the great significance of Darwin. But they were taking the underlying logic of natural selection well beyond the phenomenon of species evolution. They extended evolution to a diverse array of phenomena including psychological entities (such as self, other, and consciousness), cultural forms (such as customs and norms), formal institutions (such as government or schools), and even to the material world (causes and probabilistic regularities). In each case, "evolution" consists of the interplay between reproduction, variation, and selection. Peirce and Dewey saw ethics as a domain in which one must seek a tenuous ecology in which existing norms, established by cultural, behavioral, and intellectual

selection pressures of the past, are tempered by proposals for normative inno-
vation that must then meet the selection mechanisms of the present. Since at
least some of the selection mechanisms are themselves social norms and products of evolution, ethics must be attentive both to the principles that guide
action and to the way that the social and natural environment exert selection
pressure on our principles. Peirce and Dewey thus envisioned an "evolutionary
ethics" quite unlike that of genetic reductionism proposed a century later by
sociobiologists.

Agrarianism fits into this pragmatist framework, though it is a less abstract and more congenial way of thinking. It guards against proposals that
undo the circumstances producing virtuous habits, and stresses that "nature"
(often in the form of farms, but sometimes in the form of wilderness) provides
an environment especially capable of exerting the kind of selection pressure
on the formation of young minds and character that results in virtue and
moral strength. I have shown in some detail how this pattern of thinking
seemed to be at work in key natural resource policy decisions of the past.
Whether it could have such influence today is a matter for speculation, but I
note in closing that "slow food," the return of farmers' markets, and the rapid
growth of organic certification are all signs that point toward the salience of
agrarian ideas in our own time. That is the case for convergence in an agrarian key.

11

Convergence and Ecological Restoration

A Counterexample

Introduction: The Pragmatic Issue for Norton's Convergence Hypothesis

How does philosophy engage the world? Marx had a famous negative answer to this question in the last of his theses on Feurbach: "The philosophers have only *interpreted* the world, in various ways; the point, however, is to *change* it." If philosophy as a discipline is to respond to the critique of Marx, it requires a sustained effort to effect change beyond a mere increase in analysis and understanding. Philosophy must engage and shape policy. Action must be undertaken at the behest of philosophical ideas. If the world is not different because of the adoption of different philosophical ideas, then philosophy is meaningless: It has no engagement with and no effect on the real world in which we live.

The view that philosophy has a concrete effect on policy, action, and the world is, of course, the fundamental assumption of American pragmatism. The philosophy of pragmatism is primarily about the justification of ideas, validating them as being true or false. The truth of an idea is determined, according to pragmatism, by the efficacy of the idea in the real world. True ideas are those that "work," that have a positive effect on the activities of human beings and human institutions in the world. This philosophical worldview requires that ideas have an effect on policy and action; if they have no effect, they are meaningless. Pragmatism is thus the most powerful response to Marx's negative critique of the general impotence of the practice of philosophy.

Bryan Norton's "convergence hypothesis" purports to be a pragmatic response to the failure of environmental philosophy (and the field of environmental ethics) to solve—or even to help to solve—the environmental problems that surround us in the contemporary world. Norton has argued that environmentalists with different philosophical worldviews about the source and meaning of value in the natural world do not, in fact, disagree about fundamental environmental policies. Despite differing starting points in their environmental thinking, the policies that environmentalists advocate tend to converge around an overall goal of long-term sustainability for humans and natural ecosystems in various contexts of time and space. Because there is this convergence in policy, Norton claims that much of the theorizing and debate in environmental philosophy is pointless. Following what appears to be a pragmatic line, Norton argues that we should be devoting our philosophical energies to areas where they will do the most good—for example, refining and clarifying environmental policies devoted to long-term sustainability and educating environmental professionals and the general public—rather than continuing to engage in fruitless theoretical debates about, for example, anthropocentrism and nonanthropocentrism or the intrinsic value of natural entities.

Note that I have stated that Norton's convergence hypothesis "purports" or "appears" to be a thesis derived from pragmatism. I do not believe that the convergence hypothesis actually expresses the spirit of pragmatic thought; indeed, I believe that the convergence hypothesis, if true, would undermine the basic assumption of pragmatism that philosophical ideas must engage with actions in the real world. If the convergence hypothesis is true, then it makes no difference what philosophical ideas about the environment anyone holds: All policies will be the same. Differing philosophical ideas about humanity and its relationship to the natural world would not have different effects in the real world. How then, can ideas be subject to a pragmatic test? If the convergence hypothesis is true, then philosophy is irrelevant to the development of policy. Ideas are impotent, and Marx's critique of the practice of philosophy stands unchallenged.

But the convergence hypothesis is not true. Environmentalists with differing basic worldviews about the value and meaning of humanity and the natural world do not always tend to develop converging environmental policies based on long-term sustainability. Norton's hypothesis is an empirical claim that must be tested by examining real-life cases of the development of environmental policies from differing philosophical worldviews. In the past, I have examined the cases of development in the Amazon rain forest and the prevention of beach erosion on Fire Island, and have shown that the adoption of an anthropocentric worldview will lead to different policies than the adoption of a nonanthropocentric worldview.[1] In this chapter, I examine a third case: the practice of ecological restoration.

Norton's Theory of Convergence

Although all of the chapters in this volume examine, explain, and discuss Norton's convergence hypothesis, it will be useful to begin with a summary of Norton's position. Without attaching a specific name or label to the idea, Norton originally introduced the convergence hypothesis as "a bit of shameless speculation" in an article in 1986 in *Environmental Ethics:* "If Leopold's argument from ecological holism is sound, if the interests of the human species interpenetrate those of the living Earth, then it follows that anthropocentric and nonanthropocentric policies will converge in the indefinite future."[2] Even then, Norton was almost exclusively focused on the idea of the long-range sustainability of humans and natural systems and entities: "Showing respect for nature . . . may just be an alternative formulation of the injunction to show concern for resource stability essential to human survival over the longest term."[3]

This "shameless speculation" became the theme and thesis of Norton's important 1991 book *Toward Unity among Environmentalists.*[4] The book reviews the history of environmental thought in the United States, beginning with John Muir and Gifford Pinchot, examines the differing worldviews of environmentalists (Norton designates seven different worldviews), and looks at the convergence of policy in several different areas of environmental concern (growth in population and economics, pollution control, biological diversity, and land use). Here, the key to the argument is the commitment to scientific naturalism: "The vision of environmentalism is unified, not by a shared commitment to a single value, but by a shared belief in scientific naturalism, and its associated belief that all things in nature are related in complex, hierarchically organized systems."[5] These systems are "shaped and limited by hierarchical constraints" that are also shaped by a cultural context.[6] "Scientific naturalism thereby enforces upon all environmentalists a basically holistic, nonatomistic approach to environmental problems."[7]

Scientific naturalism thus leads to the convergence in policy: "Active environmentalists . . . [accept] an empirical hypothesis—the convergence hypothesis. Environmentalists believe that policies serving the interests of the human species as a whole, and in the long run, will serve also the 'interests' of nature, and vice versa."[8] Presumably, Norton's review and analysis of several environmental problems and policies earlier in the book offer empirical evidence for this convergence. Consider the review and analysis of U.S. Forest Service policy that Norton cites as one example of the environmentalist argument for "constraints on commercial development of natural resources."[9] Environmentalists who hold a conservationist or "wise-use" worldview (the disciples of Pinchot) dominate the Forest Service, but according to Norton, a shared policy consensus has developed with environmentalists who hold a preservationist worldview (the followers of Muir). The consensus position is "contextual management": The Forest Service no longer focuses on the production of timber and the protection of single isolated species, but also includes a consideration of the amenities and broader social values represented by forest landscapes. From the other side, preservationists now debate the variety of land-use options in and around the forest ecosystems: They do not simply demand the preservation of all natural entities. Thus, a consensus policy question emerges: "What is the proper mix of economic management and contribution to noncommercial values?" For Norton, an "essential" aspect of this consensus is "that management must take into account the important role of health and stability of the larger landscape in which productive and recreational units are embedded."[10]

It is not clear to me how this broadened contextual management of the forests represents a policy consensus or convergence. It is definitely a kind of compromise, in that Forest Service utilitarians are considering a wider range of value-producing human activities in the forests. But the "consensus" or convergence only seems possible (the way Norton describes it) if we ignore all the preservationist intuitions about the importance of nonanthropocentrism for the evaluation of nonhuman entities. The convergence of policy options that traditionally divide anthropocentrists from nonanthropocentrists only comes about if we ignore the view of the nonanthropocentrists: We consider a wider range of human value ("productive and recreational"), but we no longer consider the intrinsic value of natural nonhuman entities.

Perhaps the difficulty in demonstrating a real-life convergence is what causes Norton to offer a crucial caveat to the validity of the convergence hypothesis: He acknowledges that there are problems in testing the hypothesis: "While empirical in nature, the convergence hypothesis is not a precisely formulated hypothesis open to direct test in a series of dramatic experiments."[11] It is rather both a "very general empirical hypothesis" and "an article of environmentalists' faith."[12] This is a strange empirical hypothesis indeed. Norton thus claims that when faced with a counterexample to the convergence hypothesis, such as a case where the long-range interests of a nonhuman species appear to conflict with the long-range interests of humans, advocates of the hypothesis will dismiss the case and the evidence, "claiming the example has not yet been viewed in sufficiently long temporal terms."[13] If nothing else, such a methodology is extremely convenient for determining the absolute validity of one's own favored position.

In more recent discussions of the convergence hypothesis, Norton appears to make the position more specific, and thus (presumably) open to more direct testing, but the new characterization weakens the hypothesis considerably. He uses identical language to discuss the hypothesis in two essays first published about a decade ago.[14] Norton here describes the convergence hypothesis thus: "Provided anthropocentrists consider the full breadth of human values as they unfold into the indefinite future, and provided nonanthropocentrists endorse a consistent and coherent version of the view that nature has intrinsic value, all sides may be able to endorse a common policy direction."[15] Note that there *may* be a common policy, a convergence, so this version of the hypothesis is a much weaker claim than the original formulation in *Toward Unity*. Norton continues to specify the new version, apparently limiting its application to policies that protect the future of biological processes on Earth: "The convergence hypothesis is a general, empirical hypothesis *about policy*—it claims that policies designed to protect the biological bequest to future generations will overlap significantly with policies that would follow from a clearly specified and coherent belief that nonhuman nature has intrinsic value."[16] Now there is a significant overlap in policies about environmental issues regarding future generations; the convergence of environmental policies of all kinds seems to be melting away.

In Norton's most recent book, *Sustainability*, his major synthesis of more than twenty years of environmental philosophy, he barely mentions the convergence hypothesis, so perhaps the hypothesis has melted away.[17] Here, he claims that it is a conditional thesis, premised on a worldview that accepts dualistic categories that may be in opposition to each other, such as "human interests" and "nonhuman interests." But Norton denies the existence of these dualisms, so the convergence hypothesis "will wither away"; all we need to do is adopt the nondualistic perspective of the human place in nature expressed by deep ecologists. Since humans are not "severed from nature," there is no need for a convergence.[18]

Let us ignore the irony of Norton adopting—he uses the word "embrace"— a deep ecology perspective, since nonanthropocentric deep ecology was one of the two sides in environmental policy debates that Norton believed needed to converge with anthropocentric management practices, and instead focus on the problem of proving or disproving the convergence hypothesis. As noted above, much of *Toward Unity* is devoted to a case-by-case analysis of a wide variety of environmental problems, in an attempt to show a convergence in policy based on the environmentalist acceptance of scientific naturalism and contextual management. Yet, at the end of the book, Norton offers his caveat that the convergence hypothesis is not open to direct testing. In the later discussions of the hypothesis, however, he makes a much stronger claim of the validity of the hypothesis: "It is supported by facts both directly and indirectly; it could be falsified, but it has not been so far."[19] Norton denies that Brian Steverson's counterexample (presented in Chapter 2 of this volume) disproves his hypothesis, since Steverson gives a hypothetical example in an imaginary world, and Norton claims that the hypothesis can only be tested in the real world or "in any world that resembles the real world in most ways relevant to policy choices." Thus, Norton writes: "I do not know if the convergence hypothesis is false in Steverson's imaginary, probably impossible, world."[20]

But Norton is all too willing to imagine future cases and scenarios that allegedly confirm the convergence hypothesis. He offers for support the broad claim that since evolutionary theory teaches that all species are akin, it would be surprising that what is basically bad for humans would not also be bad for nonhuman species. The well-being of other species thus generally converges with the well-being of humans.[21] But this is a generalization that is so broad as to be almost meaningless; it does not answer specific policy questions in specific cases and it does not show that there is an actual convergence of human and nonhuman interests in the resolution of environmental problems. Norton cites as an example the increased rate of the disappearance of amphibians around the world. Suppose, he writes, we discover the causes of this problem. Then the "convergence hypothesis predicts that, once that complex of causal processes is understood, those processes that threaten amphibians are more likely than random to eventually have negative impacts on humans."[22] Setting aside the fact that this is a very weak claim for the justification of the convergence hypothesis ("more likely than random to have negative impacts"), the point is that Norton feels no hesitation in using a hypothetical case about future facts to "prove" the validity of his thesis. Apparently, only critics of the thesis are not permitted to offer thought experiments, when these thought experiments suggest a disconfirmation of the convergence hypothesis. But I can easily think of a real-life case, in the past, that shows the divergence of human interests and nonhuman interests, with no long-range negative impacts on humans: the near extinction, in the nineteenth century, of the American bison.

The refusal to admit disconfirming cases should not come as a surprise: Remember that in *Toward Unity* Norton explicitly stated that environmentalists would reject apparent cases that showed a conflict because it could be assumed that the analyses of the cases were not sufficiently long-term.[23] Finally, in his most recent book, *Sustainability*, Norton makes a theoretical rejection of any possible disconfirmation. He examines the possible validity of the opposite of the convergence hypothesis, what he calls the divergence hypothesis, in which the interests of humanity would be in conflict with the interests of nature or nonhuman species. He notes that given any proposed action that will affect the natural environment, there may be different groups of humans that will have different beliefs concerning the effects on nature and the effects on human interests. Moreover, any action that causes harm to one set of natural entities or species may have a positive effect on a different set of natural entities or species. "So if one . . . wanted to test the idea that—on the whole—human interests are at odds with the interests of nature, one would have to first figure out some way to sum, aggregate, or characterize the 'total' good of humans and set this sum in opposition to the 'total' interests of nature."[24] This test is, of course, impossible. Thus, Norton concludes that the divergence hypothesis does not make sense, or that it could not be the "subject of a reasonable disagreement."[25]

But this argument cuts both ways. If we cannot establish either the meaning or the validity of the divergence hypothesis because it is impossible to compare the aggregate of all human and nonhuman interests, then we also cannot establish the meaning or validity of the convergence hypothesis for the same reason. How would one know that human and nonhuman interests converge unless one could view all human and nonhuman interests extending out through an indefinite future? A policy of action might appear to produce convergent interests when we analyze it now, but with more information in the future we might see that the interests are really divergent; or what seem to be divergent interests now might later be seen as convergent. Norton's theoretical argument against the divergence hypothesis actually undermines the convergence hypothesis as well.

It is actually very easy to disprove the convergence hypothesis; all we need to do is cite real-life cases where the interests of humans and nonhuman species and ecosystems diverge. Norton's defense, that no hypothetical or real-life case can provide us with all the information that we require to show a true divergence, is an argument that also serves to invalidate any hypothetical or real-life case that confirms the convergence hypothesis. But enough of these theoretical arguments; the convergence hypothesis purports to be a general empirical hypothesis testable in the real world. So let us turn to a real case of environmental policy and see how these ideas about the convergence and divergence of interests actually "cash" out.

Restoration and Convergence

Consider the policy of ecological restoration. Ecological restoration is a scientific and technological enterprise, geared to the restoration, repair, and re-creation of natural ecosystems and landscapes. At one extreme, it is the mere cleanup and mitigation of systems damaged by human interference, such as the cleaning up of the *Exxon Valdez* oil spill. At the other extreme, it is an attempt to "cover up" literally an intentional disruption of natural areas, such as the re-creation and replanting of a mountainside after strip-mining for coal. There are also various middle positions, such as the sincere attempts by environmentalists to restore endangered or extinct habitats. Steve Packard's attempt to re-create the oak savannah plains of the American Midwest would be such a middle case.[26]

In a series of essays that I have written over the last sixteen years, I have criticized the moral foundations of ecological restoration.[27] I do not repeat all of my arguments here. Suffice it to say that I believe that the restoration and re-creation of damaged natural environments is a wrong direction in environmental policy, the result of a misunderstanding of the human role in shaping and determining environmental processes. Restoration ecology is a continuation of the paradigm of human scientific and technological mastery over natural processes. The underlying technological assumption is that humans can control natural processes to better effect than nature can. This will change the essential character of environmental policy, moving it away from preservation and protection, and replacing it with manipulation and control. Developers and despoilers of nature will be able to argue that anything can be done to a natural entity or system because the despoiled entity or system can be restored later. The concept of preservation will lose all substantive content. It will be a meaningless term in a world of unlimited modification of natural processes.

How does the policy of ecological restoration serve as a test case for the convergence hypothesis? Norton's convergence hypothesis states that differing environmentalist worldviews regarding the natural environment will result in a convergence in environmental policy. But the worldviews of anthropocentrism and nonanthropocentrism do not lend themselves equally to the policy of ecological restoration. Ecological restoration is a policy of action that is derived from an anthropocentric worldview; nonanthropocentrists who value the processes and entities of nature will not advocate a policy of ecological restoration.

To see that ecological restoration is an anthropocentric environmental policy, we need to examine more closely the meaning and the motivation of the restoration process. What does it mean to "restore" a natural environment? The idea that human technology and science can restore a natural environment is a perversion of the word "restore": We cannot restore a natural environment; at best we can create a perfect substitute, but this substitute is an artifact created by human beings, not a naturally occurring entity or system.

The difference between natural entities and human artifacts is the presence of human intentionality in the artifacts. A natural system that has been modified by human actions—however benign—is a system that has within it the effects of human design. But truly authentic natural entities and systems lack any conception of design (if we are to believe in a post-Darwinian science). Once we inject our intentional designs into a natural system, we no longer have a natural system; we have a garden, perhaps, a forest plantation, or a farm. We may create a landscape that appears to be a natural wilderness because for various reasons we appreciate the look and experience of wilderness—but this wilderness is a human-made artifact that merely resembles the wilderness produced by natural processes.

Since the process of ecological restoration is actually the creation of artifactual systems, a process imbued with human intentionality, it is the logical outcome of an anthropocentric worldview. Anthropocentrism dominates the practice of restoration. Our reasons and motives for performing restoration actions derive from the satisfaction of human interests. Perhaps we want to clean up an area that has been polluted and restore it to human use, or perhaps we want to restore a forest area for the benefits produced by an increase in vegetation. Perhaps we wish to re-create a historical landscape for reasons of scientific analysis, aesthetics, or nostalgia; or perhaps we want to use the restoration process as a group activity for humans as a community to feel more in touch with nature. The point is that all of these reasons and motivations are anthropocentric in character: Ecological restoration is an environmental policy that derives from an anthropocentric worldview.

Clearly, nonanthropocentrism leads in the opposite direction. A nonanthropocentric worldview will not be inclined to develop policies of action that are focused on human interests and human benefits. Nonanthropocentrism will advocate policies that are focused on nonhuman natural values and goods. Rather than advocate the technological restoration of damaged natural systems, nonanthropocentrism will encourage policies of action that prevent the occurrence of the initial harms. Nonanthropocentrism will encourage policies of action that lead to the preservation of natural entities, species, and ecosystems. Preservationist policy, based on nonanthropocentrism, is forward-looking: It sees a natural area or species and asks what can be done in the future to preserve it. Restoration policy looks backward: It sees areas damaged by human activity and asks what can be done to make these natural entities useful again. In sum, anthropocentrism and nonanthropocentrism adopt different policies of action when considering the possibility of ecological restoration. Anthropocentrists choose restoration for the purpose of advancing human interests. Nonanthropocentrists choose the preservation of natural entities and systems and the prevention of harm. There is no convergence of policy from the different worldviews.

Supporters of Norton's convergence hypothesis may make two objections to this argument. First, one might argue that restoration of a natural system or habitat also produces good results for the natural nonhuman entities in the system. Thus, there would be nonanthropocentric benefits to a policy of ecological restoration that could lead to a convergence of policy. But this objection ignores my argument that restored systems and habitats are artifacts. The nonhuman entities that inhabit a restored ecosystem are, from an ontological point of view, no longer natural entities: They are human-produced artifacts that are the result of human design and intention. They are the creations and the result of an anthropocentric worldview.

A second objection is more practical. Given a world, such as our own, in which damaged ecosystems and habitats exist, would not a committed environmentalist with a nonanthropocentric worldview advocate for the repair, mitigation, and restoration of these damaged sites? Although this might not be the first choice of the nonanthropocentric environmentalist—who would much prefer prevention of harm and preservation of undamaged systems— the existence of damaged natural systems would create a practical necessity for some policies of restoration and repair. This practical necessity would lead to a convergence in environmental policy.

I will admit that there is some truth to this second objection. Some nonanthropocentric environmentalists may be willing to compromise their views and seek a policy of restoration as "the lesser of two evils." But more tough-minded and radical nonanthropocentrists will resist this compromise and convergence. The adoption of a policy of repair and restoration of damaged ecosystems is an acknowledgement that humanity has the license to manipulate and control the natural world. Humans will manipulate and modify the environment in whatever ways please us. The natural world will have no value except for its usefulness to human projects of control and domination. Consistent nonanthropocentrism must reject this principle because it invalidates all nonhuman natural value. Nonanthropocentrism must resist anthropocentric compromises in policy and must focus all of its energies on the protection and preservation of natural entities and systems. Thus, a consistent and radical nonanthropocentrism will never converge with an anthropocentric worldview regarding the policy of ecological restoration.

Conclusion: Pragmatism and Policy Choice

Why is the rejection of Norton's convergence hypothesis philosophically important? Let us return to Marx's challenge in the last thesis on Feuerbach, and the pragmatic response to that challenge. Does philosophy have any role in changing the world? Is philosophy useful? I suspect that most philosophers believe that philosophy is of fundamental importance in the analysis and solution of real-world problems. Followers of pragmatism go further: The solution of practical problems is the basic purpose and meaning of the philosophical enterprise. But Norton's version of environmental pragmatism—with its development of the convergence hypothesis—undermines and destroys the usefulness of philosophical ideas in the solution of real-world problems. Any philosopher with a serious commitment to pragmatism must reject the convergence hypothesis.

Recall one of the original formulations of the basic idea of the philosophy of pragmatism: the story William James tells of the squirrel and the tree in the second lecture in *Pragmatism*. James is faced with a trivial "metaphysical" puzzle. A man is trying to see a squirrel that is clinging to a tree trunk. As the man moves his position, circling the tree, the squirrel continues to move, always keeping the trunk between it and its human pursuer. As the man circles the tree with the squirrel that is also circling the tree, the question is asked: Does the man circle the squirrel or not? The answer James gives is a succinct explanation of the pragmatic method:

> The pragmatic method in such cases is to try to interpret each notion by tracing its respective practical consequences. What difference would it practically make to any if this notion rather than that notion were true? . . . Whenever a dispute is serious, we ought to be able to show some practical difference that must follow from one side or the other's being right.[28]

In short, pragmatism argues that all meaningful ideas have practical consequences. Different ideas have different practical consequences. If there were no practical difference between two sets of competing ideas, then the apparent difference between the ideas would be meaningless.

But Norton's convergence hypothesis argues for this meaninglessness. According to the convergence hypothesis, different worldviews—different philosophical ideas about the meaning and value of the human relationship to the natural world—will all lead to the same policy of action regarding the natural environment. Therefore, it makes no difference what worldview we adopt regarding the natural world and its relationship to humanity. There is no pragmatic difference among ideas regarding the value of nature. Norton's convergence hypothesis thus destroys the practical effectiveness of philosophy: The practical result of all ideas is the same. It confirms Marx's criticism that philosophy is impotent, that the philosophical enterprise cannot change the world. For this theoretical reason alone, we should reject Norton's hypothesis. Fortunately, however, we also have good pragmatic and empirical reasons for rejecting the convergence hypothesis. As I have shown here and elsewhere, there are numerous examples of the divergence of environmental policy based on differing worldviews. Continued belief in the convergence of environmentalist policies from distinct and different worldviews is a dangerous illusion that threatens both a sound environmental policy and the continued development of a philosophy that can seriously engage the world.

ANDREW LIGHT

Does a Public Environmental Philosophy Need a Convergence Hypothesis?

The convergence hypothesis, which Bryan Norton rolled out at the end of *Toward Unity among Environmentalists*, is often held as offering a core challenge to one of the received dogmas of contemporary environmental ethics, namely, that a truly "environmental" ethic would have to embrace some form of philosophical nonanthropocentrism which in turn would ground some account of the noninstrumental or intrinsic value of nature. According to this largely empirical claim, "provided anthropocentrists consider the full breadth of human values as they unfold into the indefinite future, and provided nonanthropocentrists endorse a consistent and coherent version of the view that nature has intrinsic value, all sides may be able to endorse a common policy direction."[1]

One upshot of this fairly straightforward claim was to free up environmental ethicists from towing the line of the nonanthropocentric orthodoxy that had dominated the field since the early 1970s. If a more fully fleshed out, or as he later put it, "broad" anthropocentrism could provide reasons for more morally responsible environmental policies (such as claims about our obligations to future human generations that entailed substantial environmental commitments) that converged with the policies advocated by nonanthropocentrists, then it was not necessary to always start the moral defense of such policies with nonanthropocentric claims for the noninstrumental value of nature. If true, this would mean that environmental ethicists did not need to see their views as necessarily at odds with other ethical arguments aimed at promoting other aspects of human welfare. For those of us interested in doing environmental philosophy in a way that was more likely to make an impact on public policy, this view was most welcome given the overwhelming, and not necessarily inappropriate, anthropocentrism of the policy process.

In his 2005 book, *Sustainability: A Philosophy of Adaptive Ecosystem Management*, Norton claims that the convergence hypothesis is only appropriate in a world dominated by dualistic categories of analysis, namely that human interests are necessarily at odds with the "interests" of nature, whatever those may be. If we were to follow his advice in *Sustainability*, and reject all such dualistic approaches, then "the convergence hypothesis will wither away for lack of polarized interests to be brought together."[2] Such a view seems to advise that those publicly engaged environmental ethicists who agree with Norton's approach should set a priority on working with him toward the elimination of these dualisms. In this chapter, I argue that an environmental philosophy intent at making a contribution to environmental policy (what I call a "public environmental philosophy") may need to hold on to the convergence hypothesis. I do not think this is a view that Norton will necessarily disagree with, but the discussion of the importance of the convergence hypothesis will help to highlight some interesting differences between our respective approaches to what has become known as environmental pragmatism and also provide an opportunity to extend and defend the hypothesis. I begin with a discussion of our different approaches to environmental pragmatism, summarize my own pragmatist view, and then finish with a defense of what I believe is one of the most useful tools that Norton has provided us in a career that continues to produce some of the most important insights in environmental ethics.

Two Kinds of Environmental Pragmatism

In 1992 I began developing a position in environmental ethics that I called "environmental pragmatism."[3] Though not originally inspired by Norton's work, I quickly came to see his views (and those of a few others, like Anthony Weston) as allied with the general thrust of what I saw as the core elements of the position and absolutely essential for fleshing it out. At the time, no one else was using this particular term to describe the infusion of pragmatist ideas into environmental philosophy but rather, like Norton, they were describing their views as "broadly pragmatic,"[4] or, like Weston, were describing a role for the insertion of the thought of canonical pragmatist figures, such as Dewey, in environmental ethics.[5] Seeing this variety of views, with Eric Katz, I collected and commissioned what I saw as representative examples of this emerging strain of environmental thought, if not a school, in an anthology, which I titled using my preferred term: *Environmental Pragmatism* (1996). Whatever the benefits or faults of that book, at the very least, it demonstrated that a wide variety of views could be collected under this general term and that a number of people out there were looking for an alternative to the main currents of thought that had oriented the first generation of thinkers in the field.

However, my primary motivation for investigating this general line of thought was clear enough in my own head: The point of environmental pragmatism was to try to push environmental ethicists away from the various debates in value theory in which they had arguably become stuck since the early 1970s (anthropocentrism vs. nonanthropocentrism, instrumental vs. intrinsic value, subjectivism vs. objectivism, etc.) toward a more pluralist approach that would improve their ability to contribute to the formulation of better environmental policies. To my mind—then, and today—while there are many purely theoretical philosophical questions about the environment that are interesting and well worth teaching and pursuing, if, in the end, at least some elements of the field cannot contribute to the actual resolution of environmental problems, then, at the least, the field is not fulfilling the promise that many of its founders espoused at the beginning, and, at worst, it would be a failure. To strike an analogy, if environmental ethicists had nothing to offer the policy or advocacy process, it would be like a counterfactual history of medical ethics that had nothing of use to offer medical practitioners, policy makers, or patients. Given that the realms of human health and environmental health (broadly construed) clearly contain substantial, pressing, and critical moral issues, a medical ethics or an environmental ethics without a robust capacity to engage these issues on the ground would mark some kind of intellectual or moral failure.

At first glance, however, one may worry that my goal of policy relevance for environmental ethics under the name "pragmatism" is fraught with a fundamental complication. If, as I believe, the first goal of environmental pragmatism is to coax environmental ethicists away from their intramural debates, then does it actually do any good to at least appear to be adding another "school" to the meta-ethical debates already established in the field? For, as mentioned above, in the early 1990s, there were other pragmatists in environmental ethics as well who were not describing their views as "broadly pragmatic" like Norton, but rather offered a straightforward application of established pragmatist thought to environmental problems and the ongoing debates in environmental ethics. These figures, such as Larry Hickman and Kelly Parker, were included in the 1996 volume as well. In this sense, it may have appeared that *Environmental Pragmatism* was actually creating a new side to those intramural debates over value theory (most likely of interest only to other philosophers) rather than finding a way of getting around those debates and encouraging a more policy-relevant body of literature in the field.

Such a picture is not actually far off from what has happened. Now, instead of filling the pages of journals like *Environmental Ethics* with arguments between those influenced by J. Baird Callicott, Holmes Rolston, and the like, we can, and indeed have, added to those even more pages on the same debates by Deweyans, Jamesians, and Peircians. A tempest, whether it be in a teapot or not I am unsure, has emerged between various figures explicitly endorsing or denying environmental pragmatism as a school of thought,[6] and the editor of the principal journal in the field, without warning and not clearly motivated by any particular recent argument (but citing the introduction to the 1996 anthology), even editorialized against the importance of environmental ethicists being able to communicate anything to those outside of the field.[7] On this view, the hard problem of environmental ethics was not application to actual environmental issues, but getting the theoretical foundations of natural value right.

Norton and I continue to agree that the goal of environmental pragmatists should be to come up with a more pluralistic and practical environmental ethic and in that sense agree on the core idea of what environmental pragmatists should strive to achieve. But where we have parted over the years is how explicitly pragmatist environmental pragmatism needs to be. In *Toward Unity among Environmentalists*, a book that helped to cement my ideas on the relationship that environmental ethicists ought to have with environmental advocates and hence define the mission of environmental pragmatists, Norton eschewed an explicitly pragmatist metaphysics or epistemology, claiming that his pragmatism was never to be used as a premise but only as a "constant guide."[8] In his monumental work *Sustainability*, however, he has brought together what has been emerging in his work for some time, namely, a fully fledged and historically faithful pragmatist metaphysics and epistemology, relying mainly on Dewey and Peirce. Without explicitly criticizing those of us who endorse what I have come to call "methodological environmental pragmatism," the more recent Norton distances himself from those authors in the 1996 anthology who used the term, as he puts it, "broadly to include any problem-oriented perspective on environmental theory and practice" and instead embraces an environmental pragmatism that accepts the historical pragmatists' understanding of the "nature of language and logic in relation to the world of experience."[9]

The point of this chapter is not to now dive into a protracted debate with Norton about the merits of methodological environmental pragmatism versus what I call a "historical environmental pragmatism" (by which I mean a philosophical view more faithful to the pragmatist cannon) toward the goal of staking a claim as to which variety deserves the moniker "environmental pragmatism."[10] I would expect Norton to find such a discussion as tedious as I would. But because it is important for my later defense of the convergence hypothesis, I will say a bit here about my objection to the more historical environmental pragmatism that Norton now robustly defends. While I do have some reservations about Norton's Deweyan-Peircian view, my main reasons for stopping short of going beyond a methodological environmental pragmatism are not principled but rather (1) strategic and (2) more a claim that rests upon what I take to be the proper enterprise of environmental pragmatism, and, essentially, what I hope to see as a good part of the evolution of environmental ethics.

My strategic worry is simply that the climate of academic philosophy is such that a position ground in the work of one or more historical pragmatists would be a tough sell despite the not-inconsequential revival of pragmatism among figures such as Fine, McDowell, and Putnam. Most philosophers educated in both the Anglo-American and European Continental traditions are either taught from the beginning that pragmatism is a historical relic that should be rejected,[11] have it ignored in their curricula altogether, or mistakenly view it as too closely associated with a Rortyan relativism that gets little respect in philosophy departments. The side to debates on environmental values that is being offered to environmental ethicists under the name "pragmatism" is one that can too easily be ignored. If, for example, a view rejecting claims to the intrinsic value of nature is ground in some Deweyan perspective (no matter how well explicated and defended, as is Norton's view), then cannot one reject it out of hand if one does not accept, understand, or take seriously Dewey's view on anything else?

One can respond to such a worry by arguing that this sort of concern is, as I admitted before, not a principled philosophical reason. If Norton's Deweyan and Peircian environmental pragmatism gives us the best account of how to understand a critical concept like sustainability, then too bad for those unequipped or unwilling to engage it. But there are two answers to this reply, one straightforward and another that is a bit more subtle. The straightforward reply is one that, so far, has been most eloquently and thoroughly argued by Kevin Elliott: that at least some of Norton's most important substantive positions may not need the elaborate pragmatist works that he employs in *Sustainability*.[12] The other reply gets to my second reason for preferring a methodological environmental pragmatism to a historical environmental pragmatism: that the point of a pragmatic environmental philosophy should be to encourage as many ethicists and ethically inclined environmental advocates and practitioners to be more fruitfully engaged in the advocacy process regardless of their particular metaphysical and epistemological views. To continue the analogy with medical ethics, part of the point of environmental pragmatism is to make us, as a philosophical community, more "clinical."

From the beginning, my version of environmental pragmatism explicitly argued that the point of the position was not to convince environmental ethicists that they should become pragmatists in the orthodox sense or even that they needed to go back to school to learn their Dewey and others. The idea was instead to develop an approach to doing publicly engaged environmental philosophy that could allow us to set aside our debates in ethical theory—largely concerning the description of intrinsic, noninstrumental, or inherent natural value and the moral obligations that followed from that description[13]—either because we actually believed those debates were off the mark in and of themselves or because we thought they could be given up in particular contexts when we were engaged in public endeavors. As I describe in more detail below, one of the most important things that environmental pragmatism is supposed to do is encourage philosophers to pack as many ethical tools as possible into the box that they will then use to aid in the resolution of environmental problems. Some of these tools will be derived from traditional pragmatist lines of inquiry, but surely some of them will not. My core concern then is that a more historical environmental pragmatism will thin the ranks of potential publicly engaged environmental ethicists by insisting that they embrace more traditional pragmatist views all the way down.

This view has garnered the attention of several more historically oriented pragmatists in environmental ethics who have attacked it for not being pragmatist enough to warrant the name "pragmatism." For example, Ben Minteer[14] has suggested that there must be something wrong with the use of this term to describe my views as I employ it to argue that some of Eric Katz's explicitly antipragmatist views are methodologically pragmatist.[15] In turn, it would appear that Katz has accepted this description of his views endorsing a form of methodological pragmatism himself.[16] Worse still, arch antipragmatist J. Baird Callicott has employed my terminology to describe some of his work on world religions and environmental ethics as pragmatist. His claim is that there is a pragmatist element to his attempts to articulate "how already fully formed and well-articulated older cultural beliefs," such as religious beliefs, should support the same policies that one would come to from something like Aldo Leopold's land ethic.[17]

But if my view describes how Katz and Callicott—both "foundationalist" thinkers on Minteer's view—can sometimes leave their metaphysical moorings and do environmental ethics in a pragmatic and more publicly engaged way, then I count this as proof that my methodological pragmatism is setting out to do what I think a more pragmatic environmental ethics should do, namely, allow nonpragmatists to be pragmatists when it helps to make their ethics more useful in the policy process. If our hands are tied too closely to a particular metaphysics or epistemology, which is one of the things I fear happening in a historical environmental pragmatism, then we may cut short the tools that we can use and hence, as I argue below, cut short our ability to talk to people about why nature should matter to them given their core beliefs about what matters to them in a moral sense.

All of that said, none of this means that just calling oneself a pragmatist of one sort or another makes one a pragmatist. Previously, I have criticized the antipluralist elements of Callicott's work on religion and the environment, which calls into question whether this work is really consistent with my methodological pragmatism.[18] (I do, however, find some of Callicott's more recent work to be squarely consistent with methodological pragmatism.[19]) Katz's 1999 paper, which revises his views on restoration under the name of "metaphilosophical pragmatism," is also flawed to my mind, though I do not pursue those criticisms here. The point, however, is that both are trying to generate more pragmatic implications out of their more traditional views, which I count as a very positive turn in their work.

One point of disagreement that I have with both of them, however, is their rejection of the convergence hypothesis. This shared view by both Callicott and Katz troubles me, as I find the convergence hypothesis essential for providing a warrant for opening the big toolbox of moral arguments beyond the nonanthropocentric intrinsic value claims, but in such a way that allows nonanthropocentrists to do this in a consistent and coherent manner. I turn to some of those criticisms below, but first summarize the essence of my particular version of methodological pragmatism and the role of the convergence hypothesis in it.

Methodological Environmental Pragmatism in Brief

My methodological version of environmental pragmatism is fairly straightforward. The claim is essentially that, given the practical reasons for moral pluralism in environmental ethics,[20] in particular, that many people do in fact find nature valuable for a variety of reasons given the variety of experiences and modes of appreciation that something so complex as "nature" can provide, and given the democratic context in which (at least) people in developed countries will decide what to do about our environmental challenges, then, given a view about the responsibilities of environmental ethicists (explained below), we should in certain circumstances set aside our value theory debates in environmental ethics and embrace a more public form of our philosophical practice. This practice will entail adopting a strategic anthropocentrism whereby we use more enlightened, or broad, anthropocentric arguments in order to persuade a larger array of people to embrace better environmental policies because such indirect anthropocentric justifications for environmental protection can plausibly speak to our ordinary moral intuitions more persuasively than nonanthropocentric justifications. This is not suggested as a general method for applied ethics in particular or ethics in general, but only for environmental ethics as it is directly dependent on the convergence hypothesis as an activating warrant for this methodology. When the environmental community converges on the same policy, then environmental ethicists should set aside their debates on ethical theory and translate the ends of this community to as many coherent, consistent, and adequate moral reasons to appeal to as broad a slice of the public at large as is possible. In the rest of this section, I will tease out the reasons for and implications of this approach.

While there are some disagreements on the impact of environmental ethics on larger debates on environmental policy, a fair assessment would have to accept that the literature does not yet approach the impact or relevance of other "applied" fields to their respective fields of inquiry. Again, I return to my comparison with medical ethics, which appears substantially more robust than environmental ethics. In part, this could be because there are simply more people working in medical ethics, more resources available for medical ethicists, or because of the success of medical ethicists in integrating themselves into the medical establishment. But without going into a detailed comparison of the relative impact of the two fields given resources and person power, what should give us pause is how lopsided the critical mass of philosophers is, not just working on but actively involved in debates over stem-cell research and those working on an issue like global warming. On this last issue in particular, things are changing for the better, but the ranks of philosophers working on what is arguably the most important environmental challenge humanity has ever faced are remarkably thin and the relative number of articles on this topic in journals like *Environmental Ethics* is remarkably small compared to the pages of debates over value theory.[21]

I do not have the space here to fully document or prosecute this observation. Callicott strongly disagrees with this view, citing the influence of environmental ethicists on conservation biologists and a few others.[22] Avner de-Shalit and I have responded to him, claiming in part that this impact is nonetheless relatively minor given what it could be.[23] If the worry over the relative impact thus far by environmental ethicists on advocacy and policy making is an intuitively plausible concern at all, then we may fairly ask if it matters, and if it does, if there is any way to improve this situation?

It matters to me, given something that I briefly mentioned at the start of the last section: from the beginning, the field promised more than adding to the literature on value theory. Environmental ethics is one of the fields of study that arose in the academy in the late 1960s and early 1970s as a response to the growing awareness of the severity of anthropogenic environmental problems. As such, the field did not evolve as a part of professional philosophy in a vacuum, as just another interesting area of research in ethics, metaphysics, or epistemology, but instead as a specific attempt to use the tools of philosophical analysis to both better understand and better resolve a set of specific problems facing humanity. Figures like Norton (and others represented in this volume) are fulfilling this promise in the field, but I think can fairly be seen as exceptions to the general rule. Most of us have not been like the clinical medical ethicist, developing the tools needed to actively work and communicate with our colleagues in other disciplines and on the front lines of actual cases.

If we accept that the field promises more than what it has produced so far, then the next question is whether and to whom it may be responsible for failing to deliver enough. My start on this question has been to remind environmental ethicists that in addition to being a philosophical community, we are also part of the environmental community. While this connection has never been clear, the field continues at least to be part of an ongoing conversation about environmental issues, if not an outright intentional community of environmentalists. The drive to create a more pragmatic environmental ethics is not only motivated by a desire to actively participate in the resolution of environmental problems, but also to hold up our philosophical end, as it were, among the community of environmentalists. This does not mean that we cannot be critical of specific environmentalists, environmental groups, or environmentalists as a whole. But I think it does mean that we should be prepared to bring tools to the discussion of environmental problems that can be useful for the resolution of environmental problems when we have the opportunity to do so.

While the comparison is not ideal, again, consider the counterfactual history of medical ethics where it develops without any clinical application or resources to enrich ongoing debates about medical policy. If such a field would seem to not be fulfilling its potential, who would it be letting down? If we accept the fairly simple premise that there is a moral domain to human health issues, then in one sense it would be letting all of us down. But more immediately, I think a case can be made that the field would be letting down the larger medical community. That community indicated a need for ethical analysis of health problems in medical education, practice, and policy. If trained ethicists had nothing to offer that would help with the difficult and sometimes tragic choices that exist in the medical arena, then the field would be failing in some sense.

How could environmental ethicists better serve the environmental community? The answer for the methodological pragmatist begins in recognizing that if philosophy is to serve a larger community, then it must allow the interests of the community to help to determine the philosophical problems that the theorist addresses. This does not mean that the pragmatic philosopher in my sense of this term necessarily finds all the problems that a given community is concerned with as the problems for her own work. Nor does it mean that she assumes her conclusions before analyzing a problem like a hired legal counsel who does not inquire as to the guilt or innocence of her client. It only means that a fair description of the work of the pragmatic philosopher is to investigate the problems of interest to their community (as a community of inquirers). To go back to my analogy, the medical community as a whole needs an ethical analysis of stem-cell research and we should be able to produce something that is helpful to the issues that emerge in this debate.

But if we really were to take seriously that we are not just part of a discussion but part of an advocacy process, then I think we have a further public task as environmental ethicists that may be best captured by a methodological form of pragmatism. We could serve as an intermediary between the environmental community and the larger public by helping to articulate the policy recommendations of that community on these problems to those outside of their community. But articulation of the moral reasons—for example, of why the United States needs to sign on to a comprehensive international agreement on the regulation of greenhouse gases—which everyone seems to agree upon in the more limited environmental community, to a broader public should be done in terms closer to the moral intuitions of the broader public. Why? Because the issue is so pressing and important that we cannot wait for everyone to become nonanthropocentrists, nor can we wait until the dualisms that dominate our thinking concerning the relationship between humans and nature, as Norton puts it, "wither away." One thing that philosophers are well trained at doing is figuring out how commitment to one set of reasons, or philosophical positions, entails or does not entail commitment to another set. What we could help to do as a bridge between the environmental community and the broader public is to show the broader public how an embrace of their personal values, P, ought to lead to an embrace of some green goal, G. This work requires a form of "moral translation," whereby the interests of the smaller community of environmentalists is translated into a range of appeals corresponding to the various moral intuitions that are represented in the broader public arena. We can think of this work of translation as the "public task" of a methodologically pragmatist environmental philosophy. It is necessarily a pluralist project, attempting to articulate the considered interests of the environmental community in as broad a set of moral appeals as is possible so that a broad range of personal values, P_1-P_n, can be shown to entail some common G ends.

A public and pragmatic environmental philosophy would not rest with a mere description of, or series of debates on, the value of nature. A public environmental philosophy would further question whether the nonanthropocentric description of the value of nature that dominates the philosophical work of many, and possibly most environmental ethicists today, is likely to succeed in motivating most people to change their moral attitudes about nature, taking into account the overwhelming ethical anthropocentrism of most humans (amply demonstrated by studies like that of Kempton, Boster, and Hartley,[24] which shows that most people take obligations to future human generations as the most compelling reason to protect the environment). As Norton points out repeatedly in *Sustainability*, tools that chunk out a realm of the world that has a particular kind of natural value independent of other human values may not be the best tools to offer, as they do not help us to weigh competing policy priorities.

As such, a public environmental ethics would have to either embrace a broad anthropocentrism about natural value (for example, arguing that nature has value either for aesthetic reasons or, as mentioned above, that its preservation fulfills our obligations to future human generations, or that preserving or protecting it is required given some account of human virtues) or endorse a pluralism that admitted the possibility, indeed the necessity, of sometimes using what I refer to above as "strategic anthropocentric" arguments to describe natural value in more conventional human-centered terms in order to help to achieve wider public support for a more morally responsible environmental policy.

The empirically demonstrable prevalence of anthropocentric views on environmental issues in the public at large provides the stimulus for this approach rather than an antecedent commitment to any particular theory of value, pragmatist or otherwise. So, this approach does not insist that environmental ethicists should give up their various philosophical debates over the existence of nonanthropocentric natural value, nor their position on these debates. Such work can continue as another more purely philosophical task for environmental ethicists. But ethicists following this methodology must also accept the public task that requires that they be willing to morally translate their philosophical views about the value of nature, when necessary, in terms that will more likely morally motivate policy makers and the general public even when they have come to their views about the value of nature through a nonanthropocentric approach. In other work, I have provided more detail on how such a "two-task" approach would work. Here, I only note that this strategy, asking that ethicists sometimes translate their views to a language more resonate with the public, is only warranted where convergence on the ends of environmental policy has been reached and is therefore dependent on the convergence hypothesis.[25] That is, where the preponderance of views among environmentalists of various camps, as well as among environmental ethicists themselves, has converged on the same end, then the public task of the philosopher is to articulate the arguments that would most effectively motivate nonenvironmentalists to accept that end. Empirically, for many issues, this will involve making broad anthropocentric arguments (which also have the virtue of often being less philosophically contentious). But one can imagine that in some cases nonanthropocentric claims would be more appealing as well. What appeals best is, like the convergence hypothesis itself, an empirical question. Where convergence has not been achieved, however, this public task of moral translation is not warranted. Under those circumstances, we must continue with the more traditional philosophical task of environmental ethicists, our version of an environmental "first philosophy," attempting to hammer out the most plausible and defensible moral foundations for the ethical consideration of nonhuman nature.

There are many other details to complete this approach; I trust charitable interlocutors will allow for its full defense and explication elsewhere. But, to provide just one recent example, when a coalition of British evangelicals and American scientists recently set out to convince their American evangelical counterparts to support efforts to push the Bush administration to take climate change more seriously, at least some of these figures where engaging in a kind of methodological pragmatism. First, they recognized the convergence of views on the necessity of an international convention on regulation of greenhouse gases (and, of course, the science behind those views); second, they took this convergence as a warrant for action; third, they translated the reasons for such an agreement to the language of Christian fundamentalism; and, finally, they found compelling ways to articulate those reasons to their target audience (American evangelicals). The method worked. A substantial community of American evangelicals organized an effort to lobby the Bush administration to do something about global warming and also committed themselves to changing their own consumptive practices.[26] It is not that all those involved in this campaign believe the claims, for example, that a Christian God commands us to be good stewards of the Earth and that this has implications for how we should think about the threat of global warming. It is the case, though, that these figures saw that their core task was to open up the toolbox of ethical reasons for environmental protection and translate the end of a comprehensive agreement on climate change to the moral lingua franca of an audience that they believed to be particularly important to moving the Bush administration to take this issue more seriously. The strategy proved correct. Even though the Bush administration never adopted the Kyoto Protocol, or initiated its own program of mandatory cuts, at the end, at least, it acknowledged the scientific consensus on anthropogenic global warming, and, perhaps more important, the Republican Party in general acknowledged that it cannot ignore this issue any longer, nor can it cling to wholesale climate change skepticism.[27]

Given the dependence of my version of methodological pragmatism on the convergence hypothesis, I would now like to tease out a bit more of its continuing importance for the methodological environmental pragmatist, and perhaps even the historical environmental pragmatist, defending it against some criticisms along the way.

Defending Convergence

One who shares Norton's views that we should welcome, if not aim for, a withering away of the dualisms of how we understand the relationship between humans and nature that have dominated Western thinking may not agree with my embrace of the evangelical climate initiative just mentioned. When discussing such examples, I have often heard objections that they do not offer models for a responsible environmental pragmatism (or even a responsible environmental ethic), as the participants in such exercises are only leaving in place the bad old dualisms, if not completely false views that people cling to, which will continue to cause problems for achieving long-term strong sustainability.

I do not know if Norton would share those worries, but it is a question given his apparent desire for a nondualistic world. As he puts it, a view that emphasizes "placing humans within nature," leads him to

> embrace a useful formulation developed by the deep ecologists, who insist that we are not really separate from nature; our skin is but a permeable membrane. When I consider myself to belong to a place, a community, insults to my immediate environment are insults to the broader self I embrace as a member of a community. On this view, which I think is implicit in Leopold's simile of thinking like a mountain, there will be little use for the convergence hypothesis.[28]

Norton need not be assuming here a full-blown deep ecological metaphysics about the ontology of humans (that they are really, as Arne Naess puts it, a part of nature rather than apart from nature). He could be thinking of the deep ecologists' ideas in this regard as providing a helpful metaphor. But it seems there must be something more going on here than just a metaphor, that Norton really does envisage a nondualistic world. If so, again, does the evangelical climate initiative help or hinder the coming about of this nondualistic world?

On the one hand, it seems clear that we can see these as compatible long-term and short-term projects. Even conservative estimates among the climate modelers see our window of opportunity for acting on climate change, and mitigating some of the expected consequences of rising temperatures, as rapidly shrinking. We therefore need to act now and so need to offer arguments that will resonate with the many moral languages that presently exist and that we will need to appeal to in order to generate enough public support to actually do something about this problem. Achieving a deep ecological consciousness, or a nondualistic world, is instead a millennial project. We should be able to pursue both types of projects together. If correct, then we certainly need the convergence hypothesis now, as it gives us hope for agreement in the short run on environmental policies given the divides that do exist among environmentalists, and, as this particular example shows, the divides that will persist as we successfully bring more and more diverse groups who did not previously see themselves as environmentalists into the environmental fold. Someday, some of us may hope, we can afford to have the convergence hypothesis wither away, but that day may be a long way off.

On the other hand, some will demur, we cannot pursue both strategies at the same time. Let us call one form of this objection the worry about compatibility of ends and another the worry about compatibility of consistent motivations. The first worry is that we cannot hope to pursue both strategies because the short-term approach that works within established, potentially dualistic, value sets will forestall or even block our evolution to a nondualistic world. The second worry is that there is something unsavory, if not outright immoral, about advocating a view that one thinks is false, in this case, implicitly endorsing a conservative Christian set of values that one finds untenable, if only because one has trouble with, what Gerry Cohen calls, "the God premise."

I cannot answer the compatibility of ends objection here, as it is of necessity an empirical objection. How do we know that using the convergence hypothesis now in the way that my methodological pragmatism does will block our evolution to a nondualistic world? Only time will tell, and even then, how we could assess progress would be a sticky evaluative question. But beyond this answer, I also think it is important to take heart in the original articulation of the hypothesis. If it really is the case that provided antithetical anthropocentric and nonanthropocentric "theories are formulated in their most defensible form (defensible, that is, in their own lights as independent theories), applications of the two theories would approve many, perhaps all, of the same policies,"[29] then perhaps a broad anthropocentric world (World[1]) would in the end be identical to a nonanthropocentric world (World[2]). And if that is true, perhaps both would be identical to Norton's nondualistic world (World[3]), so there is not so much to worry about after all. A world where people have different motivations to agree on the same environmental policies just puts us in the same condition of sustainability.

What I mean by the idea of World[1]–World[3] being identical is that, crudely put, they could contain the same stuff. They could have the same species richness and diversity, the same quality of resources available for future generations, the same scope of sense of place values, the same levels of integrity, ecosystem health, or whatever else one wants in a sustainable world. I say "could" in describing what we might find in these worlds rather than Norton's more forceful "would" because we, of course, cannot know what any particular policy would necessarily deliver, whatever the motivation, but only what it could aspire to deliver. The issue for me on what World^1–World^3 could contain is answered by asking the question: What sort of environmental initiative could not be justified directly or indirectly from the starting point of broad anthropocentrism, nonanthropocentrism, or nondualism? If we admit that indirect moral reasons, for example, to protect endangered species, stabilize the climate, or advance ecosystemic health, can be sufficient to ground policies promoting these ends, then the three worlds start to look, if you will, aspirationally identical to me. If we add in the temporal dimension of what we can most plausibly achieve soonest, then World^1 seems most compelling for the strategic reasons I mentioned in the last section. Essentially, if the three worlds look identical, then I do not feel that we need to worry about the road that got us there.[30]

Callicott, however, has raised a few objections to the convergence hypothesis that may weaken my response to the compatibility of ends claim. In "The Pragmatic Power and Promise of Theoretical Environmental Ethics,"[31] he seeks to defend more traditional projects in environmental ethics—the pursuit of a nonanthropocentric account of the intrinsic value of ecosystems and species—in part by taking to task what he assumes is a common goal of all environmental pragmatists: a critique of theory in environmental ethics, especially accounts of intrinsic value. In fact, oddly, given that Norton never articulates the convergence hypothesis specifically as a claim about intrinsic versus instrumental accounts of natural value, for Callicott, that is the root of the position: "Because the concept of intrinsic value in nature makes no difference to environmental practice and policy, debate about it is a waste of time and intellectual capital that could better be spent on something more efficacious."[32]

While this is not an accurate statement of the convergence hypothesis, it may reflect how many more traditionally oriented environmental ethicists unfortunately have come to take the pragmatic turn in the field: They believe that we think what they are doing is a waste of time. Such a view is unfortunate and I do not think reflects the views of any serious environmental pragmatist. Nonetheless, Callicott uses this caricature to launch some more interesting criticisms of the convergence hypothesis itself, which are flawed in the end, partially because of this misunderstanding of the hypothesis.

First, Callicott argues that the hypothesis is not credible because "it is hard to believe that all Earth's myriad species, for example, are in some way useful to human beings,"[33] and then he goes on to give examples of how there are many species that do not seem to be useful to us or to larger ecosystems so they must not be something that anthropocentrists could ever mount a case for protecting, but which would be well worth protecting if one accepted a claim that, I suppose, all of nature has direct intrinsic value that generated moral obligations to protect it.

The first answer to this objection is one that Norton has raised repeatedly but that never seems to stick on the minds of those who read it. The convergence hypothesis is an empirical hypothesis and so, certainly, there may be instances of divergence. Second, as I suggest above, the issue is whether one *can* make a claim that a given species could be protected through a broadly anthropocentric value set rather than if anyone in particular has yet made that claim or made it on the basis of utility. Here too we can clearly see Callicott's error in assuming that the hypothesis turns on the intrinsic-instrumental distinction rather than the anthropocentric-nonanthropocentric distinction.[34] For example, one could also bring in broadly virtue-based arguments for why destroying a species is something that we should not do, which may have nothing to do with relative instrumental utility. To do so, for example, may be an instance of hubris, or, if stewardship is a virtue, an abrogation of that understanding of human flourishing. Whatever difficulties we would have mounting such a case, they would not seem to be any more or less difficult than mounting the nonanthropocentric alternative.

Next, Callicott argues that if we look at the "formalities" or "structural features" rather than "contents" of anthropocentric-based versus nonanthropocentric environmental policies, then we are likely to see divergence rather than convergence.[35] The gist of the argument (which is a reprise of similar comments that Callicott made in his aforementioned 1995 piece) is that the importance of arguments for intrinsic value is that they will shift the burden of proof away from those who wish to preserve or protect nature onto those who wish to develop or destroy it. Intrinsic value claims will in this sense be like rights claims and work as moral trumps protecting repositories of natural value.

I have two responses here in addition to those I have previously made.[36] First, if we are really talking about environmental policies in general, such as the Clean Air Act, the Clean Water Act, or any other of the more than twenty pieces of environmental legislation passed in the United States from the late 1960s to 1980, then we should not assume that they were based (or in the case of future hoped-for legislation on issues like climate change, would be based) on any single set of narrowly defined values that we could label as anthropocentric or nonanthropocentric or allocating intrinsic or instrumental value to nature. There are no general structural features to anthropocentric- or nonanthropocentric-inspired policies because most environmental policies (especially if one closely investigates the legislative record) are based in a myriad of intuitions that would fall into one, both, or neither of these camps.

To imagine that there are policies that are based on one narrow set of values is to imagine policies that rarely exist in a democracy. Given that pragmatists are by and large concerned with the application of environmental ethics to democratic environmental policy making, then we would assume that values undergirding any policy would and should be plural.

Second, if there were something more morally straightforward than an omnibus bill, such as some kind of environmental bill of rights based in a recognition of the intrinsic value of nature, there would be no reason to believe that it would be more sound, effective, trumping, or workable than a comparative set of rights to humans to have sustainable environments or granting some rights to future generations of humans that could have environmental implications. Either alternative could do what Callicott wants: shift the burden of proof away from destruction of nature to protection of it. In fact, such an avenue may be more likely given the simple fact that it is actually happening now. Dozens of countries currently have laws granting rights to a safe, healthy, or sustainable environment to their populations,[37] and it is now only a matter of time before we begin to see the implications of these laws. If Callicott were to reply by claiming that rights to nature would be different in kind to environmental rights to humans because they would grant rights to things other than humans that could trump human rights, then I would point out that rights often do conflict. Whoever we grant environmental rights to—humans or natural entities themselves based on intrinsic-value claims—they will be in conflict with other rights, and the resolution of such conflicts will be based on a myriad of historical and legal issues, not on the fact that rights have been granted to something other than humans.

Let us now turn to the second general worry concerning my application of the convergence hypothesis, the problem of compatibility of consistent motivations. My methodological environmental pragmatism is quite clear on this issue. Other easily defensible moral prohibitions against lying and deceiving should be sufficient in most cases to take care of the worry that there may be something unsavory or immoral about articulating the implications of moral frameworks with which one does not agree.

As I have put it elsewhere,[38] I cannot walk up to a Christian evangelical gathering and say something like, "Jesus sent me here today to talk to you about climate change and your responsibilities to him to preserve and protect this precious world that he has given you" because it would simply be a form of deception that is independently objectionable. I find nothing wrong, however, with pointing out the compelling argument for stewardship in a book that this community takes very seriously and with helping them to see how some values and duties that they derive from that book strongly entail taking seriously this particular problem and how the responsibilities they find sufficient to motivate them to action provide reasons to do something about this problem. I can imagine, however, that some more adamant atheists, say Richard Dawkins or Sam Harris, would still find participation in such an activity objectionable. But I would find such views as compelling as the objections of the strong moral monist who claimed that there was one and only one true moral foundation for why nature has value that should be respected in a moral sense and that any argument to protect nature for any other moral reason must be actively rejected. I have independent reasons to disagree with such positions and nothing in my methodological pragmatism would insist that moral monists adopt this position. The pragmatist must be a pluralist.

One could also raise a similar objection that methodological pragmatism would appear to endorse the development of any argument for a given converged-upon policy—even, say, an ecofascist argument just to make sure that the fascists are green, too. But just as we have independent moral reasons to condemn lying and deceiving (which I think overcome objections that have been raised to this view that it is "merely" rhetorical), we have independent moral reasons to reject fascism, racism, and other contemptible views. Those reasons are sufficient to reject working with such communities or making those arguments.[39]

Hopefully, by now we may see an ultimate compatibility between my methodological environmental pragmatism and Norton's version of historical environmental pragmatism. Norton (or Nortonians) embrace the same pluralism and, for example, appreciate the talents of someone like Aldo Leopold, who was able to appeal to a large array of audiences by using a large array of reasons toward common ends. Norton's pluralism may be more principled than mine, but it gets us in the same place and therefore should, as Elliott puts it, be able to move forward as more a political than metaphysical thesis, ultimately proving it compatible with methodological pragmatism.[40] When it comes to the convergence hypothesis, when we take seriously the immediate problems with the world we now live in, the necessity (even moral propriety) for building a broad consensus on these problems, and the possible responsible role that environmental ethicists can take in it, then we can readily see that it is a hypothesis we cannot live without and should, as I have tried to do, make use of in a more robust way. Those holding steady to Norton's historical environmental pragmatism should be able to use this methodology to good ends until, and if, we ever reach that nondualistic world.

If part of the motivation for methodological pragmatism is our connection to the environmental community, we should remember that the origins of the convergence hypothesis are also in that community and were not, as is often forgotten today, a hypothesis invented by Norton. In *Toward Unity*, the convergence hypothesis is introduced by Norton as something that is taken as an "article of faith" by the environmental community (which he apparently deduced from interviewing leaders of that community while in Washington,

D.C., on leave writing the book) rather than something that he had come up with himself: "Although they are fascinated with the disagreement raging over the center, or centers, of environmental values, *active environmentalists have made* their peace over this issue by accepting an empirical hypothesis—the convergence hypothesis. *Environmentalists believe* that policies serving the interests of the human species as a whole, in the long run, will serve also the 'interests" of nature, and vice versa."[41]

If the convergence hypothesis did emanate from the environmental community itself, then, consistent with the arguments I have made here, we can fairly ask what that community expects should follow in general from this hypothesis and what we can do in particular in response to it. The environmental community may not care about the metaphysical or epistemological foundations of our views, pragmatist or otherwise, despite their inherent value. While continuing to articulate and flesh out those views, I hope that my methodological environmental pragmatism, or whatever we wind up calling it, offers another public role for environmental philosophy given the faith that environmental advocates place in that hypothesis and, I hope, that they will eventually place in us.

13

DONALD A. BROWN

The Importance of Creating an Applied Environmental Ethics

Lessons Learned from Climate Change

Introduction

Over the last thirty years, environmental ethics literature has been growing rapidly.

Yet, for the most part, environmental ethics has failed to influence environmental policy making. In fact, in 2003 Eugene Hargrove, the editor and founder of the journal *Environmental Ethics*, acknowledged this failure of environmental ethics to penetrate public policy making in an editorial in the same journal.[1]

In the experience of one who has been monitoring the environmental ethics literature from deep inside the policy world, Hargrove's claim that environmental ethics is rarely considered by policy makers is right on the mark. Environmental ethics literature is almost never read by policy makers and infrequently considered in day-to-day decision making about pressing environmental issues.[2] Yet, the need for ethically based environmental decisions is as acute as ever since humans continue to gravely threaten human health and the environment. In fact, a strong case can be made that global trends in regard to climate change, loss of biodiversity, and water resources are particularly ominous. For this reason, the failure of the environmental ethics literature to penetrate environmental policy making is worthy of serious reflection.

In this chapter, I examine the causes for this failure of environmental ethics to penetrate public policy and look at some of the mistaken assumptions that have informed much of the current environmental ethics literature that has led to its avoidance in solving pressing environmental problems. After this, I consider the role that environmental ethical analysis could play in the implementation of environmental policy, explaining why the failure of ethical analyses of specific environmental problems appears to be more vital than ever to improving environmental decision making. Next, I take up issues initially raised by Bryan Norton's work on the potential convergence of ethical conclusions about specific environmental problems despite differences in ethical theories. Finally, I look at these issues from the standpoint of climate change.

Causes of Failure of Environmental Ethics to Penetrate Environmental Policy

There are two reasons why environmental ethics has not penetrated environmental policy formation. The first is that scientific, economic, and legal (and not ethical) discourses are the exclusive languages spoken in the temples of environmental policy making. Each of these technical languages rests on a set of unexamined norms that pretend to be ethically neutral but hide numerous ethical controversies.

For instance, scientific journals usually require high levels of proof before drawing conclusions about human causes of adverse effects to health and the environment. Yet, as we shall see, understanding specific environmental impacts of human actions with high levels of scientific certainty is often beyond our scientific ability. For this reason, environmental decisions must often be made in the face of pervasive scientific uncertainty. Yet, decision making in the face of uncertainty always raises ethical questions, including: a) Who should have the burden of proof given the nature of potential impacts? b) What quantity of proof should satisfy this burden? c) What assumptions should be made about potential but uncertain impacts? d) Do potential victims of climate impacts have rights to be protected from risks created by human activities that have uncertain impacts? These normative questions, however, are rarely expressly considered in day-to-day decision making despite the frequent need to make environmental decisions in the face of uncertainty.

Scientists and policy makers seldom spot the ethical questions raised by the application of science to public policy. For political reasons, most policy makers are taught to categorize potential environmental problems into two classes: (a) projects that will harm the environment, and (b) those that are safe. Framing problems into only two categories leaves out a large percentage of potential projects that could have adverse impacts on human health and the environment, or could, in combination with other not-tested factors, cause environmental harm.

Because the scientific literature is also usually based only on two frames, that is, (1) identify causes of environmental harm when certain statistical tests are satisfied or (2) conclude that there is no scientific basis to assert that harm will be caused, the issues of who should have the burden of proof and what quantity of proof should satisfy that burden is not considered in the scientific literature.

Sometimes scientists create a two-frame analysis of a problem where the questions looked at are reduced to whether a proposed site for disposal of waste is "suitable" or "unsuitable."[3] What makes such a limited framing particularly problematic from an environmental ethics perspective is the propensity of decision makers to assume that if a site or project is not proven to be "unsuitable," applying the logical fallacy of "appeal to ignorance," a proposed site must be "suitable."[4] That is, the absence of proof of harm is often treated by both policy makers and scientists as the basis for concluding that no harm will result.

Uncertainty is a very frequent attribute of problems faced by environmental decision makers both because of theoretical and practical reasons.

Theoretical uncertainty in environmental decision making is frequently encountered for a variety of reasons including the lack of clear understanding of how complex ecological systems work and the resulting inability to predict with confidence the impacts of human activities on ecological systems. In fact, complex systems are known to contain thresholds that if exceeded could result in rapid nonlinear changes in these systems. Knowing where these thresholds exist may be key to describing the response of ecological systems, yet these thresholds are often poorly understood.

These uncertainties are the basis for lack of confidence in environmental models that are often used to predict future states of ecological systems that are stressed by human activities. A recent book entitled *Useless Arithmetic: Why Environmental Scientists Can't Predict the Future* identifies some of the many limits in models used to predict various projects' impacts on human health and the environment.[5]

To deal with these uncertainties, environmental scientists sometimes try to put upper and lower bounds on likely impacts, but these bounds must often rely upon the assessor's subjectively derived probabilities when there is no empirical basis for determining the probability of different outcomes. But subjective probabilities are sometimes nothing more than the semieducated guesses of the assessors. As a result, many environmental predictions have turned out to be wrong.

Another common problem that environmental decision makers must frequently face is what to do about potential effects of environmental exposures on human health. Yet, these connections are often not well understood particularly in regard to cumulative and synergistic risks created by exposures to multiple hazardous substances. Uncertainty about connections between human health and environmental stressors is common because epidemiological tools usually relied upon to understand the causes of human disease are often unhelpful in environmental controversies because many diseases caused by environmental exposures are believed to be multicausal. Yet, epidemiological methods for determining causation depend upon being able to isolate individual potential causes to develop hypotheses that can be tested.

It is now known that many different types of stressors can impair the functioning of the immune systems that can make people more vulnerable to other environmental exposures.[6] Because of the ability of many stressors to interact to cause disease, epidemiological tools are often unhelpful for sorting out the environmental causes of diseases. Yet, the political culture puts pressure on government regulators not to act until they have high levels of confidence about causes of harm.

For some environmental problems, the causes of scientific uncertainty are not theoretical limitations but practical realities. That is, because of limits of time and money, collecting the data to understand impacts of human activities on human health and the environment is not an option for decision makers, even in cases where there are no theoretical problems. For instance, relatively theoretically unproblematic problems such as determining the direction of groundwater flow often force a policy maker to make a decision in the face of uncertainty because of prohibitive costs of gathering sufficient data needed to determine groundwater flows with high levels of scientific confidence.[7] That is, as it costs more than $10,000 to drill a well that identifies the stratagraphic setting of a project, a step necessary to determine groundwater flow direction, and since many wells may be necessary to reach high levels of confidence about a site's geology in places where the geology is varied, decision makers are often forced to limit the number of wells to that which is economically reasonable. For these and other reasons, decision makers are often plagued by questions about how much data are enough given high costs of requiring additional data. Because data are not practically available, environmental decision makers must frequently make decisions in the face of uncertainty.

Environmental decision makers are also frequently plagued by time constraints. Although it may be theoretically possible to perform a long-term study on which to make a decision, to wait too long may doom projects in which investors need quicker answers. For instance, to have confidence in groundwater background conditions, several years of seasonable varying data may be necessary, yet waiting several years to make a decision on a proposed project is often deemed to be politically unacceptable. In case after case, decision makers tell potential project managers to give them as much data as they can in a time frame that is reasonable. Yet, these shortcuts frequently guarantee that a decision will need to be made in the face of uncertainty.

For these reasons, the dirty little secret in environmental decision making is that decisions must be made under conditions of pervasive scientific uncertainty. Yet, as we have seen, decision making in the face of uncertainty raises several different types of unacknowledged ethical questions. Yet, these ethical issues are usually hidden from the public and rarely exposed to ethical scrutiny.

The ethical questions raised by scientific uncertainty for the most part remain unexamined and decision makers usually make decisions that are poorly guided by ethical considerations. In such cases, the ethical problem is not differences between whether the decision should protect human interests or ecological concerns because most projects will hurt both interests if they are injurious. For instance, if groundwater gets contaminated by hazardous substances, both adverse human health and ecological impacts can be foreseen, and the decision maker is usually required by law to deny a proposed project if any adverse impacts are determined. The most pressing ethical problem is not whether humans or the environment will be harmed, but who should have the burden of proof in cases where there is great pressure on the decision maker to authorize a project unless he or she can prove that harm will be caused.

In addition, where prescriptive questions are acknowledged by environmental decision makers, those empowered to make decisions often rely upon traditional cost-benefit analyses or other economic balancing tests. That is, when values issues arise about the impact of human actions on human health and the environment, policy makers assume that they should be guided by traditional economic analyses of policy options. Yet, standard economic analyses raise a host of ethical questions, including whether:

a. rights to human health and security should be jeopardized by a proposed action that could be justified on narrow utilitarian grounds;
b. issues of distributive justice should be considered when harms and benefits are very disaggregated;
c. future generations' rights may be harmed because of discounting methods employed in standard cost-benefit analyses that greatly diminish the value of benefits that are experienced in the future; and
d. all values should be reduced to monetary terms measured in markets.

Policy makers are taught to use scientific tools to determine the environmental impacts of human activities, economic tools to determine and balance competing values, and the law to look for relevant prescriptions where they exist to guide decision making. Ethics simply never comes up in day-to-day environmental decision making. The only priests allowed into the temple of environmental decision making are scientists, engineers, economists, and lawyers. Each of these disciplines is based upon norms that may be ethically problematic in some environmental controversies.

Environmental ethics literature occasionally has acknowledged problems with this narrow instrumental rationality employed in decision making, yet even this literature is rarely tied to specific environmental controversies. But because certain value-neutral policy languages structure specific environmental controversies, most environmental ethics literature is much too abstract to play a role in environmental decision making. For these reasons, a first-order problem for environmental ethics is not deciding the appropriate meta-ethical guidance; it is rather to get ethics considered at all in policy making.

The second reason why environmental ethics literature has not been influential in policy making stems from its preoccupation with abstract ethical questions. A large percentage of the environmental ethics literature has focused on meta-ethical issues and an attempt to ground environmental ethics in new biocentric, ecocentric, feminist, virtue, or other ethical theories. Even when environmental ethics papers turn to specific controversies such as protection of biodiversity, they rarely focus on the specific scientific, economic, or legal issues that are in contention and that will likely determine actual public policy outcomes. Therefore, the environmental ethics literature rarely has engaged with the issues in play in environmental controversies.

In fact, a strong case can be made that the field of environmental ethics that bloomed in the late 1970s was based, at least in part, on a misdiagnosis of the causes of ethical failure. In the beginning, the environmental ethics literature often assumed that the narrow anthropocentric ethical footing that underlay twentieth-century and Western culture caused the emerging environmental crisis. As a result, this literature has largely consisted of philosophers talking to each other about how to reform, replace, or extend dominant anthropocentric ethical norms. Yet, what is most needed from ethical analysis of environmental problems is not a new agreement on the ultimate grounding of an environmental ethic, but help in dislodging a certain type of instrumental rationality that prevents any serious ethical reflection on the potential impacts of human behavior on human health and the environment.

The Need for an Applied
Environmental Ethics

From inside the environmental policy temple, the primary cause of ethical failure does not appear to be meta-ethical inadequacy, but the failure to examine the hidden ethical assumptions of scientific, economic, and legal arguments.

The fact that meta-ethical failure is not the cause of the existing environmental crisis becomes apparent when one examines specific environmental controversies through an ethical lens. As we shall see from the example of climate change, when one looks at the ethical dimensions of controversial concrete environmental decision making, one often finds that even anthropocentric ethical theories do not support many decisions. That is, more often than not, environmentally harmful decisions fail to pass anthropocentrically based ethical analyses once decision making is scrutinized by express ethical reflection.

For this reason, if environmental ethics is to be relevant to public policy, it must demand an opportunity in policy making for ethical reflection upon the scientific, economic, and legal discourses in which environmental problems are defined and responded to. To do this, environmental ethicists must understand the scientific, economic, and legal issues entailed by specific environmental controversies. Therefore, rather than teaching policy makers about environmental ethics, environmental ethicists must become competent communicators in scientific, economic, and legal discourses in which environmental problems are defined and decided. If they wish to be relevant, environmental ethicists need to follow and examine the specific scientific, economic, and legal justifications for environmental decisions. If they do so, ethicists can make enormous contributions to environmental policy by uncovering the hidden ethical assumptions embedded in the scientifically and economically based prescriptions.

For all these reasons, we need an environmental ethics literature that is much more applied to particular controversies and to how they are debated in civil society than it has been so far. An applied environmental ethics would be sensitive to the factual context in which any environmental controversy arises and the arguments that are made for or against taking protective action in regard to these controversies. In particular, the world needs an environmental ethics literature that pays attention to specific economic and scientific justifications for or against particular projects that could cause environmental harm and then analyzes these justifications through an ethical lens.

A Convergence among Environmentalists?

If an applied environmental ethics focuses on justifications for specific environmental problems rather than on meta-ethical issues, one can ask: Does this mean there is never any need for express reflection on different ethical approaches to solve environmental problems?

Bryan Norton, in *Toward Unity among Environmentalists*, argued that despite philosophical differences among environmentalists there is no reason why common policy goals cannot be achieved in environmental decision making.[8] Norton's thesis predicted that biocentric, ecocentric, and human-based philosophical positions actually converge when environmental decision makers make decisions in real cases. If Norton is right, there is hardly any need to spend much time on meta-ethical disputes, a preoccupation of the majority of the environmental ethics literature.

As we have seen above, the first-order problem for environmental ethics is to open up policy languages to express ethical reflection. This conclusion, by itself, however, does not guarantee that there are never any potential disputes among different ethical premises worthy of reflection once the policy languages are open to express ethical analysis. The conclusion about the need to start with the actual disputes does, however, agree with part of the pragmatists' agenda that advises that ethical analyses should not begin with a particular ethical theory but instead start with a definition of the problem under consideration.

Norton's thesis has been very controversial and has been attacked particularly by some biocentric and ecocentric theorists who have argued that anthropocentric theories are not sufficient to protect biodiversity and ecological integrity.

Some have pointed out that Norton's thesis and its opposition have too infrequently been tested by empirical analysis (e.g., see Chapter 5 in this volume). Until there is exhaustive testing of the Norton hypothesis, it may be difficult to draw final conclusions about whether the Norton hypothesis is right all of the time, most of the time, or rarely. If opening up policy making to express ethical reflection is needed initially to reform environmental policy making, one could be critical of the environmental ethics literature and its meta-ethical focus without necessarily agreeing that there will always be a convergence on values among environmentalists on all issues once ethical reflection is initiated.

Climate change policy making proves to be an interesting empirical test of both Norton's theory and the idea that a first-order problem is to open up policy justifications to express ethical reflection as previously argued in this chapter.

Lessons Learned from Climate Change

The following are conclusions relevant to this chapter drawn from the "White Paper on the Ethical Dimensions of Climate Change,"[9] a product of the Collaborative Program on the Ethical Dimensions of Climate Change (EDCC). The EDCC was created because:

- Human-induced climate change raises many profound ethical questions, yet these ethical issues have not been addressed adequately in climate change policy debates and discussions.

- Given that those most responsible for climate change are not the same people as those most vulnerable to adverse climate change impacts, an equitable approach to climate change may be practically necessary to achieve a globally acceptable climate change solution.
- Climate change policy options are often discussed exclusively in the languages of science and economics that frequently hide or ignore important ethical questions.
- An ethical analysis of climate change policy options must be mindful of the scientific, economic, and social contexts that frame the ethical inquiry.

This program began by working with environmental scientists, economists, and policy makers in 2005 and by following issues in contention in actual climate change negotiations. The program then identified the most important ethical issues raised by the current state of the international debate on climate change. These issues had to be teased out of the scientific and economic justifications for or against taking action on climate change. They included the following high-priority issues that need to be faced to move the climate change agenda forward:

- Who should have responsibility for damages caused by climate change?
- What ethical principles should guide the selection of an atmospheric greenhouse gas (GHG) target?
- What ethical principles should guide allocation of GHG emissions limitations among nations to assure that the atmospheric target will be achieved?
- What does ethics have to say about the use of scientific uncertainty as justification for nonaction on climate change?
- What does ethics have to say about the use of cost arguments as justification for nonaction on climate change?
- What do ethics have to say about the need of nations to act to reduce GHG emissions despite the fact that other nations have not acted?
- What do ethics have to say about justifications for nonaction on climate change on the basis that new, less-costly technologies will be invented in the future?
- What elements of procedural justice should be followed to assure that victims of climate change can adequately participate in global climate change decisions?

Because ethical analysis must be sensitive to the factual context that sets the context for environmental issues, the "White Paper" began discussion of each of these issues by describing the scientific, economic, and legal background and premises of these issues.[10] It then did an ethical analysis of each of these issues that included identification of which conclusions could be based on an overlapping ethical consensus despite different ethical starting points. The authors were surprised to see that many ethical conclusions could be stated with relatively high levels of confidence and could be based upon overlapping ethical consensus positions, thus confirming the Norton hypothesis. For instance, no matter what meta-ethical approach was the initial starting point, the "White Paper" concluded that:

- All nations need to reduce their GHG emissions to their fair share of safe global emissions as soon as possible, unless the victims of climate change consented to be put at risk to higher levels.
- Atmospheric targets for GHGs must be set at the lowest level possible, unless victims of climate change consented to higher levels.
- The argument that a nation need not reduce its GHG emissions because of scientific uncertainty about consequences of timing and magnitude does not withstand minimum ethical scrutiny.
- If nations justify their refusal to take action to reduce GHG emissions on the basis of cost to them alone, their position is ethically unsupportable because no person or nation has a right either to harm others as a means to achieve their economic health or to endanger others' lives, health, or security.
- The use of cost as a basis for determining the limits of national responsibility to reduce GHG emissions (to be distinguished from the use of cost to determine the least-costly methods to achieve a specific goal) is ethically problematic because responsibility for reducing emissions should be derived from rights theories and principles of distributive justice, not on cost to the polluter.
- A nation's use of cost-benefit analysis (CBA) as a prescriptive justification for its unwillingness to reduce GHG emission to levels consistent with just allocations is ethically problematic.
- Since principles of justice would give all people equal rights to use the atmosphere in absence of morally relevant criteria that would entitle people to different levels of use, those who advocate that use of cost as a basis for determining responsibility for GHG reductions bear the burden of identifying morally relevant criteria that justify the use of cost of reductions as a basis for determining responsibility.
- CBAs that aggregate costs and benefits in analyses of climate change policies fail to satisfy principles of justice that require a just

sharing of harms and benefits among people who will be affected by climate change policy.

- Although some developing nations can make a presentable ethical argument that they could increase GHG emissions without exceeding their just share of global emissions, some of the developed nations cannot make this argument because they have already exceeded their just share of global emissions that are needed to stabilize atmospheric concentrations at safe levels.

- The duty to cease activities that harm others is not diminished if others who are contributing to the harm fail to cease their own harmful behavior. This is so because no nation or person has a right to continue destructive behavior on the basis that others who are contributing to the damage have not ceased their destructive behavior.

- Given basic human rights to life, health, and security, those who might be harmed by climate change policy options have a right to free, informed consent to being exposed to climate change risks. In order to give free, informed consent about climate change policy options, persons must:

  a. not be forced to consent,
  b. be in possession of all relevant information, and
  c. understand policy options.

Although many issues looked at in the "White Paper" were found to be resolvable on the basis of ethical consensus, not all issues could be resolved by appealing to an overlapping ethical agreement. For instance, the following issues were identified as not resolvable on the basis of a consensus ethical position, at least at the early stages of the program's ethical analyses:

- How to allocate each nation's just share of safe global emissions other than the conclusion that the allocation must be made on ethically relevant criteria.

- If nation states have responsibility to reduce GHG emissions, what can be said about the ethical responsibility of other units of government, organizations, and individuals or other nonstate actors within those nations states?

- What ethical principles should be followed for determining liability within nations given disparities among those who have benefited from past GHG emissions and those who have not, and differences

of historical emissions levels among government subdivisions, organizations, and individuals?

- Given that scientific confidence about adverse impacts from climate
  change has increased over time, when did the science of climate
  change become certain enough to create duties to act?
- To what extent is ability to pay for GHG reductions relevant criteria
  for establishing responsibility for GHG emissions?
- What ethical principles should be followed to assure that the interests of future generations are adequately represented in climate
  change negotiations?

Conclusion

From this analysis of pressing climate change issues, the following can be
concluded:

The Norton thesis is more frequently right than wrong on most high-
priority climate change issues, but not always so. However, at least in the case
of climate change, when there are ethical conflicts about how to resolve particular issues, they are not caused by differences between anthropocentric
and nonanthropocentric considerations. The conflicts come from differences
in various anthropocentric theories including, but not limited to, differences
between rights-based and consequences-based ethical considerations and
competing approaches to distributive and procedural justice.

However, it must be admitted that not all environmental problems may
be as easily resolvable on the basis of overlapping ethical consensus as climate change seems to be. Ethical conclusions on climate change policies do
not create conflicts among those who support anthropocentric and nonanthropocentric ethical premises largely because climate change is already killing people, with the result that what is needed to protect humans from harm
is often the same as what is needed to protect plants, animals, and ecosystems. In the formulation of climate change policies, little turns on distinctions between anthropocentric and nonanthropocentric ethical premises.
When it comes, however, to protection of biodiversity, anthropocentric-based
prescriptions may differ from nonanthropocentric obligations. However, even
in the case of protection of biodiversity, one often can ground the need for
protection on human interests as well as ecocentric and biocentric ethical
considerations.

The most important lesson from climate change, however, is that environmental ethics needs to look at concrete justifications for or against environmental protection as a starting point before doing any ethical analysis.
This is a first-order problem for environmental ethics that can only be solved
by close attention to actual issues in contention.

In the case of climate change, as well as other environmental problems, an applied environmental ethics is needed that follows scientific and economic justifications for action or nonaction on potential environmental problems. Only then will environmental ethics play its appropriate role in helping guide policy and environmental decision making.

14

Who Is Converging with Whom?

An Open Letter to Professor Bryan Norton
from a Policy Wonk

Dear Bryan:

Well, now you see what comes from mixing philosophy with the real world. You try to make a sensible case about how humans and nonhumans can just get along, and now a number of your fellow thinkers are very unhappy with you. No harm done, I suppose; after all, this is just academic business as usual, nothing that the rest of us should worry about. Nevertheless, I do think you've put your finger on a real problem here. The question is: are you ready to go the distance?

Let me first make sure I understand this whole convergence idea. What you're saying, basically, is that what's good for nature is probably good for us humans, too, so sensible folks will eventually come to recognize that we're all in the same boat, or maybe ark. Is that sort of it? I guess I need to stifle for a moment the "duh" that involuntarily arises from within me, since obviously some very smart professors think your hypothesis is claptrap. But are those professors interested in hardscrabble reality, as you claim to be? After all, they identify themselves as nonanthropocentrists, which sort of seems to me like saying they aren't people, since how would a person really take on a nonperson perspective unless he or she was a nonperson? I mean, why would we think that a person's nonperson perspective would be the same as a nonperson's actual perspective? No reason that I can see, though no doubt I'm missing something here. And anyway, policy and politics—which lie at the heart of your convergence idea—are realms of people; this seems sort of definitional, so how you could take a nonpeople perspective on something that's in the realm of people beats the daylights out of me.

Oh, and let me be clear. I like critters. From the worms that keep my garden soil happy (let's forget about the aphids that terrorize my tomatoes) to the nighthawks and bats darting in the moonlight above my tent when I am out in the wilderness, I think they're all great. And when the last tiger goes, it will be a sad day for us anthropocentrists, but I doubt the butterflies will much care. Anyway, just want to get my bona fides on the table here.

So it turns out that these nonanthropocentrists (would misanthropes be a better name?) actually don't want to converge with you. This suggests to me that there's either a problem with your hypothesis or a problem with the philosophers who are mad at you. You are interested in what actually happens in the world, but the nonanthropocentrists are committed to a posture of philosophical purity. You talk about contextualization, but philosophical purity demands an absence of context. You talk about pragmatism, but the whole point of reasoning from alleged first principles, as nonanthropocentrists must do, is to avoid compromise with the other. You are concerned with uncertainty, but nonanthropocentrism can only exist if founded on fundamentalist certainty. I particularly love this word "intuition" that the nonanthropocentrists use to describe the origins of their beliefs. Invoking "intuition" seems like a way to ground the beliefs simultaneously in something like rationality (intuitions come from the brain, after all) and something like religion (but, like faith, they are not subject to probing or falsification through rational inquiry or even philosophy). In any case, unless I totally misunderstand what's going on here, for the nonanthropocentrists to acknowledge convergence would be for them to accept that their position is not metaphysical but normative, in which case, what would they have to philosophize about?

This simultaneous appeal to rationality and faith is the funny thing about nonanthropocentrism. It must be scientifically true, right, if it's to make any sense? I mean, if it turned out that we could kill off thousands and thousands of species without any additional adverse affects on people, then nonanthropocentrism wouldn't be anything more than a statement about the intrinsic yet arbitrary value of critters. Yet it's not like scientists really have much of an understanding about how the health of particular species influences the health of whole ecosystems, or about how the health of particular ecosystems influences the vitality of human society, or, maybe most important, how efforts of humans to manage ecosystems and species actually do what they set out to do. The ugly reality is, of course, that we do kill thousands and thousands of species, and somehow manage to keep soldiering along. So you also need some pretty powerful faith to back up the apparent rationality—not just faith that science will untangle all this eventually (but that is necessary), but also faith in the intrinsic value of every species. Talk about odd bedfellows.

Wait a minute . . . something is making me uncomfortable here. As bizarre as these nonanthropocentrists are, they do seem to have something that you don't. Empiricism, pragmatism, and contextualism are fine, but what's at the heart of it all? Politics may be the art of the possible, but it's also the pursuit of the desirable. Your anthropocentrism, weak as it is, seems, oddly enough, a bit soulless. What if it turns out that what's good for people isn't necessarily good for other species? That is to say, what if humans can continue willy-nilly to pursue their interests with scant attention to environmental consequences beyond those that cause discernible diminution of human living conditions? This is not implausible; in fact, the last couple hundred years of history seem to endorse this possibility rather robustly. The idea that six billion folks could inhabit this poor planet at a rather higher overall standard of living than was possible for the one billion living in the mid-nineteenth century would, at that time, have quite reasonably seemed absurd. Proclamations that we have already exceeded the planet's carrying capacity notwithstanding, convergence seems itself to depend on the belief that we cannot keep going as we are going now. And it's true, we cannot; just as it is true that the Earth could not have sustained six billion humans using the technological infrastructure of 1850. The worrisome possibility for me is not so much that our current environmental depredations are unsustainable, but quite the contrary—that we will continue to worm our way out of them because of our incredible technological creativity.

And here's another thing that bugs me: You emphasize that your position is in fact a hypothesis, and thus empirically testable. But this does not, of course, mean that those tests could ever settle the question one way or the other. I'm a bird watcher and am thrilled at the recovery of the bald eagle, which I take it is in some way connected to the banning of DDT insecticide. So one might construe this as empirical support for the idea of convergence. Yet others have argued that banning DDT has resulted in millions of human deaths from malaria that could otherwise have been prevented. And malaria contributes to poverty, which is one driver of environmentally destructive behavior (so, of course, is affluence, but that is another problem). And DDT has been replaced by poisons of shorter environmental residence time but higher short-term toxicity—thus increasing the health risk for those who actually apply the DDT-substitutes. You don't have to accept these arguments—they're all contestable and contextual—to see that just because convergence is a testable hypothesis doesn't mean (a) that anthropocentrists and nonanthropocentrists will interpret the data in ways that support convergence or (b) that the actual decisions we make are in any way optimal over the long term for protecting a wide range of human values including nonanthropocentrism.

As a political question, it seems to me that the problem with the nonanthropocentrists is not that their position is rooted in a belief, it's that the belief is a ridiculous basis for political action and thus for policy. After all, many if not all of the important political movements of the past century have been grounded in values about how a good society ought to behave. Imagine applying some version of convergence to the civil rights movement and you'd be saying that segregationists and integrationists would ultimately converge because what was good for African Americans would turn out to be good for the rest of us as well, and both would come to recognize this fact when civil rights laws were enacted and enforced. This might be true, but it's a lot less powerful, and a lot more contestable, than arguing that segregation was simply wrong from any reasonable moral foundation upon which Americans might choose to stand. But if I understand you correctly, the convergence hypothesis is not based on a notion of the intrinsic values of biodiversity but on your modest and wholly sensible intuition that if we keep on going the way we're going, we will exceed the planet's carrying capacity, induce a failure in ecosystem services, and basically fall off a cliff. This could well be true—but it might also be true that we'll continue to muddle through, much as we have in the past, and—perhaps most alarming—continue to remake our environment in ways that would render it unrecognizable to early twenty-first-century humans, but perhaps comfortably familiar to our distant progeny.

We can continue to argue until we're blue in the face about the question of how much biodiversity we need to survive. This argument is very good for scientists, of course, because we keep expecting them to settle the question and this means we keep giving them research funding. I have nothing against supporting scientists, but as an empirical matter, it doesn't seem like a very good way to solve the political disputes that inevitably arise around questions of species and biodiversity protection. After all, we've got thirty years or more of science behind us since the enactment of the Endangered Species Act, but the politics has grown more, not less, bitter and intractable; the science more, not less, fraught with complexity and uncertainty.

So, it seems to me that the argument for species and biodiversity preservation will have the most political potency when it's rooted explicitly in the wide range of *anthropocentric* values. And here's where you've got the real convergence problem. Consider two really good reasons why people might want to protect species and biodiversity: (1) We like them: They give us abiding pleasure and profound appreciation of our place in nature and of the diversity and complexity of life; and (2) We need them: Many peoples' livelihoods and communities depend on the sustainability of certain ecosystems and species. These are only two of the many anthropogenic values that ought to line up on the side of preservation, but they illustrate what seems to me, policy wonk that I am, the heart of the real convergence problem. How is it possible, for example, that in the battle over the protection of the Western spotted owl, the environmentalists and the loggers ended up on opposite sides of the argument? Why wasn't it blindingly obvious that sustainable management of the Western forests was necessary to protect both the owls and the communities in which the loggers lived? How could it be that the logging companies, whose commitment was simply to extract maximum board feet from the forests without regard to biodiversity consequences, could have ended up as the allies of the loggers, who were put out of jobs predominantly by the combination of overlogging and increased automation of the logging industry?

Those questions are meant as provocations, of course, but the fact that philosophers are worried about how to reconcile anthropocentrism with nonanthropocentrism rather than seeking to discover creative grounds upon which traditionally adversarial anthropocentric perspectives might converge around species preservation suggests to me, at least, that the philosophical debate is far removed from the political reality. The exploitation of renewable resources like trees, fish, and even game animals, which I imagine can have no place at all on the agenda of nonathropocentrism ("they're not resources, they're living things!"), seems like a political venue where a variety of anthropocentric values that are traditionally in conflict could line up on the side of species and biodiversity protection. This seems to me like an example of a real convergence problem, Bryan. Have at it.

IV

Reply by Bryan G. Norton

15

BRYAN G. NORTON

Convergence and Divergence

The Convergence Hypothesis
Twenty Years Later

Introduction: Conceiving Convergence

In 1985, having received the Gilbert White Fellowship from Resources for the Future, I went to Washington, D.C., and began work on what would become *Toward Unity among Environmentalists*.[1] Having spent two previous years working in the D.C. area, I had made a number of contacts in the activist community there, and returning to the capital allowed me to continue working with those contacts. My prior work in environmental ethics had equipped me with a number of theoretical concepts and distinctions, and in *Why Preserve Natural Variety?* (1987), I organized my arguments for protecting species and habitats into the standard categories of human-based reasons (Part A) and reasons based on the intrinsic value of natural objects (Part B).[2] I say this because I think I detect in some of my critics an attribution of some kind of primal animus against nonanthropocentrism and the intrinsic-value attributions usually associated with it. In fact, my early work was quite sympathetic to nonanthropocentrism, as I attempted to give arguments for environmental protection the strongest formulation I could.

Prolonged exposure to activists and their concerns, however, kept challenging me and my comfortable use of these theory-based categories. For example, when I examined the various players and groups, I generally found practical people working for well-defined goals—but in explaining those goals, they never resorted to the justifications we ethicists use. Similarly, in judging groups in terms of their effectiveness in achieving goals I thought worthy, I could find no basis for a sharp separation in either policy effectiveness or even in rhetoric between groups that could be categorized as "anthropocentric" in their goals and others that could be categorized as biocentric or ecocentric.

As I thought more strategically and less theoretically about rationales for protecting species and other natural phenomena, I found myself increasingly troubled by my attempts to fit what I saw unfolding in policy arenas into the framework of definitions and distinctions that had become common fare for me and my colleagues in environmental ethics. As I read *Deep Ecology* by William Devall and George Sessions, for example, I learned that we should expect environmentalists to be easily sorted into two categories according to the motives driving their work: (1) "deep ecologists," who accept "biospecies egalitarianism" and work to save nature for its own sake; and (2) "shallow" ecologists, who work to protect nature as a "resource" for human beings.[3] These categories were presented, quite openly, as evaluative—one did not have to read far to realize that deep ecologists are the "good guys" in this narrative and that the shallow ecologists need moral correction—but I found myself very uncomfortable with the implications of these judgmental categories. In applying them, I found that Gifford Pinchot, who set aside 172 million acres of forest for the American people and as a habitat for wildlife, not to mention all of the leading national environmental groups, were classified together with developers and mining interests *against* truly "deep" environmentalists such as Devall and Sessions. This exclusivity seemed counterproductive, strategically and politically.

Thus, in response to what I saw as an overly sharp distinction between two approaches to environmental values and valuation based on *motives*, I proposed the convergence hypothesis (CH). I was reacting to a very strong tendency evident in the early 1980s, to overemphasize motives and values appealed to as the "litmus test" separating true, green environmentalists from environmentalists in disguise, who at best were "shallow" and not to be trusted when the going gets tough. Shying away from classifications—especially dualistic ones based on distinctions between types of motives—I thought it useful to look not at motives for actions, but at actions themselves. I noted the many times that the national environmental groups, even though they often emphasize the good effects of their efforts on humans and their well-being, were actually leaders in protecting habitat for other species, and generally strong advocates for endangered and threatened species. Accordingly, I found it counterproductive to lecture them for their lack of motives considered "pure" by some environmental ethicists.

Looking at the problem of assigning and/or measuring the value of species from a policy perspective, I saw a range of effective efforts to protect species and that these efforts were generally justified by proximate values rather than ultimate values. For example, the activists working on endangered species might disagree about whether conservation corridors creating larger populations and merged gene pools of isolated stocks was a good policy, but I never heard them disagree about whether populations or species should be valued for their contribution to humans or in their own right.

In what follows, I discuss the CH from three standpoints. I will (1) discuss in more detail the meaning and possible verification of the CH, (2) respond to several specific criticisms of the hypothesis that appear in the critical chapters published in this volume, and (3) end by sketching and referring to recent work elsewhere in order to explain why an improved vocabulary for understanding environmental values and valuation may render the CH less necessary.

Convergence or Divergence?

I proposed the CH to help me understand the phenomenon I experienced: Activists can work together for shared policy goals pretty much regardless of the rationales they might—upon questioning—articulate as the justifications for their actions. Further, in reading the great conservationists of the past, from John Muir to Aldo Leopold to Rachel Carson, I saw them gliding seamlessly from concerns about the impact of bad environmental policies on humans to appeals to "rights of nature," and concerns about the health and welfare of animals and their populations. Their decisions as to which values to tout seemed more dependent on the audience they hoped to reach, rather than on some abstract commitment to a particular value system that must—for purity's sake—motivate their every action. This apparent flexibility in ultimate values seemed to me to be just good politics and good strategy; what surprised me, initially, was the vociferous and negative reaction many environmental ethicists had to my emphasis on cooperation among those with different and shifting viewpoints on values.

What I learned, in fact, was that the CH has mostly provoked skepticism among environmental ethicists; at first, I was in the mood of Sarewitz: "Duh." What's to disagree with? Maybe it is too obvious to say. But I cannot deny that most authors who address the CH seem to be on a mission to stamp out dangerous nonsense. It was not until I read Christopher Stone's important book *Earth and Other Ethics* that the intellectual terrain became clearer.[4] Writing as an attorney and legal scholar who looked to the formal study of ethics for pieces of reasoning useful in developing particular cases in particular situations, Stone drew a distinction between "monism" and "pluralism" among ethical theories, defining monism as the view that the enterprise of ethics "is conceived as aiming to produce, and to defend against all rivals, a single coherent and complete set of principles capable of governing all moral quandaries." He also noted that monistic approaches likewise assume that, for each quandary, those principles will yield one, uniquely correct, answer.[5]

As it turns out, most of the invective against my CH has not been directed at the empirical claim that, if one looks at actions, one will not find a sharp dichotomy in actions or policies advocated by anthropocentrists and nonanthropocentrists, but rather at the inference that the CH presupposes pluralism. What makes the CH a threat to monists is that it proceeds toward action without resolving metaphysical differences. Recognizing the "wicked" nature of environmental problems, we are comfortable submitting questions of what a community should do to a fair democratic procedure within that community. Those, such as Callicott and Westra, who have established their careers on the advocacy of intrinsic value in nature as placing limits on the range of morally acceptable human action, have found the hypothesis threatening because, if it were true, it may be taken to lessen the importance of their own theoretical work. If intelligent, long-sighted anthropocentrists advocate the same policies as nonanthropocentrists, their claim to be the single-handed saviors of the natural world would be diminished. As a result, these authors set out to find one or more examples of an action that would be taken by a nonanthropocentrist that would not be taken by an anthropocentrist. These arguments are examined in more detail below.

The CH, when viewed as an empirical hypothesis about policy and about the policy implications of popular (and unpopular) theories of morality, should not be seen as threatening unless one is committed to a narrowly monistic view of ethics. The hypothesis was formulated in a context that assumed the existence of two divergent theories of value and two groups of activists that can be divided according to their acceptance or rejection of these underlying theories. I did not *create* this context or the assumptions that governed it; rather, I *found* a literature in environmental ethics that insisted upon the separation of "deep" from "shallow" environmentalists on the basis of their motives.[6]

Motive-based distinctions among environmentalists also infected the survey research of political scientists and sociologists of the environmental movement, as they asked leading questions and characterized the answers as revealing two different "paradigms," the "Old Dominant Social Paradigm" and the "New Environmental Paradigm." I have argued elsewhere that that this polar separation of advocates had no explanatory role in characterizing the behavior of environmentalists.[7] When I finally took off lenses colored by philosophical assumptions and definitions, what I saw were environmentalists with differing philosophies and viewpoints, but all equally committed, pursuing pretty much the same policies of habitat protection. They all advocated protection of riparian corridors, tried to maintain as large as possible populations of indigenous but threatened species, strongly defended the Endangered Species Act, and so on.

Thus, when viewed as an empirical hypothesis about policy and about the policy implications of theories of morality, the CH predicts that, in an uncertain world and when considered over longer periods of time, sincere efforts to protect nature and natural systems will converge on efforts to protect the full range of values of humans. I learned, however, that it is difficult to formulate the CH as a testable hypothesis. There are two reasons for this: one derives from the nature of the theories that I wish to assert are convergent in action; the other is inherent in the idea of the CH itself. My attempts to state the CH, therefore, have been less precise and less uniform than would be ideal—a fact that is pointed out in the preceding chapters by many of my critics and even by my supporters.

In the first case, it is difficult to formulate this hypothesis because theoreticians differ wildly in what intrinsic value is, what it means to have it, and what entities in fact have it. Similarly, anthropocentrists differ regarding how far into the future our obligations to future people extend. So there are really several "families" of both anthropocentric and nonanthropocentric theories of environmental value. My attempts to state the CH, therefore, have had to hedge between statements that are too vague to be much help and statements that are representative of only a few members of each "family." The CH can only be assessed intelligibly if we identify internally consistent versions of the two central doctrines of anthropocentrism and nonanthropocentrism. If, for example, one fails to specify whether nonanthropocentrism assigns intrinsic value to individuals or only to systems, one cannot associate the position with a particular strategy or policy, so comparisons of the policies implied by the two value positions are impossible.

Stenmark (this volume), writing in criticism of the CH, carries this criticism further; he acknowledges (in contrast to anthropocentrists such as the Brundtland Commission and the Rio Declaration, which lay out policies that are argued to be in the broad interest of humans) that there is a dearth of specific policy recommendations offered by nonanthropocentrists. So it is even difficult to begin to test the convergence hypothesis. Rather than fault the nonanthropocentrists for this apparent oversight, he gives them a "free pass" by avoiding discussion of specific policies and compares the "goals" of anthropocentrists with those of nonanthropocentrists. So, his attack on the CH is not based on specified policies, but on the claim that "the goals for environmental policy making that anthropocentrists, biocentrists, and ecocentrists envision are not the same."[8] Goals, however, are notoriously ambiguous with respect to the specific actions and policies they are taken to imply. For example, in my work on endangered species and biodiversity, I would probably state the following goal: "To protect wild species, their habitats, and the integrity of the ecosystems on which they depend indefinitely." What, exactly, is it that nonanthropocentrists—if they ever deign to offer actual policy implications of their "ideas"—disagree with in this goal? And, if I add to this "goal" the trailer that I would do so to benefit future generations of humans who will love and need these wild species and habitats, what *policy* difference will be signaled by that addition to my goal statement, in distinction to the goals statement of a nonanthropocentrist, who might add "for the benefit of animals, ecosystems, species, and so forth," to their statement of goals.

There is also, however, a difficulty built into the notion of convergence. Because convergence is hypothetical upon gaining more scientific evidence, and because in practice the preponderance of scientific evidence is always subject to change, one never knows—at any given time with any given stock of scientific knowledge—all that one would want to know to determine whether the policies advocated by the two ideologies should be close, identical, or convergent.

In spite of these two problems in precise formulation, I still believe the CH, if stated in more general terms, is valid within contexts that embody two exclusive types of values—human-regarding and nonhuman-regarding ethics. The point can be made using an alternative formulation that does not require precise formulation of each of the rival theories of value: In general, differences in the *actions and behaviors of environmentalists* cannot be illuminatingly *explained* by appeal to *anthropocentric as opposed to nonanthropocentric motives.*

Let me try one more way to explain, if not justify, the CH. Imagine two worlds very similar to our own, similarly populated and rich in resources but badly frayed by the aggressive extraction of those resources in the search of wealth and consumption. Each of these parallel worlds will henceforth have their environments controlled by one of two omniscient "managers." One of the managers is programmed to unfailingly decide and act, based on full knowledge, in every way to protect the full range of human interests over indefinite time. The other manager sets out, with perfect skill and full knowledge, to manage to protect nature and natural systems because of their "intrinsic value." The CH says we can expect that the policies advocated by these two omniscient managers will converge upon a range of policies that are wise from both a human and a nonhuman perspective (whatever it means to talk about a "nonhuman perspective"). The effect of this thought experiment is to minimize the role of scientific uncertainty; omniscient managers have the same knowledge, so if these managers create different worlds, based on different ideologies, the divergence between the two managers' actions should be a measure of how predictive the CH is. By equalizing the scientific knowledge of our two managers, we focus exactly on the question of whether, and exactly how, ideological ideas affect policy. The story of the two managers is only an illustrative story, however; it is, of course, unrealistic to talk about environmental decision making without recognizing uncertainty. What we do not know is a bigger barrier to choosing right actions than differences about what motives are used to justify the actions.[9]

One way to see the plausibility of the hypothesis is to consider its denial, the divergence hypothesis (DH), which would claim that, as we better understand and refine our statements of anthropocentric and nonanthropocentric theories of environmental value, the policies proposed by the advocates of these theories will diverge further and further.[10] So stated, the DH would seem to fly in the face of the Darwinian understanding of nature by which we and other species are "fellow travelers in the odyssey of evolution," and by which all species are dependent upon the habitats that support their life needs.[11] According to the DH, the human species has developed or will develop a set of needs that are, even in the long term, quite independent of the well-being of other species. I do not believe that this very general argument, by itself, establishes the CH in enough detail to be useful, because of course humans have developed many needs based in cultural practices, which have to some degree developed independently of needs that serve only the physical necessities of existence. Nevertheless, any theory of divergence that ignores survival and physical needs related to flourishing—needs shared by humans and other species—is implausible in a context of evolutionary and ecological theory. For example, the flourishing of all species depends on some level of stability (admittedly dynamic) of habitats. Humans have developed almost airtight houses with central heat and air conditioning, which seems to insulate them from the necessities imposed by nature, but does that mean human long-term interests are ultimately at odds with the necessities of other species and healthy ecosystems? Divergence theorists might think so; guided by the CH, I focus on the full range of human values (including love for wildlife) and about effects on the well-being of future generations.

Take, for instance, the problem of global climate change. It may be true that, in the short run (leading up to the present, for example), pursuit of legitimate human interests in economic development have led to the release of greenhouse gases. Some economists have speculated that the overall human benefit-to-cost ledger for greenhouse warming may be positive at least in the short run, as growing seasons lengthen and marginal areas open for agriculture. When one adds, however, the qualification that I have insisted upon since the first formulation of the CH, that we must consider the well-being of humans *in the long run*, it is becoming abundantly clear that humans will suffer great losses, probably imposed by our selfishness upon future generations, if we do not respond effectively to the challenge of climate change.[12] In this case, then, because humans have responded to needs partially determined by cultural accretions, they can modify cultural practices more rapidly than plants and animals can change biologically. It is nevertheless true that climate change threatens many human values, including many cultures and perhaps even human survival itself. As in many other cases, what appear to be discrepancies in what is "good" for humans and what is "good" for nature, adopting a time horizon that is sufficiently long for calculating human well-being will erase those discrepancies.

One example, of course, does not prove or disprove the DH, but it does illustrate the danger—almost never heeded by nonanthropocentrists, who usually narrow the range of human interests, and then argue that these incomplete and artificially narrowed economic interests will not coincide with the expansive attributions of intrinsic value that they apply to natural objects. More is said about this mischaracterization of human values in the next section. Here, I ask: "Given our current policies are bad for both humans and for nature as well, why not advocate policies that are good for both humans and nature?" I do not understand, for example, why Westra finds the CH so abhorrent; I always thought she was saying that protecting "integrity" of natural systems would be (if we would only try it) good for humans as well as good for natural systems. In endorsing divergence, she seems to believe that humans can only protect nature if they harm themselves and their human cohorts. What surprises me is the extent to which the advocates of the DH apparently believe that we face a war between humans and nature; that humans wield all of the artifactual tools, and it is up to our generation to sacrifice human values in order to protect nature. In the end, the philosophical preferences come down to this: Choose, with Callicott and Westra, to act on the divergence hypothesis, and then argue that because of the "intrinsic value" of nonhuman species, we as a species should take it in the neck to serve the interests of other species. If that is the future of environmental ethics, then the theoreticians will have proved their necessity: Without them, who would be there to assign the blame on those who did not sacrifice enough to save nature and its intrinsic value?

Finally, having recognized the problems in formulating a testable version of the CH, I do not see why anyone would object to the following, very weak, formulation of the CH as a working hypothesis: Given the pervasive damage done both to humans and nonhumans by our past and current actions, in most situations there is some action that will provide benefits for both humans and nonhumans. Let us get together behind this vast area of opportunities that benefit both humans and nature, and we will see whether there are any left over when we have implemented all of the policies that benefit both.

Responses to My Critics

I am faced with so many artfully constructed arguments and criticisms that I am at a loss as to how to respond to all of them. With so many red flags brandished at me, which way should I charge? If I were to give the full answer each deserves, I am sure I would once again be criticized for the excessive length of my recent work. Unsatisfactory as it may seem, I will have to content myself with verbal nods in the direction of supporting arguments, give a few hints as to how some criticisms might be answered, and concentrate on a few key criticisms in hopes that this combination of inadequate responses will move the discussion forward. Let me start by discussing the relationship between pragmatism and environmental values because confusion over my position on this topic leads to some remarkable claims by Callicott and Katz.

Who Is a Pragmatist?

When surveying some of the criticisms of my work in environmental pragmatism and the CH, both in this book and elsewhere, I have been surprised by what seem to me to be odd conceptions of pragmatism and by odd characterizations of philosophical positions as pragmatic or not pragmatic. For example, in a series of papers, J. Baird Callicott has argued that his work is "pragmatic"; indeed, he apparently thinks his work is more pragmatic than mine.[13] Eric Katz, in contrast, argues in this volume that my positions are not really pragmatist positions, even though I explicitly argue for those positions in pragmatist terms. What is almost as surprising is that neither author backs up these surprising claims with anything like a careful definition or explanation of what they believe pragmatism is or what criteria might be used to apply the label to practicing philosophers.

Let me start, then, by listing the four "interrelated substantive themes" that create what Richard Bernstein calls the "pragmatic ethos."[14] He lists these themes as: (1) antifoundationalism, (2) fallibilism, (3) the social character of the self, and (4) recognition of radical contingency. I would add to Bernstein's excellent list an emphasis on the role of language and symbolic expression as conventional tools of understanding and communication; a rejection of representationalism in epistemology and its companion, the correspondence theory of truth; pragmatists emphasize action rather than pure thought, as in the understanding of problems and possible solutions. All of this can be understood as elaboration of Bernstein's four themes, which add up to a renunciation of the search for knowledge of a reality beyond symbolized experience. It also marks the end of certainty and a rejection of a priori knowledge. One manifestation of this complex of ideas is a tendency, in discussion in the public policy arena, to favor a problem-oriented approach that expects theory to emerge from action, in specific problem contexts rather than to develop and refine theory in the abstract and then to apply that theory to determine right action in specific situations.[15]

If these characterizations of pragmatism are at all accurate, then Callicott's claim that his viewpoint is pragmatic is truly remarkable and clearly implausible. He has explicitly declared himself a "foundationalist," thereby departing sharply from Bernstein's first theme.[16] As is explored in more detail below, his ethical views are based on and built out of *individual* and apparently presymbolic affects, which clashes with Bernstein's third, "emphasis on community" theme. The distance between Callicott and pragmatists' action-oriented conception of language is evident in a recent essay in which he describes his conceptual enterprise as "rectifying names."[17]

Callicott's explanation of "rectifying names" is charmingly appropriate for his own views, but anachronistic at best. He implies a view of language that is mainly denotative, reminiscent of Locke and Hume, who saw words as labels for ideas; by adding some rationalistic assumptions about natural kinds in nature, these ideas apparently stand in for Aristotelian essences in Callicott's view of language. Words, on this refuted theory of language, are symbols that denote pre-existent categories in the real world—natural kinds. Without such kinds, what would the "names" of general terms refer to? Because he has an essentially denotative ideational theory of meaning whereby concepts are names of kinds in nature, he has not freed himself from the pre-Kantian conception of the mind as a sensorium of ideas that are copies of bits of reality. Pragmatists view language not as a series of labels but as a means of communication among members of a community bound by shared symbols. A true pragmatist would never fall into this form of essentialism, or the foundationalism it supports, because a true pragmatist recognizes the conventional nature of language—that language is tied to actions and behaviors more than to "ideas." Callicott's apparent commitment to language as labels of prior "kinds" apparently means he also rejects Bernstein's fourth theme: radical contingency.

In addition, even if we tolerantly take Callicott's apparently denotative conception of language to be a misleading slip in the interest of dropping the names of Confucius and Shakespeare, reading further in the essay, one learns how easy it is to become a nonanthropocentrist. All one has to do is to "attribute" noninstrumental value to some or many objects in nature and then, in one's rhetoric against developers, one should no longer make economic arguments but rather assert that a contested wetland has intrinsic value. This "rectification of names" then changes the entire decision process; merely by asserting that a wetland, for example, has intrinsic value, the burden of proof has been shifted and, I guess, the bulldozers stop. As anyone with more than a frivolous study of pragmatism knows, the philosophy can appear in some surprising guises; but Callicott's attempt to solve environmental problems by adjusting the rhetoric could not be further from the core ideas of pragmatism. Pragmatists do not think of language as labels for ideas, they see language as conventional, as woven into interpersonal communication in the service of cooperative action. Language is a tool for changing the world; but Callicott's pseudopragmatism totally misses the point, as the only function of the newly named objects of intrinsic value is to characterize a new form of rhetoric. If Callicott means to claim that his views reflect philosophical pragmatism, he is simply mistaken. If he means to claim that discussions of intrinsic value have actually been useful to environmental activists, he should advance some data, not anecdotes about pupfish. Others observing the same policy landscape have reported evidence conflicting with even this weak Callicottian claim.[18]

Perhaps Callicott means to claim that his views are "pragmatic" only in the sense that they are *useful* to environmental activists in that he claims environmentalists will do better in their battles with developers if, as suggested above, they declare a development-targeted wetland to have "intrinsic value." But even this explanation of his point seems to tout intrinsic value for its *rhetorical* effectiveness, rather than as an effective guide toward the best policies for a community in real situations. And, of course, compared to the pragmatists' approach that starts from specific problems and builds toward general theory, Callicott's whole approach to environmental ethics for the past thirty years has been to build and defend a theory in abstract terms, and then to use it to solve problems such as decisions about wetland protection generically without any social or environmental context.[19] If this is pragmatism, Immanuel Kant, for example, would be a pragmatist because he uses his categorical imperative to help people know what to do in any situation where they are considering lying or breaking a promise. What Callicott has lost, in contrast to Kant, is that whereas Kant tried to offer objective criteria of right action that would actually *justify* a choice not to lie, Callicott's "principles" are constructed out of subjective and emotive affects of individuals who happen to feel a particular way. As such, they have no argumentative force against skeptics, so the most Callicott is offering for activists to apply are rhetorical devices that might work in some cases.

I turn now to Katz's equally surprising claim that my positions in *Sustainability* are not really pragmatist positions at all.[20] I credit Katz for at least trying to offer a very general characterization of pragmatism before engaging in classificatory pronouncements. Unfortunately, however, while he gets his very partial characterization of pragmatism right, he seems to totally miss the point of my pragmatic analysis. He characterizes pragmatism as the philosophical "worldview [that] requires that ideas have an effect on policy and action; if they have no effect, they are meaningless."[21] As he seems to see, pragmatists do not think *all* "ideas" are important because they have an impact; some ideas are, in fact, rejected for lack of impact on experience or action. Peirce's pragmatic criterion has as its function to separate those ideas that have empirical impact and those that do not: "Consider what effects, which might conceivably have practical bearings, we conceive the object of our conception to have. Then, our conception of these effects is the whole of our conception of the object."[22] I may be wrong in my judgment—if the CH proves empirically false—but I am clearly using Peirce's criterion when I say that the idea of intrinsic value in nature fails the pragmatic test. If adding the idea of intrinsic value to that of enlightened human interest creates no difference in mandated behaviors, and indicates no real changes in behavior from following "broad anthropocentrism," then the CH is a classic case of pragmatic reasoning. The "metaphysical" idea that nature has "intrinsic value" is shown to have at best only ideological and rhetorical use. Our "conception of it has no conceivable bearings."

So, I proudly state that I am a pragmatist. This also means, of course, that I am a fallibilist, and I may be proved wrong eventually. Even if I am proved wrong about the CH, however, by the discovery of important divergences between human well-being and the interests of nature, this would only make me a *mistaken* pragmatist, not a *nonpragmatist*.

Some Proposed Counterexamples to the CH

I found Holmes Rolston III's thoughtful discussion and analysis both interesting and challenging and I am not sure I have convincing answers to all of his points. First, let me say that I do not disagree that motives are important in many situations—motives do matter in courts of law, for example; intent and motive can be definitive in separating accidental harms from assaults. My point is not, then, that motives never matter. Again, it is very important to remember that the CH is a hypothesis about *policies*; my point is that motives ought not to divide possible allies who seek similar policies for different reasons.

Having clarified that point, I must also say that Rolston mentions some of the most difficult cases for the CH. The first type of case he mentions are cases where protection of a species has very high human costs, and he mentions the problem of protecting Bengal tigers in Nepal and the needle-mouthed fly in California. A first step in gaining clarity in cases like these is to ask exactly what *policy* is being proposed. Since 1987, the general policy criterion I have advocated is to apply the safe minimum standard (SMS) of conservation, which says: "Always save the resource (in this case, the species in question), provided the (human) costs are bearable." Furthermore, I have argued that the SMS rule is consistent with and supports the current legal status of the Endangered Species Act, which mandates protection of a species unless the protection conflicts with important regional or national interests. In that context, the issue shifts to determining, in particular cases, what level of costs become unbearable.

In the case of the flies, we are talking about where to locate development for human habitation, in a wealthy community where developers and some home buyers are demanding expansion into the habitat of an endangered species in a context where the possibility of building elsewhere or of increasing the density of human habitation elsewhere exists. Giving up those economic opportunities and fulfillment of preferences for more sprawl seem not to be unbearable costs for developers (who can build elsewhere) or for potential dwellers (who can buy a house elsewhere). In this case, the endangered species clearly wins—the costs are bearable.

The tiger case, however, involves choosing between a species and fulfillment of basic human needs including food and access to resources that are necessary for human life. I have always found the tiger case one of the most difficult cases to resolve, as Rolston does, and anyone who has a simple answer to it invites suspicion. In such cases, both the anthropocentrist and the nonanthropocentrist face serious dilemmas, depending on the situation. Nonanthropocentrists such as Steverson (this volume) seem to believe that accepting the intrinsic value of all species means a species should be saved no matter what the costs—that there should be no exceptions to endangered species legislation, period. This sounds reasonable, but imagine that a huge asteroid, large enough to wipe out all human life and most other complex life forms if it strikes Earth, is hurtling earthward. Suppose also that the technology is available that could probably explode or divert the asteroid, but the chances of success will be greatly increased, because of the angle of the approach, if the rocket launcher and the equipment needed to service it is placed on the habitat of the needle-mouthed fly. Saving most of life on Earth thus depends on the likely extinction—by our act—of a species. Our obligation is stronger than the SMS, he thinks, as he believes that we should save "as many species as possible." Would Steverson then consider it "possible" to save species if the cost is most of life on Earth? I hope not; but if not, he, just like the rest of us, is on a slippery slope represented by having to decide, with no clear criterion, when it is "possible to pay the costs" in order to save a species. Or, he could bite the bullet and say that it is "possible" to use other sites (so the fly must be saved for the two years before the asteroid actually hits), and it seems that he favors the fly over most of life on Earth. I would give the rockets their best chance. What would Rolston and other nonanthropocentrists do? I would like to think they would (regretfully) impinge on the habitat of the fly—implying that even if all species have intrinsic value, that value is not nonnegotiable, even though a strict deontology based on the intrinsic value of all species would demand forbearance from intentionally damaging the fly's habitat. One can also, by varying the case, create a dilemma for anthropocentists: Suppose occupying the fly's habitat for the rocket attempt, rather than another space, would increase the likelihood of success, but only by .001

percent. Would *that* be a bearable cost? If the anthropocentrist thinks not, then we could change the case to increase that percentage gradually until the anthropcentrist feels the dilemma.

My main point, here, is that whatever the motive or the rule that guides one's policy with respect to species, there will be difficult cases and dilemmas that cause anguish. I find the strong, Kantian interpretation of Steverson's "possibility" test—never act so as to knowingly cause an extinction—too inflexible. My rule, SMS, seems to me a pretty good one, no matter what one's motives. If, however, nonanthropocentrists want a more restrictive basis for determining individual cases, this will require that they provide an alternative criterion, and provide a philosophical justification for it. In the end, we will either have to follow an inflexible rule like Steverson's or we will have to argue about what costs are bearable to save any particular species. If Steverson admits that "possibility" assessments count costs to determine what is feasible, then it is hard to distinguish this rule from SMS. It involves an assessment of costs. I do not think, therefore, that Steverson has provided a clear counterexample *in policies advocated*. This same answer applies directly to at least some of the four cases of Stenmark (this volume), who cites human population policies.

In the tiger case, Rolston raises one of the most difficult cases possible, and makes a very perceptive point: In many cases where human actions threaten species, they do so as a result of a long series of choices that have been bad for humans as well as bad for nature. Often, bad choices affecting population, lack of land reform, and so forth create dilemmas in which there are no good choices. In cases like the Bengal tiger, Rolston wonders why the tiger species should be extinguished for our failures, and suggests we mend our ways on our own terms. This is a courageous choice, but I would make this point: Since the dilemma of the tiger resulted from choices that *can be easily criticized on purely human grounds*, we cannot think of the tiger case as a clear counterexample to the CH, which expects that decisions made for the actual good of humans will converge with decisions made to advance nonhuman interests. It says nothing about the case in which humans horribly mismanage their own affairs, mistreat each other, fail to provide fair access to resources, and so forth. So, when Stenmark (this volume), mentions "human population policies" as a counterexample to the CH, I need only point out that human population policies have caused famine, destruction of human and natural habitats for species valued by humans, and untold human misery to show that this is clearly *not* a case where the full range of human values have been protected for the present and the future *at the expense of nature*. These terrible policies were pursued *at the expense of human beings* as well, creating havoc in the natural world, so this policy does not conflict with multigenerational anthropocentrism.

In the tiger case, growing populations regulated only by each family's choice, failure of land reform, and so forth created terrible *human problems*. If they had been effectively addressed, then both humans and nonhuman species would be better off. That judgment is certainly consistent with the CH. So I do not know what to say except to try to create a win-win situation; if we fail—and we probably are failing—I doubt that declaring the tiger to have intrinsic value will create a more just system, or save the tiger in the face of human folly.

In other words, I think the tiger case may, at this point, be a case on which it is impossible for *anyone—anthropocentrists and nonanthropocentrists alike, to have a compelling position*, however one comes down on the continuum of invasive management of human cultures in order to achieve a world-scaled goal. One eventually has to count the costs of protection, as I argue above, and I think reasonable people can disagree about what the costs are, who suffers them, and at what point the human costs become unbearable, even as we agree that there is a strong obligation to act to protect all species. I cannot fault Rolston for drawing the line perhaps somewhere nearer protection of the tiger; indeed, I find the tiger dilemma virtually paralyzing in its difficulty, so I would have to study the situation a lot more deeply to make specific recommendations in this complex case. However, the existence of cases in which, as a result of long-standing failure of humans to act in their own interests, we now face only bad choices, does not represent a failure of the CH, but rather a failure of human-oriented management.

I also must react to Rolston's discussion of regrettable and unacceptable experiments that have terribly mistreated animals in order to advance human medicine or other human ends. I abhor the mistreatment of animals and have spent years of my life working with zoos, aquaria, and other facilities that keep wild animals in captivity. What I learned in that work is that ethics of human-animal relations are fascinating and very difficult. With respect to individual animals, I do believe that individuals of many species have moral standing. I am not sure how I would characterize the obligations I feel to individual animals, except to say that I strongly endorse norms for human actions that affect morally considerable animals. I would say that, if I knew a clear and compelling theory and explanation of human rights and justifiable interests, I believe a similar or analogous theory of ethics would apply to many animals. What I do not know is whether or not that makes me a nonanthropocentrist. In any case, I have concentrated on environmental, not animal, ethics and I have argued since 1982 that I do not think distinctively environmental values, such as the value we place on ecosystems and species, are well explained using an individualistic ethic, whether human or biocentric.[23] I have thus devoted quite a few pages to explaining a special kind of values, which I call "communal values," such as landscape and ecological integrity, and healthy and fair institutions.[24] So I remain an anthropocentrist in environmental ethics (in the sense, explained above, that I reject the theoretical apparatus developed to characterize one kind of environmental values). Since my professional concern has been with environmental values and environmental policies in this area, I choose to accept the CH as a working hypothesis.

Finally, while it often seems that Rolston and I are very far apart in environmental ethics, I think these disagreements about whether we should posit values independent of human beings, capable at least in some cases of "trumping" human values, have more to do with our theories of epistemology than with any differences about policies and problem solutions. He seems comfortable with theoretical terms for which I can see no operational meaning, so I believe that Rolston's attributions of intrinsic value to species and ecosystems cannot be justified epistemologically; they are ideology, not verifiable. I fear, therefore, that they cannot form the basis of strong arguments for protecting species or other policies unless people are already convinced species and ecosystems have that intrinsic value. Again, full treatment of this topic would be beyond the topic of convergence.[25]

Legal Standing and an Incorrect Interpretation

J. Baird Callicott develops a complex argument that the Endangered Species Act, together with judicial interpretations of it, have "objectified" intrinsic values in species, by which I think he means that passing legislation protecting species creates legal rights, which include the possibility of anyone bringing suit on behalf of an endangered species. Since the suit can be brought in the name of a species itself, Callicott interprets this legal gambit as attributing "intrinsic value" to the object. By coupling this argument with another argument that anthropocentrists would not accept the same policies regarding species, he concludes that the CH is false. To put the argument in his own words: "If we can identify a public policy that is clearly based on nonanthropocentric intrinsic values, and it would not be the same policy had it been based exclusively on anthropocentric instrumental values, then the convergence hypothesis will be unequivocally falsified. There is one such public policy—the U.S. Endangered Species Act of 1973. Therefore, the convergence hypothesis is false."[26]

It might be fun to try to figure out how Callicott can claim his first premise as, thanks to the legislature and the courts, "the ESA is 'clearly' (my emphasis) based on non-anthropocentric intrinsic values." In fact, his argument is so confusing that space available here is inadequate to address the confusions piled on ambiguities as he constructs his legalistic argument. Here is a sampling of his "clear" reasons that the ESA "objectifies" intrinsic value in species: "To repeat: The ESA does *not* provide intrinsic value, legal rights, and standing for listed species; rather, it provides *implicit* intrinsic value, *operational* legal rights, and *de facto* standing for listed species."[27] De jure standing, he says, comes with the first court recognition of standing for a species. This is "clear"? Not to me, I am afraid, especially since this conflation of legal standing with moral desert for standing then leads into a discussion of Kant's idea of intrinsic worth or dignity. Are we to believe that Kant, here cited as the locus classicus for moral dignity beyond price, but who was also the locus classicus for deriving his moral obligations from pure reason, would lend his support to rights by legislation? I have no idea how Callicott intends to connect *operational* moral rights as might be "provided" by a legislature with the Kantian idea of moral dignity.[28]

Rather than trying to sort out that mess, let me concentrate on the second, hardly defended, premise of his argument—that the ESA would not "be the same policy had it been based exclusively on anthropocentric instrumental values"—because addressing this aspect of his argument has more promise to illuminate our real differences.[29] What, exactly, is the *policy* that anthropocentrists and nonanthropocentrists fail to agree upon? Callicott argues that, by granting de facto and de jure standing to species as a matter of law, the legislature and courts have, in their passage and interpretation of the ESA "objectified" "intrinsic value" in nature—a moral value. He further argues that failure on the part of anthropocentrists to interpret the act as conferring intrinsic value somehow affects their viewpoint on legal standing. So far, this sounds like a difference of legislative interpretation, not policy. He goes on, however, to argue that no anthropocentrist could consistently attribute standing in some cases that could be brought by nonanthropocentrists, and he thinks this results in a difference in "policy." This is a trivial problem that can be dealt with by simply invoking the distinction between legal and moral rights/values. One need not attribute independent moral value or "intrinsic" value to an object in order to ascribe it standing in courts of law, as is made obvious by the case of "corporations" that are "considered persons" before the law, but persons who are merely instrumental to stockholders. My policy regarding species, which has been stated in several of my books and articles, is the SMS: Save the species provided the costs are bearable.[30] Use of the SMS is motivated by the belief that species are of great, but unquantifiable value, and that even in a situation of uncertainty, all affordable efforts must be taken to protect species. If the protection of species is forwarded, as Callicott claims it is, by granting legal standing to species, and allowing any citizen to sue on the behalf of an endangered species, then I would argue in court for the "legal fiction" that species can be considered "persons before the law" (like corporations). Since I am committed to always protecting species if the costs are bearable, then I will gladly endorse a convention regarding

standing for species if it is effective in achieving this goal. Callicott's difference of interpretation is just that; he haş identified no convincing case where
an enlightened anthropocentrist and a self-consistent nonanthropocentrist
would pursue *different policies*, but only that they would give different interpretations and arguments for the policies they would likely share.

This, however, is not really our main disagreement. Why does Callicott
take it as obvious that I must, as an anthropocentrist, reduce all human value
to economic measures, a position I have criticized in almost all of my writings? His answer: "An ESA based on purely anthropocentric instrumental
values would require the value of endangered species to be quantified on the
monetary metric and be subjected to comparison with other anthropocentric
instrumental values in Benefit–Cost Analysis (BCA) exercises."[31] In other
words, Callicott's only argument that anthropocentrists would engage in different policies and different acts is by *defining* anthropocentrism as "strong"
anthropocentrism. Strong anthropocentrism is precisely the view he describes,
that all environmental values are measurable as individual preferences or willingness to pay. Indeed, he tries to associate me with this position, as he completely negates my actual position with an offhand remark that "from all
Norton says about the matter, it would seem to be appropriate, when finally
economists are able to do it well, to quantify *all* important anthropocentric
instrumental environmental values in the monetary metric for purposes of
making trade-offs . . ."[32]

How can Callicott accuse me of economic reductionism? I have been far
more critical of that position than he, having provided extended arguments to
that effect in every one of my books. How can Callicott ignore such obvious
textual evidence that, while I believe all values are human values, I also recognize important human, environmental values *that cannot be interpreted in
terms of willingness to pay or fulfillment of individual preferences*?

I think there are two reasons for Callicott's blindness. The first reason
is the one he gives, almost offhandedly in his chapter in this volume. He
notes that I mention, on a pluralistic system such as mine, that one must
sometimes face "trade-offs" among those values and then (without citing
one scintilla of textual evidence, because there is none) he follows a quota-
tion from me about multiple human values with an addition, "But in order
for those trade-offs to be made intelligently, the competing anthropocentric
instrumental values at stake must be quantified in a common metric."[33]
This is a position I directly contradict time and again in *Sustainability*. In
particular, I devote section 4.1, described as a "pivotal" chapter in my
book, to refuting and replacing the rational-choice model for dealing with
trade-offs among human value. There, I argue that environmental problems
are "wicked problems" and that they are not susceptible to solution by "algorithmic" models. Since rational-choice models are algorithmic, the pivotal

chapter of my book is devoted to dismissing them in search of more appropriate models. I find such a model in chapters 7, 8, and 10, where I reject "methodological individualism"—the view that all values must be values of "human individuals"—arguing for "communal" values. Since communal values are not individual values, as noted above, they cannot be represented in terms of individual preferences. So, Callicott, by illegitimately associating my position that all environmental values are human values with rational choice models (which I reject) turns my position into a straw man. I believe in "broad" anthropocentrism, and my whole approach to environmental values and valuation has been to introduce a variety of environmental values, associating these with different "scales" of our environment, and to show that reductionistic, individualistic models like rational choice and the microeconomic methods associated with it, must be resisted as incomplete, not just in practice, but in principle.[34]

As a pluralist about environmental values, believing that humans value nature in many ways; we must sometimes, as pluralists, "trade off" some things we value for other things we value more. This is simply a consequence of our finitude; we cannot do everything we would like to do. Admitting that we make trade-offs does not commit us to quantifying all values, as is clear from countless cases where humans, appealing only to human values, "trade off" one kind of good for other goods. Because it is convenient for his argument, Callicott decrees that anyone who accepts the necessity of sometimes trading off among goods that we cannot simultaneously maximize *must* capitulate to quantification of economic values in order to make a trade-off. He then uses this decree as a general premise from which he argues that because I recognize the need for trade-offs, I *must* become an "Economist" (theorists who claim all environmental values are economic/commodity values).[35] His decree, however, seems not to govern people's actual behavior. There are many situations where people make trade-offs and make them in a rational, rule-guided way, even though economic measurement of costs and benefits are impossible or prohibited. For example, in battlefield medicine, physicians often have to practice "triage," which requires that they decide, based on prognosis based on available treatment options, to let some injured soldiers die so that they can save the lives of multiple soldiers with lesser injuries. In fact, physicians have a set of rules that guide such decisions, but the rules are not quantified and they have nothing to do with costs and benefits—a physician who, for example, chose to save a soldier who is better educated and more likely to have a positive impact on human welfare if he lives, even though the prognosis is less positive than another injured combatant, would be violating well-established decision guidelines and would be subject to moral censure and perhaps legal liability. This example shows that Callicott's claim that the only way to make trade-off decisions is through cost-benefit analysis is simply false. So, any argument he makes based on this premise is unsound. Unfortunately for his criticism of my work, all of his points depend directly on this false premise.

Many decision rules then, including the ones employed in triage, allow "rational" choices without reference to economics or quantification. In the triage case, physicians are in one sense dealing with commensurate values—human lives, some of which will be saved and others not. We also, of course, make trade-off decisions among goods that are incommensurable, as for example when a young person who has a powerful drive to get an education is offered a scholarship at a distant university that will necessitate separation from the love of his or her life. These kinds of decisions are, in fact, made every day and, even if the young person does calculate the likely increment in income from a good education, that is probably not the definitive formulation of the value of the education; and even if it were, the value of the education cannot be placed on the same scale of value with one's love. They are incommensurable. For this and other reasons, anthropocentrists should not be Economists; and I have written hundreds of pages explaining why not and in developing alternative ways to consider plural values. If Callicott could ever give up his prejudice that decision models must be monistic and comprehensive, then he would see that pluralism opens the door to a procedural approach rather than posing a metaphysical choice that must be resolved philosophically.

If Callicott had read further in the book he cites, he would have found that in chapter 8, I discuss the values people derive from love of place, from projecting their present values as "community performatives"—commitments to protect their place. And in chapters 7 and 10, I develop an extended argument that these values cannot be parsed as individual preferences, but rather constitute a whole new category of value, the aforementioned "communal value."[36] Since economic values are a construction out of individual values, and communal commitments to place are not commitments to individual well-being, but communitarian commitments, they cannot be, ipso facto, economic values. Similarly, I have argued for more than twenty years that nature has "transformative" value, which—while accruing to humans—cannot be treated as the fixed individual preference values of economics.

Since Callicott clearly can read, but refuses to credit me with the positions I describe in plain English, we must suspect that another, less-explicit argument is being employed. Here is that argument: "In the literature of academic environmental philosophy and ethics. . . . values are classified dichotomously as (A) instrumental or (B) intrinsic. The value of something as a means to an end other than itself is instrumental. The value of something for itself, for its own sake, as an end in itself, is intrinsic."[37] Notice that the first sentence quoted here simply states a fact about the linguistic habits of academic environmental philosophers. In another recent paper, Callicott makes the same pronouncement, but leaves off any reference to the context of environmental ethics, making the "fact" about the language and concepts of environmental ethics into a pronouncement about the nature of all human value: "We subjects value objects in one or both of at least two ways—instrumentally or intrinsically—between which there is no middle term."[38] And, as one reads on in Chapter 9 in this volume, one learns that this fact/pronouncement becomes the basis for some remarkable restrictions about what one can or cannot say about values. Treated as a pronouncement, this is simply a bit of a priori rationalist dogma.

Callicott simply defined "intrinsic" value as "noninstrumental" value so as to make the only available choice seem to be between "anthropocentric and instrumental" values and "noninstrumental and intrinsic." This definition, of course, is simply vacuous. Intrinsic value is defined negatively: It is value that "is left over when all its instrumental value has been subtracted. In other words, 'intrinsic value' and 'noninstrumental value' are two names for the same thing."[39] The definition provides no guidance in identifying objects that have this kind of value, how to recognize it, and so forth. When Callicott asserts that we subjects can value objects in one of two ways, he is not summarizing experience; he is forcing all environmental values into his either-or, dualistic categories. He has defined it as necessarily true that anthropocentrists cannot value anything other than humans noninstrumentally.

The problem is that this commitment does not come from examining people's values as stated, because in common parlance, most people are pluralists about environmental values, and draw no such sharp distinction between values that are instrumental, intrinsic, or whatever.[40] Callicott uses his philosophical theory to force pluralistic expressions of human value into two possible motives. He is not asserting that this distinction is useful in understanding our experience (which it is not); he is rather asserting that our experience must conform to a fixed form of reason. I, however, do not find this "dichotomous" thinking helpful and I have tried to reform academic environmental philosophy by avoiding the either-or choice that Callicott places at the center of his ethic.

Callicott's victory by definition is supplemented with another sleight of hand. Having declared that all anthropocentric values—again, I guess, by definition—are "instrumental," and having characterized all "instrumental" values as involving economic trade-offs (as noted above), Callicott has defined the categories of ethics so that anyone who is an anthropocentrist is necessarily committed to the reduction of all human value to economic value. This generalization defies common sense and ordinary language. In the process of pronouncing this tendentious definition, he has eliminated his toughest competition—weak/broad anthropocentrism—by definition. Now, however, having won the argument by definition, one wonders how Callicott would argue for his restrictive set of definitions, which are essential to "convict" me of holding positions I directly dispute. If he simply leaves it, as he does in Chapter 9, as a casual observation of the linguistic habits of academic environmental philosophers, then my answer is that, indeed, academic philosophers did, in the 1970s, fall into the unfortunate lingo of past dualisms. That unfortunate fall necessitated my efforts to change the linguistic conventions of environmental ethics and valuation by eliminating metaphysics and creating categories more descriptive of how humans actually value nature, in a multiscalar way. I believe these action-oriented categories will be more useful in understanding how people actually do value nature. If, however, Callicott wants to use it as a *premise* in his argument to show that I cannot be an anthropocentrist without being an economic reductionist, he needs more support than citing the linguistic habits of his cronies in a specialized field generally considered a rather esoteric endeavor.

I can see two possibilities. First, perhaps he thinks the definitions are true, a priori. But since they apparently rule out substantive philosophical positions such as weak/broad anthropocentrism, then he is apparently committed to a synthetic a priori: Some substantive positions in environmental ethics are false because they conflict with the a priori categories of traditional, dualistic philosophy. Since I do not believe in synthetic a priori knowledge, I reject this argument out of hand. We might, of course, carry on an epistemological argument at this point, but pursuing that would be premature because I doubt Callicott would go this route.

Rather, I think he would argue that the distinctions between intrinsic and instrumental value are well established in ordinary language, and he has a right to use them in argument. The problem with this argument is that its premise—that the distinctions as he uses them are enshrined in ordinary language—is simply false. Long before anyone proposed the distinction between anthropocentric and nonanthropocentric environmental ethics, it was common, for example, to value paintings or other works of art for their "intrinsic" merit, even though nobody believed this entailed that paintings have value beyond the human context in which they were painted or valued. Similarly, people throughout history have been comfortable talking about "intrinsically valuable" human experiences, from religious experiences to experiences of awe at seeing the Grand Canyon. In ordinary language, intrinsic valuing was often a special kind of human valuing, and for Callicott to define all intrinsic valuing as nonanthropocentric is lexically incorrect as a description of ordinary speech. Human beings can love other species; they can value aspects of nature "noninstrumentally" in the sense that—while they do not question that it is a human value—they recognize it is a special kind of value. We pluralistic environmentalists have no problem with this perfectly normal

speech—we value things in many ways, and these ways vary across a continuum from consumptive values to recreational values, transformative values,
spiritual values, and so forth. But for Callicott, committed to his set of definitions for whatever reasons, anthropocentric pluralists contradict themselves
every time they say that they value something noninstrumentally.

The oddity of the linguistic and analytic framework that Callicott attempts to impose in order to save his idea of value as distinct from human
value can be seen by listing some of the consequences of his definitions, and
the legislative and juridical interpretation of the values comprehended by his
definitions. Consider the following, apparently odd consequences of his
position:

1. No anthropocentrist can attribute the kind of value that Callicott
   calls "noninstrumental" or "intrinsic." Therefore, it was impossible
   for nature to have intrinsic value before the twentieth century (except for a brief existence while St. Francis of Assisi was alive).
2. The legislature of some countries, some states, and some municipalities afford legal standing to endangered species. Therefore,
   endangered species have intrinsic value in some jurisdictions and
   not in others at the same time.
3. If a legislature and the courts first grant standing to species, and
   then withdraw it, the species gains, and then loses, intrinsic value.
4. If a species indeed has intrinsic value, it has it because of a legislative or juridical act. Most nonanthropocentrists I know would reverse this argument: Legislatures should protect species and give
   them standing because species have intrinsic value.
5. Since I value nature noninstrumentally (not as a fulfillment of my
   "preferences," but as providing powerful experiences capable of
   transforming those preferences), I am a nonanthropocentrist.

I conclude that Callicott cannot defend his definitions on the grounds
that they rest on the logic of ordinary language concepts. His only refuge,
then, is to support his definitions as true a priori. This reinforces the point I
have made for years: The real difference between anthropocentrists and
nonanthropocentrists has more to do with epistemological disagreements
than with environmental ethics and values.

Now, however, having shown that Callicott's argument that anthropocentrists cannot value nonhuman objects noninstrumentally or intrinsically applies only if we accept his nonstandard and tendentious definitions, we must
return to the larger argument. Callicott cannot believe what he reads in my
texts—that I am truly a broad anthropocentrist who recognizes many types
of human value—because he is trapped in the definitional web that he so

desperately wove to save his concept of "nonanthropocentric value" that he thinks any human but noninstrumental value is an oxymoron. That, however, is a problem with his definitions, not mine. I urge him to consider a truly pragmatic, conventional view of language in which language is used for communication—rather than invoked as harboring a priori rules forcing language users to toe the line and accept his dualistic and metaphysical categories of value.

Having dealt with several of the more severe criticisms of my work, I close this response-oriented part by mentioning in passing my reactions to other critical essays, generally the ones that treat my work more gently. As noted, I am reassured by the fact that two authors who have significant experience in the world of policy, Brown and Sarewitz, endorse the CH. In general, it has been philosophers, especially those of a nonanthropocentric bent, who have violently opposed the CH. I am appreciative, also, that Paul Thompson sees parallels and echoes between my community-based approach and the old agrarian movements. I welcome this kind of commentary, as it clarifies the implications of adaptive management to have it seen through another value lens. I do think sustainability theory has a lot to learn from good farmers; and the agrarian ideas may prove the most effective form of "sense of place"—which I include as a definitional aspect of adaptive management—in many areas of the United States.

Douglas MacLean provides an analysis of one of my early attempts to develop a theory of intergenerational ethics suitable as a value theory for sustainability management; an experiment in trying to apply Rawls's contractual model to justify protection of ecological and other ecophysical systems. As I explain in *Sustainability*, I decided during the 1990s not to develop a contractual model because I think it merely shifts the problem of what we owe the future into another unanswerable question: How can future generations be represented in contractual bargaining? Worries about Rawls's model, including some mentioned by MacLean, convinced me to develop a model based on acts of commitment called "community performatives."[41]

The Future of the Convergence Hypothesis

As noted by Andrew Light, I take a somewhat different viewpoint on the CH in my book *Sustainability*. In that book, I tried to reform our language for discussing environmental values and policy and proposed that, once my linguistic scrubbing of the old, vestigial, dualistic categories is complete, the CH will no longer be essential. I tried, that is, to propose a pluralistic vocabulary rich enough to include all people and all values in a deliberative process, and set out to replace the illusory separation of humans from nature that originated in dualistic metaphysics and still infects our language today with a pluralistic but procedural approach to hearing and integrating multiple values through deliberative processes and social learning. In *Sustainability*, viewing the conceptual landscape prospectively, I saw the CH withering away for lack of polarized rhetoric demanding the application of it. Light points out, which I had noticed, that the CH remains useful in any discourse that retains dualisms of humans and natural objects (or "intrinsically valued" and "instrumentally valued" nonhumans). And, despite my efforts and commitment to transcend dualisms, I acknowledge that, if it withers, the CH will do so slowly, as there will remain for decades to come pockets of philosophers who insist on a divergence hypothesis. What I had not considered is Light's very nice point that, if anthropocentrism and nonanthropocentrism advocate the same policies, and they are being replaced by a better, less-dualistic explanation of policy, we can expect a triangular convergence, which may provide yet more ways to model, explain, and justify environmental values. Since my linguistic coup will no doubt remain a long-term project for some time to come, Light is correct in saying that the CH has a bright future, in which expanding knowledge of the many factors affecting human well-being, from climate to ecological systems to survival needs, is likely to find more and more ways in which doing the right thing for humans is also doing the right thing for wild animals and natural systems. Even if the dualisms of modernism and the modernist hangover we suffer currently fade away, the CH has a bright future. An empirical hypothesis that also functions like an act of faith and as a working hypothesis, the CH directs attention toward policies with positive implications for values of humans and nature, and away from fruitless debates over which motives for environmental policies are morally most pure.

Contributors

Donald A. Brown is associate professor of environmental ethics, science, and law at Pennsylvania State University and director of the Ethical Dimensions of Climate Change Program housed in Penn State's Rock Ethics Institute. Brown is also director of the Pennsylvania Environmental Research Consortium, an organization comprised of fifty-six Pennsylvania universities and the Pennsylvania Departments of Environmental Protection and Conservation and Natural Resources. He has written about and lectured extensively on climate change issues over the last twenty years, with a focus on the need to integrate environmental science, economics, and law in environmental policy making. His latest book is *American Heat: Ethical Problems with the U.S. Response to Global Warming* (2002).

J. Baird Callicott is Regents' Professor of Philosophy and chair of the Department of Philosophy and Religion Studies at the University of North Texas. He is the coeditor in chief of the *Encyclopedia of Environmental Ethics and Philosophy* (2008) and author or editor of a score of books and author of more than a hundred journal articles, encyclopedia articles, and book chapters in environmental philosophy and ethics. He has served the International Society for Environmental Ethics as president and Yale University as bioethicist-in-residence. He is perhaps best known as a contemporary exponent of Aldo Leopold's land ethic and is currently exploring an Aldo Leopold Earth ethic in response to global climate change.

Eric Katz is professor of philosophy at the New Jersey Institute of Technology. He is the author of *Nature as Subject: Human Obligation and Natural Community* (1997), and editor of *Death by Design: Science, Technology, and Engineering in Nazi Germany* (2006). He has coedited (with Andrew Light) the collection *Environmental Pragmatism* (1996) and (with Andrew Light and David Rothenberg) the collection *Beneath the Surface: Critical Essays in the Philosophy of Deep Ecology* (2000), and (with Andrew Light and William Thompson) the textbook *Controlling Technology*, 2nd ed. (2003).

Andrew Light is associate professor of philosophy and environmental policy and director of the Center for Global Ethics at George Mason University. He is also a Senior Fellow at the Center for American Progress in Washington, D.C. He works primarily on the ethical dimensions of environmental policy and emerging technologies, with special attention to restoration ecology, nanotechnology, and, more recently, climate change. He has authored, coauthored, and edited seventeen books, including *Environmental Values* (2007), *Philosophy and Design* (2007), *The Aesthetics of Everyday Life* (2005), *Moral and Political Reasoning in Environmental Practice* (2003), *Technology and the Good Life?* (2000), and *Environmental Pragmatism* (1996).

Douglas MacLean is a professor of philosophy at the University of North Carolina at Chapel Hill. He is also an affiliate faculty member in the Institute for the Environment. His research focuses on moral philosophy and public policy and he has published extensively on risk, energy policy, and the philosophy of environmental valuation.

Robert E. Manning is professor of natural resources in the Rubenstein School of Environment and Natural Resources at the University of Vermont. Manning teaches courses on the history, philosophy, and management of national parks, wilderness, and related areas, and conducts a program of research for the U.S. National Park Service and other agencies. He is the author of *Studies in Outdoor Recreation* (1999, 2nd ed.) and *Parks and Carrying Capacity: Commons without Tragedy* (2007), and coeditor (with Ben Minteer) of *Reconstructing Conservation: Finding Common Ground* (2003).

Ben A. Minteer is an assistant professor of environmental ethics and policy in the Human Dimensions unit of the School of Life Sciences and an affiliate assistant professor of philosophy at Arizona State University. His research focuses on the linkages between environmental ethics and policy goals and the history and philosophy of conservation and environmentalism. He is author or editor of several books, including most recently *The Landscape of Reform: Civic Pragmatism and Environmental Thought in America* (2006) and *Reconstructing Conservation: Finding Common Ground* (2003).

Bryan G. Norton is Distinguished Professor of Philosophy, Science, and Technology in the School of Public Policy, Georgia Institute of Technology. Norton specializes in environmental ethics, biodiversity policy, sustainability theory, public participation, and in spatial scaling aspects of environmental problems. He is author of *Why Preserve Natural Variety?* (1987), *Toward Unity among Environmentalists* (1991), *Searching for Sustainability* (2002), and *Sustainability: A Philosophy of Adaptive Ecosystem Management* (2005). He has also edited and coedited several volumes, and he has published widely in the journals of several disciplines.

Holmes Rolston III is University Distinguished Professor and professor emeritus of philosophy at Colorado State University and a founder of environmental ethics as a philosophical discipline. His books include *Philosophy Gone Wild* (1986), *Environmental Ethics* (1988), *Conserving Natural Value* (1994), and *Science and Religion: A Critical Survey* (2006, new ed.). He gave the Gifford Lectures, University of Edinburgh, 1997–1998, published as *Genes, Genesis and God* (1999). Advocating environmental ethics, he has lectured on seven continents. He is featured in Joy A. Palmer, ed., *Fifty Key Thinkers on the Environment* (2001), and is past and founding president of the International Society for Environmental Ethics.

Daniel Sarewitz is professor of science and society, and director and cofounder of the Consortium for Science, Policy, and Outcomes at Arizona State University. His work focuses on revealing the connections between science policy decisions, scientific research, and social outcomes. He is the author of *Frontiers of Illusion: Science, Technology, and the Politics of Progress* (1996); the coeditor of three other books; and the author of many scholarly and general-audience articles about the interactions of science, technology, and society. From 1989 to 1993, he worked on R&D policy issues as a staff member in the U.S. House of Representatives.

Mikael Stenmark is head of department and professor of philosophy of religion at the Department of Theology, Uppsala University, Sweden. His books include *How to Relate Science and Religion: A Multidimensional Model* (2004), *Environmental Ethics and Environmental Policy Making* (2002), *Scientism: Science, Ethics and Religion* (2001), and *Rationality in Science, Religion and Everyday Life* (1995). He has also published articles in journals such as *Religious Studies, Faith and Philosophy, Zygon: Journal of Religion and Science, Heythrop Journal,* and *Environmental Ethics.*

Brian K. Steverson is the John L. Aram Chair in Business Ethics in the School of Business at Gonzaga University. His research areas are environmental ethics, business ethics, and metaethical issues related to evolutionary emotivism. Steverson's work has appeared in the journals *Environmental Ethics, Environmental Values,* and *Ethics, Place, and Environment.*

Paul B. Thompson is the W. K. Kellogg Professor of Agricultural, Food and Community Ethics at Michigan State University, where he teaches in philosophy and in the College of Agriculture and Natural Resources. His book, *Food Biotechnology in Ethical Perspective,* was released in a second edition in 2007, and two edited volumes, *What Can Nanotechnology Learn from Biotechnology?* and *The Ethics of Agricultural Intensification,* were published in 2008.

Laura Westra is professor emerita (philosophy) at the University of Windsor. She is the founder of the Global Ecological Integrity Group (GEIG), and has organized several conferences of that group in conjunction with the IUCN Commission on Law and Environment (CEL), Special Ethics Group (ESG). She is also the cochair of the IUCN-CEL Specialist Indigenous Peoples Group. Most of Westra's work is on environmental ethics, policy, and law, with special emphasis on human rights and global justice. Westra has published more than eighty articles and chapters in books, and twenty books/monographs in these areas.

Notes

1 UNITY AMONG ENVIRONMENTALISTS?

1. Richard Routley, "Is There a Need for a New, an Environmental Ethic?" *Proceedings, 15th World Congress of Philosophy* 1 (1973): 205–210.

2. A short list of important work advancing the nonanthropocentric position in environmental ethics in the 1980s and 1990s would include: Paul Taylor, *Respect for Nature* (Princeton: Princeton University Press, 1986); Holmes Rolston III, *Environmental Ethics* (Philadelphia: Temple University Press, 1988) and *Conserving Natural Value* (New York: Columbia University Press, 1994); J. Baird Callicott, *In Defense of the Land Ethic* (Albany: State University of New York Press, 1989) and *Beyond the Land Ethic* (Albany: State University of New York Press, 1999); Robin Attfield, *The Ethics of Environmental Concern* (Athens: University of Georgia Press, 1991); Lawrence E. Johnson, *A Morally Deep World: An Essay on Moral Significance and Environmental Ethics* (Cambridge, UK: Cambridge University Press, 1993); Laura Westra, *An Environmental Proposal for Ethics: The Principle of Integrity* (Lanham, MD: Rowman & Littlefield, 1994); Richard Sylvan and David Bennett, *The Greening of Ethics: From Human Chauvinism to Deep Green Theory* (Tucson: University of Arizona Press, 1994); Eric Katz, *Nature as Subject: Human Obligation and Natural Community* (Lanham, MD: Rowman & Littlefield, 1996); and Robert Elliot, *Faking Nature: The Ethics of Ecological Restoration* (London: Routledge, 1997).

3. Two authoritative statements of the deep ecology approach are Bill Devall and George Sessions, *Deep Ecology: Living as if Nature Mattered* (Salt Lake City, UT: Gibbs Smith 1985); and Arne Naess, *Ecology, Community and Lifestyle*, trans. David Rothenberg (Cambridge: Cambridge University Press, 1989).

4. This attitude has been expressed by many contributors to the field, including Holmes Rolston, J. Baird Callicott, Laura Westra, and Eric Katz, among others.

5. Steven Cohen, *Understanding Environmental Policy* (New York: Columbia University Press, 2006), p. 15.

6. *National Environmental Policy Act of 1969*, Public Law 91-190, *U.S. Code* 42 (January 1, 1970), §§ 4321–4347.

7. Caldwell was one of the key advisors to the legislative construction of NEPA in the late 1960s. See Lynton Keith Caldwell, *The National Environmental Policy Act: An Agenda for the Future* (Bloomington: Indiana University Press, 1998); quote on p. 6. Italics in original.

8. *National Environmental Policy Act*, Sec. 2.

9. *National Environmental Policy Act*, Sec. 101, *U.S. Code* 42, § 4331.

10. Harold Glasser offers a different interpretation of the value foundations of NEPA, suggesting that it is in fact consistent with the (nonanthropocentric) deep ecology approach of Arne Naess. According to Glasser, NEPA is congruent with deep ecology in that it "symbolizes an effort to integrate deep problematizing with value-based considerations." I think this reading of the Act requires a considerable stretch of the imagination; even Glasser, for example, acknowledges that there is no explicit nonanthropocentric language to be found in NEPA. See Glasser, "Naess's Deep Ecology Approach and Environmental Policy," in *Philosophical Dialogues: Arne Naess and the Progress of Ecophilosophy*, ed. Nina Witoszek and Andrew Brennan (Lanham, MD: Rowman & Littlefield, Inc., 1999), pp. 360–390; quote on p. 370.

11. *Clean Water Act*, Sec. 404, *U.S. Code* 33, § 1344.

12. Alyson C. Flourney, "Building an Environmental Ethic from the Ground Up," *UC Davis Law Review* 37 (2003–2004): 53–80; quote on p. 62.

13. Flourney, "In Search of an Environmental Ethic," *Columbia Journal of Environmental Law* 28 (2003): 63–118; esp. p. 105.

14. Flourney does note, however, that there is room for alternative interpretations of some statutory provisions that may comport with nonanthropocentric arguments, but these are clearly minority elements and far from the primary (i.e., anthropocentric) justifications. As she puts it, "Most of our environmental laws, as implemented, reflect predominantly an ethical impulse that is both anthropocentric and utilitarian." See Flourney, "Building an Environmental Ethic," p. 67.

15. This is not to say that individuals working within conservation and environmental organizations do not hold alternative views. Along these lines, a recent study of land management conservation organizations in England showed that a majority of the managers and conservation practitioners interviewed held intrinsic-value-of-nature views, even while they acknowledged these values were not reflected in formal organizational policy. See W. F. Butler and T. G. Acott, "An Inquiry Concerning the Acceptance of Intrinsic Value Theories of Nature," *Environmental Values* 16 (2007): 149–168.

16. For example, Mark Sagoff, *The Economy of the Earth* (Cambridge: Cambridge University Press, 1988) and *Price, Principle, and the Environment* (Cambridge: Cambridge University Press, 2004).

17. Deborah Stone, *Policy Paradox: The Art of Political Decision Making*, 2nd ed. (New York: Norton, 2001), p. 34.

18. However, see J. Baird Callicott's argument in Chapter 9 (this volume) for an alternative view of the moral standing of species that Callicott believes has emerged under subsequent judicial and legislative interpretation of the Endangered Species Act.

19. Eric Katz, *Nature as Subject: Human Obligation and Natural Community* (Lanham, MD: Rowman & Littlefield, 1997), p. 166.

20. J. Baird Callicott, "The Pragmatic Power and Promise of Theoretical Environmental Ethics: Forging a New Discourse," *Environmental Values* 11 (2002): 3–25; quote on p. 14. Italics in original.

21. Josh Donlan et al., "Re-wilding North America," *Nature* 436 (2005): 913–914.

22. The Rewilding Institute, http://www.rewilding.org/.

23. J. Baird Callicott, "Environmental Philosophy IS Environmental Activism: The Most Radical and Effective Kind," in *Environmental Philosophy and Environmental Activism*, ed. Don E. Marietta Jr. and Lester Embree (Lanham, MD: Rowman & Littlefield), pp. 19–35.

24. See especially Bryan G. Norton, "Environmental Ethics and Weak Anthropocentrism," *Environmental Ethics* 6 (1984): 131–148; and "Why I Am Not a Nonanthropocentrist: Callicott and the Failure of Monistic Inherentism," *Environmental Ethics* 17 (1995): 341–358.

25. It is important to note that Norton was not the only (nor the first) philosopher to advance an anthropocentric project in the field's first two decades of development (i.e., the 1970s and 1980s). John Passmore's *Man's Responsibility for Nature* (New York: Scribner, 1974), in addition to being one of the first single-author works in environmental ethics, similarly rejected the notion that modern environmental problems required the replacement of Western (i.e., anthropocentric) ethics with a new nonanthropocentric moral philosophy.

26. See the discussion of transformative value in Bryan G. Norton, *Why Preserve Natural Variety?* (Princeton, NJ: Princeton University Press, 1987).

27. Norton, "Environmental Ethics and Weak Anthropocentrism," pp. 131–148.

28. Norton's effort to make environmental ethics more relevant to environmental policy discourse and decision making has gained momentum since the mid-1990s. Much of this work has emerged under the banner of "environmental pragmatism," which received its philosophical coming-out party in Andrew Light and Eric Katz, eds., *Environmental Pragmatism* (London: Routledge, 1996). This "policy turn" (as Robert Frodeman puts it), though, includes philosophers outside the pragmatist tradition who nevertheless share the pragmatists' concern that environmental philosophy has not engaged policy making as much as it should. The latter includes work beyond the usual broad discussions of environmental protection, such as concrete normative analyses of actual environmental dilemmas, study of the intersection of politics and environmental values in public decision making, philosophical investigations of environmental science policy, and related issues and problems. For a good discussion of this emerging multidimensional policy focus within environmental philosophy, see Robert Frodeman, "The Policy Turn in Environmental Philosophy," *Environmental Ethics* 28 (2006): 1–20.

29. Bryan G. Norton, *Toward Unity among Environmentalists* (New York: Oxford University Press, 1991), p. 12. Italics in original.

30. Ibid., p. 240.

31. Ibid., p. 201.

32. Ibid., p. 203. Italics in original.

33. See Bryan G. Norton, "Epistemology and Environmental Values," *The Monist* 75 (1992): 208–226; and "Why I Am Not a Nonanthropocentrist," pp. 341–358.

34. See, e.g., Light and Katz, *Environmental Pragmatism*. Norton's debt to pragmatist philosophy became increasingly explicit and direct in the years since the publication of *Toward Unity*. In fact, his most recent book, *Sustainability: A Philosophy of Adaptive Ecosystem Management* (Chicago: University of Chicago Press, 2005), may be read as his attempt to work out the implications of a pragmatist epistemology and philosophy of language for a comprehensive, integrated model of environmental valuation.

35. Space limitations of the present volume did not permit the inclusion of Steverson's rejoinder to Norton's reply. But see Brian K. Steverson, "On Norton's Reply to Steverson," *Environmental Ethics* 19 (1997): 335–336.

36. The convergence idea, we should remember, describes the potential policy compatibility *within* the environmental philosophy and advocacy community; the suggestion that there is common ground between environmentalists and other groups/interests (e.g., labor parties, property rights advocates, resource developers, etc.) is another argument, though one that merits more scrutiny by environmental ethicists. I thank an anonymous reviewer for Temple University Press for emphasizing this important point.

37. See, for example, Bryan G. Norton, "Why I Am Not a Nonanthropcentrist"; Callicott, "The Pragmatic Power and Promise of Theoretical Environmental Ethics"; and Ben A. Minteer, "Environmental Philosophy and the Public Interest: A Pragmatic Reconciliation," *Environmental Values* 14 (2005): 37–60. An interesting empirical study of the impact of environmental ethics in law and policy is Christopher Stone, "Do Morals Matter? The Influence of Ethics on Courts and Congress in Shaping U.S. Environmental Policies," *UC Davis Law Review* 37 (2003–2004): 13–51.

2 CONTEXTUALISM AND NORTON'S CONVERGENCE HYPOTHESIS

1. An early attempt at arguing for this convergence can be found in Bryan G. Norton, "Environmental Ethics and Weak Anthropocentrism," *Environmental Ethics* 6 (1984): 131–148. That argument has been developed and refined in Norton's "Conservation and Preservation: A Conceptual Rehabilitation," *Environmental Ethics* 8 (1986): 195–220, and his *Toward Unity among Environmentalists* (New York: Oxford University Press, 1991). Recently, James Sterba has argued for a similar kind of convergence regarding principles of justice. See "Environmental Justice," in *Morality in Practice*, ed. James P. Sterba, 4th ed. (Belmont, CA: Wadsworth, 1994), pp. 499–506.

2. Norton, *Toward Unity among Environmentalists*, p. 187.

3. Ibid., chap. 12.

4. Ibid., pp. 226–227.

5. Ibid., pp. 225–226. This baseline principle of species preservation was developed by S. V. Ciriacy-Wantrup in his *Resource Conservation: Economics and Politics* (Berkeley and Los Angeles: University of California, Division of Agricultural Sciences, 1959) as a way of dealing with the inherent limitations of quantifying resource benefits. Norton also defends the use of the SMS approach in his *Why Preserve Natural Variety?* (Princeton, NJ: Princeton University Press, 1987), p. 36.

6. Ibid., p. 224.

7. Arne Naess, "The Shallow and the Deep, Long-Range Ecology Movement: A Summary," *Inquiry* 16 (1973): 95.

8. Norton, *Toward Unity among Environmentalists*, p. 224.

9. Ibid., p. 225.

10. Ibid., p. 240.

11. Ibid.

12. The key articles are Bryan G. Norton, "Context and Hierarchy in Aldo Leopold's Theory of Environmental Management," *Ecological Economics* 2 (1990): 119–127; "Sustainability, Human Welfare, and Ecosystem Health," *Environmental Values* 1 (1992): 97–111; "Should Environmentalists Be Organicists?" *Environmental Values* 12 (1993): 21–30; and, coauthored with Robert E. Ulanowicz, "Scale and Biodiversity Policy: A Hierarchical Approach," *Ambio* 21 (1992): 244–249.

13. Norton, "Sustainability, Human Welfare, and Ecosystem Health," p. 105.

14. Norton, "Should Environmentalists Be Organicists?" p. 28.

15. Norton, *Why Preserve Natural Variety?* chap. 4.

16. Ramon Margalef, "On Certain Unifying Principles in Ecology," *American Naturalist* 97 (1963): 357–374. Norton also cites Eugene P. Odum, "The Strategy of Ecosystem Development," *Science* 164 (1969): 262–270.

17. Norton cites Ulanowicz on this point in "Scale and Biodiversity Policy," p. 247.

18. Norton, *Why Preserve Natural Variety?* p. 84. The idea of ecosystemic autogeny advanced by Norton is similar to the Gaia hypothesis that the biosphere is a self-regulating system, and to the idea that ecosystems are autopoietic entities, as recently suggested by Callicott. See J. E. Lovelock, *Gaia: A New Look at Life on Earth* (Oxford: Oxford University Press, 1979); and J. Baird Callicott, "Aldo Leopold's Metaphor," in *Ecosystem Health: New Goals for Environmental Management,* ed. Robert Costanza, Bryan G. Norton, and Benjamin D. Haskell (Covelo, CA: Island Press, 1992), pp. 42–56.

19. An oft-cited source for hierarchy theory is R. V. O'Neill, D. L. Angelis, J. B. Waide, and T.F.H. Allen, *A Hierarchical Concept of Ecosystems* (Princeton, NJ: Princeton University Press, 1986). Norton relies on an earlier work, T.F.H. Allen and Thomas B. Starr, *Hierarchy: Perspectives for Ecological Complexity* (Chicago: University of Chicago Press, 1982).

20. Norton, *Toward Unity among Environmentalists,* p. 148.

21. Ibid., p. 148.

22. Ibid., p. 151.

23. Ibid., p. 147.

24. Ibid., p. 153.

25. Norton, *Why Preserve Natural Variety?* p. 36.

26. For example, see Norton and Ulanowicz, "Scale and Biodiversity Policy," p. 248.

27. Ibid., p. 246. Italics in original.

28. Ibid., p. 248.

29. Ibid., p. 249.

30. Costanza, Norton, and Haskell, *Ecosystem Health,* is an outstanding collection of essays by authors supportive of this approach.

31. Norton, "Sustainability, Human Welfare, and Ecosystem Health," p. 105.

32. Norton and Ulanowicz, "Scale and Biodiversity Policy," p. 244. Italics in original.

33. Norton discusses these difficulties in "A New Paradigm for Environmental Management," in Costanza, Norton, and Haskell, *Ecosystem Health,* pp. 23–41. David J. Rapport has labeled this branch of ecological science "clinical ecology." See Rapport,

"What Is Clinical Ecology?" in Costanza, Norton, and Haskell, *Ecosystem Health*, pp. 144–156. Additionally, a growing branch of scientific ecology, restoration ecology, is built on the premise that ecological science is capable of generating the kind of knowledge of ecological systems necessary to restore damaged or "ailing" systems to some healthy state. See, for example, William R. Jordan III, Michael E. Gilpin, and John D. Aber, eds., *Restoration Ecology* (Cambridge: Cambridge University Press, 1987).

34. Norton, *Toward Unity among Environmentalists*, p. 151.

35. Ibid., p. 140.

3 CONVERGENCE AND CONTEXTUALISM

1. In Brian K. Steverson, "Contextualism and Norton's Convergence Hypothesis," *Environmental Ethics* 17 (1995): 135–150 (original; reprinted in Chapter 2 of this volume).

2. Bryan G. Norton, "Conservation and Preservation: A Conceptual Rehabilitation," *Environmental Ethics* 8 (1986): 195–220. See also Norton, *Toward Unity among Environmentalists* (New York: Oxford University Press, 1991), esp. pp. 237–243, where I argued that the divergence hypothesis, which describes environmentalists as split into two policy camps because they have opposed ultimate values, was not really accurate even in the early days of Muir and Pinchot (see pp. 34–38).

3. Steverson, "Contextualism and Norton's Convergence Hypothesis," p. 148 (orig.; p. 33 in this volume).

4. The safe minimum standard criterion was proposed to cover cases in which (a) the benefits of protection of a resource are difficult or impossible to characterize, enumerate, or count, and in which (b) loss of the resource is irreversible. I, and others, have been impressed with the robustness, if not the precision, of the safe minimum standard criterion, and with its apparent application to the case of species protection. See S. V. Ciriacy-Wantrup, *Resource Conservation: Economics and Policies* (Berkeley: University of California Press, 1963); Richard Bishop, "Endangered Species and Uncertainty: The Economics of the Safe Minimum Standard," *American Journal of Agricultural Economics* 60 (1978): 10–18; Bryan Norton, *Why Preserve Natural Variety?* (Princeton, NJ: Princeton University Press, 1987), esp. pp. 35–39, 119–123; and Norton, *Toward Unity*, esp. pp. 152–153, 225.

5. While I find this intuitionistic interpretation of deep ecologists' moral position somewhat surprising, there is no doubt that it is Steverson's intention to attribute an intuitionistic logic to them (Steverson, "Contextualism and Norton's Convergence Hypothesis," p. 137 in orig.; p. 23 in this volume). Appeals to intuitions in ethics are ambiguous, as has been pointed out by B.A.O. Williams, who distinguishes between *intuitionism* as a faculty, allowing the a priori grasp of ethical truths, and not-yet-theorized individual reactions to concrete ethical quandaries. But, referring to "axiological intuitions," it is clear that Steverson thinks deep ecologists subscribe to the model of intuitionistic, a priori ethics that, as Williams says, "has been demolished by a succession of critics." B.A.O. Williams, *Ethics and the Limits of Philosophy* (Cambridge, MA: Harvard University Press, 1985, pp. 93–95. In my own approach to ethics, I give great weight to intuitions of the second sense (which Williams calls "spontaneous convictions"), but these have nothing in common with the a priori, general axiological principles of Steverson's deep ecologists. See Norton, *Toward Unity*, esp. pp. 86–93. At first

it may seem curious that Steverson, who does not reveal his own theoretical views, is so willing to accept the "intuition" of deep ecologists without examination; but that is of course the fate of self-evident intuitions—the very classification of them as such sets them above discussion. Accordingly, I take it as a compliment that Steverson criticizes what he takes to be the management consequences of contextualism—suggesting that something is asserted by that method, and that such assertion can be debated and perhaps revised or even refuted. What is odd in this situation is that, according to Steverson's argument, an empirical hypothesis is being held to account by comparison to an intuitively known principle.

6. Steverson, "Contextualism and Norton's Convergence Hypothesis," p. 139 (orig.; p. 25 in this volume).

7. Ibid., p. 137, (orig.; p. 23 in this volume), for example.

8. Note that the consideration of this open question could be characterized, among theorists who accept the safe minimum standard criterion as the best available criterion of action, as the question of the "level" (individual, species, or ecosystem) at which to apply the safe minimum standard criterion. If the "resource" referred to is "nature," or "the complex processes of nature," then species might, in some cases, appear less important than a process. Incidentally, while I recognize that deep ecologists object to use of the term "resource" because it reduces nature to instrumental value only, I am using the term here in the neutral sense (as I think Ciriacy-Wantrup intended), to refer to anything that is the object of conservation efforts.

9. Joe Alper, "Everglades Rebound from Andrew," *Science* 257 (1992): 1853.

10. Stuart Pimm, personal communication with author.

11. Steverson, "Contextualism and Norton's Convergence Hypothesis," p. 138 (orig.; p. 24 in this volume).

12. See Bryan G. Norton, Michael Hutchins, Elizabeth F. Stevens, and Terry L. Maple, *Ethics on the Ark: Zoos, Animal Welfare, and Wildlife Conservation* (Washington, DC: Smithsonian Institution Press, 1995). The chapters in Part II of this book discuss the problem of identifying conservation targets from several perspectives.

13. In "Contextualism and Norton's Convergence Hypothesis," p. 146 (orig.; p. 31 in this volume), for example, Steverson describes species as the "objects of ultimate concern." This characterization, I think, links the general intuition that species have intrinsic value with the question of conservation targets in Steverson's mind. He believes (falsely, I argue below) that determining what is of ultimate value in conservation efforts implies clear answers to the practical question of conservation targets.

14. Bryan G. Norton, "Biological Resources and Endangered Species: History, Values, and Policy" in *Protection of Global Biodiversity: Converging Strategies*, ed. Jeffrey McNeeley and Lakshman Guruswamy (Durham, NC: Duke University Press, 1998), pp. 247–264.

15. This use of the term *landscape* is explained in Bryan G. Norton and Robert E. Ulanowicz, "Scale and Biodiversity Policy," *Ambio* 21, no. 3 (June 1992): 244–249.

16. Steverson, "Contextualism and Norton's Convergence Hypothesis," p. 147 (orig.; p. 32 in this volume).

17. Ibid., p. 147 (orig.; p. 32 in this volume).

18. Despite the centrality of this attribution to his criticism, Steverson does not provide a citation; this statement does not state a view I have ever held. It is apparently

attributed as an inference from other views I have stated, but an inference he thinks I would make under the counterfactual condition of complete knowledge.

19. Steverson, "Contextualism and Norton's Convergence Hypothesis," p. 149 (orig.; p. 34 in this volume).

20. Ibid., p. 150 (orig.; p. 34 in this volume).

21. See M. Faber, R. Manstetten, and J. Proops, "Toward an Open Future: Ignorance, Novelty, and Evolution," in *Ecosystem Health: New Goals for Environmental Management*, ed. Robert Costanza, Bryan G. Norton, and Ben Haskell (Covelo, CA: Island Press, 1992) for a detailed analysis of the problems of prediction in environmental management, and of the necessity to go beyond a characterization merely of "uncertainty."

22. See Norton, *Why Preserve Natural Variety?* chaps. 3 and 4, for discussion and references.

23. One must assume, of course, that Whittaker's Law operates within some limits, as was pointed out by an anonymous reviewer of an earlier version of this chapter. Since depauperate landscapes provide open territory for the invasion of plants and animals, a cascading crash in species diversity would eventually be blunted and reversed by a countervailing force of invasion. Just as a highly complex and organized system resists entry by more species, the cascading effects of adding species eventually slow. But within the current situation, these exceptions are irrelevant, at least on the global scale. The relevance of Whittaker's Law to the current situation, in which a cascade of species and diversity loss is beginning and accelerating, seems to be to caution avoidance of species loss, provided the costs of protection are affordable.

24. See Reed Noss and Jeffrey Murphy, "Endangered Species Left Homeless in Sweet Home," *Conservation Biology* 9 (1995): 229–231, for a practical plea for good judicial sense, and more emphasis on habitat protection. According to Noss and Murphy, "If habitat destruction is the leading threat to biodiversity, then protecting natural habitats should be the most effective way to conserve biodiversity."

25. Linda Brubaker, "Vegetation History and Anticipating Future Vegetation Changes," in *Ecosystem Management for Parks and Wilderness*, ed. James K. Agee and Darryl R. Johnson (Seattle: University of Washington Press, 1988).

26. Norton, *Toward Unity*, p. 83.

27. Ibid., p. 83.

28. See Kai Lee, *Compass and Gyroscope* (Covelo, CA: Island Press, 1993) for a useful analysis of the political context of social learning in pursuit of environmental goals. Also see Bryan G. Norton, "Reduction or Integration: Two Approaches to Environmental Values," in *Environmental Pragmatism*, ed. Andrew Light and Eric Katz (London: Routley Publishers, 1996) for a proposal for a pragmatist approach to environmental policy and ethics.

4 WHY NORTON'S APPROACH IS INSUFFICIENT
FOR ENVIRONMENTAL ETHICS

1. Ken Saro-Wiwa, "Right Livelihood Award Acceptance Speech," Stockholm, Sweden, 9 December 1994.

2. Carl Walters, *Fish on the Line* (Vancouver: David Suzuki Corporation and the Fisheries Centre, University of British Columbia, 1995).

3. *The Globe and Mail,* Toronto, Canada, 13 March 1995.

4. Kent H. Redford and Allyn M. Stearman, "Forest Dwelling Native Amazonians and the Conservation of Biodiversity: Interests in Common or in Collision?" *Conservation Biology* 7, no. 2 (1993): 248–255.

5. Robert Ulanowicz, "Ecosystem Integrity: A Causal Necessity," in *Perspectives on Ecological Integrity,* ed. Laura Westra and John Lemons (Dordrecht: Kluwer Academic Publishers, 1995), pp. 77–87.

6. Walters, *Fish on the Line,* pp. 50–52.

7. Monica Hammer, Ann Mari Jansson, and Bengt-Owe Jansson, "Diversity, Change and Sustainability: Implications for Fisheries," *Ambio* 22, nos. 2–3 (1993): 97–105. Italics in original.

8. Laura Westra, *An Environmental Proposal for Ethics: The Principle of Integrity* (Lanham, MD: Rowman & Littlefield, 1994); see Laura Westra "Ecosystem Integrity and Sustainability: The Foundational Value of the Wild," in Westra and Lemons, eds., *Perspectives on Ecological Integrity,* pp. 12–33.

9. Reed F. Noss, "What Should Endangered Ecosystems Mean to the Wildlands Project?" *Wild Earth* 5, no. 4 (1995–1996): 21.

10. Robert Goodland, "Environmental Sustainability and the Power Sector, Part I: The Concept of Sustainability," *Impact Assessment* 12, no. 3 (1994): 276.

11. Laura Westra, "Environmental Racism and the First Nation People of Canada: Terrorism at Oka," in *Canadian Studies in Applied Ethics,* ed. W. Cragg and A. Wellington (Toronto: Broadview Press, 1997); see also J. Baird Callicott, *In Defense of the Land Ethic* (Albany: State University of New York Press, 1989), esp. chap. 10, pp. 177–201.

12. Mark Sagoff, *The Economy of the Earth: Philosophy, Law and the Environment* (Cambridge: Cambridge University Press, 1988).

13. Ibid.

14. Donald Scherer and Thomas Attig, eds., *Upstream/Downstream* (Philadelphia, PA: Temple University Press, 1990).

15. Robert E. McGinn, "Technology, Demography, and the Anachronism of Traditional Rights," *Journal of Applied Philosophy* 11, no. 1 (1994): 57–70.

16. Walters, *Fish on the Line.*

17. Bryan G. Norton, "Why I Am Not a Nonanthropocentrist: Callicott and the Failure of Monistic Inherentism," *Environmental Ethics* 17 (1995): 341–358; see also Norton, "Environmental Ethics and Weak Anthropocentrism," *Environmental Ethics* 6, no. 2 (1984): 131–148.

18. Goodland, "Environmental Sustainability and the Power Sector, Part I," pp. 275–304.

19. Robert E. McGinn, "Technology, Demography, and the Anachronism of Traditional Rights," *Journal of Applied Philosophy* 11 (1994): 57–70.

20. Sagoff, *The Economy of the Earth.*

21. Eric T. Freyfogle, *Justice and the Earth: Images for Our Planetary Survival* (New York: Free Press and Macmillan, 1993), p. 27.

22. J. A. Hutchings and R. A. Myers, "What Can Be Learned from the Collapse of a Renewable Resource? Atlantic Cod, *Gadus Morhua,* of Newfoundland, Labrador," *Canadian Journal of Fisheries and Aquatic Science* 51 (1994): 2126–2146; see Hammer, Jansson, and Jansson, "Diversity, Change and Sustainability: Implications for Fisheries,"

and M. C. Beveridge, M. Lindsay, G. Ross, and L. A. Kelly, "Aquaculture and Biodiversity," *Ambio* 23, no. 8 (1994): 497–502.

23. William E. Rees and Mathis Wackernagel, *Our Ecological Footprint* (Gabriola Island, BC: New Society Publishers, 1996), p. 16.

24. Ibid., p. 4.

25. Ibid., pp. 14–16.

26. Ibid., pp. 55–57.

27. Laura Westra and Peter Wenz, eds., *The Faces of Environmental Racism: The Global Equity Issues* (Lanham, MD: Rowman & Littlefield, 1995).

28. Robert Ulanowicz, *Ecology: The Ascendent Perspective* (New York: Columbia University Press, 1997).

29. Donald A. Brown, "The Role of Law in Sustainable Development and Environmental Protection Decisionmaking," in *Sustainable Development: Science, Ethics and Public Policy*, ed. John Lemons and Donald A. Brown (Dordrecht: Kluwer Academic Press, 1995), pp. 64–76.

30. Thomas Muir and Anne Sudar, "Toxic Chemicals in the Great Lakes Basin Ecosystem," in *Science Advisory Board Report to the International Joint Commission* (Burlington, Ontario: Environmental Canada, 1987), p. 18.

31. Laura Westra, "Ecosystem Integrity and Sustainability: The Foundational Value of the Wild," in Westra and Lemons, eds., *Perspectives on Ecological Integrity*, pp. 12–13; Westra, *An Environmental Proposal for Ethics: The Principle of Integrity*, pp. 24–27, 41.

32. McGinn, "Technology, Demography, and the Anachronism of Traditional Rights," pp. 57–70.

33. Bryan G. Norton, *Toward Unity among Environmentalists* (New York: Oxford University Press, 1991), p. 222.

34. Brown, "The Role of Law in Sustainable Development and Environmental Protection Decisionmaking," pp. 64–76.

35. Donald Pauly, "Principles of Marine Ecology Applied to the Establishment of Marine Fisheries Reserves," 125th Meeting of the American Fishery Society, Tampa, Florida, 1995.

36. Westra, *An Environmental Proposal for Ethics*; Westra, "Ecosystem Integrity and Sustainability: The Foundational Value of the Wild."

37. Westra, *An Environmental Proposal for Ethics*.

38. Reed F. Noss, "The Wildlands Project: Land Conservation Strategy," *Wild Earth*, special issue (1992): 10–25; Reed F. Noss and A. Y. Cooperrider, *Saving Nature's Legacy* (Washington, DC: Island Press, 1994).

39. James J. Kay and E. Schneider, "The Challenge of the Ecosystem Approach," *Alternatives* 20, no. 3 (1994): 1–6; reprinted in Westra and Lemons, eds., *Perspectives on Integrity*, pp. 49–59.

40. Norton, *Toward Unity among Environmentalists*, p. 246.

41. Gary E. Varner, "Can Animal Right Activists be Environmentalists?" in *People, Penguins and Plastic Trees*, ed. Christina Pierce and Donald VandeVeer, 2nd ed. (Belmont, CA: Wadsworth Publishing Co., 1995): 254–273.

42. Norton, *Toward Unity among Environmentalists*, p. 246.

43. James Karr and Ellen Chu, "Ecological Integrity: Reclaiming Lost Connections," in Westra and Lemons, eds., *Perspectives on Ecological Integrity*, pp. 34–48; see

Noss and Cooperrider, *Saving Nature's Legacy*; and Reed F. Noss, "Maintaining Ecological Integrity in Representative Reserve Networks," World Wildlife Fund Canada/ World Wildlife Fund/United States Discussion Paper, January 1995.

44. Brown, "The Role of Law in Sustainable Development and Environmental Protection Decisionmaking," p. 67.

45. Bryan G. Norton, "A New Paradigm for Environmental Management," in *Ecosystem Health*, ed. Robert Costanza, Bryan G. Norton, and Benjamin D. Haskell (Washington, DC: Island Press, 1992), p. 24.

46. Westra, *An Environmental Proposal for Ethics*; see also G. Daily, ed., *Nature's Services* (Washington, DC: Island Press, 1997), esp. pp. 1–10.

47. Bryan G. Norton, "Environmental Ethics and Weak Anthropocentrism," *Environmental Ethics* 6, no. 2 (1984): 131–148; Norton, "Why I Am Not a Nonanthropocentrist," pp. 341–358.

48. See, for instance, William Aiken, "Ethical Issues in Agriculture," in *Earthbound: New Introductory Essays in Environmental Ethics*, ed. Tom Regan (New York: Random House, 1984), pp. 247–288, and Tom Regan, *The Case for Animal Rights* (Berkeley: University of California Press, 1983), to mention but two other opponents of arguments for holism of the ecocentric/biocentric variety.

49. Norton, "Environmental Ethics and Weak Anthropocentrism," p. 133.

50. Ibid.

51. Regan, *The Case for Animal Rights*, p. 50; Holmes Rolston III, *Environmental Ethics: Duties to and Values in the Natural World* (Philadelphia, PA: Temple University Press, 1988); Kenneth Goodpaster, "On Being Morally Considerable," *Journal of Philosophy* 75 (1978): 308–325; Paul W. Taylor, *Respect for Nature: A Theory of Environmental Ethics* (Princeton, NJ: Princeton University Press, 1986).

52. Norton, "Why I Am Not a Nonanthropocentrist."

53. Noss, "Maintaining Ecological Integrity in Representative Reserve Networks."

54. Klaus Meyer-Abich, *Revolution for Nature*, trans. Mattthew Armstrong (Cambridge, UK: White Horse Press, 1993).

55. Aldo Leopold, *A Sand County Almanac and Sketches Here and There* (New York: Oxford University Press, 1949).

56. Karr and Chu, "Ecological Integrity," pp. 34–48.

57. Robert Goodland and Herman Daly, "Universal Environmental Sustainability and the Principle of Integrity," in Westra and Lemons, eds., *Perspectives on Ecological Integrity*, pp. 102–124.

58. Goodland, "Environmental Sustainability and the Power Sector, Part I," pp. 275–304; Westra, "Ecosystem Integrity and Sustainability: The Foundational Value of the Wild," in Westra and Lemons, eds., *Perspectives on Ecological Integrity*, pp. 12–33.

59. Westra, *An Environmental Proposal for Ethics*.

60. Kristin Shrader-Frechette, *Nuclear Power and Public Policy* (Dordrecht: Kluwer Academic Publishers, 1982); Shrader-Frechette, *Risk and Rationality* (Berkeley: University of California Press, 1991); McGinn, "Technology, Demography, and the Anachronism of Traditional Rights."

61. Noss and Cooperrider, *Saving Nature's Legacy*; Hans Lenk, "Ecology and Ethics: Notes about Technology and Economic Consequences," *Research in Philosophy and Technology* 12 (1992): 157–176.

62. Ernest Partridge, "On the Rights of Future Generations," in Scherer and Attig, eds., *Upstream/Downstream*, pp. 40–66; Richard De George, "The Environment, Rights and Future Generations," in *Ethics and Problems of the 21st Century*, ed. Kenneth E. Goodpaster and Kenneth M. Sayre (Notre Dame, IN: University of Notre Dame Press, 1979), pp. 93–105; Ruth Macklin, "Can Future Generations Correctly Be Said to Have Rights?" in *Responsibilities to Future Generations*, ed. Ernest Partridge (Buffalo, NY: Prometheus, 1981); Kavka, Gregory, "The Paradox of Future Individuals," *Philosophy and Public Affairs* 2, no. 2 (1982): 92–112; Derek Parfit, *Reasons and Persons* (Oxford: Oxford University Press, 1984).

63. Norton, "Why I Am Not a Nonanthropocentrist."

64. Richard De George, "The Environment, Rights and Future Generations," in Goodpaster and Sayre, eds., *Ethics and Problems of the 21st Century*, pp. 93–105.

65. Westra, "Integrity, Health and Sustainability: Environmentalism without Racism," in *The Science of the Total Environment*, ed. C. L. Soskolne and R. Bertollini (Oxford: Elsevier, 1996); Rita Colwell, "Global Change: Emerging Diseases and New Epidemics," President's Lecture, American Association for the Advancement of Science, 10 February 1996; Janice D. Longstretch et al., "Effects of Increased Solar Ultraviolet Radiation on Human Health," *Ambio* 24, no. 3 (1995): 153–165.

66. Theo Colborn, Dianne Dumanoski, and John Peterson Myers, *Our Stolen Future* (New York: Dutton, 1996), pp. 116, 186.

67. Ibid., p. 89.

68. Ibid., pp. 88–89.

69. Ibid., p. 81.

70. Ibid., pp. 251–260.

71. Jon Cohen, "Tobacco Money Lights Up a Debate," *Science* 272 (1996): 488–494.

5 CONVERGENCE IN ENVIRONMENTAL VALUES

1. See, for example, Bryan G. Norton, "Conservation and Preservation: A Conceptual Rehabilitation," *Environmental Ethics* 8 (1986): 195–220; *Toward Unity among Environmentalists* (New York: Oxford University Press, 1991); "Applied Philosophy vs. Practical Philosophy: Toward an Environmental Philosophy Integrated According to Scale," in *Environmental Philosophy and Environmental Activism*, ed. Don E. Marietta and Lester Embree (Baltimore, MD: Rowman & Littlefield, 1995), pp. 125–148; "Why I Am Not a Nonanthropocentrist: Callicott and the Failure of Monistic Inherentism," *Environmental Ethics* 17 (1995): 341–358; "Integration or Reduction: Two Approaches to Environmental Values," in *Environmental Pragmatism*, ed. Andrew Light and Eric Katz (London: Routledge, 1996), pp. 105–138; and "Convergence and Contextualism: Some Clarifications and a Reply to Steverson," *Environmental Ethics* 19 (1997): 87–100 (reprinted in this volume).

2. For example, Norton, "Applied Philosophy vs. Practical Philosophy."

3. J. Baird Callicott, "Environmental Philosophy IS Environmental Activism: The Most Radical and Effective Kind," in Marietta and Embree, eds., *Environmental Philosophy and Environmental Activism*, pp. 19–35; Callicott, "Intrinsic Value in Nature: A Metaethical Analysis," *Electronic Journal of Analytic Philosophy* 3 (1995): http://ejap .louisiana.edu/archives.html; Laura Westra, "Why Norton's Approach Is Insufficient for Environmental Ethics," *Environmental Ethics* 19 (1997): 279–297; Brian Steverson,

"Contextualism and Norton's Convergence Hypothesis," *Environmental Ethics* 17 (1995): 135–150. The Westra and Steverson papers are reprinted in this volume.

4. Ben A. Minteer and Robert E. Manning, "Pragmatism in Environmental Ethics: Pluralism, Democracy, and the Management of Nature," *Environmental Ethics* 21 (1999): 191–207.

5. See especially Callicott, "Environmental Philosophy IS Environmental Activism," as well as his chapter in this volume.

6. Callicott, "Environmental Philosophy IS Environmental Activism," p. 22.

7. Norton, "Why I Am Not a Nonanthropocentrist."

8. Callicott, "Intrinsic Value in Nature."

9. Westra, "Why Norton's Approach Is Insufficient for Environmental Ethics," p. 290 (orig.; p. 58 in this volume).

10. See, for example, Willet Kempton, James Boster, and Jennifer Hartley, *Environmental Values in American Culture* (Cambridge, MA: MIT Press, 1995).

11. Steverson, "Contextualism and Norton's Convergence Hypothesis," p. 139 (orig.; p. 24 in this volume).

12. Ibid., 22.

13. Norton, "Convergence and Contextualism," p. 99 (orig.; pp. 46–47 in this volume).

14. Callicott, "Intrinsic Value in Nature," p. 9, emphasis added.

15. Callicott, "Environmental Philosophy IS Environmental Activism."

16. Westra, "Why Norton's Approach Is Insufficient for Environmental Ethics," p. 293 (orig.; p. 61 in this volume).

17. See Ben A. Minteer, "No Experience Necessary? Foundationalism and the Retreat from Culture in Environmental Ethics," *Environmental Values* 7 (1998): 333–348.

18. Don Dillman, *Mail and Telephone Surveys: The Total Design Method* (New York: John Wiley and Sons, 1978).

19. Material was drawn primarily from the following sources: Robin Attfield, *The Ethics of Environmental Concern* (Athens: University of Georgia Press, 1991); John Black, *The Dominion of Man: The Search for Ecological Responsibility* (Edinburgh: Edinburgh University Press, 1970); J. Baird Callicott, *In Defense of the Land Ethic* (Albany: State University of New York Press, 1989); Warwick Fox, *Toward a Transpersonal Ecology* (Albany: State University of New York Press, 1995); Eugene Hargrove, *Foundations of Environmental Ethics* (Englewood Cliffs, NJ: Prentice Hall, 1989); Samuel Hays, *Conservation and the Gospel of Efficiency* (Cambridge, MA: Harvard University Press, 1959); Hans Huth, *Nature and the American* (Lincoln: University of Nebraska Press, 1990); Max Oelschlaeger, *The Idea of Wilderness* (New Haven, CT: Yale University Press, 1991); Holmes Rolston III, *Environmental Ethics: Duties to and Values in the Natural World* (Philadelphia, PA: Temple University Press, 1988); Roderick Nash, *The Rights of Nature: A History of Environmental Ethics* (Madison: University of Wisconsin Press, 1989); Donald Worster, *Nature's Economy: A History of Ecological Ideas* (Cambridge: Cambridge University Press, 1994).

20. Minteer, "No Experience Necessary?"

21. See, for example, Stephen Kellert, "Historical Trends in Perceptions and Uses of Animals in 20th Century America," *Environmental Review* 9 (1985): 19–33; and Robert E. Manning, "The Nature of America: Visions and Revisions of Wilderness," *Natural Resources Journal* 29 (1989): 25–40.

22. Minteer and Manning, "Pragmatism in Environmental Ethics."

23. These statements were partly adapted (with modifications made for regional differences) from the forest attitude research conducted by Bruce Shindler, Peter List, and Brent Steel in the Pacific Northwest. See Bruce Shindler, Peter List, and Brent Steel, "Managing Federal Forests: Public Attitudes in Oregon and Nationwide," *Journal of Forestry* 91 (1993): 36–42; and Brent Steel, Peter List, and Bruce Shindler, "Conflicting Values about Federal Forests: A Comparison of National and Oregon Publics," *Society and Natural Resources* 7 (1994): 137–153.

24. Robert McCullough, *The Landscape of Community* (Hanover, NH: University Press of New England, 1995); Richard Judd, *Common Lands, Common People* (Cambridge, MA: Harvard University Press, 1997).

25. Callicott, "Intrinsic Value in Nature."

26. Callicott, "Environmental Philosophy IS Environmental Activism," p. 22.

27. Benjamin Barber, *A Place for Us* (New York: Hill and Wang, 1998), p. 42.

6 THE RELEVANCE OF ENVIRONMENTAL ETHICAL THEORIES FOR POLICY MAKING

1. Bryan G. Norton, *Toward Unity among Environmentalists* (New York: Oxford University Press, 1991), p. 86.

2. Ibid., pp. 226–227.

3. Paul Taylor, *Respect for Nature: A Theory of Environmental Ethics* (Princeton, NJ: Princeton University Press, 1986), p. 12.

4. Holmes Rolston III, *Environmental Ethics* (Philadelphia, PA: Temple University Press, 1988), p. 230.

5. J. Baird Callicott, "Environmental Philosophy Is Environmental Activism: The Most Radical and Effective Kind," in *Environmental Philosophy and Environmental Activism*, ed. Don E. Marietta Jr. and Lester Embree (Boston, MA: Rowman & Littlefield, 1995), p. 22.

6. J. Baird Callicott, "Animal Liberation: A Triangular Affair," in J. Baird Callicott, *In Defense of the Land Ethic* (Albany: State University of New York Press, 1989), p. 28.

7. Taylor, *Respect for Nature*, p. 155.

8. Callicott, "Animal Liberation: A Triangular Affair," p. 21.

9. Tom Regan, *The Case for Animal Rights* (Berkeley: University of California Press, 1983), p. 240.

10. Taylor, *Respect for Nature*, p. 129.

11. Holmes Rolston III, *Conserving Natural Value* (New York: Columbia University Press, 1994), p. 82 (emphasis added).

12. Rolston, *Environmental Ethics*, p. 226.

13. Carl-Henric Grenholm, "Etik och djurförsök" ["Ethics and Animal Experimentation"], *Årsbok 1997 för Föreningen lärare i Religionskunskap*, pp. 93–94 (my translation).

14. Andrew C. Kadak, "An Intergenerational Approach to High-Level Waste Disposal," *Nuclear News*, July 1997, p. 50.

15. James P. Sterba, "The Welfare Rights of Distant People and Future Generations: Moral Side-Constraints on Social Policy," *Social Theory and Practice* 7 (1981): 107.

16. World Commission on Environment and Development, *Our Common Future* (Oxford: Oxford University Press, 1987), p. 1.

17. Ibid., p. xiv.

18. Regan, *The Case for Animal Rights*, p. 357.

19. Aldo Leopold, *A Sand County Almanac and Sketches Here and There* (London: Oxford University Press, 1949), pp. 224–225.

20. Rolston, *Environmental Ethics*, p. 144.

21. World Commission, *Our Common Future*, p. 9.

22. Ibid., p. 105.

23. Ibid., p. 49.

24. Ibid., p. 102.

25. Ibid., p. 144.

26. Rolston, *Conserving Natural Value*, p. 233. Italics in original.

27. Arne Naess, *Ecology, Community and Lifestyle* (Cambridge: Cambridge University Press, 1989), p. 29.

28. Ibid., pp. 140–141.

29. Callicott, "Animal Liberation: A Triangular Affair," p. 27.

30. William Aiken, quoted in J. Baird Callicott, "The Conceptual Foundations of the Land Ethic," in Callicott, *In Defense of the Land Ethic*, p. 92.

31. Sandy Irvine and Alec Ponton, *A Green Manifesto: Policies for a Green Future* (London: Macdonald Optima, 1988), p. 23.

32. World Commission, *Our Common Future*, p. 166.

33. Ibid., pp. 147, 166.

34. Holmes Rolston III, "Winning and Losing in Environmental Ethics," in *Ethics and Environmental Policy*, ed. Frederick Ferré and Peter Hartel (Athens: University of Georgia Press, 1994), p. 231.

35. See Rolston, *Conserving Natural Value*, p. 68.

36. World Commission, *Our Common Future*, pp. 13, 147.

37. Rolston, *Conserving Natural Value*, p. 27.

38. Bill Devall and George Sessions, "Deep Ecology," in *The Environmental Ethics and Policy Book*, ed. Donald VanDeVeer and Christine Pierce (Belmont, CA: Wadsworth, 1994), p. 217.

39. Callicott, "Animal Liberation: A Triangular Affair," p. 34.

40. Rolston, *Conserving Natural Value*, p. 91.

41. Regan, *The Case for Animal Rights*, p. 357.

42. Taylor, *Respect for Nature*, p. 175.

43. Regan, *The Case for Animal Rights*, p. 356.

44. Taylor, *Respect for Nature*, p. 183.

45. World Commission, *Our Common Future*, p. 1.

46. Ibid., p. 137.

47. Ibid., p. 138.

7 CONVERGING VERSUS RECONSTITUTING ENVIRONMENTAL ETHICS

1. Bryan G. Norton, *Why Preserve Natural Variety?* (Princeton, NJ: Princeton University Press, 1987), p. 136.

2. Ibid., p. 135.

3. Ibid., chaps. 8, 9.

4. Bryan G. Norton, *Toward Unity among Environmentalists* (New York: Oxford University Press, 1991), p. 86.

5. Bryan G. Norton, "Convergence and Contextualism: Some Clarifications and a Reply to Steverson," *Environmental Ethics* 19 (1997): 87–100 (reprinted in this volume).

6. Norton, *Toward Unity*, p. 239.

7. Millennium Ecosystem Assessment, *Living beyond Our Means: Natural Assets and Human Well-Being: Statement from the Board* (2005); available at http://www .millenniumassessment.org/documents/document.429.aspx.pdf, p. 5.

8. Millennium Ecosystem Assessment, *Our Human Planet: Summary for Decision-Makers* (Washington, DC: Island Press, 2005).

9. Millennium Ecosystem Assessment and World Health Organization, *Ecosystems and Human Well-Being: Health Synthesis* (Geneva, Switzerland: World Health Organization, 2005).

10. Millennium Ecosystem Assessment, *Ecosystems and Human Well-Being: Opportunities and Challenges for Business and Industry* (Washington, DC: World Resources Institute, 2005).

11. Millennium Ecosystem Assessment, *Ecosystems and Human Well-Being: Wetlands and Water Synthesis* (Washington, DC: World Resources Institute, 2005).

12. Millennium Ecosystem Assessment, *Ecosystems and Human Well-Being: A Framework for Assessment* (Washington, DC: Island Press, 2003).

13. Norton, *Why Preserve Natural Variety?* pp. 227–233, quote on p. 231.

14. Bryan G. Norton, "Convergence Corroborated: A Comment on Arne Naess on Wolf Policies," in *Philosophical Dialogues: Arne Naess and the Progress of Ecophilosophy*, ed. Nina Witoszek and Andrew Brennan (Lanham, MD: Rowman & Littlefield, 1999), pp. 394–401.

15. Ibid., p. 398.

16. Ibid., p. 397.

17. Bryan G. Norton, Michael Hutchins, Elizabeth F. Stevens, and Terry L. Maple, eds., *Ethics on the Ark: Zoos, Animal Welfare, and Wildlife Conservation* (Washington, DC: Smithsonian Institution Press, 1995), p. 115.

18. William Booth, "Developers Wish Rare Fly Would Buzz Off," *Washington Post*, 4 April 1997, p. A10.

19. Norton, "Convergence and Contextualism," p. 100 (orig.; p. 47 in this volume).

20. Norton, "Convergence Corroborated," p. 397.

21. Aldo Leopold, *A Sand County Almanac* (New York: Oxford University Press, 1969; orig. 1949), pp. 221–225.

22. Ibid., pp. viii–ix.

23. Bryan G. Norton, "Why I Am Not a Nonanthropocentrist: Callicott and the Failure of Monistic Inherentism," *Environmental Ethics* 17 (1995): 341–358, quote on p. 341.

24. James J. Kilpatrick, "Brutality and Laughter in the Lab," *Washington Post*, 23 July 1985, p. A15.

25. Norton, *Toward Unity*, p. 251.

26. U.S. Fish and Wildlife Service, *Final Environmental Impact Statement: Proposed Use of Steel Shot for Hunting Waterfowl in the United States* (Washington, DC: U.S. Government Printing Office, 1976).

27. Sanjay Kumar Nepal and Karl E. Weber, *Struggle for Existence: Park-People Conflict in the Royal Chitwan National Park, Nepal* (Bangkok, Thailand: Asian Institute of Technology, 1993); Nabina Shrestha, *Protected Species of Nepal* (Kathmandu: IUCN Nepal, 1997); Steffen Straede and Finn Helles, "Park-People Conflict Resolution in Royal Chitwan National Park, Nepal: Buying Time at High Cost?" *Environmental Conservation* 27 (2000): 368–381.

28. Holmes Rolston III, "Saving Nature, Feeding People, and the Foundations of Ethics," *Environmental Values* 7 (1998): 349–357.

29. Bryan G. Norton and Anne C. Steinemann, "Environmental Values and Adaptive Management," *Environmental Values* 10 (2001): 473–506, quoted on p. 473, pp. 476–477.

30. Bryan G. Norton, "Pragmatism, Adaptive Management, and Sustainability," *Environmental Values* 8 (1999): 451–466, quote on p. 459.

31. Norton, "Convergence and Contextualism," p. 100 (orig.; p. 47 in this volume).

32. Norton, "Why I Am Not a Nonanthropocentrist."

33. Bryan G. Norton, "Environmental Ethics and Weak Anthropocentrism," *Environmental Ethics* 6 (1984): 131–148.

34. Norton, *Toward Unity*, pp. 11–12.

35. Ibid., pp. 187–204.

36. Norton, "Convergence and Contextualism," p. 87 (in original article abstract).

37. Norton, *Toward Unity*, pp. 3–12.

38. Ibid., p. 3.

39. Norton, *Why Preserve Natural Variety?* pp. 10–11, chap. 10.

40. Norton, *Toward Unity*, pp. 3–13.

41. Norton, "Pragmatism, Adaptive Management, and Sustainability," p. 451.

42. Norton, *Toward Unity*, p. 5.

43. Bryan G. Norton, "Biodiversity and Environmental Values: In Search of a Universal Earth Ethic," *Biodiversity and Conservation* 9 (2000): 1029–1044, quoted on p. 1029, p. 1039, p. 1043.

44. Ibid., pp. 1039–1041.

45. Bryan G. Norton, "Objectivity, Intrinsicality and Sustainability: Comment on Nelson's Health and Disease as 'Thick' Concepts in Ecosystemic Contexts," *Environmental Values* 4 (1995): 323–332, quote on p. 323.

46. Norton, "Biodiversity and Environmental Values," p. 1043.

47. Allan Luks, "Helper's High," *Psychology Today* 22 (1988): 39, 42; and Stephen Post, "Altruism, Happiness, and Health: It's Good to Be Good," *International Journal of Behavioral Medicine* 12 (2005): 66–77.

48. Norton, *Toward Unity*, pp. 226–227.

49. Ibid., pp. 6, 187.

50. Bryan G. Norton, "Thoreau's Insect Analogies: Or, Why Environmentalists Hate Mainstream Economists," *Environmental Ethics* 13 (1991): 235–251, quote on p. 235.

51. Norton, *Toward Unity*, p. 251.

52. Ibid., p. 252.

53. Ibid., p. 237.

54. Holmes Rolston III, "Environmental Virtue Ethics: Half the Truth but Dangerous as a Whole," in *Environmental Virtue Ethics,* ed. Ronald Sandler and Philip Cafaro (Lanham, MD: Rowman & Littlefield, 2005), pp. 61–78.

55. Peter S. Wenz, *Environmental Ethics Today* (New York: Oxford University Press, 2001), p. 169.

56. Ibid., p. 172.

57. Roger L. DiSilvestro, *Reclaiming the Last Wild Places: A New Agenda for Biodiversity* (New York: John Wiley & Sons, 1993), pp. xiv–xv.

58. Holmes Rolston III, "Winning and Losing in Environmental Ethics," in *Ethics and Environmental Policy: Theory Meets Practice,* ed. Frederick Ferré and Peter G. Hartel (Athens: University of Georgia Press, 1994), pp. 217–234.

59. Socrates, *Apology,* 41d.

60. Wallace Stegner, "The Wilderness Idea," in *Wilderness: America's Living Heritage,* ed. David Brower (San Francisco, CA: Sierra Club Books, 1961), pp. 97–102.

61. Walt Whitman, *Leaves of Grass* (Ithaca, NY: Cornell University Press, 1961; facsimile of 1860 ed.), p. 319.

62. Philip Cafaro, "Thoreau's Environmental Ethics in *Walden,*" *Concord Saunterer,* n.s., 10 (2002): 17–63, quote on p. 43.

63. Philip Cafaro, "Thoreau, Leopold, and Carson: Toward an Environmental Virtue Ethics," *Environmental Ethics* 22 (2001): 3–17, quote on p. 14.

64. Rolston, "Winning and Losing in Environmental Ethics," p. 220.

65. Ibid., p. 222.

66. Ibid., p. 221.

67. Ibid., p. 233.

68. See Rolston, "Winning and Losing."

8 ENVIRONMENTAL ETHICS AND FUTURE GENERATIONS

1. The views of these figures are usefully discussed in Bryan G. Norton, "Conservation and Preservation: A Conceptual Rehabilitation," *Environmental Ethics* 8 (1986). They are also discussed in Norton, *Toward Unity among Environmentalists* (New York: Oxford University Press, 1991).

2. This model is described in Norton, *Toward Unity.* It is further developed in Norton, "Integration or Reduction: Two Approaches to Environmental Values," in *Environmental Pragmatism,* ed. A. Light and E. Katz (London: Routledge, 1996), pp. 105–138.

3. Edmund Burke, *Reflections on the French Revolution* (New York: C. E. Merrill), par. 165.

4. John Rawls, *A Theory of Justice* (Cambridge, MA: Harvard University Press, 1971).

5. See Rawls, *A Theory of Justice,* pp. 284–298. For further discussion of savings rates and future generations, see Rawls, *Political Liberalism* (New York: Columbia University Press, 1993), pp. 271–275.

6. Rawls, *A Theory of Justice,* p. 284.

7. I do not claim that these are the only reasons for discounting. Derek Parfit was one of the first philosophers to carefully identify and discuss different reasons for discounting. See Derek Parfit, *Reasons and Persons* (Oxford: Oxford University Press, 1984). My taxonomy and discussion is somewhat different from his.

8. Someone might doubt that people are generally happier or better-off as a function of wealth. Some empirical evidence supports this doubt, but the assumption that

well-being is a function of wealth is nearly universally shared among economists. For the sake of exposition about the reasons for discounting, I will grant that assumption here. For doubts about the connection between well-being and wealth, see Tibor Scitovsky, *The Joyless Economy: The Psychology of Human Satisfaction*, rev. ed. (New York: Oxford University Press, 1992); R. E. Lane, *The Market Experience* (New York: Cambridge University Press, 1991); Robert Samuelson, *The Good Life and Its Discontents: The American Dream in the Age of Entitlement* (New York: Knopf, 1997); and Michael Argyle, "Causes and Correlates of Happiness," in *Well Being: The Foundations of Hedonic Psychology*, ed. D. Kahneman, E. Diener, and N. Schwartz (New York: Russell Sage Foundation, 1997).

9. Nicholas Stern, *The Economics of Climate Change: The Stern Review* (Cambridge: Cambridge University Press, 2007), available online at http://www.hm-treasury .gov.uk/independent_review_economics_climate_change/sternreview_index.cfm.

10. See, for example, the critical reviews of *The Stern Review* by William Nordhaus and Martin Weitzman in the *Journal of Economic Literature* 45(2007): 686–724.

11. Martin Weitzman, "The *Stern Review* of the Economics of Climate Change," *Journal of Economic Literature* 45 (2007): 688.

12. Ibid., p. 7.

13. John Rawls, *A Theory of Justice*, p. 27. See also T. M. Scanlon, *What We Owe to Each Other* (Cambridge, MA: Belknap Press, 1998).

14. There are other ways, of course, to respond to considerations of distributive justice. I discuss one consequentialist alternative below. Another alternative is to reject consequentialism and defend a different ethical theory that better captures our intuitions about justice and the nature of respect that recognizes the separateness of persons.

15. Stern, *The Economics of Climate Change: The Stern Review*, p. 60.

16. Partha Dasgupta, "Commentary: *The Stern Review*'s Economics of Climate Change," *National Institute Economic Review* (January 2007): 4–7, quote on p. 6.

17. Ibid. Italics in original.

18. Roy Harrod, *Towards a Dynamic Economics* (London: Macmillan, 1948), p. 40.

19. Kenneth Arrow, "Discounting, Morality, and Gaming," in *Discounting and Intergenerational Equity*, ed. P. R. Portney and J. P. Weyant (Washington, DC: Resources for the Future, 1999), pp. 13–21.

20. Ibid.

21. There is an interesting question about whether actions we take now can affect the well-being of people in the past. Aristotle, for example, defends such a view. See *Nicomachean Ethics* 1101a, 22–35. But I choose to ignore this question here.

22. Although philosophers commonly attribute this maxim to Jeremy Bentham, I have not been able to find it in Bentham's writing. It is quoted and attributed to Bentham by John Stuart Mill, *Utilitarianism* (Indianapolis: Hackett, 1979), p. 60.

23. John Broome, "Why Economics Needs Ethical Theory," in *Welfare, Development, Philosophy and Social Science: Essays for Amartya Sen's 75th Birthday, Vol. 3*, ed. K. Basu and R. Kanbur (Oxford: Oxford University Press, forthcoming). This issue of temporal dissociation is explored in depth by Thomas Nagel, *The Possibility of Altruism* (Princeton, NJ: Princeton University Press, 1978), pp. 27–78.

24. F. P. Ramsey, "A Mathematical Theory of Saving," *Economic Journal* 38 (1928): 543–559, quote on p. 543.

25. Broome, "Why Economics Need Ethical Theory."

26. William Nordhaus, "A Review of *The Stern Review* on the Economics of Climate Change," *Journal of Economic Literature* 45 (2007): 686–702, quote on pp. 692–693. See also Nordhaus, *A Question of Balance* (New Haven: Yale University Press, 2008), pp. 165–191.

27. Ibid., p. 18.

28. Ibid., p. 33.

29. Martin Weitzman, "A Review of *The Stern Review* on the Economics of Climate Change," *Journal of Economic Literature* 45 (2007): 703–724, quote on p. 705.

30. Ibid.

31. Broome, "Climate Change," p. 16.

32. Proposals like this are familiar in the philosophical literature. See, for example, J. Feinberg, "The Rights of Animals and Unborn Generations," in *Rights, Justice, and the Bounds of Liberty: Essays in Social Philosophy* (Princeton, NJ: Princeton University Press, 1980), pp. 159–184.

33. Philosophers have debated the issue whether causing a person to exist (or whether coming into existence) is a way of being benefited. If it is, then it would seem that a possible person (perhaps an unfertilized egg or a sperm) that never comes into existence is thereby harmed. Many philosophers find such claims implausible.

34. This example is due to Derek Parfit, who is largely responsible for calling the attention of philosophers to the nonidentity problem. See Parfit, *Reasons and Persons*.

35. I discuss this argument more fully in Douglas MacLean, "A Moral Requirement for Energy Policies," in *Energy and the Future*, ed. D. MacLean and P. Brown (Lanham, MD: Rowman & Littlefield, 1983), pp. 180–196.

36. This argument has been developed by Thomas Hill Jr., "Ideals of Human Excellence and Preserving the Natural Environment," *Environmental Ethics* 5 (1983): 211–224; see also Hill, "Finding Value in Nature," *Environmental Values* 15 (2006): 331–341.

37. J. Baird Callicott, "Environmental Philosophy IS Environmental Activism: The Most Radical and Effective Kind," in *Beyond the Land Ethic* (Albany: State University of New York Press, 1999), pp. 27–43.

38. Ibid., pp. 32–33.

39. The classic defense of this view can be found in Joseph Butler, *Five Sermons, Preached at the Rolls Chapel and a Dissertation upon the Nature of Virtue*, ed. Stephen L. Darwall (Indianapolis, IN: Hackett, 1983).

40. Bernard Williams, "Must a Concern for the Environment Be Centered on Human Beings?" in *Making Sense of Humanity and Other Philosophical Papers* (New York: Cambridge University Press, 1995), pp. 233–240.

41. See Bernard Williams, "The Human Prejudice," in *Philosophy as a Humanistic Discipline* (Princeton, NJ: Princeton University Press, 2006), pp. 135–152.

9 THE CONVERGENCE HYPOTHESIS FALSIFIED

1. As amended by Public Law 94-325, June 30, 1976; Public Law 94-359, July 12, 1976; Public Law 95-212, December 19, 1977; Public Law 95-632, November 10, 1978; Public Law 96-159, December 28, 1979; Public Law 97-304, October 13, 1982;

Public Law 98-327, June 25, 1984; Public Law 100-478, October 7, 1988; Public Law 100-653, November 14, 1988; Public Law 100-707, November 23, 1988; and Public Law 108-136, November 24, 2003.

2. *Tennessee Valley Authority v. Hiram Hill et al.*, 437 U.S. 153 (1978), emphasis added.

3. A. Myrick Freeman III, *The Measurement of Environmental and Resource Values: Theory and Methods* (Washington, DC: Resources for the Future, 1993).

4. Eugene C. Hargrove, "Toward Teaching Environmental Ethics: Exploring Problems in the Language of Evolving Social Values," *Canadian Journal of Environmental Education* 5 (2000): 1–20.

5. Freeman, *Measurement*.

6. Dianna Norris, Norm Phelps, and D. J. Schubert, *Canned Hunts: The Newest American "Sport"* (Silver Springs, MD: Fund for Animals, 2001).

7. Freeman, *Measurement*.

8. M. E. Power et al., "Challenges in the Quest for Keystones," *BioScience* 46 (1996): 287–309.

9. G. R. Van Blaricom and J. A. Estes, eds., *The Community Ecology of Sea Otters* (New York: Springer-Verlag, 1988).

10. Robert Costanza et al., "The Value of the World's Ecosystem Services and Natural Capital," *Nature* 387 (1997): 253–260.

11. David Ehrenfeld, "Why Put a Value on Biodiversity?" in *Biodiversity*, ed. E. O. Wilson (Washington, DC: National Academy Press, 1988), pp. 212–216, p. 215.

12. Christopher D. Stone, *Should Trees Have Standing? Toward Legal Rights for Natural Objects* (Los Altos, CA: William Kaufmann, 1974), first published as an article in *Southern California Law Review* 45 (1972): 450–501.

13. *Friends of the Earth Inc. et al. v. Laidlaw Environmental Services (TOC), Inc.,* No. 98-822; 528 U.S. 167; 120 U.S. 693; 145 L. Ed. 2d 610; 2000.

14. *Coho Salmon (Onchorynchus Kisuch) v. Pacific Lumber Company*, 61 F. Supp. 2d 1001 (1999), emphasis added.

15. Ibid., p. 11.

16. Rachel Carson, *Silent Spring* (New York: Houghton Mifflin, 1962); Stewart Udall, *The Quiet Crisis* (New York: Holt, Reinhart, and Winston, 1963).

17. Aldo Leopold, *A Sand County Almanac and Sketches Here and There* (New York: Oxford University Press, 1949); Wallace Stegner, "Aldo Leopold's Legacy," in *Companion to A Sand County Almanac: Critical and Interpretive Essays*, ed. J. Baird Callicott (Madison: University of Wisconsin Press, 1987), pp. 133–145.

18. Leopold, *Sand County*, pp. 210–211.

19. Ibid., p. 211.

20. Ibid., p. 223.

21. J. Baird Callicott, "The Philosophical Value of Wildlife," in *Economic and Social Values of Wildlife*, ed. Daniel J. Decker and Gary Goff (Boulder, CO: Westview Press, 1987): 214–221.

22. John Muir, *A Thousand Mile Walk to the Gulf* (Boston, MA: Houghton Mifflin, 1916), p. 98 (emphasis added).

23. Christopher D. Stone, "*Should Trees Have Standing?* Revisited: How Far Will Law and Morals Reach? A Pluralist Perspective," *Southern California Law Review* 59 (1985): 1–54.

24. *Sierra Club v. Rogers C. B. Morton*, 70 U.S. 34 (1972).

25. *Palila v. Hawaii Department of Land and Natural Resources*, 471 F. Supp. 985, 987 (D. Hawaii 1979).

26. *Palila v. Hawaii Department of Land and Natural Resources*, 852 F.2d 1106, 1007 (9th Cir. 1988).

27. Amartya Sen, "Approaches to the Choice of Discount Rates for Social Benefit-Cost Analysis," in *Discounting for Time and Risk in Energy Policy*, ed. R. Lind (Washington, DC: Resources for the Future, 1982), pp. 325–353.

28. See, for example: John O'Neill, "The Varieties of Intrinsic Value," *The Monist* 75 (1992): 119–137; Robert Elliot, "Intrinsic Value, Environmental Obligation and Naturalness," *The Monist* 75 (1992): 120–160; Tom Regan, "Does Environmental Ethics Rest on a Mistake?" *The Monist* 75 (1992): 161–182; Eugene C. Hargrove, "Weak Anthropocentric Intrinsic Value," *The Monist* 75 (1992): 183–207; Jim Cheney, "Intrinsic Value in Environmental Ethics: Between Subjectivism and Objectivism," *The Monist* 75 (1992): 227–235.

29. For a good summary, see Carl Wellman, *Theories of Rights* (Totowa, NJ: Rowman and Allanheld, 1985).

30. Immanuel Kant, *Foundations of the Metaphysics of Morals*, tr. Lewis White Beck (New York: Bobbs Merrill, 1959), p. 53; originally published in 1785.

31. Jeremy Bentham, *Introduction to the Principles of Morals and Legislation* (Oxford: The Clarendon Press of Oxford University, 1789); John Stuart Mill, *Utilitarianism* (London: Longmans, 1863).

32. W. J. Baumol, *Welfare Economics and the Theory of the State* (Cambridge, MA: Harvard University Press, 1952).

33. John Rawls, *A Theory of Justice* (Oxford: The Clarendon Press of Oxford University, 1971).

34. *Northern Spotted Owl v. Hodel*, 716 F. Supp. 479 (W.D. Wash. 1988); *Northern Spotted Owl v. Lujan*, 758 F. Supp. 621 (W.D. Wash. 1991); *Hawaiian Crow ('Alala) v. Lujan*, 906 F. Supp. 549, 542 (D. Hawaii 1991); *Mt. Graham Red Squirrel v. Yeutter*, 930 F.2d 703 (9th Cir. 1991); *Mt. Graham Red Squirrel v. Madigan*, 954 F.2d 1441, 1459 (9th Cir. 1992); *Mt. Graham Red Squirrel v. Espy*, 986 F.2d 1568, 1581 (9th Cir. 1993); *Mt. Graham Red Squirrel v. Madigan*, 954 F.2d 1441, 1459 (9th Cir. 1992); *Florida Key Deer v. Stickney*, 864 F. Supp. 122 (1994); *Marbled Murrelet v. Pacific Lumber Co.*, 880 F. Supp. 1343, 1346 (N.D. Cal. 1995); *Loggerhead Turtle v. County Council of Volusia County, Florida*, 896 F. Supp. 1170, 1177 (M.D. Fla. 1995); *Hawksbill Sea Turtle v. FEMA*, 126 F.3d 461, 466 (3d Cir. 1997); *Coho Salmon (Onchorynchus Kisutch) v. Pacific Lumber Co.*, 61 F. Supp. 2d 1001 (N.D. Cal. 1999); *Cetacean Community v. Bush*, 249 F. Supp. 2d 1206 (D. Haw. 2003).

35. Donald G. Kyle, *Spectacles of Death in Ancient Rome* (New York: Routledge, 1998).

36. Kant, *Foundations*.

37. Roger Sawyer, *Slavery in the Twentieth Century* (London: Routledge and Kegan Paul, 1986).

38. John F. Decker, *Prostitution: Regulation and Control* (Littleton, CO: F. B. Rothman, 1979); James K. Inciardi, *The War on Drugs: Heroin, Cocaine, Crime, and Public Policy* (Palo Alto, CA: Mayfield, 1986).

39. D. J. Rothman et al., "Bellagio Task Force Report on Transplantation, Bodily Integrity, and the International Traffic in Organs," *Transplantation Proceedings* 29 (1997): 2739–2745.

40. S. Savage-Rumbaugh, S. G. Shanker, and T. J. Taylor, *Kanzi: The Ape at the Brink of the Human Mind* (New York: Oxford University Press, 1998).

41. Tom Regan, *The Case for Animal Rights* (Berkeley: University of California Press, 1983); Peter Singer, *Animal Liberation: A New Ethics for Our Treatment of Animals* (New York: Avon, 1977); Kenneth E. Goodpaster, "On Being Morally Considerable," *Journal of Philosophy* 75: 308–325; Paul W. Taylor, *Respect for Nature: A Theory of Environmental Ethics* (Princeton, NJ: Princeton University Press, 1986); Gary Varner, *In Nature's Interests* (New York: Oxford University Press, 1998).

42. Henry Cohen, "Federal Animal Protection Statutes," *Animal Law* 1 (2000): 143–153.

43. J. Baird Callicott, "On the Intrinsic Value of Non-human Species," in *The Preservation of Species*, ed. Bryan G. Norton (Princeton, NJ: Princeton University Press, 1986): 138–172.

44. For example, Jonathan Aldred, "Existence Value, Welfare, and Altruism," *Environmental Values* 3 (1994): 381–402.

45. A. M. Vargas, P. Lockhart, P. Marinari, and P. Gober, "The Reintroduction Process: Black-Footed Ferrets as a Case Study," in *Proceedings: American Zoo and Aquarium Association Western Regional Conference*, Denver, Colorado, May 15–19, 1966): 829–834.

46. Aldred, "Existence Value."

47. United Nations, *Fact Sheet No. 2 (Rev. 1), The International Bill of Human Rights* (Geneva: United Nations, 1996); J. E. Nowak, R. E. Rotunda, and J. Nelson Young, *Handbook on Constitutional Law*, Hornbook Series (St. Paul, MN: West Publishing, 1976).

48. Kant, *Foundations.*

49. Mark Sagoff, *The Economy of the Earth: Philosophy, Law, and the Environment* (Cambridge: Cambridge University Press, 1988).

50. Mark Sagoff, "At the Shrine of Our Lady of Fatima *or* Why Political Questions Are Not All Economic," *Arizona Law Review* (1981): 1283–1298.

51. E. H. Buck, M. L. Corn, and P. Baldwin, "IB100072: Endangered Species: Difficult Choices," *CRS Issue Brief for Congress* (Washington, DC: National Council for Science and the Environment, 2001).

52. Warwick Fox, "What Does the Recognition of Intrinsic Value Entail?" *Trumpeter* 10, no. 3 (1993): 101.

53. M. Litvin, "Clash over Property Rights," *Nations Business* 82 (1994): 57–59.

54. *Babbitt v. Sweet Home Chapter Communities for a Great Ore*, 515 U.S. 687 (1995).

55. R. A. Epstein, *Takings, Private Property, and the Power of Eminent Domain* (Cambridge, MA: Harvard University Press, 1985); J. S. Burling, "Property Rights, Endangered Species, Wetlands, and Other Critters—Is It against Nature to Pay for Taking?" *Land and Water Law Review* 27 (1992): 309–362.

56. L. E. Dwyer, D. D. Murphy, and P. R. Ehrlich, "Property Rights Case Law and the Challenge of the Endangered Species Act," *Conservation Biology* 9 (1995): 725–741.

57. D. J. Coyle, "Taking Jurisprudence and the Political Cultures of American Politics," *Catholic University Law Review* 42 (1992): 817–862.

58. *Palila v. Hawaii Department of Land and Natural Resources*, 852 F.2d 1106, 1007 (9th Cir. 1988).

59. *Marbled Murrelet v. Pac. Lumber Co.*, 880 F. Supp. 1343, 1346 (N.D. Cal. 1995).

60. Ibid.

61. *Loggerhead Turtle v. County Council of Volusia County, Florida*, 896 Supp. 1170, 1177 (M.D. Fla. 1995).

62. *Loggerhead Turtle v. County Council of Volusia County, Florida*, 148 F.3d 1231 (11th Cir. 1998).

63. Ibid.

64. *The Cetacean Community v. Bush*, 249 F. Supp. 2d 1206 (D. Haw. 2003).

65. *The Cetacean Community v. Bush*, 386 F.3d 1169 (9th Cir. 2004).

66. Ibid. Quoting *Best Life Assurance Co. v. Commissioner*, 281 F.3d 828, 834 (9th Cir. 2002).

67. Ibid.

68. Ibid.

69. Ibid. Quoting Stone, *Should Trees Have Standing?* p. 5.

70. Katherine A. Burke, "Can We Stand for It: Amending the Endangered Species Act with an Animal-Suit Provision," *University of Colorado Law Review* 75 (2004).

71. *Defenders of Wildlife v. Hodel*, 658 F. Supp. 43, 47–48 (D. Minn. 1987) and *Defenders of Wildlife, Friends of Animals and Their Environment v. Hodel*, 851 F.2d 1035 (8th Cir. 1988). The complex history of the case is summarized in *Defenders of Wildlife*, 504 U.S. at 559: "The District Court granted the Secretary's motion to dismiss for lack of standing. *Defenders of Wildlife v. Hodel*, 658 F. Supp. 43, 47–48 (Minn. 1987). The Court of Appeals for the Eighth Circuit reversed by a divided vote. *Defenders of Wildlife v. Hodel*, 851 F.2d 1035 (1988). On remand, the Secretary moved for summary judgment on the standing issue, and respondents moved for summary judgment on the merits. The District Court denied the Secretary's motion, on the ground that the Eighth Circuit had already determined the standing question in this case; it granted respondents' merits motion, and ordered the Secretary to publish a revised regulation. *Defenders of Wildlife v. Hodel*, 707 F. Supp. 1082 (Minn. 1989). The Eighth Circuit affirmed, 911 F.2d 117 (1990). We granted certiorari, 500 U.S. 915, 111 S. Ct. 2008, 114 L.Ed.2d 97 (1991)."

72. *Defenders of Wildlife v. Hodel*, 851 F.2d 1035 (1988).

73. *Lujan v. Defenders*.

74. Ibid.

75. *Tennessee Valley Authority v. Hill*, emphasis added.

76. Stephen M. Johnson, "Private Plaintiffs, Public Rights: Article II and Environmental Citizen Suits," *Kansas Law Review* 49 (2001): 383; Robert B. June, "Citizen Suits: The Structure of Standing Requirements for Citizen Suits and the Scope of Congressional Power," *Environmental Law* 24 (1994): 761.

77. *Bennett v. Plenert*, Not Reported in F. Supp., No. Civ. 93-6076-HO (D. Or., Nov. 18, 1993).

78. *Bennett v. Spear*, 520 U.S. 154, 162 (1997).

79. Robert A. Anthony, "Zone-Free Standing for Private Attorneys General," *George Mason Law Review* 7 (1999).

80. *Bennett v. Spear.*

81. Preeti S. Chaudhari, "*Bennett v. Spear*: Lions, Tigers, and Bears Beware. The Decline of Environmental Protection," *Northern Illinois University Law Review* 18 (1998): 553.

82. *Tennessee Valley Authority v. Hill.*

83. Ibid.

84. Ibid.

85. *Rancho Viejo, LLC v. Norton*, 334 F.3d 1158, 1158.

10 CONVERGENCE IN AN AGRARIAN KEY

1. Thomas C. Hilde and Paul B. Thompson, "Agrarianism and Pragmatism," in *The Agrarian Roots of Pragmatism*, ed. Paul B. Thompson and Thomas C. Hilde (Nashville, TN: Vanderbilt University Press, 2000), pp. 1–21.

2. Phillip Cafaro, "Split Decision" (Book Review), *Conservation Biology* 21 (2007): 888–890.

3. Bryan Norton, "The Constancy of Leopold's Land Ethic," *Conservation Biology* 2 (1988): 93–102.

4. Bryan G. Norton, *Sustainability: A Philosophy of Adaptive Ecosystem Management* (Chicago: University of Chicago Press, 2005).

5. Paul B. Thompson, "Agrarianism as Philosophy," in Thompson and Hilde, eds., *The Agrarian Roots of Pragmatism,* pp. 25–50, and Thompson, "The Reshaping of Conventional Farming: A North American Perspective," *Journal of Agricultural and Environmental Ethics* 14 (2001): 217–229.

6. Paul B. Thompson, "Expanding the Conservation Tradition: The Agrarian Vision," in *Reconstructing Conservation: Finding Common Ground*, ed. Ben A. Minteer and Robert E Manning (Washington, DC: Island Press, 2003), pp. 77–92.

7. Donald W. Meinig, *The Shaping of America: Volume 2* (New Haven, CT: Yale University Press, 1993).

8. Thomas Jefferson, *Writings*, ed. Merrill D. Peterson (New York: Literary Classics of the United States/Library of America, 1984), p. 291.

9. Ibid., p. 290.

10. Ibid., p. 818.

11. See Meinig, *The Shaping of America.*

12. Gary Wills, "American Adam," *New York Review of Books*, 6 March 1997, pp. 30–33.

13. See Char Miller, *Gifford Pinchot and the Making of Modern Environmentalism* (Washington, DC: Island Press, 2001).

14. Bryan G. Norton, *Toward Unity among Environmentalists* (New York: Oxford University Press, 1991).

15. Miller, *Gifford Pinchot*, p. 169.

16. Theodore Roosevelt, *The Rough Riders/An Autobiography*, ed. Louis Auchincloss (New York: Literary Classics of the United States/Library of America, 2004), p. 306.

17. Ibid., p. 374.

18. Ibid., p. 350.

19. Theodore Roosevelt, *Letters and Speeches*, ed. Louis Auchincloss (New York: Literary Classics of the United States/Library of America, 2004), p. 716.

20. See Thompson, "Agrarianism as Philosophy."

21. Roosevelt, *Letters and Speeches*, p. 443.

22. Quoted in Miller, *Gifford Pinchot*, p. 171.

23. L. H. Bailey, *Report of the Commission on Country Life, with an Introduction by Theodore Roosevelt* (New York: Sturgis & Walton, 1911). See also Paul A. Morgan and Scott J. Peters, "The Foundations of Planetary Agrarianism: Thomas Berry and Liberty Hyde Bailey," *Journal of Agricultural and Environmental Ethics* 19 (2006): 443–468.

24. Morgan and Peters, "The Foundations of Planetary Agrarianism."

25. Holmes Rolston III, *Genes, Genesis and God: Values and Their Origins in Natural and Human History* (Cambridge: Cambridge University Press, 1999).

26. See Paul B. Thompson, "Mark Sagoff's Kantian Environmental Philosophy," *Ethics, Place and Environment* 9 (2006): 344–350; and Mark Sagoff, "Reply to My Critics," *Ethics, Place and Environment* 9 (2006): 365–372.

11 CONVERGENCE AND ECOLOGICAL RESTORATION

1. Eric Katz and Lauren Oechsli, "Moving beyond Anthropocentrism: Environmental Ethics, Development, and the Amazon," *Environmental Ethics* 15 (1993): 49–59; Eric Katz, "Biodiversity and Ecological Justice," in *Biodiversity and Landscape: A Paradox of Humanity*, ed. K. C. Kim and R. D. Weaver (Cambridge: Cambridge University Press, 1994), pp. 61–74; Eric Katz, "A Pragmatic Reconsideration of Anthropocentrism," *Environmental Ethics* 21 (1999): 377–390.

2. Bryan G. Norton, "Conservation and Preservation: A Conceptual Rehabilitation," *Environmental Ethics* 8 (1986): 195–220; quote on p. 220.

3. Ibid., p. 220.

4. Bryan G. Norton, *Toward Unity among Environmentalists* (New York: Oxford University Press, 1991).

5. Ibid., p. 239.

6. Ibid.

7. Ibid., p. 240.

8. Ibid.

9. Ibid., pp. 103–107; quote on p. 103.

10. Ibid., p. 106.

11. Ibid., p. 240.

12. Ibid.

13. Ibid.

14. See Bryan G. Norton, "Convergence and Contextualism: Some Clarifications and a Reply to Steverson," *Environmental Ethics* 19 (1997): 87–100 (reprinted in Chapter 3 in this volume); and Norton, "Convergence Corroborated: A Comment on Arne Naess on Wolf Policies," in *Philosophical Dialogues: Arne Naess and the Progress of Philosophy*, ed. Nina Witoszek and Andrew Brennan (Lanham, MD: Rowman & Little-

field, 1999; reprinted in Bryan G. Norton, *Searching for Sustainability: Interdisciplinary Essays in the Philosophy of Conservation Biology* (Cambridge: Cambridge University Press, 2003), pp. 78–87.

15. Norton, "Convergence and Contextualism," p. 87 (orig.; p. 36 in this volume); Norton, *Searching for Sustainability*, p. 78.

16. Norton, "Convergence and Contextualism," p. 99 (orig.; p. 46 in this volume); Norton, *Searching for Sustainability*, p. 78.

17. Bryan G. Norton, *Sustainability: A Philosophy of Adaptive Ecosystem Management* (Chicago: University of Chicago Press, 2005), pp. 508–510.

18. Ibid., p. 510.

19. Norton, "Convergence and Contextualism," p. 99 (orig.; p. 47 in this volume); Norton, *Searching for Sustainability*, p. 78.

20. Norton, "Convergence and Contextualism," p. 99 (orig.; p. 46 in this volume).

21. Ibid.; Norton, *Searching for Sustainability*, p. 81.

22. Norton, "Convergence and Contextualism," p. 100 (orig.; p. 47 in this volume); Norton, *Searching for Sustainability*, pp. 81–82.

23. Norton, *Toward Unity*, p. 240.

24. Ibid., p. 509.

25. Ibid.

26. See Steve Packard, "Just a Few Oddball Species: Restoration and Redesign of the Tallgrass Savanna," *Restoration and Management Notes* 6, no. 1 (Summer 1988): 13–22. I discuss Packard's work in the expanded version of "The Big Lie," reprinted in my book *Nature as Subject: Human Obligation and Natural Community* (Lanham, MD: Rowman & Littlefield, 1997).

27. Eric Katz, "The Big Lie: Human Restoration of Nature," *Research in Philosophy and Technology* 12 (1992): 231–241. A slightly different version of "The Big Lie" was published as "Restoration and Redesign: The Ethical Significance of Human Intervention in Nature," *Restoration and Management Notes* 9, no. 2 (Winter 1992): 90–96. See also Katz, "The Call of the Wild: The Struggle against Domination and the 'Technological Fix' of Nature," *Environmental Ethics* 14 (1992): 265–273; "Artefacts and Functions: A Note on the Value of Nature," *Environmental Values* 2 (1993): 223–232; and "Imperialism and Environmentalism," *Social Theory and Practice* 21, no. 2 (Summer 1996): 271–285. These essays on the ethics of restoration are reprinted in Katz, *Nature as Subject*, pp. 93–146. Other discussions of restoration are: Katz, "The Problem of Ecological Restoration," *Environmental Ethics* 18 (1996): 222–224; and "Another Look at Restoration: Technology and Artificial Nature," in *Restoring Nature: Perspectives from the Social Sciences and Humanities*, ed. Paul H. Gobster and R. Bruce Hull (Washington, DC: Island Press, 2000), pp. 37–48. For critical commentary on my views, see Yeuk-Sze Lo, "Natural and Artifactual: Restored Nature as Subject," *Environmental Ethics* 21 (1999): 247–266; Andrew Light, "Ecological Restoration and the Culture of Nature: A Pragmatic Perspective" in Gobster and Hull, eds., *Restoring Nature*, pp. 49–70; and Steven Vogel, "The Nature of Artifacts," *Environmental Ethics* 25 (2003): 149–168.

28. William James, *Pragmatism*, Lecture II (Indianapolis, IN: Hackett, 1981), pp. 25–26.

12 DOES A PUBLIC ENVIRONMENTAL PHILOSOPHY NEED A CONVERGENCE HYPOTHESIS?

1. Bryan G. Norton, "Convergence and Contextualism," *Environmental Ethics* 19 (1997): 87–100; quote on p. 87 (orig.; p. 36 in this volume). There is some disagreement about what is meant by anthropocentrism and nonanthropocentrism. For reasons that I do not specify here, I take the view that the distinction should be drawn over the issue of whether or not one believes that direct moral obligations can be extended to entities other than humans. Following Norton's discussion of "weak anthropocentrism," there seems to be no reason that an anthropocentrist could not value nonhuman individuals or collective entities like species or ecosystems for indirect reasons. Nonanthropocentrists, then, are those who extend direct moral obligations to things other than humans. This last category is admittedly very large, but still meaningful insofar as it marks a departure from most of the history of Western ethics.

2. Bryan G. Norton, *Sustainability: A Philosophy of Adaptive Ecosystem Management* (Chicago: University of Chicago Press, 2005), p. 510.

3. Andrew Light, "Environmental Pragmatism and Valuation in Nature," in *Human Ecology: Crossing Boundaries*, ed. Scott Wright (Fort Collins, CO: Society for Human Ecology, 1993), pp. 23–30.

4. Bryan G. Norton, *Toward Unity among Environmentalists* (New York: Oxford University Press, 1991), p. x.

5. Anthony Weston, "Beyond Intrinsic Value: Pragmatism in Environmental Ethics," *Environmental Ethics* 7 (1985): 321–339.

6. See, for example, Ben A. Minteer, "No Experience Necessary? Foundationalism and the Retreat from Culture in Environmental Ethics," *Environmental Values* 7 (1998): 333–347; Minteer, "Intrinsic Value for Pragmatists?" *Environmental Ethics* 23 (2001): 57–75; J. Baird Callicott, "Silencing Philosophers: Minteer and the Foundations of Anti-Foundationalism," *Environmental Values* 8 (1998): 499–516; Callicott, "The Pragmatic Power and Promise of Theoretical Environmental Ethics," *Environmental Values* 11 (2002): 3–26.

7. Eugene Hargrove, "What's Wrong? Who's to Blame?" *Environmental Ethics* 25 (2003): 3–4.

8. Norton, *Toward Unity*, p. x.

9. Norton, *Sustainability*, p. 77.

10. For those keeping track, prior to 1997, I called methodological environmental pragmatism "metaphilosophical environmental pragmatism," and what I then termed "philosophical environmental pragmatism" I now call "historical environmental pragmatism." I only point this out because as recently as 2007 there were still several references to people endorsing "metaphilosophical environmental pragmatism" despite the abundant references in my work to "methodological environmental pragmatism." See Kevin Elliott, "Norton's Conception of Sustainability: Political or Metaphysical?" *Environmental Ethics* 29 (2007): 3–22.

11. See, for example, J. Baird Callicott, "Fallacious Fallacies and Nonsolutions: Comment on Kristin Shrader Frechette's 'Ecological Risk Assessment and Ecosystem Health: Fallacies and Solutions,'" *Ecosystem Health* 3 (1997): 133.

12. Elliott, "Norton's Conception of Sustainability."

13. See Callicott, "The Pragmatic Power and Promise," for confirmation that this has been the core set of issues for the field since its inception.

14. Ben A. Minteer, "Deweyan Democracy and Environmental Ethics," in *Democracy and the Claims of Nature*, ed. Ben A. Minteer and Bob Pepperman Taylor (Lanham, MD: Rowman & Littlefield, 2002), pp. 33–48.

15. Andrew Light, "Environmental Pragmatism as Philosophy or Metaphilosophy?," pp. 325–338.

16. Eric Katz, "A Pragmatic Reconsideration of Anthropocentrism," *Environmental Ethics* 21 (1999): 377–390.

17. Callicott, "Silencing Philosophers," 507.

18. Andrew Light, "The Case for a Practical Pluralism," in *Environmental Ethics: An Anthology*, ed. Andrew Light and Holmes Rolston III (Cambridge, MA: Blackwell, 2003), pp. 229–247.

19. For example, J. Baird Callicott et al., "Biodiversity in the Big Thicket," *Ethics, Place, and Environment* 9 (2006): 21–45.

20. See Light, "The Case for a Practical Pluralism."

21. That said, the corps of philosophers working on climate change is exceptionally good, including Chrisoula Andreou, Don Brown, Simon Caney, Steve Gardiner, Dale Jamieson, Henry Shue, and Clark Wolf. Interestingly, though I cannot pursue the issue or its implications here, I would not count any of these figures as traditionally oriented environmental ethicists in the sense of primarily being concerned with the sort of projects engaged in by figures like Callicott and Rolston. It should also be pointed out that arguably the best work produced by these figures and others has been published in more mainstream philosophical journals such as *Philosophy and Public Affairs*. I believe that this is partially because none of these figures are substantially departing from more traditional forms of ethical theory in pursuit of a moral response to global warming.

22. See, for example, J. Baird Callicott, "Environmental Philosophy Is Environmental Activism: The Most Radical and Effective Kind," in *Environmental Philosophy and Environmental Activism*, ed. Don E. Marietta and Lester Embree (Lanham, MD: Rowman & Littlefield, 1995), pp. 19–36; and Callicott, "The Pragmatic Power and Promise."

23. Andrew Light and Avner de-Shalit, "Environmental Ethics: Whose Philosophy? Which Practice?" in *Moral and Political Reasoning in Environmental Practice*, ed. Andrew Light and Avner de-Shalit (Cambridge, MA: MIT Press, 2003), pp. 1–27.

24. Willett Kempton, James S. Boster, and Jennifer A. Hartley, *Environmental Values in American Culture* (Cambridge, MA: MIT Press, 1997).

25. Andrew Light, "Taking Environmental Ethics Public," in *Environmental Ethics: What Really Matters? What Really Works?* ed. David Schmidtz and Elizabeth Willott (Oxford: Oxford University Press, 2002), pp. 556–566.

26. See J. Eilperin, "Warming Draws Evangelicals into Environmentalists Fold," *Washington Post*, 8 August 2007, p. A1. For more on the Evangelical Climate Initiative, go to http://www.christiansandclimate.org/.

27. Again, I do not have the space here to fully defend this assertion, but it was the case that none of the major Republican candidates during the 2008 U.S. Republican presidential primary were climate skeptics (with the exception of Fred Thompson).

More important, as one senior Republican U.S. senator from a southern state put it to me over a year before the 2008 election the important issue now, for him, is that most Americans believe in anthropogenic global warming and so the party has no choice but to address the issue.

28. Norton, *Sustainability*, p. 510.

29. Ibid., p. 508.

30. Katie McShane offers a very interesting set of reasons why we should continue to work out nonanthropocentrism even if the convergence hypothesis is true given that ethics is not just about policy making but also includes substantial questions about "how to feel, what attitudes to take toward different things in the world, which to care about and how to care about them." Katie McShane, "Anthropocentrism vs. Nonanthropocentrism: Why Should We Care?" *Environmental Values* 16 (2007): 170. I cannot reply to McShane here, but only say that formally my methodological pragmatism is designed to be agnostic on the question of the truth of anthropocentrism versus nonanthropocentrism, so there is nothing necessarily incompatible with this particular aspect of my views and hers. I certainly also think there is more to ethics than just serving public policy, as should be evident in my recent book with John O'Neill and Alan Holland, *Environmental Values* (London: Routledge, 2008). It would, of course, be absurd that there would be no differences between the possible worlds I just sketched. How much those differences matter in the service of sustainability, however, would be an interesting question to pursue.

31. Callicott, "The Pragmatic Power and Promise."

32. Ibid., p. 12.

33. Ibid., p. 13.

34. See McShane, "Anthropocentrism vs. Nonanthropocentrism," p. 171, for a good account of why the intrinsic-instrumental distinction is not the operative distinction for testing the hypothesis.

35. Callicott, "The Pragmatic Power and Promise," p. 14.

36. See Light and de-Shalit, "Environmental Ethics."

37. See Tim Hayward, *Constitutional Environmental Rights* (Oxford: Oxford University Press, 2005).

38. Light, "Taking Environmental Ethics Public."

39. I can imagine pushing this distinction between the evangelical Christian case and the ecofascist case by finding other independently morally objectionable views widely held by fundamentalist Christians and then arguing that the last thing we want to do is offer anything to such communities that would demonstrate how the background values they hold actually can fruitfully address the problems we encounter in the world. Teasing out an answer here would take some time and so will need to be addressed elsewhere, but I think the objection is not insurmountable. It would require, however, a not insignificant investigation of the nature and scope of liberal tolerance and what we personally mind or do not mind in terms of how people treat each other and how they think about each other. I do not seem to mind that some of the evangelical climate enthusiasts believe that I will go to hell because I am a Jew. I do mind, however, that there are fascists who would like to cleanse the world of people like me. Perhaps the difference is that the evangelicals are, to my mind, speculating about my possible future in a possible afterlife (a view that I do not share) rather than suggest-

ing something about my possible future in the here and now (a here and now that I am reasonably sure does exist). Also, obviously, wanting to work with religious believers to solve environmental problems does not entail that one condone all religious belief or practice or that one cannot make a distinction between, on the one hand, someone's committed belief in their own personal basis for morality and, on the other hand, some form of fanaticism.

40. Elliott, "Norton's Conception of Sustainability." Indeed, Elliott claims at the end of this article that the political version of Norton's thesis in *Sustainability* is a version of my metaphilosophical (now methodological) pragmatism.

41. Norton, *Toward Unity*, p. 240, emphasis added. Some have suggested to me that we have forgotten that the origins of the hypothesis are due in part to the way Norton later discussed it. See, for example, Bryan G. Norton, *Searching for Sustainability* (Cambridge: Cambridge University Press, 2003), p. 78: "The convergence hypothesis which I have offered"; and Norton, *Sustainability*, p. 508: "I have introduced into the bifurcated discourse of environmental values what I call the convergence hypothesis." But I take this to be only shorthand for introducing these discussions rather than claiming that the hypothesis is something that Norton invented *de novo* rather than, to my mind more admirably, naming it and introducing it to environmental ethicists from the larger environmental community to help set us straight.

13 THE IMPORTANCE OF CREATING AN APPLIED ENVIRONMENTAL ETHICS

1. Eugene Hargrove, "What's Wrong? Who's to Blame?" *Environmental Ethics* 25 (2003): 3–4.

2. This conclusion is drawn from my experience working in environmental policy for more than thirty years at state, federal, and international levels. During this time, I have followed environmental ethics literature and written or edited several books, as well as many book chapters and journal articles.

3. Kristin Shrader-Frechette, "Methodological Rules for Four Classes of Scientific Uncertainty," in *Scientific Uncertainty and Environmental Problem Solving*, ed. John Lemons (Cambridge, MA: Blackwell, 1995).

4. Ibid.

5. Orrin H. Pilkey and Linda Pilkey-Jarvis, *Useless Arithmetic: Why Environmental Scientists Can't Predict the Future* (New York: Columbia University Press, 2007).

6. U.S. Environmental Protection Agency (U.S. EPA), *Framework for Cumulative Risk*, EPA/630/P-02/001F(Washington, DC: Author, 2003).

7. John Lemons, "Uncertainties in the Disposal of High-Level Nuclear Waste," in *Scientific Uncertainty and Environmental Problem Solving*, ed. John Lemons (Cambridge, MA: Blackwell, 1996).

8. Bryan G. Norton, *Toward Unity among Environmentalists* (New York: Oxford University Press, 1991).

9. Donald Brown et al., "White Paper on the Ethical Dimensions of Climate Change" (University Park: Rock Ethics Institute, Pennsylvania State University, 2006); available at http://rockethics.psu.edu/climate/whitepaper-intro.htm.

10. Ibid.

15 CONVERGENCE AND DIVERGENCE

1. Bryan G. Norton, *Toward Unity among Environmentalists* (New York: Oxford University Press, 1991).

2. Bryan G. Norton, *Why Preserve Natural Variety?* (Princeton, NJ: Princeton University Press, 1987).

3. Bill Devall and Georde Sessions, *Deep Ecology: Living as if Nature Mattered* (Salt Lake City, UT: Gibbs M. Smith, 1985).

4. Christopher Stone, *Earth and Other Ethics: The Case for Moral Pluralism* (New York: Harper and Row, 1987).

5. Stone, *Earth and Other Ethics*, p. 116.

6. See, for example, John Passmore, *Man's Responsibility for Nature* (New York: Charles Scribner's Sons, 1974), chaps. 4, 5.

7. Norton, *Toward Unity*, pp. 64–73.

8. Mikael Stenmark, "The Relevance of Environmental Ethical Theories for Policy Making," *Environmental Ethics* 24 (2002): 135–148; quote on p. 141 (orig.; p. 86 in this volume).

9. Norton, *Toward Unity*.

10. Although he does not clearly explain what he thinks such a hypothesis would imply about policy, Callicott apparently endorses the divergence hypothesis. See J. Baird Callicott, "The Pragmatic Power and Promise of Theoretical Environmental Ethics," *Environmental Values* 11 (2002): 3–26, esp. p. 14.

11. Aldo Leopold, *A Sand County Almanac* (Oxford: Oxford University Press, 1949), p. 109.

12. Note that Donald Brown, one of the writers in this volume who has experience in actual policy contexts, agrees with this assessment, while decrying the failure of environmental ethicists to recognize the key role of empirical science in policy development. See Brown, Chapter 13 of this volume.

13. J. Baird Callicott, "Environmental Philosophy IS Environmental Activism: The Most Radical and Effective Kind," in *Environmental Philosophy and Environmental Activism*, ed. Don E. Marietta and Lester Embree (Lanham, MD: Rowman & Littlefield, 1995), pp. 19–36; Callicott, "Silencing Philosophers: Minteer and the Foundations of Anti Foundationalism," *Environmental Values* 8 (1999): 499–516; and Callicott, "The Pragmatic Power and Promise."

14. Richard J. Bernstein, "Pragmatism, Pluralism, and the Healing of Wounds," in *Pragmatism: A Reader*, ed. Louis Menand (New York: Vintage/Random House, 1997).

15. My elaborations do not, I think, depart from Bernstein's characterization in that they can be justified by reference to his list; they reflect my special interest in the pragmatics of language and the postfoundational epistemology of W.V.O. Quine (see Quine, "Two Dogmas of Empiricism," in his *From a Logical Point of View* (New York: Harper and Row, 1950); and Quine, "Epistemology Naturalized," in his *Ontological Relativity and Other Essays* (New York: Columbia University Press, 1969). My approach is also informed by Rudolf Carnap's interpretation (in the last years of his career) of philosophical questions as involving pragmatic choices. See Carnap, "Empiricism, Semantics, and Ontology," in his *Meaning and Necessity* (Chicago: University of Chicago Press, 1949). These elaborations are developed in the appendix to my book, *Sustain-*

ability: A Philosophy of Adaptive Ecosystem Management (Chicago: University of Chicago Press, 2005).

16. Callicott, "Silencing Philosophers."

17. Callicott, "The Power and the Promise."

18. Eugene Hargrove, "What's Wrong? Who's to Blame?" *Environmental Ethics* 25 (2003): 3–4; Christopher Stone, "Do Morals Matter? The Influence of Ethics on Courts and Congress in Shaping U.S. Environmental Policies," *UC Davis Law Review* 37 (2003): 13–52; Donald Brown, Chapter 13 in this volume.

19. Callicott, "The Power and the Promise," p. 14.

20. Norton, *Sustainability.*

21. Eric Katz, Chapter 11 in this volume, p. 185.

22. Charles Sanders Peirce, "How to Make Our Ideas Clear," in *Pragmatism: A Reader*, ed. Louis Menand (New York: Vintage/Random House, 1997), quote on p. 36.

23. Bryan G. Norton, "Environmental Ethics and Nonhuman Rights," *Environmental Ethics* 4 (1982): 17–36; and "Environmental Ethics and Rights of Future Generations," *Environmental Ethics* 4 (1982): 319–337.

24. Norton, *Sustainability*, esp. section 7.1.

25. Bryan G. Norton, "Epistemology and Environmental Values," *Monist* 75 (1992): 208–226; and Norton, "Values in Nature," in *Contemporary Debates in Applied Ethics*, ed. A. I. Cohen and C. H. Wellman (London: Blackwell, 2005).

26. J. Baird Callicott, Chapter 9 in this volume, p. 143.

27. Ibid., p. 151. Emphasis in original.

28. Ibid., pp. 152–155.

29. Ibid., p. 143.

30. Norton, *Why Preserve Natural Variety?*

31. J. Baird Callicott, Chapter 9 in this volume, p. 166.

32. Ibid., p. 145.

33. Ibid.

34. Bryan G. Norton and Douglas Noonan, "Ecology and Valuation: Big Changes Needed," *Ecological Economics* 63 (2007): 664–675.

35. As defined in Norton, *Sustainability.*

36. Norton, *Sustainability.*

37. Callicott, Chapter 9 in this volume, p. 143.

38. Callicott, "The Power and the Promise," p. 16.

39. Ibid., p. 21.

40. Ben A. Minteer and Robert E. Manning, "Convergence in Environmental Values: An Empirical and Conceptual Defense," *Ethics, Place, and Environment* 3 (2000): 47–60; reprinted as Chapter 5 in this volume.

41. This idea was first developed in print in "The Ignorance Argument: What Must We Know to Be Fair to the Future?" in *Economics, Ethics, and Environmental Policy*, ed. Daniel W. Bromley and Jouni Paavola (Oxford: Blackwell, 2002). These ideas were developed in more detail in "Intergenerational Equity and Sustainability," the only original essay in my anthology of essays, *Searching for Sustainability* (Cambridge: Cambridge University Press, 2003). There, I criticize the economic model for measuring sustainability and offer an account in terms of opportunities and constraints. This detailed argument was shortened and woven into the larger argument of *Sustainability* as chapter 8.

Index